Ego Psychology:
THEORY & PRACTICE

Ego Psychology:
THEORY & PRACTICE

Gertrude and Rubin
BLANCK

COLUMBIA UNIVERSITY PRESS
New York & London 1974

Gertrude and *Rubin Blanck* are in private practice.
They contribute to the professional journals in psychoanalysis,
psychotherapy, clinical social work, and clinical psychology.
They teach in a program of continuing education at the
Institute for the Study of Psychotherapy, and have conducted
workshops, seminars, and lectures in various parts of
the United States and Europe.

Library of Congress Cataloging in Publication Data

Blanck, Gertrude.
    Ego Psychology: Theory and Practice

    Bibliography: p. 365
    1. Psychotherapy. 2. Psychoanalysis. I. Blanck,
Rubin, joint author. II. Title.
[DNLM: 1. Ego. 2. Psychotherapy—History. WM240 B641f 1974]
RC480.5.B58   616.8'917   73-17287
ISBN 0-231-03615-9

CONTENTS

FOREWORD

I T WOULD BE DIFFICULT to overestimate the impact that advances in ego psychology have had upon psychoanalysis. Nevertheless, for many years following the publication of Heinz Hartmann's *Ego Psychology and the Problem of Adaptation* in 1939 the application of this new dimension to analytic therapy languished. This was true even after 1952, when Hartmann's epochal work was translated into English by David Rapaport. It was commonplace to hear the most seasoned analysts say that while they found ego psychology interesting, it appeared to have little relevance to technique.

In the meantime, the results of psychoanalytic treatment were being viewed with increasing skepticism, and indeed pessimism, by even the most thoughtful and fairminded participants in the psychotherapeutic scene. The most skillful analysts found themselves altogether too often confronted by impasses in the treatment, not only of borderline cases, but of severe neuroses.

Meanwhile, persistent advances were being made in studies in early ego development, particularly implemented by direct observation of infants and children, refined considerations of pregenital phases, studies in superego development, in narcissism, in the nature of psychic trauma, and in kindred basic phenomena. A few foresighted individuals began to apply these findings to therapeutic technique, particularly with regard to levels of object relations. The extraordinary delicacy with which this enables an analyst to reach his patient at effective empathic levels much earlier than had previously been considered possible gives enormous impetus to the growth of the therapeutic alliance. Furthermore, it makes possible earlier interpretations at levels which do not violate fundamental analytic principles. It enriches the

therapeutic dialogue in preconscious terms of great complexity, because knowledge of the progression and vicissitudes of ego functioning has been made so much more explicit. Respect for the patient's
autonomy, wherever it resides, and the emergence of dormant, often
unsuspected autonomous capacities, are further advantages of such
therapeutic knowledge.

Among the pioneers in this exciting enterprise have been Gertrude
and Rubin Blanck. Their mastery of ego psychology, beautifully illustrated by their exegesis of the work of the most profound thinkers in
this field, is exemplified in chapters devoted to Hartmann, Jacobson,
Mahler, Spitz, and others. Rich clinical applications of ego psychology
abound in later chapters. Clarity, precision, specificity—these are
the hallmarks of the Blancks' therapeutic endeavors. Their compas-
sion and empathy for the most difficult and demanding of psychologically ill human beings adds a dimension indispensable to the successful use of psychoanalytically oriented psychotherapy.

                                              Nathaniel Ross, M.D.

ACKNOWLEDGMENTS

MANY HAVE CONTRIBUTED to the thinking that led us to write this volume. Most must, perforce, remain anonymous—our patients, from whom we have learned much and whom we hope we have helped in that mutual process—and our students, whose interest and enthusiasm have been constant sources of stimulation and inspiration. Our colleagues who have contributed case material are acknowledged in the chapters where that material appears.

Among those to whom we are also indebted are Dr. Nathaniel Ross for his unwavering support, encouragement, and unstinting exchange of theoretical ideas, as well as for his reading of the manuscript; Dr. Margaret S. Mahler for her theoretical contributions, which deserve the widest dissemination, and for her reading of the manuscript and validating the correctness of our summation of her theoretical views; Dr. René A. Spitz for reading the chapter which summarizes his work and particularly for making some important clarifications and additions from his most recent research; and Dr. Otto F. Kernberg for making his material available. We are obviously also greatly indebted to the other theorists whose works we have summarized, and from which we have extrapolated techniques, and we hope we have done them justice.

Special acknowledgment is due our teacher, Martin S. Bergmann, whose exemplary scholarship and devotion to theoretical exploration we hope we have emulated to some degree.

We also owe thanks to Mrs. Barbara B. Frank for her painstaking work on the manuscript.

Ego Psychology:
THEORY & PRACTICE

If there are certain things to which
hitherto psycho-analysis has not given
adequate consideration, that is not because it has overlooked their effects
or wished to deny their significance,
but because it pursues a particular
path which had not yet carried it so
far, and, moreover, now that these
things have at last been overtaken,
they appear to psycho-analysis in a
different shape from that in which they
appear to other people.

Sigmund Freud, 1923

INTRODUCTION

Anyone who hopes to learn the noble game of chess from books will soon discover that only the openings and end-games admit of an exhaustive systematic presentation and that the infinite variety of moves which develop after the opening defy any such description. This gap in instruction can only be filled by a diligent study of games fought out by masters. The rules which can be laid down for the practice of psychoanalysis are subject to similar limitations.[1]

THUS FREUD BEGINS HIS SERIES of papers on the technique of psychoanalysis. Despite his bold acknowledgment of the limitations on conveying precise rules of technique to the student of psychoanalysis, he did succeed in establishing a relatively distinct of procedures for the psychoanalyst to follow. The psychotherapist has no such guidelines. Because the scope of psychotherapy is so much broader than that of psychoanalysis, it is difficult to elaborate concise and even consistent technical rules. Despite the ever-widening area of applicability of psychoanalysis to patients formerly regarded as unanalyzable, psychoanalysis remains a circumscribed form of treatment designed for a particular type of patient and having a clearly defined goal.

Ideally, indications for treatment should be determined by diagnosis; practically, other considerations do play a role. This means that despite its "widening scope," [2] psychoanalysis is the treatment of choice for those whose psychic structures have developed to the point where solutions to conflict are distinctly neurotic. Viewing the same matter from the angle of psychoanalytic developmental psychology,

[1] S. Freud, *Standard Edition*. Vol. 12, p. 123.
[2] L. Stone, "The Widening Scope of Indications for Psychoanalysis."

which is our principal vantage point, suggests reserving psychoanalysis for those who have acquired an intact ego and a distinct identity. This leaves a rather large segment of the patient population to the psychotherapist.

The term *psychoanalysis* has treble meaning: it is a personality theory, a research tool, and a therapy. As a therapy, it would be subsumed logically under the broader term *psychotherapy,* literally defined as treatment of the psyche, were it not that generally accepted usage has it otherwise. By tacit consensus, psychoanalysts and psychoanalytically oriented psychotherapists refer to psychoanalysis as something separate and different from psychotherapy. Thus, psychotherapy has, by exclusion, acquired the connotation of all psychological treatment other than psychoanalysis.

Definition by exclusion leaves problems in its wake. The limitless applicability of psychotherapy has led to proliferation of theory and technique in many directions, some quite far from the psychoanalytic. It has even led to elaboration of techniques without theory. Many of these are fads which pass. Some disappear only to appear again in slightly altered form. There are, of course, many well-intentioned and thoughtful attempts to solve certain therapeutic problems. The severe pathologies which are relegated to the psychotherapist cannot always await elaboration of theory while treatment is urgently needed. Therefore, much empiricism and even pragmatism prevail. Also, there is pressure to discover forms of brief therapy because psychoanalytically oriented therapy takes so long. During World War II, for example, brief therapy such as hypnosis, sodium amytal sessions, and the like were tried in the military hospitals in an effort to treat the immediate trauma and return the serviceman to active duty. Great hope was held out for these forms of treatment because they promised shortcuts that could be applied to civilians after the war, but one hardly hears of them anymore and the many books that appeared on them are out of print.

There is no gainsaying that psychoanalytic psychotherapy takes a long time. But we agree with Greenacre that the so-called brief therapies, as we know them today, eventually take longer because " 'brief psychotherapies' are sometimes paradoxically extended over very long times indeed, being repeatedly ended and reopened, because little was consolidated in the treatment and all sorts of extraneous and unnecessary interferences entered." [3] At this stage of our knowledge, there are still no shortcuts. We are aware that the nonanalytic therapies in current vogue are briefer—especially those based on academic rather than psychoanalytic psychology. Most of these, while decrying the simplistic thinking of Watson and Pavlov, are nevertheless modernized versions of behaviorism and conditioning. But the reasons for the wide gap between psychoanalytic and academic psychology, while most interesting, remain beyond our scope to explore here. However, it is pertinent to point out the fundamental theoretical difference between them. While the nonanalytic therapies disregard the unconscious and strive for behavioral change, psychoanalytically oriented psychotherapy takes the unconscious very much into account and has structural change as its optimal goal. And such far-reaching personality change does take longer than behavioral change. But it is hazardous to choose a form of therapy out of considerations such as brevity and expediency. These are too superficial to be relevant to scientific theory building. It is conceivable that brief therapies based on psychoanalytic developmental psychology will evolve in the future, without discarding such fundaments of psychoanalysis as the unconscious and the development of psychic structure. But for the time being it seems to us that the more desirable road is not necessarily the shorter, but the one that takes fully into consideration theory as it has evolved to this point. Upon that foundation we can hope for progressive theory building which will, in turn, dictate more efficient techniques.

Another position which includes some of the psychoanalytic—because, by definition, it borrows from it—is the eclectic. Most persons attracted to the profession of psychotherapy value open-mindedness and liberalism. This makes eclecticism deceptively appealing. While academic psychologists tend to assail psychoanalytic theory as unscientific because its experiments cannot be patterned after those of the physical sciences, eclectics consider psychoanalysis too dogmatic. Again, we would extend ourselves too far beyond our subject were we to attempt to deal with both these criticisms here. The "nonscientific" argument has been ably answered repeatedly. That any science is

[3] P. Greenacre, "The Role of Transference," pp. 677–78.

based on a certain amount of dogma is self-evident and contains no negative connotation. Were this not so, everything in every discipline once proven would have to be proved over and over again ad infinitum. Eclecticism, while appearing to be less "rigid" than classical psychoanalytic theory, tends to be nihilistic in that it puts together incompatible parts of varied theories. In that process, theoretical foundations are discarded, leaving no opportunity for theory building.

A third point of view, this one closer to the so-called dynamic or depth psychologies, is represented by the environmental or cultural schools of Horney, Sullivan, *et al.* Their theories regard the individual as reactive to his environment, both sociological and psychological; therefore, attempt to treat is from that position. Behavior is altered, not by reinforcement or conditioning, but by dynamic interaction between the patient and a therapist who, in effect, constitutes a new and presumably more benign environment. From this position come such broad technical approaches as interpersonal relations, interaction, corrective emotional experience, emotional reeducation, and the like. Here is a fundamental difference from the psychoanalytic view, within which the concept of internalization is basic.

The theoretical position from which our technical procedures are drawn is psychoanalytic developmental psychology. This book is intended only as a description of techniques derived from that theory. Those who are seeking an eclectic approach or a survey of all the different forms of psychotherapy will not find them here. The concepts of internalization and of object relations are so basic to psychoanalytic developmental psychology that they will reverberate throughout our discussion of theory and technique. Internalization, briefly defined, is the process of making part of oneself that which was formerly external. It goes hand in hand with the concept of object relations because object representations become increasingly internalized as structuralization proceeds. This describes also the essence of the difference between the psychoanalytic and the environmental and interpersonal schools. Psychoanalytic psychology is developmental psychology in that it accounts for the structuralization of the personality from birth onward. While the most rapid and fundamental features of structuralization take place in the early years of life, development is a process which continues throughout life.

There is an abundant and adequate literature on the technique of psychoanalysis. Therefore, we shall not concern ourselves with psychoanalysis as a therapy except to compare it with the technique of psychotherapy. While there is an even more abundant literature on the technique of psychotherapy, much of it represents the diverse and varied schools and systems to which we have alluded. The relatively few works on the technique of psychotherapy which are psychoanalytically oriented do not exploit the discoveries of psychoanalytic developmental psychology, sometimes called ego psychology. It is for this reason that we believe it useful to add a work describing the applicability of ego psychological concepts to the existing literature on the technique of psychotherapy. Psychoanalysis as a theory is the conceptual base for both forms of treatment, psychoanalysis and psychotherapy. It is only in the technical application of theory that these forms of treatment differ, sometimes slightly, sometimes markedly.

Freud's theoretical work is so extensively written about elsewhere that we shall not attempt to recapitulate at length. The best exposition of Freud's work exists in his own writings. One encounters scholars, particularly in the fields of psychology and sociology, who regard it as essential to their education to have "read" Freud. This is much to their credit, even if their reading leads them to dismiss his work as inconsistent, unscientific, outdated, and so on. But Freud cannot be read as one would read a textbook. He has to be studied in the chronology of his writings and with minute attention to the theoretical views which he postulated, revised, discarded, and elaborated upon, as well as to those to which he did not have the opportunity to return and reconsider. Freud in 1895 is different from Freud in 1926 and still more different in 1938. His major work, *The Interpretation of Dreams,* written in 1899 and published in 1900, although a masterpiece of enormous value, has not been updated to include the structural theory he proposed in 1923. It is our gain that Freud did not use his productive lifespan to go back and revise systematically, although revise he did. His time was better spent continuing to evolve theory. He left us with the task of continuously and systematically reviewing what he had already done. To know what remains valid, we are obliged to study, not read. It has become fashionable these days to quote superseded theory to prove Freud wrong—but we shall not discuss that further, either, because it has no place in scientific theory building.

While Freud's own writings and those of his "pupils" provide an ample literature for the student of Freudian theory before 1940 or so, there is little in the way of a comparable unified literature on contemporary Freudian ego psychology, usually referred to simply as *ego psychology* or, lately, as *psychoanalytic developmental psychology*. We account for this by the fact that, after Freud's death, there was no longer a single mind evolving theory. Rather, a number of investigators whose works to some extent build one upon the other, but to a much greater extent are complementary, contribute to the totality of modern Freudian theory. The writings of these theorists constitute primary sources. But unification of the theory is attained only by reading each of these authors separately. We are unable to account for the surprising fact that they are little known outside of psychoanalytic circles, but we have encountered this phenomenon frequently enough to be convinced that a single volume presenting the theories of the major ego psychologists would be a contribution. We shall attempt this here, at the same time offering this unification of theory as the conceptual base upon which our technical suggestions rest. We have chosen to summarize the works of Heinz Hartmann alone, as well as with his collaborators, Ernst Kris and Rudolph M. Loewenstein. These contributions constitute the foundation stones of contemporary ego psychology. To them must be added the theories of Edith Jacobson and the observational studies of Margaret S. Mahler and René A. Spitz. We add Otto F. Kernberg and Heinz Kohut as contributors to the technique of working with the more severe pathologies. There are many other important contributors whose work we do not summarize, although we will allude to some of their work in our discussions of technique. A listing of their names would almost repeat the bibliography. The reason for our choice is that, although many valuable contributions to theory have been made and continue to be made, we have chosen for special emphasis those theorists whose contributions are fundamental to theory building. From their theories, we have extrapolated technical procedures, some of which are well known and are practiced daily. Therefore, we do not claim priority in the sense of having discovered each technique, but we think that, by unifying theory and technique, we give clarity to the former and conceptual rationale to the latter.

Our summaries of the contributions of these giants of theory building are not all inclusive and offer no substitute for reading the primary sources. We do think, however, that they will be useful for acquiring an overall grasp of the interrelatedness of the works of these theorists before delving into their original writings.

We do not present either past or current theory as finite. There is much room at the frontier of knowledge in both theory and technique. We expect that, as investigation flourishes, much presently held theory will be elaborated; some will be revised, some discarded. We do insist that this cannot be done out of hand but only on the basis of metapsychological considerations, which include full exposition of the theory to be superseded and of the effects of the proposed innovation.

This book is not intended to innovate theory. Instead, we shall elaborate techniques, adhering to the same principle that proposals regarding technique, no less than theory, require full explanation from the innovator. As far as possible, we shall explain the theoretical rationale for our proposals, why they are necessary in a given situation, and what they are designed to accomplish. For introducing technique no less than for theory, metapsychological responsibility is called for. The oft-heard remark, "I don't know what it does but it works," is too pragmatic for didactic purposes.

The contention that attempts to treat the more disturbed patient by classical psychoanalytic methods have failed is largely correct. Because of this, there exists sincerely held opinion that psychoanalytic theory is to be discarded in the treatment of the unanalyzable patient. We propose that failure lay, not in inherent defect in theory, but in the application of technique which had been designed for treatment of the neuroses.

Psychoanalytic theory, as represented by psychoanalytic developmental psychology, now provides enough understanding of human development to make possible a systematized presentation of a technique of psychotherapy different in some respects from that of psychoanalysis.

The point at issue is not whether psychoanalytic theory is correct, but only· whether its application is indicated by the diagnosis. To demonstrate how treatment choice is determined, we shall describe in detail the diagnostic features to be considered and the principles which may be used as guides in the therapist's decisions. Although psychotherapy offers much more scope for technical innovation than does psychoanalysis, it is by no means a free field; the therapist is limited by the needs of the patient, as measured by diagnostic considerations which approach the quantitative.

Disciplined departure from psychoanalytic procedure was first presented systematically by Eissler. He introduced the term *parameter* and defined it as the least possible departure from the classical model dictated by the structure of the ego. His technical proposal came at a time when the ego psychologists had elaborated Freud's structural theory to the point where knowledge about the ego made more sophisticated conceptualization of psychoanalytic technique feasible. By basing the parameter on the crucial diagnostic feature of ego structure, the psychoanalyst could depart from classical technique, although, however, such an act would have to be reconciled before treatment could be successfully terminated. Eissler was aware that, in a sense, he was not proposing a new technique, but rather a conceputalization of a technique Freud had already recommended. Since Eissler, there have been innumerable attempts to deal with the patient whose structure is less developed than that of the neurotic by using techniques usually termed *deviations,* or *modifications* of classical psychoanalytic technique. While these are well and good for the neurotic structures, if they are kept within Eissler's guidelines, we think it blurs the technique of psychoanalysis proper if one attempts to compress within it techniques designed for the less structured personalities. Psychoanalysis as a treatment is better reserved for the neuroses. We remind ourselves here that Freud even recommended a trial analysis after which the patient was to be dismissed if it was found that his ego was not capable of enduring it. Thus Freud was the first to suggest that the way the ego functions in the treatment proper could also be regarded as a diagnostic indicator of its structure.

It keeps matters less cluttered if we reserve the term *modified psychoanalytic technique* for those structures which can tolerate the use of a parameter, including Eissler's stricture that the parameter be self-eliminating. This maintains both the precision and the boundaries of psychoanalytic technique and yet makes room for a technique of psychoanalytically oriented psychotherapy which, while using the same theory as psychoanalysis, leans more heavily on those aspects of theory recently formulated by the investigators of development in the early months of life. This is, of course, because the less-structured personalities to be treated by the psychotherapist are to be understood in terms of developmental failure. However, this is not to be taken too simplistically. Although early development is critical for structuralization, Spitz cautions that the psychic structure of the adult is quite different from that of the child. "Some of these disturbances of early infancy, be they psychogenic affections or psychosomatic conditions, bear a striking resemblance to disturbances with which we are familiar also in the adult. I have stated that these resemblances do not make the two, the disturbance in the infant and the psychiatric disease in the adult, either homologous or even analogous." [4]

We shall describe the diagnosis and treatment of failure in structuralization in detail. Heretofore, specific techniques for the treatment of such cases were not systematically conceptualized. *Heretofore,* in our frame of reference, means before Hartmann introduced the concepts of the arrival of the infant with "inborn ego apparatuses" into an "average expectable environment," [5] thus expanding psychoanalysis from a psychology of conflict to a normal developmental psychology as well.

The method of any therapy is dictated by the goal. Psychoanalytic procedures were designed specifically to make the unconscious conscious and thereby to effect structural change (alteration in relationships among id, ego, and superego). To this end all diversionary goals are subordinated. In psychotherapy, there is not a single goal; there are many. We shall elaborate upon the differences in technique between psychoanalysis and psychotherapy. Here it may be stated that for the application of psychoanalytic technique, we require not only a well-developed ego but also an individual who is highly motivated. In the practice of psychotherapy, everyone, regardless of diagnosis and

[4] R. A. Spitz, *The First Year of Life,* p. 293.
[5] H. Hartmann, *Ego Psychology and the Problem of Adaptation.*

sometimes even of motivation, is a potential patient. The ego of the patient, unless psychotherapy has been decided upon for practical reasons, is, by definition, impaired. In psychoanalysis, ego building is usually incidental to the major technical purpose. In psychotherapy, the treatment per se consists of an attempt to heal the damaged ego. Ego building becomes the very fabric of treatment and procedures must be designed specifically for this purpose.

Sometimes the goal in psychotherapy is the halting or reversing of processes of decompensation. With a suicidal patient, one may try just to keep him alive before concerning oneself with enabling him to function. In marital or parent-child problems, one may try to extricate the individuals and their personal problems from the interpersonal battleground. With an adolescent or young adult, one may try to help him to use psychotherapy as the springboard away from childhood.

Since psychotherapy is the treatment of choice for the more severe pathologies, we cannot be as optimistic prognostically as are authors of texts on the technique of psychoanalysis. Also, the techniques of psychotherapy which we are proposing are still in the pioneering stage. They extrapolate from developmental theory methods of treatment which seem logically to follow. We have used these techniques ourselves, as have many of our students. It would be futile to attempt to quantify our results. We can only say that the ego-building devices we suggest to our students and use in our own practices help in varying degrees. There have been astonishing successes and outright failures. As to the broad category of "borderline," it ranges from borderline psychotic structure on the one hand to borderline neurotic on the other, with most cases falling in between. We believe that prognosis is a factor of the ego structure; the borderline neurotics therefore present more favorable prognoses than do borderline psychotics. And it must be acknowledged that the most severe pathologies are essentially irreversible. This does not at all mean that maintaining the patient at whatever may be his optimal level of functioning is not worthwhile. But we do not expect, in the long run, that greater theoretical knowledge and improved techniques will ever bring psychotherapy to as favorable a prognostic position as psychoanalysis. This does not imply that psychoanalysis is a superior form of treatment. In fact, considered

from the point of view of the skills and versatility demanded, psychotherapy is more difficult. From the patient's side, the best form of
treatment is always that which is suited to his structure.

The psychotherapist, then, addresses his treatment to a far wider
range of the diagnostic spectrum than does the psychoanalyst. He is
even called upon to treat those who may not be capable of knowing
whether they wish to be patients. If the potential patient is a child, he
is brought by his parents. If the patient is a marital partner, because
of the tendency of marital partners to project their difficulties upon
each other, a husband may be forced by his wife to seek treatment, or the wife may be forced by the husband. Persons brought before the courts are sometimes remanded for treatment. Favorable as
this may appear to those who welcome infiltration of twentieth-century psychology into the judiciary, it does pose a problem for the psychotherapist who is to treat a person on a court order that may not
coincide with that person's motivation. Even patients who come without coercion may lack the kind of motivation essential for psychoanalysis. Much of what we shall have to say about the beginning phases
of psychotherapy, therefore, will focus on the problem of how to help
the unmotivated person become a patient in the sense of accepting
the need for treatment and finding the capacity to enter into a therapeutic alliance.

It is, of course, not at all difficult to recognize the resistance of the
person who is consciously reluctant. The more subtle problem of the
person who professes to want treatment but whose resistance is (by
definition) unconscious is well known and tolerated, especially by psychoanalysts. But there is a tendency to dismiss the consciously unwilling person as untreatable. We shall show that it matters only slightly
in psychotherapy whether the initial reluctance is conscious or unconscious. It is obvious that conscious reluctance presents obstacles, but
techniques for dealing with them can be devised.

There is a third type of patient whose first approach to the therapist must be regarded somewhat differently. It may be said that he
lacks resistance. The very nature of his problem involves such impairment of the defensive function that he cannot resist. Also impaired
are such functions as judgment and decision making, leaving him
with no volition in relation to treatment. Therapy that furthers ego

development can help this type of patient to reach the—for him —desirable state of *becoming* resistant.

Thus the variety of goals in psychotherapy exceeds that of psychoanalysis. For didactic purposes, we find it useful to think that quantitatively, and certainly qualitatively, there are as many goals as there are patients. This attitude avoids fitting the patient into a particular frame of reference, a preconceived diagnostic category, a particular school of thought, or the limitations of a given therapist's knowledge and skill. It also tends to minimize countertransference phenomena.

We shall have little more to say about the important matter of countertransference. Strictly defined, it is unconscious excessive libidinal or aggressive feelings toward the patient, of which the therapist is unaware. In training psychotherapists we find that pointing out these unconscious attitudes is always a most delicate matter and, as in psychotherapy itself, often serves to reinforce resistance if it is not well timed. We know of no better way of ensuring that countertransference will be minimal than that of recommending that the therapist himself be psychoanalyzed. Hopefully, he will then not need to use the patient for the gratification of his unconscious needs. Greenson refers to psychoanalysis as "that impossible profession" [6] and would probably extend his views to include psychotherapy. He means that this is the only profession in which the working day consists of deliberate abstention from gratification of otherwise acceptable human needs. The lawyer, physician, teacher, and the like may perform professional services in the context of peripheral relationships with client, patient, or student. Within limits, he may be friendly or aloof; kind, indifferent, perhaps even verging on cruel; humorous or grim. While such attitudes do indeed have some effect upon his services and may impair them, never, in these other professions, are they central to the services themselves. Yet the very tool of psychotherapy is the disciplined personality of the therapist. Therefore, he is constrained to improve this tool (it can never be perfected) and to use it solely in the patient's interest.

It is sometimes feared that such insistence upon discipline will constrict spontaneity. Spontaneity, we find, fuses with disciplined tech-

[6] R. R. Greenson, "That Impossible Profession."

nique when the therapist gains experience; then his responses acquire "secondary autonomy." [7] He becomes capable of being himself with the patient without overstepping the bounds of professional efficacy. It is then no longer difficult or artificial for the therapist to use tamed spontaneity, intuition, and the capacity to empathize, along with a body of knowledge. Trained also to self-examination by his own analysis, he will scrutinize his feelings and ensure that his behavior is in the best interest of the patient rather than in the service of his own needs. Sometimes a patient's needs happen to coincide and mesh with those of the therapist, but in a busy work day not every need of every patient can be so obligingly compatible. When the patient's need is not consistent with that of the therapist, there can be no question that the therapist must put his own aside. This is not a hardship when the professional ego acquires secondary autonomy because professional behavior becomes automatic and pleasurable for its own sake.

Self-discipline in the interest of the patient resembles maternal behavior when the child, in the developmental phases of infancy, is best mothered by a person who understands his needs, especially the need to grow psychologically, and who lends herself to this purpose even when it involves frustrating herself. To illustrate, she may find it highly pleasing to continue to understand him without words when it would be more growth promoting to encourage him to verbalize, but if she were to indulge herself in this pleasure she would retard the development of important ego functions such as speech, and especially the attainment of new levels of object relations. The "good-enough mother" [8] foregoes her exercise of intuitive understanding for the sake of furthering development. Similarly, the disciplined therapist who, let us say, enjoys exhibiting his brilliance, withholds an interpretation for the sake of awaiting the patient's arrival at it, at the expense of accomplishing a satisfying tour de force for himself.

It remains for us to describe what we believe to be necessary talent for the practice of psychotherapy. Formal institute requirements usually consist of a prescribed number of courses, a certain number of supervisory hours, and personal treatment. None of these, even inten-

[7] H. Hartmann, *Ego Psychology and the Problem of Adaptation.*
[8] D. W. Winnicott, "Transitional Objects and Transitional Phenomena," p. 94.

sive personal psychoanalysis, assures talent. We are in accord with
Greenson that talent involves at its core the capacity to empathize,
but we would go beyond him in asserting that such capacity is, at our
state of knowledge, no longer an endowment of unknown genesis. Referring as it does to the ability to feel *with* another person (as distinguished from sympathy, which is the ability to feel *for*), it derives
from that period in the therapist's own life when he has been felt
with. Specifically, we think that the therapist should have had a good
symbiotic experience at the phase-specific period in his life when empathy in the mother-child dyad is essential to further development.
We know of no sounder basis for the acquisition of talent for the profession. In addition to having had the kind of life experience that includes adequate symbiosis in infancy, there must also have been adequate resolution of the separation-individuation crisis. Symbiosis alone
would tend to have a stultifying effect by causing the therapist to
duplicate this experience with patients who do not necessarily need it.
An individual who has emerged from the "symbiotic membrane" [9]
has, in that process, also had experience in attenuating separation
anxiety. He has a well-crystallized identity which, in his professional
work, will reflect in the capacity to respect his patient's autonomy.

Sometimes it is said that the potential psychotherapist should have
intuition. We prefer to speak of empathy because the origin of empathy can be traced to a normal developmental phase and thereby be
accounted for by the quality of the infantile experience. Intuition, on
the other hand, remains a mysteriously acquired and much less reliable capacity which sometimes lends itself to rationalization of
countertransference. To react to the patient with one's own feelings
of the moment, or to provoke the patient to react in order to get
some "action," provides no assurance of the correctness of one's
technical behavior. Intuition cannot be taught, duplicated, or validated, so it would be a desirable gift only if there were none else.
In that case, the practice of psychotherapy would have to be restricted
to those who possess this elusive endowment. Capacity to empathize
is steadier, more reliable and, above all, many be bent in the direc-

[9] M. S. Mahler, "Autism and Symbiosis; Two Extreme Disturbances of Identity."

tion of acquiring and combining knowledge of theory and technique with professional self-discipline.

There is also a place for art in psychotherapy. We would define art as the creative application of sound theory. By this definition, all technique is an art. Regarded in this way, technique need not lean as heavily as was heretofore thought upon the individual therapist's possession of mysterious gifts. Some practitioners are nevertheless unusually gifted and we by no means disparage such innate qualities. As we shall demonstrate in the description of proposed interventions in our case material, there is much scope for individual creativity in such matters as the phrasing of an interpretation and in the timing of the intervention. A good sense of timing is exceedingly difficult to teach, but it can be gained with experience. Freud used the word *tact* to describe the knack for making timely interventions. It may be that the therapist who combines intuition and empathy with knowledge of theory acquires tact most easily.

Although we shall present definite guidelines, we shall present few rules as such. To the small extent that rules can be provided, they are useful, although their constraint may endanger creativity. We do believe, however, that one can present technique in a way that encourages professional growth along with increasing knowledge of psychoanalytic developmental psychology and its application to psychotherapy. From our experience in teaching and supervising beginning therapists, we know that if theory is well understood, technical interventions resolve themselves—not into rules, but into logical moves which flow easily from theory.

Our material deals in the main with ambulatory out-patients, most of whom are able to present themselves for treatment in the therapist's office and, in some degree, to function. Therapy for the overt psychotic who needs to be treated in a hospital setting is beyond our scope because special techniques obtain in those situations. Our main thrust is to help therapists who treat the large population of psychotherapy out-patients who live in the community.

1

THEORY

1

PSYCHOANALYTIC DEVELOPMENTAL PSYCHOLOGY: HISTORICAL ROOTS

PSYCHOANALYTIC THEORY BUILDING was reviewed by Rapaport in historical perspective and was found by him to have developed through four distinct phases. The first of these, the prepsychoanalytic period, was characterized by a primitive concept of *ego* meaning person, self, or consciousness. Defense referred to the dissociation of memory from consciousness. The term *repression* was used at that time to represent this simple concept of defense. It was not until forty years later that repression took its place as only one of several mechanisms of defense, thereby altering in meaning. But before that major revision in theory could be made, the term *ego* had to be redefined.

By grouping the development of psychoanalytic theory into phases, Rapaport also demonstrated how essential it is to study this theory in historical perspective. Much in the vocabulary has changed in meaning as terms and even whole concepts have become more sophisticated. Examples are *repression, ego, self, narcissism,* and, outstandingly, the concept of anxiety. In this first period of psychoanalytic theory, anxiety was regarded as an end product of repression. Affect so dammed up became transformed into anxiety.

Freud's last definition of *ego* appeared in *An Outline of Psycho-Analysis,* written in 1938. In tracing the development of Freud's thinking about the ego, Hartmann pointed out that Freud defined it there as an organization with constant cathexis and assigned to it functions such as defense, reality testing, perception, memory, attention, judgment. In *The Interpretation of Dreams,* Freud described the psychic apparatus as consisting of two antithetical forces, one which constructs the wish and the other which exercises censorship, thereby bringing about distorted expression of the wish. He spoke also of a critical agency which directs our waking life and determines our voluntary, conscious action. The germ of his thinking about the ego is recognizable here, too. But he still regarded *conscious* and *ego* as synonymous and defined it as a sense organ for perception, for thought processes, and thus for the reception of external and internal stimuli. In dealing with the concept of primary and secondary processes, Freud also referred to functions which we can now recognize and ascribe to the ego. Primary process is directed toward free discharge of excitation, whereas secondary process, by using memory traces, employs thought as trial action. Here, again, we see the beginnings of what later came to be regarded as major functions of the ego— namely, perception, motility, anticipation, and delay.

The defensive function of the ego was the principal focus of interest in Freud's early work. Although he did not elaborate until 1923, he had already noted as early as 1896 that defenses can be unconscious. In *Notes upon a Case of Obsessional Neurosis,* first published in 1909, defenses such as regression, undoing, isolation, and displacement were described. It remained for Anna Freud in 1936 to emphasize the defensive function of the ego and to elaborate upon the various mechanisms of defense. (Note that the dates of first publication are not the same as those given in the bibliography for *The Standard Edition.* First dates of publication are given in this chapter to show historical development.)

In *Formulations on the Two Principles of Mental Functioning,* first published in 1911, Freud's ideas concerning primary and secondary processes were further developed. Here he juxtaposed them with the reality principle. Consciousness (ego) has to attend to considerations other than pleasure. The ego functions of attention and memory are recognized. Motor discharge is thought of as capable of being organized into behavior; thought may substitute for action. In this paper, too, Freud introduced the term *ego instincts.* Later he abandoned it, but here he distinguished ego instincts from sexual instincts by the greater ability of the former to adhere to the reality principle. Freud referred also to a pleasure ego which can only wish and try to avoid pain, whereas the reality ego can strive for that which is useful.

Also in 1911, Freud completed his remarkable study of the Schreber case.[1] He provided a psychoanalytic view of psychosis, homosexuality, and secondary narcissism. He suggested, but did not elaborate, that modification of the ego as a consequence of pathological development results in disturbances in libidinal processes. This has far-reaching influence on both theory and technique in ego psychology.

In On Narcissism: An Introduction, first published in 1914, Freud developed his theory of ego drives and ego libido. Although this theory was later discarded, it is noteworthy because the accompanying concept that the ego can become instinctualized is basic to contemporary ego psychology.

In 1915 Freud first published his paper The Unconscious, in which he proposed the metapsychological principle that mental processes are to be studied in their dynamic, topographic, and economic aspects. Later theoretical developments dictated the addition of two more metapsychological considerations—the genetic and the adaptive. For understanding the changing concept of ego, it is of interest to consider the evolution of the dynamic position out of these changes. By 1915 it was regarded that although what is repressed remains unconscious, so do those impulses which tend toward opposing the repressed. Thus, the topographical point of view began to yield to the structural.

But before this could eventuate, the second phase of psychoanalysis was reached, ushered in by Freud's discovery that traumatic events which his patients reported as memories had not really occurred and were, in fact, fantasies. Theoretical interest became focused, therefore, on the instincts as the agency that created the fantasies. This middle era in theory building is regarded as the period of instinct theory. Nevertheless, as Hartmann pointed out, there were threads of ego psychology in Freud's thought while psychoanalysis was still largely

[1] S. Freud, Psychoanalytic Notes on an Autobiographical Account of a Case of Paranoia (Dementia Paranoides).

an id psychology. Freud had, in 1938, in *An Outline of Psycho-Analysis,* assigned the function of self-preservation to the ego, thus making a clear distinction between id and the instincts of the lower animals.

The third phase, that of the structural theory, provided the foundation for contemporary ego psychological thought. With the publication of *The Ego and the Id* in 1923, Freud demonstrated the value of the constructs id, ego, and superego. His new definition of *ego* is still held today. Now it is no longer synonymous with self, but one of a tripartite personality structure. The ego has both unconscious and conscious elements and the added function of defense. Because behavior was not well explained by instinct theory alone, the ego and its functions have since then become the major focus of psychoanalytic investigation. In the presently held position of Arlow and Brenner, the structural theory is superior to the topographical (conscious, preconscious, unconscious) and therefore supersedes it. Others do not agree that one theory replaces the other, finding rather that both are useful but need to be integrated.

Although the concept of conflict was central in Freud's thought from the beginning, with the introduction of the structural theory a far more sophisticated psychology of conflict arose. Conflict was no longer regarded simply as force and counterforce, but the result of tension between two of the psychic institutions. Tension between ego and id, for example, produces anxiety and forces the ego to take defensive measures against this intolerable affect. Shortly after publishing *The Ego and the Id,* Freud added *Inhibitions, Symptoms and Anxiety* (1926). It was the inevitable step in elaboration of the structural theory. In it, Freud postulated the so-called second theory of anxiety, superseding the first or toxic theory. The second theory described anxiety as the consequence of conflict and showed that the ego can respond to it as a signal for invoking defense. Hartmann, in his search through Freud's work for his thoughts about ego functions, found that the concept of signal anxiety suggests an anticipatory function. Conflict, anxiety, and defense lead to symptom formation. This is seen as the end result of the conflict and its resolution by means of compromise between id and ego. The wish emanating from the id is at once defended against by the ego and at the same time permitted attentuated discharge in the disguised form of a symptom.

When theory building reached this stage it became necessary to revise the definition of *repression*. Freud had already noted as early as 1909 that there are other mechanisms of defense, but it remained for Anna Freud to systematize the entire concept. This she did in 1936 with the publication of *The Ego and the Mechanisms of Defence*. Here, she showed that the ego has at its disposal not only repression, now redefined, but nine additional mechanisms. Repression, by that time, could no longer be regarded as the simple process of dissociation from consciousness. It had to be seen as an unconscious act of the ego, in response to the signal of anxiety, to employ countercathectic energy in keeping the material out of consciousness. Here we are using the economic aspect of metapsychology to explain the energic factor in the defensive process. Countercathexis operates against the cathectic energy which would otherwise allow the material into consciousness. In addition to repression, the nine mechanisms of defense specifically listed by Anna Freud are: regression, reaction formation, undoing, introjection, identification, projection, turning against the self, reversal, and sublimation (displacement of instinctual aims). These may be used singly or in combination, and are not to be regarded as exhaustive. For example, there are the well-known defenses of rationalization and intellectualization. Also, there are defensive methods other than the "mechanisms," such as the use of one drive against another.

When psychoanalytic attention focused so sharply on the defensive function of the ego, radical alteration in technique was dictated. Anna Freud made technical suggestions to the effect that much could be learned about the ego of the patient if the analyst were to observe its defensive functioning which, in the analytic situation, appears in the form of resistance. Modern psychoanalytic technique demands that the analyst divide his attention between ego and id instead of engaging in the uncovering of id content only. This has even more far-reaching implications for the technique of psychotherapy because, in the treatment of the nonneurotic structure, much more and sometimes all of the treatment is concerned with the ego.

The fourth or contemporary phase of theory-building began in 1937 with Hartmann's presentation of a series of lectures before the Vienna Psychoanalytic Society. It was not, however, until 1958 that these were published in their entirety in English as *Ego Psychology and the Problem of Adaptation.* Rapaport described the contemporary phase of psychoanalytic theory building as characterized by increasingly sophisticated development of the concept of object relations and appreciation of its central role in the development of the personality. Again, Hartmann's search through Freud's writings for the origins of modern ego psychological concepts revealed that, in 1921, in *Group Psychology and the Analysis of the Ego,* Freud referred to identification early in life as involving an emotional tie with another person. Also, in this same paper, in explaining hysterical symptomatology, Freud stated that identification replaces object choice by means of two successive defense mechanisms, regression and introjection of the object. He here described love as enriching the ego with properties of the object.

In *Mourning and Melancholia,* first published in 1917, Freud regarded the ego as the repository of abandoned objects. It is in this essay that we find the famous poetic statement, "the shadow of the object fell upon the ego." [2] These references to the relationship between ego and object, so painstakingly gleaned by Hartmann, presage the modern position not only concerning object relations but also concerning ego identifications and the complexity of processes of internalization. To Hartmann, they are clear indications that Freud had thought about object relations before that term was coined. Thus, Freud did not neglect interpersonal relations, as is sometimes charged, although he left the elaboration of many of its facets to his successors.

Hartmann is regarded as the father of modern ego psychology. His work is the direct outcome of the introduction of the structural theory because Freud's revised concept of *ego,* which that theory proposed, opened up many theoretical questions about the development of the ego and its functions. Hartmann's particular interest lay in functions of the ego in addition to the defensive.

The structural theory led to investigation of the ego by other theorists as well. Although the Hartmann position has prevailed and in its turn has germinated the thinking of the theorists who worked with

[2] S. Freud, *Mourning and Melancholia,* p. 249.

him and who built upon his foundation, it is of some historical interest to know about these others. Glover proposed a concept of ego nuclei, by which he meant that the ego is not, at first, an entity but consists rather of loosely arranged clusters which only gradually come together to form a coherent structure. Melanie Klein, in an attempt to answer questions about the ego, condensed Freud's theories about childhood development into the first year of life and even included the resolution of the oedipus complex in that short lifespan. Her theories, widely questioned elsewhere, are nevertheless still prevalent in Britain and South America. Despite serious questions about major aspects of her theory and even graver questions about their technical implications, she nonetheless pioneered in the investigation of infantile mechanisms of projection and introjection at a time when little was known about these processes in early life. Federn was also an ego psychologist in the strict sense of the term, since his investigations yielded information about the psychotic ego. Because Federn's work remained within the realm of psychopathology while psychoanalysis was on the verge of becoming a normal developmental psychology, it fell to Hartmann to bring it there. Hartmann's contributions far transcend their intrinsic value because, like Freud, his work is germinal. Eissler and Eissler [3] refer to it as exerting a fertilizing influence. He brought ego psychology at once to an acme and to a point of departure for Jacobson, Mahler, Spitz, and the many others who proceeded to build upon his formulations.

[3] R. S. Eissler and K. R. Eissler, "Heinz Hartmann: A Biographical Sketch."

❧ 2 ❧

PSYCHOANALYSIS AS A NORMAL DEVELOPMENTAL PSYCHOLOGY: HARTMANN'S THEORIES AND HIS WORK IN COLLABORATION WITH KRIS AND LOEWENSTEIN

H ARTMANN'S SMALL VOLUME, *Ego Psychology and the Problem of Adaptation,* first published in German in 1939, recapitulated the lectures he had given at the meetings of the Vienna Psychoanalytic Society two years earlier. He continued to work for three decades thereafter, making important contributions himself and also in the now famous collaboration with Kris and Loewenstein.

Hartmann was a synthesizer. He brought together concepts from anatomy, psychology, biology, and sociology, thereby contributing immeasurably to the expansion of psychoanalytic conceptualization without, however, impairing its intrinsic scientific validity. Inspired by the broadened opportunities for theory building provided by the structural theory, Hartmann's interest turned to the ego. Psychoanalysts had begun to be baffled by the observation that, momentous as its discovery had been, the theory of the progression of psychosexual phases did not completely explain empirical data. Particularly was a drive theory inadequate to explain relatedness between self and object. As Hartmann put it, "But, as for the present, the concepts of developmental phase, conflict, trauma have become much more complex for us, and, I think, they will become ever more complex before we again reach that beautiful, peaceful state of affairs when both simple and general formulations become possible." [1]

[1] H. Hartmann, *Essays in Ego Psychology,* p. 209.

Hartmann was also an organizer of psychoanalytic theory construction, reflecting in his philosophy the central theme of the new ego psychology he was to propose—that the ego, as it develops, acquires an organizing function. Valuable as is his work for psychoanalysis, it is even more so for psychotherapy. The intact ego of the psychoanalytic patient is amenable to the methods of free association, lifting of repressions, interpretation of transference, and the like. But the ego of the psychotherapy patient is modified because of developmental failures that prevent acquisition of even neurotic structure, and it is these heretofore dark areas of developmental theory that Hartmann has illuminated so brilliantly. By his providing the instrument of normal development against which to measure pathology, we have come to understand the nature of failures in development. By now, combining Hartmann's groundbreaking discoveries with the contributions of the theorists who later elaborated on the details of normal and pathological development, we are better able to understand the minutiae of pathology, to trace its origin to the locus of developmental failure, and to formulate therapeutic techniques for pathologies more severe than neurosis.

Hartmann's work begins with a major thrust—the concept of adaptation, which he defines as "primarily a reciprocal relationship between the organism and its environment." [2] He then examines this reciprocity from both sides, suggesting that, on the side of the organism, functions develop which may then be used for adaptation. Thus, the organism develops the capacity to act upon itself—autoplastic activity; and the capacity to effect responses from the environment —alloplastic activity.

Beginning with the autoplastic, Hartmann examined the nature of the organism itself. He postulated that: ". . . Mental development is not simply the outcome of the struggle with instinctual drives, with love-objects, with the superego, and so on. For instance, we have reason to assume that this development is served by apparatuses which function from the beginning of life." [3]

These are known as *apparatuses of primary autonomy.* With this, Hartmann revised a major assumption of psychoanalytic theory—

[2] H. Hartmann, *Ego Psychology and the Problem of Adaptation,* p. 24.
[3] *Ibid.,* p. 15.

that the ego arises out of the id, out of that segment of the id which
comes into contact with the outside world. By postulating the existence of inborn ego apparatuses such as perception, intention, object
comprehension, thinking, language, recall phenomena, productivity,
motor development, and the like, he provided a new frame of reference; the developing organism has these potentialities available. Thus
theory acquired the concept of the *undifferentiated matrix.* "Strictly
speaking, there is no ego before the differentiation of ego and id, but
there is no id either, since both are products of differentiation." [4] That
the concept of the *undifferentiated matrix* is not as radical a revision
of Freud as some suppose is asserted by Hartmann himself, who shows
that, in *Analysis Terminable and Interminable,* Freud indicated that,
before the ego exists, its lines of development are already determined.
Thus, Freud suggested that there may be genetic givens contained in
the as-yet undeveloped ego.

Under normal developmental conditions, the inborn ego apparatuses, which develop into functions, remain in the *conflict-free sphere.*
In traumatic developmental circumstances, they may become involved
in conflict. Elaborating this theme, Hartmann points out that adaptation develops not only progressively, in a straight line, but also regressively, through detours in fantasy. The unconscious is so basic that
man cannot escape from it, nor would escape be desirable. How
would the infant develop without maternal projections, unconscious
fantasies, as well as conscious hopes? Would love be possible without
this irrational factor? If we grant this irrationality, the myth of the
"fully analyzed" individual and of normality as perfection are dispelled. "The normal human being is free neither of problems nor of
conflicts. Conflicts are part of the human condition." [5] Borrowing a
title from an author of the time, R. Musil, Hartmann describes the
hypothetically perfect human being as *A Man without Qualities.*

On the side of the environment or, as Hartmann terms it, the *average expectable environment,* is foremost the mother and her maternal needs which reciprocate the infant's needs. Behind the mother
stand her husband, the concept of family, and the entire social structure. Nor does it end there, because:

[4] *Ibid.,* p. 12.   [5] *Ibid.,* p. 13.

Man does not come to terms with his environment anew in every generation; his relation to the environment is guaranteed by—besides the factors of heredity—an evolution peculiar to man, namely, the influence of tradition and the survival of the works of man. . . . The works of man objectify the methods he has discovered for solving problems and thereby become factors of continuity, so that man lives, so to speak, in past generations as well as in his own. Thus arises a network of identifications and ideal-formations which is of great significance for the forms and ways of adaptation.[6]

Processes of adaptation are influenced by constitution, external environment, and ontogenesis. This summary delineates the separate identities of each of the reciprocating partners in adaptation. We proceed to Hartmann's description of their interaction and its results.

Hartmann's synthesis of theory transcended tying in the relationships of the several social and biological sciences, including medicine. He also integrated the concepts of maturation and development. In a later work,[7] he used the term *maturation* for those processes which are biological, and reserved *development* for those that combine the biological and psychological. In his original work, he deals with the nature-nurture controversy by stating, "Psychology and biology are for us simply two different directions of work, two points of view, two methods of investigation, and two sets of concepts." [8] Observing that the first social relationships are crucial for maintaining biological equilibrium, he concludes that the infant's first object relations are of primary concern to psychoanalysis. He asks, "Is the relationship of the child to his mother, or the care of children not a biological process?" [9] and replies, "In our opinion the psychological is not an 'antithesis' to the biological, but rather an essential part of it." [10]

Evolution, to Hartmann, is a "process of progressive 'internalization'" [11] for, in the development of the species, the organism achieves increased independence from its environment, the result of which is that ". . . reactions which originally occurred in relation

[6] *Ibid.*, p. 30.
[7] H. Hartmann, E. Kris, and R. M. Loewenstein, "Comments on the Formation of Psychic Structure."
[8] H. Hartmann, *Ego Psychology and the Problem of Adaptation*, p. 34.
[9] *Ibid.*, p. 33.   [10] *Ibid.*, p. 34.   [11] *Ibid.*, p. 57.

to the external world are increasingly displaced into the interior of
the organism." [12] The biological functions are easily disrupted by the
drives because there is no stimulus barrier to internal excitation. (To
illustrate the seminal quality of Hartmann's work, Jacobson and
Schur, years later, elaborate on this fundamental concept of the biological disruption caused by drive discharge to the interior.) This
close relationship of inner world and drives makes possible a better
capacity to adapt, because man's view of objective reality does not
have to depend on the shifting strength of the drives, as is true of
other animals whose goals and aims are closely intertwined with instinct. The more independent an organism becomes, the greater its independence from the stimulation of the immediate environment.
Adaptive capacity is also increased in man by the possibility to with-
draw from the external world, to think, and to return to it with improved mastery.

Having dealt with the interdependence of infant and mother, organism and environment, Hartmann then proceeds to consider an
aspect of the reciprocal relationship apart from adaptation or its con-
verse. To develop this concept—*fitting together*—he considers
the task of maintaining equilibrium by means of the various regulating processes. He concludes that there is a rank order in the ego functions that serve adaptive processes, and that adaptation must also
serve *fitting together*. He finds that there are four regulatory processes: the equilibrium between individual and environment; the
equilibrium of instinctual drives; the structural equilibrium of mental
institutions; and, since the ego is now postulated as inborn and not
merely an equilibrium of itself, the synthetic function is a specific apparatus of equilibrium at the disposal of the individual.

Out of his consideration of these regulating factors, Hartmann is
forced to propose that there are processes of adaptation in the broader
and narrower senses, as well as broader and narrower reality principles. This seeming confusion is the result of heuristic necessity, of having to refer to postulates not yet proposed because they cannot be discussed simultaneously. Therefore, we have to consider the spiraling
situation wherein the infant, born into an average expectable environ-

[12] *Ibid.*, p. 40.

ment with apparatuses of his own serving adaptation, enters into a system of reciprocal relations in which his own regulating systems perform adaptive services, not only upon himself and his environment, but also, through his effect on his environment, upon himself again, calling for further adaptive accommodations which introduce new configurations and equilibria. In this circular, interdependent interchange, even the most effective forms of reality adaptation cannot guarantee optimal adaptation. An example is that of the adult woman who has attained reality adaptation if she has developed evenly, in phase-specific steps, and has reached psychological adulthood. This adaptation, in and of itself, will not serve her well enough if she has an infant, unless she also has the capacity for partial and temporary regression in order to become a partner in the mother-child dyad. Temporarily abandoning her higher forms of development, mother and infant fit together, serving both the maternal requirements and the infant's needs. The subjective reality principle, or, in Hartmann's terms, the reality principle in the narrower sense, takes precedence over the objective (broader) reality principle of the woman's effective, individuated identity as an adult.

For the child, differentiation then takes place within an average expectable environment and those functions which derive from the apparatuses of primary autonomy develop outside the area of conflict. Motility, intentionality, perception, and the like will follow the innately programmed developmental course, always provided that the mothering person is present and not so grossly interfering that she adversely affects the development of the ego and its functions. Maturation, which proceeds according to a biological timetable, is less vulnerable to disruption than is ego development.

The term *autonomous ego* is frequently, but incorrectly, ascribed to Hartmann. He speaks of the "relative independence of ego development," [13] "ego constitution," [14] and "autonomous ego development." [15] But these mean that the ego has innate givens upon which to rely and which will develop in concert with the innate givens available to the drives and the anatomical constitution; such independence can only be relative, however, because there can be but one

[13] *Ibid.*, p. 41.   [14] *Ibid.*, p. 101.   [15] *Ibid.*

indivisible whole. "And in regard to the ego aspect, too, some of us are agreed that we have to consider it as a partly primary, independent variable, not entirely traceable to the interaction of drives and environment; also that it partly can become independent from the drives in a secondary way. That is what I meant by the terms *primary* and *secondary autonomy* in ego development." [16]

As thought processes develop, involving delay of drive discharge, intelligence serves the ego by aiding the organization of percepts and memory traces, making meaningful action possible. This organization of the inner world—the world of internalizations—is the very process of structuralization. As this proceeds, certain forms of behavior change in function. A process which had originated as a defense— for example, the essential mechanism of reaction formation in toilet training—acquires adaptive autonomy when the purpose changes to maintenance of hygienic habits and orderliness. With change in function, the activity becomes pleasurable in its own right, whereas when it is still in its archaic defensive form it counteracts pleasure. The end result of change in function is attainment of secondary autonomy. We referred to this process in the Introduction in discussing how the disciplined professional behavior of the therapist becomes pleasurable.

In the many papers which Hartmann wrote following *Ego Psychology and the Problem of Adaptation,* he enlarged upon his original thoughts. Because the unconscious is not subject to Aristotelian logic, turning away from reality is possibly, but not necessarily, pathological. Rational action may come about by means of detours, analogous to the use of denial in fantasy by children. Although the healthy ego has to be able to endure suffering and depression, it must also be able to regress, as in sleep and orgasm.

While Hartmann saw his theoretical task as elaborating on the understanding of the derivation and functioning of the construct *ego,* he did not lose sight of the totality of the personality: ". . . hence we need a model of psychic structure which shows the interrelations of drive, intellect, adaptation, integration, etc., by assigning them their place in relation to those centers of mental functioning which in analysis we call systems." [17]

[16] H. Hartmann, *Essays in Ego Psychology,* p. 105.   [17] *Ibid.,* p. 81.

To the already well-known concept of *intersystemic* conflict, Hartmann adds that of *intrasystemic* conflict: the ego can be in conflict with elements within itself. For example, it can both oppose and gratify the drives. Autonomous functions might become entangled with defense; insight might conflict with rationalization. Also, the theme of ego building is given prominence in Hartmann's continuing study of the ego.

What do we mean when we say that we help the patient's ego; or, strengthen his ego? This certainly cannot be adequately described by referring only to the redistributions of energy between the id and the ego, or between the superego and the ego; shifts from certain spheres of the ego to other functional units within the ego are involved. No definition of ego strength would I consider complete which does not refer to the intrasystemic structures. . . .[18]

Neurosis, he believes, is not adequately treated unless the therapeutic work has concerned itself also with the interaction of the neurosis with normal functioning. We have found this to be particularly useful, not only in the psychoanalysis of neurosis, but in its applicability to aspects of psychotherapy such as marital counseling.

A major theoretical proposition put forth by Hartmann is that of *neutralization*, that process which moves both libidinal and aggressive energies from the instinctual to the noninstinctual mode, thereby rendering them available to the ego. Noting that Freud's proposals about sublimation preceded his dual drive theory, it seemed logical to Hartmann to enlarge the concept of sublimation by including within consideration of drive-taming processes the vicissitudes of the aggressive drive. Recently there has been much dissatisfaction expressed with the concept of neutralization, largely by theorists who are not clinicians. These theorists wish to move psychoanalytic energic concepts away from nineteenth-century hydrodynamics toward greater compatibility with twentieth-century physics. It is our opinion that this might make theory appear much neater, but at the expense of clinical usefulness. Criticism of Freud's and Hartmann's energic concepts has not yet led to formulation of a more useful theory.

To continue with Hartmann on this matter: The capacity to neutralize drive energy, working in a circular, expanding interaction with

[18] *Ibid.,* pp. 145–46.

the capacity to delay drive discharge, places energies for ego building (structuralization) and expanding ego functions at the disposal of the infant. The hungry infant of three months has already achieved some capacity to neutralize drive energy. Thus, he uses the sensation of hunger in conjunction with memory traces of past gratification to summon his mother by his cry, which, by then, has changed from the objectless cry of the neonate to a purposeful one. Object relations are built by transferring energy—which was formerly invested only in the drives—to the ego, for negotiation with the environment.

The concept of neutralization expands understanding of psychosis. While Freud regarded psychosis as conflict between ego and reality, Hartmann redefines it as a failure of neutralization, resulting in the inability of the ego to assume its organizing role and to mediate between the drives and reality. The derivation of energy for the defensive function of the ego is also more incisively explained; neutralized aggression is the energic source for the defense mechanisms. The ego that cannot employ defense is, of course, seriously impaired: "If frustrations, and particularly narcissistic injuries, which in other individuals would be of minor importance, are frequently capable of inducing a detachment of libido and precipitating a schizophrenic process, this is essentially due to the deficiency or to the lack of stablized power of object relations and certain ego functions." [19]

Anticipating Jacobson and Kohut, Hartmann conceived of narcissism as the cathexis of self representations, not of the ego as Freud first proposed or even of the self of poststructural theory. This opened the way for Jacobson to formulate a concept of identity based upon ego and superego identifications, originating with self and object representations which differentiate, developmentally, in the processes of structuralization and internalization. The mode of narcissism may be instinctual or neutralized, allowing room for it to develop normally or pathologically, in accordance with the way that structuralization in general takes place.

Hartmann also proposed a progression in the development of object relations. They proceed from the objectless stage of primary narcissism, through the stage in which the object is experienced as exist-

[19] *Ibid.*, p. 194.

ing only to fulfill the infant's needs, to the level of object constancy. Object constancy is defined as cathexis of the constant mental representation of the object regardless of the state of need. This definition has far-reaching implications for development and provides a therapeutic goal of utmost importance in the treatment of borderline patients, most of whom begin treatment at the level of need gratification. For them, a large part of the therapeutic task becomes one of raising the level of object relations to approach constant representation. That the image of the object is retained regardless of the state of need means not only that the individual has cathected the object with neutralized libido, but also that he has reached a stage of development which makes him less dependent upon the environment. Self and object representations, and the drives, are no longer vulnerable to splitting. Identity is maintained by continuous cathexis not only of object but of self representations. On this solid foundation, Spitz, Mahler, and Jacobson build their elaborations of psychoanalytic developmental psychology.

In the years immediately after World War II, Hartmann, in collaboration with Kris and Loewenstein, presented a series of propositions which may be regarded, in the historical sense, as ushering in an era of extension of ego psychology. We shall list the essential theoretical formulations contained in this series of papers.

To the three aspects of metapsychology—the dynamic, the topographic, and the economic—was added a fourth, the genetic. "The genetic approach in psychoanalysis does not deal only with anamnestic data, nor does it intend to show only 'how the past is contained in the present.' Genetic propositions describe why, in past situations of conflict, a specific solution was adopted; why the one was retained and the other dropped, and what causal relation exists between these solutions and later developments." [20]

The authors attempt to clarify terms and especially to make room for consideration of ego functioning beyond the defensive function. They discuss the role of deprivation in structure building. While carefully avoiding the viewing of frustration simplistically, as the source of aggressive drive manifestations, they pave the way for later theo-

[20] H. Hartmann and E. Kris, "The Genetic Approach in Psychoanalysis," p. 17.

rists to elaborate on its value for development. They also describe the concept of identification as a process which may serve two purposes, the already-known defensive one, and one serving normal development. They further discuss identification as a varying process, depending upon the level of development at which it takes place. Imitation, therefore, is a forerunner of true identification, representing as it does the outer limit of what the child can accomplish with perception and wishing. Identification proper is a process of internalization, whereas imitation is not. Therefore, identification makes for a greater degree of independence from the object. This is the road to autonomy.

The authors' discussion of the superego anticipated Kohut by ten years. Particularly clarifying is the distinction they draw between superego as a discrete structure, and superego forerunners. They separate genetic roots from functional entity. The beginning introjections, incorporations, and identifications are variously described in the literature as primitive, archaic forms of superego, or as precursors or preoedipal superego. Hartmann and Loewenstein prefer to reserve superego as term and concept for that structure which develops from the oedipal conflict. In that struggle, the disparate aspects become integrated and merge into a new structure which is the superego. An oversimplified analogy is that flour, eggs, and shortening, if described as forerunners or archaic forms of a cake, would hardly be described correctly. The cake becomes an entirely new form. To refer to the ingredients of what are to become combined to form the superego as archaic forms of the structure itself is to deny the essence of the ego's capacity, namely its organizing function. To them the superego is ". . . a dynamically partly independent center of mental functioning with aims of its own." [21] Its development does not proceed in the direction of increased detachment from the ego, but is bound up with it. The ego ideal is regarded as one of the functions of the superego, as are also conscience and moral values. In summary then, superego development depends upon ego development and ". . . Once the superego as a system is set up, its normal functioning is constantly bound to certain activities of the ego; and the further evolution of the superego does not diminish the developing ego's influence, but tends to in-

[21] H. Hartmann and R. M. Loewenstein, "Notes on the Superego," p. 65.

crease it." [22] Jacobson further developed this interesting spiral effect of ego development enhancing superego development and discussed how both are mutually reinforcing.

In all, the contributions of Hartmann and his collaborators may be read in retrospect as well as in prospect, as we are presenting them here, because so many of their formulations, postulates, and propositions provide points of departure for the theory to follow. Retrospective reading convinces one not only that Hartmann is rightly called the father of ego psychology, but shows which of his traits are replicated in his theoretical progeny.

We shall summarize briefly the basic theoretical formulations of Hartmann and his collaborators. These include:

1. The concept of human adaptation, involving autoplastic modification of the self, alloplastic modification of the environment, and the effects of these ongoing processes. Adaptation is both progressive and regressive and also serves fitting together.

2. Modification of Freud's thoughts about the origin and development of the ego. Hartmann's postulate is that the neonate is equipped with an undifferentiated matrix within which there exist apparatuses of primary autonomy. After ego and id differentiate, these will serve ego. There is, therefore, an implied existence of an innate ego constitution as well as other innate factors which come into play after differentiation.

3. Apparatuses of primary autonomy that develop outside the sphere of conflict. This postulate moved psychoanalysis as a science into the realm of the study of normal behavior, by which psychoanalysis became a normal developmental psychology as well as a psychopathology. Development is no longer regarded as solely conflict-borne because a conflict-free sphere is also held to exist.

4. Introduction of the concept of an average expectable environment. By introducing this concept, Hartmann affirmed the crucial importance of the maternal contribution to development, leading to subsequent study of the mother-child dyad and to elaboration of our understanding of that essential aspect of human interchange—object relations.

[22] *Ibid.*, p. 64.

5. The theme of developing levels of object relations by enunciating the several stages from primary narcissism, through need gratification, to object constancy.

6. The idea that the patient is to be regarded as a whole. One must not lose sight of this whole out of concern for a specific facet of behavior or psychopathology.

7. A description of the development of psychic structure, the inner world, the environment, and the network of inheritances already available to the neonate. This description, while complex, is clinically accurate.

8. The concept of secondary autonomy—change in function. This concept provides understanding of defense, adaptation, and ego effectiveness.

9. Adding considerations of intrasystemic conflict to the already-known concept of intersystemic conflict. This addition provides precision to understanding ego functioning and led to elaboration of techniques for ego building in therapy not heretofore possible.

10. Redefinition of narcissism as libidinal cathexis of the self representations (not of ego or self), which preserved the clarity of the structural theory.

11. Emphasis upon the essential role of frustration to development. This emphasis led to elaboration of the processes of acquisition of identity and of the use of the aggressive drive in the service of development.

12. The concept of neutralization, which radically revised energic concepts and techniques for treating psychotic and borderline structures.

13. In collaboration with Kris and Loewenstein, Hartmann's redefinition of terms and their proposal of the genetic aspect, which added a dimension to metapsychology.

14. Insight into processes of superego formation. Distinguishing the superego from its forerunners both lent clarity to earlier concepts and added to them.

Finally, it was Hartmann who, in concurrence with Freud, proposed that the tenets arrived at by means of clinical observation needed to be rounded out by observational studies. He said: "Many of us expect psychoanalysis to become a general *developmental psychology;* to do so, it must encompass these other roots of ego development. . . . This naturally gives new importance to the direct observation of developmental processes by psychoanalysts (first of all the direct observation of children)." [23] [24]

[23] H. Hartmann, *Ego Psychology and the Problem of Adaptation,* p. 8.
[24] See page 40, quotation from Freud.

❧ 3 ❦

THE CONTRIBUTIONS OF
RENÉ A. SPITZ

EXPERIMENTATION WITH HUMAN BEINGS is severely limited for
obvious reasons. While experimental psychologists do design and
conduct such studies, they are largely in the area of conscious behavior. Spitz is critical of experiments which, for the sake of quantification, exclude fundamental aspects of human psychology, such as affects, from their design. To Spitz, affects, although they are abstract
and defy measurement, explicate behavior. He thinks that research
methods restricted to that which can be measured "arrest the advancement of knowledge." [1] Observation of infants and young children is a more difficult method that does not lend itself readily to
measurement or even to statistical analysis. It is subject to the danger
of adultomorphic speculation, and it demands the objectivity of the
true scientific investigator. Spitz and Mahler combine this latter quality with a profound knowledge of psychoanalysis as a theory of
human behavior which constitutes a conceptual base. Freud had proposed that observational design could provide the data needed to validate psychoanalytic theory. He said: "The direct observation of children has the disadvantage of working upon data which are easily
misunderstandable; psycho-analysis is made difficult by the fact that it
can only reach its data, as well as its conclusions, after long detours.
But by cooperation the two methods can attain a satisfactory degree
of certainty in their findings." [2]

Although it would certainly not be desirable to devise experiments

[1] R. A. Spitz, *The First Year of Life*, p. 85.
[2] S. Freud, *Standard Edition*, Vol. 7, p. 201.

that are cruel and have irreversibly destructive effects, unfortunately such situations do exist in real life. Man's inhumanity to man gave Spitz the material for his study on the hospitalized infant,[3] through which we have learned about the deleterious effects of the absence of a mothering person. Spitz found that marasmus and death are the fate of the unmothered infant. His conclusion illustrates how a brilliant investigator creates new theory. Drawing upon animal psychology and ethology, he combines facts from these sciences with psychoanalytic theory and his observational data to propose a new concept. It is essential to life, he concludes, that the neonate's innate equipment be "quickened" [4] through interchange with the mother. He says that "Only a reciprocal relation can provide the experiential factor in the infant's development, consisting as it does of an ongoing circular exchange, in which affects play the major role.[5] From the beginning of life, it is the mother, the human partner of the child, who mediates every perception, every action, every insight, every knowledge." [6]

To illustrate our theme, that of the technical implications of theory—the dyadic relationship is central to transference phenomena. Capacity to engage in transference has its roots in ". . . the multiform, silent ebb and flow, the mute invisible tides, powerful and at the same time subtle, which pervade these relations." [7] Spitz studied infants born to mothers in prison. It was administrative policy there to separate the child from the mother after several months. The emotional plight of the child thus removed from the maternal object taught Spitz about so-called anaclitic depression. Important as these studies are, they are forerunners of Spitz' major observational investigations which illuminate the theory of the developmental steps whereby the neonate organizes his ego within the dyadic relationship.

Spitz announces his theme:

. . . we shall study these reciprocal relations and try to apprehend what goes on between mother and child. Basing ourselves upon direct observations and experiments on infants, we shall present our findings and ideas on object relations—their beginnings, development, stages, and certain

---

[3] R. A. Spitz, "Hospitalism: An Inquiry into the Genesis of Psychiatric Conditions in Early Childhood."
[4] R. A. Spitz, *The First Year of Life*, p. 95.   [5] *Ibid.* .   [6] *Ibid.*, p. 96.
[7] *Ibid.*, pp. 204–205.

anomalies. We shall also attempt to throw some light on how these relations ensure survival and how they serve the unfolding of the psychic and somatic sectors of personality.[8]

He studies the very tools—the ego functions—with which the infant acquires awareness of the maternal partner. This leads to consideration of perception itself, its antecedents and the vicissitudes of its development. Affects in particular influence perception and the development of object relations, and anxiety is foremost among these affects. The intricacies of interactive processes and their effect upon each partner are detailed, contributing significantly to the understanding of communication. Spitz found also that there are critical nodal points of development, points at which asynchronous maturation of the innate equipment enforces adaptive development of psychic structure. Failures at such points result in deviant psychic organization. The role of culture is affirmed and delineated. Discrete forms of infant pathology are correlated with failures in phase-specific development.

The oral cavity is designated as the cradle of perception because, at birth, it is the only area of the body that is integrated and operational. The central nervous system receiving stations are not yet cathected or activated. Therefore, the sensorium plays a relatively subordinate role in the early weeks. Tactile sensations are received by skin and labyrinth and, as early as the second week of life, stimulate the infant to turn his head toward the body of the person holding him. But it is the "snout" region which has the most specific and reliable reflexes because it is of survival-specific importance in food ingestion. These reflexes trigger the only directed (not intentional) behavior in the neonate. This is not to say that the infant's first sensations are perceptions proper, since perception only evolves in conjunction with experience. Spitz therefore distinguishes between the coenesthetic sensing of the neonate and the diacritic perception of which he will become capable later. Coenesthetic reception is on the level of deep sensibility, is experienced in terms of totalities, and is largely visceral. Adults who retain remnants of this form of reception are usually gifted. For most adults, coenesethetic reception atro-

[8] *Ibid.*, p. 3.

phies, giving way to modes of response through localized, discrete senses and to semantic symbols. Still referring to the first months of life, Spitz describes how signs and signals reach the infant selectively, filtered through his innate stimulus barrier, complemented by the protective screen provided by the mother, the infant's external auxiliary ego. These affect tension, equilibrium, posture, temperature, vibration, skin and body contact, rhythm, pitch, tone. Coalescing within the affective climate of the mother-child relationship, these constitute the first communications.

Since the maternal partner is so vital to the child's development, Spitz finds it pertinent to consider her abilities. These depend upon her own level of development and on her reality. He believes that, already during pregnancy, potential for coenesthetic response becomes activated. Regressive behavior is widely observed in pregnant women. Such preparation for the dyadic relationship equips the prospective mother for participation in the affective interchanges with the neonate that are so important to his ongoing development. The infant can provide gratification to the mother on all levels—conscious, preconscious, and unconscious—as well as to all her psychic structures —id, ego, and superego. This, of course, is predicated on the assumption that the child is wanted and arrives at a phase-specific time for the mother. If progress through her own developmental phases was adequate, a woman arrives at the developmental phase of parenthood [9] with capacity for empathy and for regression in the service of the ego.[10] Having attained identity, the regression is reversible. Regressive potential, nevertheless, is great. The mother "has to defend herself against the gamut of seductions offered by her baby." [11] She also has to be most flexible because the drives of the infant mature rapidly, shifting their aims. Since the mother is the principal object of these drives, her responses have to be attuned to the shifts and changes. She has to provide an ever-changing attunement and new stimulations as the infant's needs demand. In describing communication within the dyad, Spitz refers repeatedly to a circular interaction, or an action-reaction-action cycle. Communication cannot,

[9] T. Benedek, "Parenthood as a Developmental Phase."
[10] E. Kris, *Psychoanalytic Explorations in Art.*
[11] R. A. Spitz, *The First Year of Life,* p. 26.

of course, be on exactly the same plane for both mother and infant. The baby's mode is expressive, originating as it does from affects; it is self-centered, not directed toward an as yet nonperceived object. The mother's responses are obviously directed, but anyone listening to a mother cooing to her baby notes the regressed form taken by this directed communication, attuned as it is to the infant's affective receptivity.

Most of the interchanges between mother and infant take place in the nursing situation, during which the infant stares at the mother's face: ". . . when the infant nurses at the breast, he *feels* the nipple in his mouth while at the same time he *sees* the mother's face. Here contact perception blends with distance perception." [12] As hunger is satiated and the nipple is relinquished, or as the nipple is lost and regained, the visual percept remains constant. It is little wonder, therefore, to find that, as early as the beginning of the second month of life, the infant follows the moving face of the adult with his eyes. This event is the precursor of object formation and object constancy. However, ". . . the nursing situation is not merely an experience of gratification. It initates the transition from exclusive contact perception to distance perception. It activates the diacritic perceptual system, which gradually replaces the original and primitive coenesthetic organization." [13] Thereby, the shift from contact perception to distance perception is influenced by rhythms of unpleasure as well as of pleasure. During the period of life which is dominated by affective experience (coenesthetic sensing), awareness of an outside related to need gratification comes about through repetitive experiences in the nursery—feeding, changing, bathing, and the like. Memory traces are laid down, correlated with the rhythm of gratification and frustration and with an awareness of the mothering person who is sensed but is not quite perceived yet. Thus the infant begins to form meaningful constellations out of a universe of amorphous sensation. Still on a primitive level, there are nevertheless signs that cognitive processes have begun to encroach progressively on the totality of emotional response. The shift to discriminative (diacritic) modes takes place, at first so tentatively that it can only be maintained as long as the "dia-

[12] *Ibid.*, p. 65.   [13] *Ibid.*, p. 75.

logue" continues. External signs that this important shift is occurring can be observed as early as the beginning of the second month of life when there appears to be awareness of the configuration of the human face. By the third month, it can be demonstrated. Spitz has shown that the child responds with a smile to the gestalt of two eyes, a nose, and a mouth. It matters not yet if this be a person or a Halloween mask. What does matter is that it be full face and in motion; the child does not respond to a profile nor to a mask or a human face that is not moving.

The period of coenesthetic sensing is an essential precursor to the establishment of the first organizer of the psyche, the indicator of which is the smiling response. The relationship between neonate and mothering person is a biological-psychological one, the proportions of which shift with development. At first biology is dominant. It is through the dialogue that the relationship alters to become a predominantly social experience. This primitive object relationship serves first to ensure survival of the human infant who is altricial, incapable of providing for himself at the beginning of life. Precocial animals are not long dependent upon the mother for survival. This often-overlooked distinction between man and some other animals invalidates simplistic extrapolation from animal psychology to human behavior.

Indicators are the external signs that internal shifts are taking place. Spitz' concept of *organizer of the psyche* is borrowed from embryology, in which it is defined as a center radiating its influence. Before the emergence of an organizer, transplanted tissue will assume the qualities of the surrounding tissue. Afterward, it acquires and retains an "organized" identity and can only take its own form. Applying this term to psychoanalytic developmental psychology, Spitz finds it a useful way to describe the attainment of new levels of integration in the developmental process.

The smiling response is observable when the psyche has become sufficiently organized to be able to link affect to intentionality. This response signals the shift from reception of inner stimuli to perception of the external; from cathexis of the inside to cathexis of the periphery. It is a vital precursor of object relations proper. It occurs when capacity to suspend the unconditional functioning of the pleasure principle is attained and is, of course, a movement in the direction of

the reality principle. Demonstrable existence of memory traces shows
that a topical division into conscious and unconscious is beginning to
take place. The infant is capable, also, of displacement of cathectic
charge; pleasurable response previously produced by the active gratifying ministrations of the feeding adult is now displaced to a memory
trace and is triggered and anticipated by the perception of the moving face. In effect, this is the precursor of the process of thought, and
it means, of course, that a rudimentary ego has come into being and
that the synthetic function is operative.

Further and increasingly complex developmental tasks arise. As
signs and signals from the periphery are perceived, the stimulus barrier becomes less operative and the ego must take over the function
which the stimulus barrier served. Also, it is consistent to assume that,
with the shift from inner reception to outer perception, there is a general movement away from total passivity and toward activity. It is finally to be considered that social relations have begun, involving the
ego function of volition. This will lead ultimately to the capacity to
love. Toward that goal, however, the infant still has a long way to
travel. Between the third and eighth months of life, his continuing
ego development will lead toward establishment of the libidinal object proper.

The process of fusion involves the coming together of the two
drives—aggression and libido—under the dominance of libido.
This comes about at approximately six months of age and Spitz
thinks that failure in fusion leads to deviant or deficient, mostly
pathologic development. Fusion occurs in the context of the relationship with the libidinal object, at the point when there is realization
that the formerly "good" (gratifying) object and the "bad" (frustrating) one are, in fact, one and the same person. The resultant coming
together of the two drives and the two object representations thus
consists of a double process which can occur only if the experiences
have been sufficiently gratifying for libido to unite with aggression,
but also sufficiently frustrating to provoke development of structure
(differentiation between self and object representations) to proceed.
With neutralization of the drives having begun with the predominance of gratifying over frustrating experiences, now also postponement of drive discharge becomes possible as memory traces of gratifi-

cation and of a gratifying object continue to accumulate. With delay of discharge, thought can be interposed before action—a process which leads ultimately to a capacity to weigh consequences, to consider alternatives, and even to decide to take no action at all.

Within the increasing complexity of development, one feature emerges with outstanding clarity; the infant becomes aware of his specific mother. With the improvement in visual perception that comes with maturation, but certainly primarily out of psychological experience with her, the mother (the libidinal object proper)—and to a slightly lesser extent other familiar persons—is recognized. No longer will a stranger or a Halloween mask elicit a smile. On the contrary, the approach of a stranger provokes withdrawal and often crying. This observable phenomenon—eight-month anxiety or stranger anxiety—marks the attainment of a new level of object relations and with it the second major organization of psychic structure. With the attainment of this level of development, of which eight-month anxiety is the indicator, the following psychological events take place.

Drive attenuation makes possible mental activity of far greater complexity than heretofore. Memory traces have greater clarity and are more extensive. The libidinal object proper is established. Anxiety becomes focused around specific object loss. Directed action is now possible and enables the infant to learn or invent devices for keeping the mother near him.

Aided by development of locomotion, he can also keep himself near her. Since it is not possible, and not even desirable, for the mother to be continuously available, the child has to cope with separation and separation anxiety. If the anxiety is in tolerable doses, development is accelerated. Also, increase in physical capacity leads to pleasure in its exercise. Greenacre, a theorist whose work elaborates another aspect of this stage of the toddler's development, refers to the expanding and pleasurable nature of the child's exploration of his environment as a "love affair with the world." [14] Optimally, these forays take place within the watchful orbit of the mother lest the child's enthusiasm carry him so far that severe and therefore traumatic separation anxiety ensues.

[14] P. Greenacre, "The Childhood of the Artist," p. 57.

Spitz details some of the mechanisms employed by the infant to cope with tolerable separation anxiety. By imitation, the precursor of identification, the child begins the long process of internalization. He attempts to provide himself with the gratifications that had been provided by the object. "To the extent to which the infant's own potentialities are developed in the course of the first year of life, he will become independent of his surround." [15] This accords with Hartmann's assertion that, as internalization proceeds, so does greater independence from the environment.

With increasing locomotion, tactile experience is reduced. However, the need for mother is only slightly lessened at this point. Therefore, her voice assumes a new kind of importance, signifying that she is still present and, by her admonitions, that she still cares for the child. By this means, diacritic sensory perception stimulates further movement away from the archaic coenesthetic sensing when tactile contact played such an important role. Up to this point, global words served as a sort of communication. The word "Mama," for example, contained complex statements and feelings. Now, however, the need for more precise communication becomes pressing; abstract thought has to be expressed overtly. The first abstraction to be formed is often the semantic "no," accompanied by a head-shaking gesture. This is the indicator of yet a third organizer of the psyche. Spitz' concept is that each "no" from the mother constitutes a frustration, experienced as an aggression and a prohibition which interrupt an initiative. It forces the child back into passivity. The memory trace of the experience carries an affective charge, which assures its permanency. Displeasure causes conflict; an aggressive thrust against both passivity and displeasure forces confrontation with the fact that it is the libidinal object who is the source of the displeasure. The child resolves this in an active mode by identifying with the aggressor, doing as she does, shaking his head and saying "no." This single word is an expression both of negation and of judgment. It is the first abstraction in the sense of adult mentation. Its inception heralds a new form of interchange with objects and will attain greater and greater intricacy. With this gesture, action is replaced by message, enhancing distinc-

[15] R. A. Spitz, *The First Year of Life*, p. 4.

tion between self and object representations. From this point on, communication will assume predominantly semantic form.

The process of fusion, which must have taken place a few months earlier, is an essential percursor to attainment of this third level of ego organization, *semantic communication.* Dominance of libidinal over aggressive cathexis of the "libidinal object proper" [16] prevents response with rage or rebellion to the frustration of "no." The solution provided by identification with the aggressor preserves the object and at the same time creates a self-regulating structure. Where these complex processes of fusion and neutralization have failed, aggression predominates and makes for rage, noncompliance, and even violence. Perhaps more prophetically than he realized at the time, Spitz said:

From the societal aspect, disturbed object relations in the first year of life, be they deviant, improper, or insufficient, have consequences which imperil the very foundation of society. Without a template, the victims of disturbed object relations subsequently will themselves lack the capacity to relate. They are not equipped for the more advanced, more complex forms of personal and social interchange without which we as a species would be unable to survive. They cannot adapt to society. . . . The only path which remains open to them is the destruction of a social order of which they are the victims. Infants without love, they will end as adults full of hate.[17]

Spitz' emphasis upon object relations, so pertinent to normal development, thus also highlights the unquantifiable pitfalls which tend to veer development in pathological directions. The building of object relations: ". . . take place as a constant interaction between two very unequal partners, the mother and the child. . . . The very perfection of a relation between two beings as closely attuned to each other and linked by so many tangibles and intangibles entails the possibility of serious disturbances if they are out of tune." [18] However, it is reassuring to note that the infant's need for a human partner is of such overriding importance that it far outweighs the inevitable mechanical failures in the mothering process.

The concept of *critical periods* is an important outgrowth of Spitz' observation of the confluence of biological maturation and ego development. Basing himself on Freud's dynamic and economic proposi-

[16] *Ibid.,* p. 161.   [17] *Ibid.,* p. 300.   [18] *Ibid.,* p. 205.

tions formulated as the Nirvana principle, Spitz considers the maintenance of energy tension within a rather generous optimal zone as one
of the primary innate homeostatic regulating principles already
functioning at birth. That presupposes that the phylogenetically programmed progression of maturation is synchronous with and parallel
to that of the progression of development which varies according to
environmental factors. Obviously, asynchronicities must arise between
the rigid progression of maturation and the constantly changing development. According to Spitz, these asynchronicities correspond to
critical periods and to the organizers. They mark the ego levels at
which the device for discharging tension becomes inadequate. Agita-
tion ensues, eventuating in the elaboration of a better discharge for-
mula (through trial and error and the law of effect). The new for-
mula reestablishes synchronous progression for awhile, until the next
asynchronicity becomes sufficiently frustrating to enforce the elaboration of the next higher structural device to cope with accumulating
tension (and later active conflict). An important function of the maternal object is to regulate the frustrations of the critical periods; not
to remove frustration, but, when necessary, to impose it, for optimal
frustration is structure (and ego) building. One of the major perils of
our pharmacological culture is the avoidance of development—
preventing frustration with the help of tranquilizers or amphet-
amines. The result is disturbed structure formation and disorder in
ego and superego development. Orderly (in the sequential meaning of
the term) development is, in fact, an underlying tenet of Spitz'
thought about normal development. In this regard, he points out also
that, in relation to the organizers of the psyche, inadequate establishment of one level of organization leads to deviant development in the
next. He sums up the three stages in psychic organization:

The first of the organizers of the psyche structures perception and establishes the beginnings of the ego. The second integrates object relations
with the drives and establishes the ego as an organized psychic structure
with a variety of systems, apparatuses, and functions. The third organizer
finally opens the road for the development of object relations on the
human pattern, that is, the pattern of semantic communication. This
makes possible both the emergence of the self and the beginning of social
relations on the human level.[19]

[19] R. A. Spitz, *A Genetic Field Theory of Ego Formation: Its Implications for Pathology*, pp. 96–97.

In substantial concurrence with Hartmann about the undifferentiated matrix, Spitz nevertheless prefers the term *nondifferentiation* to extend the concept beyond ego and id. He wishes to include nondifferentiation between psyche and soma, inside and outside, drive and object, I and non-I, and different regions of the body.

Spitz also differs slightly with other theorists in that he places less emphasis on body ego. It seems to us that this is because ego psychological thought has advanced the timetable of development. When Freud said that "the ego is first and foremost a bodily ego," [20] it was within his frame of reference, namely that the ego develops out of the id in contact with reality. It was also at a historical period in psychoanalytic theory building when ego and self were not yet clearly distinguished and defined. It seems more consistent with present-day knowledge about the first days and weeks of life to consider that, just as there is not yet awareness of the maternal object, there is also no awareness of the body. The body ego, therefore, or the corporeal self, can only exist when differentiation between self and object representations is well advanced. Spitz says in this vein: "I think of constituent parts of the ego which have as their prototype innate, mostly phylogenetically transmitted physiological functions as well as innate behavior patterns." [21]

Just as Spitz thinks that imprinting, important in animal behavior as an innate behavior pattern, is negligible in the human infant after the first few weeks, so does it remain consistent with his views that phylogenetically transmitted physiological functions are a far cry from a body ego. These thoughts accord well with the concept of a nondifferentiated matrix in which apparatuses exist as potential. Thus Spitz preserves nondifferentiation as a concept and clarifies that apparatuses of primary autonomy are not yet concerned with the corporeal self. He does, in considering later phases of development, place great emphasis upon awareness of the body and its utility in furthering independence. In that regard, autoerotic activity is held to be important to the attainment of identity.[22]

Much more than the issue of body ego remains to be clarified in

[20] S. Freud, *The Ego and the Id, Standard Edition,* Vol. 19, p. 26.
[21] R. A. Spitz, *The First Year of Life,* p. 104.
[22] R. A. Spitz, "Autoerotism Reexamined: The Role of Early Sexual Behavior Patterns in Personality Formation."

psychoanalytic developmental psychology. The undifferentiated or
nondifferentiated matrix, first postulated by Hartmann some thirty-
five years ago, still contains much to be explored. Spitz has demonstrated dramatically and unquestionably that mothering is essential
not only to development but to life itself. Yet the extent of the contribution from the child's side of the dyad remains relatively unclear.
Mahler has found wide variation—from the infant who cannot engage in the dyadic experience, on the one extreme, to the child who
can extract psychological supplies essential to development from even
an emotionally impoverished environment, on the other. We think,
therefore, that the matter of innateness, which Spitz and Mahler have
to a large extent validated, nevertheless remains an area to be investigated more precisely.

Most recently, Spitz has become engaged in exploration of the
mind-body problem (which has puzzled philosophers and psychologists
through the ages); of the role of the dimension of time in neonatal
development; and of the first affective experiences. The original unorganized, random discharge in the neonate gives way to the higher
state of conditioned reflex, which operates in both psyche and soma.

From the interface with the soma it (conditioned reflex) reaches into the
psyche by introducing an outstandingly psychological function. That
purely psychic function, however, mobilizes a typical somatic apparatus
with which we are familiar from neurophysiology, namely, the alertness
system. This in its turn activates the attention cathexis, which I, for one,
would hesitate to assign exclusively either to psyche or to soma.[23]

In a profound extension of affect theory, Spitz proposes that the
birth cry is

an experience when affect and percept meet for the first time and also as
the first experience of *time* in the form of duration of unpleasure. The factor of duration moves in a direction opposite to the Nirvana principle of
immediate discharge. The addition of the time dimension promotes an active preference for percepts with survival value. Affects, thereby, direct
and quicken perception.

The bond between affect and perception is ". . . a bridge, made of
duration, anticipation, and meaning; a bridge to span the void across
the chasm in front of the soma . . ."[24]

[23] R. A. Spitz, "Bridges: On Anticipation, Duration, and Meaning," pp. 727–28.
[24] *Ibid.*, p. 734.

4

THE CONTRIBUTIONS OF MARGARET S. MAHLER

MORE THAN THOSE OF ANY of the other theorists, Mahler's contributions lend themselves to direct hypotheses about the nature of borderline phenomena and to transposition into technical procedures. Her conclusions are based upon observation of children and their mothers in interaction in a specially designed nursery school setting. As with Spitz' work, some of her observational material had always been available, but it required a creative scientist to link observation with psychoanalytic theory and to innovate elaborations of that theory. Others of her observations were facilitated by special design—for example, by having her trained collaborators observe the response of the toddler to the mother's absence, by skillful interviewing of the mother, and the like. Her methodology meets as closely as possible—in working in depth with human beings—the insistence of experimental psychologists upon replicability. Before this study of normality and pathology, Mahler had already had many years' experience in the study of childhood psychosis. Out of that work, she proposed that there are three phases of development leading, at approximately the fourth year of life, to the establishment of identity; these are the autistic, and symbiotic, and separation-individuation phases. Her later observational studies rounded out and refined this scheme.

Ego psychological theory building is based on Hartmann's postulate of the undifferentiated matrix. The infant who is to develop normally arrives at birth with adequate inborn apparatuses of primary autonomy and encounters an average expectable environment, the major part of which is his particular mother. Mahler proceeds to describe how, from birth on, there begins a complex, multiform, and circular developmental process. The first weeks of life are spent in "a state of primitive hallucinatory disorientation, in which need satisfaction belongs to his (the neonate's) own omnipotent, *autistic* orbit." [1] In that state, the goal is homeostasis. At first, the infant is objectless. Shortly after, he is unable to distinguish his own from his mother's tension-reducing operations. Then he begins to separate those experiences that feel pleasurable from those that feel painful. Next, at approximately the second month of life, he becomes dimly aware of a need-satisfying object; the symbiotic phase is about to begin.

The term *symbiosis,* borrowed from biology, is defined in that science as the living together of two dissimilar organisms in close association or union, especially where this is advantageous to both; it is to be distinguished from parasitism. Mahler uses it metaphorically: "The essential feature of symbiosis is hallucinatory or delusional, somatopsychic omnipotent fusion with the representation of the mother and, in particular, the delusion of a common boundary of the two actually and physically separate individuals." [2]

Mahler regards both autism and symbiosis as two parts of that phase which Freud designated as primary narcissism. At about the third month of life, with the dim awareness that needs are gratified by an object, symbiosis proper begins.

Central to Mahler's conclusions from her observation of infants is that optimal symbiotic gratification is essential to development. There can be such extreme communicative mismatching between mother and infant that psychosis ensues. From the side of the infant, mismatching can be the consequence of a defect in the inborn apparatuses. There are infants who are unable to engage in the symbiotic union. (Mahler believes that this observation does away with the commonly held concept of the schizophrenogenic mother.) She has also observed the opposite; some infants, especially well endowed, have an unusual capacity to extract from the environment whatever they need for their development. If symbiotic deprivation is severe,

---

[1] M. S. Mahler, *On Human Symbiosis and the Vicissitudes of Individuation,* pp. 7–8.
[2] *Ibid.,* p. 9.

the result is symbiotic psychosis or regression to autism. Mahler believes that, actually, childhood psychosis consists of a combination of both symbiotic and autistic pathology. However, the symbiotic psychotic child has some awareness of the symbiotic object, but this is only to the extent of attempting to merge with its "good" aspect and to ward off reingulfment by its "bad" aspect. In autistic childhood psychosis, capacity to retain some memory traces of good mothering is lost and regression is to objectlessness. With an adequate symbiotic experience, however, ego building proceeds. The groundwork for formation of a body image is laid. A rudimentary capacity to mediate between inner and outer perception becomes operative. "The ego is molded under the impact of reality, on the one hand, and of the instinctual drives, on the other." [3] Ego functions are acquired, especially the important function of delay. This comes about because, with gratification, needs become less imperative. Memory traces of pleasure are linked with perception of the mother's ministrations. This also leads to elaboration of higher levels of object relations. By the second part of the first year, the symbiotic partner has become so specific that she is no longer interchangeable.

Thus Mahler established that the etiology of childhood psychosis lies in gross failure of symbiosis. But the psychotic child does not, even with treatment, usually attain such improved status that he can arrive at our consultation rooms in adulthood as an ambulatory patient. We do see persons who have been insufficiently gratified in the symbiotic phase. But the difference between gross failure and insufficiency is often the difference between psychosis and attainment of a borderline structure. Sometimes we see patients such as Mr. Baker [4] who have had a "taste" of symbiotic gratification at the phase-specific time. Because it is less than completely satisfying, it leaves a hunger which, if circumstances so lend themselves, becomes gratified later, out of phase. Neither the life situation of later symbiotic gratification nor therapy designed to provide it as a benign experience can usually correct this structural flaw, although logically one is tempted to think it should. This is because developmental processes can proceed despite less than ideal symbiosis, albeit in a distorted direction. As an exam-

[3] *Ibid.*, pp. 10–11.   [4] Chapter 7, this volume.

ple, there is the rather common result of inadequate phase-specific symbiosis—premature ego development. This comes about if the maternal partner fails in her function of constituting an auxiliary ego. The infant has to take over her functions. If there has been barely enough symbiotic experience to avert psychosis proper, the result is a particularly difficult-to-reach borderline structure—a narcissistically arranged pseudo self-sufficiency which leaves little room for much therapeutic intervention of any sort, let alone provision of symbiosis. We shall later describe the case of Mr. Xavier [5] who had regressed to this narcissistic state—after a relatively satisfactory symbiotic phase—as the result of traumatic object loss (in the form of hospitalization) in the early part of the separation-individuation phase.

Although there is no direct pathway back to the infantile situation and therefore there is none to direct correction of the failures of that period of life, revival in the transference does provide reparative opportunity. Transference is used most effectively if it is not confused with constitution of the therapist as a real object. Distortions and deviant development as exemplified by the case of Mr. Howe [6] must be corrected before object relations can proceed to the higher level necessary for transference and working alliance. In the case of Mr. Howe as well as in others, we shall emphasize interpretation rather than provision of experience as the therapeutic route. Here, it is more appropriate to stress that, more often than not, an attempt to provide belated symbiotic experience runs the danger of reinforcing fixation.

For the technical purposes with which we are here concerned— treatment of the adult borderline structures—it is the next phase, separation-individuation, that has the most meaningful developmental significance. The subphases of separation-individuation are differentiation, practicing, rapprochement, and separation-individuation proper in the sense of formation of discrete identity, separateness, and individuality. Mahler's use of the word *separation* never means physical separation but refers to the child's psychological awareness of his separateness. We shall discuss the subphases of separation-individuation in normal development as the backdrop for understanding how shortcomings of that phase make for pathology that extends into later life.

[5] Chapter 14, this volume.   [6] Chapter 15, this volume.

In that regard, therefore, it is essential to keep in mind that an individual may never, in reality, experience physical separation and perhaps *for that very reason* may not reach the psychological milestone of separation-individuation. *In agreement with Mahler, we regard failure to have attained object constancy in the process of separation-individuation as the core problem in the borderline states.* As such, it will constitute the main thrust of our discussion of technique.

With optimal symbiosis, *differentiation,* the first subphase of the separation-individuation phase, is begun. Assured of symbiotic pleasure and of the "safe anchorage," [7] and aided by maturational processes, especially locomotion, there is "expansion beyond the symbiotic orbit." [8] "The more nearly optimal the symbiosis, the mother's 'holding behavior,' has been; the more the symbiotic partner has helped the infant to become ready to 'hatch' from the symbiotic orbit smoothly and gradually . . . the better equipped has the child become to separate out and to differentiate his self representations from the hitherto fused symbiotic self-plus-object representations." [9]

From about ten to sixteen months of age, the *practicing* subphase proceeds. Maturation of locomotion propels the infant away from his mother, making for greater physical separation and providing opportunity for exploration of wider segments of reality. The birth of the child as an individual comes about when, in response to the mother's selective response to his cueing, the child gradually alters his behavior. "It is the specific unconscious need of the mother that activates, out of the infant's infinite potentialities, those in particular that create for each mother 'the child' who reflects her own *unique* and individual needs. This process takes place, of course, within the range of the child's innate endowments." [10]

Thus, the mother conveys a "mirroring frame of reference." [11] Developing our own theme that the roots of later pathology lie in these important phases and subphases of development, we can see here that, in the practicing subphase, inadequate mirroring, insufficient mutual cueing, and the like fail to provide an adequate frame of reference for beginning delineation of identity. When the practicing period begins,

[7] M. S. Mahler, *On Human Symbiosis and the Vicissitudes of Individuation,* p. 17.
[8] *Ibid.*   [9] *Ibid.,* p. 18.   [10] *Ibid.,* p. 19.   [11] *Ibid.*

massive shifts in cathexis accompany it—shifts from the symbiotic
orbit to the autonomous apparatuses. Even though, normally, the
mother remains emotionally available, the threat of object loss exists.
At best, it is minimal. In pathogenic situations, it can be traumatic.
As an example of the latter, a mother may welcome too wholeheartedly her toddler's increasing independence as freeing her, too. This
rather common form of abandonment can prevent confident acquisition of identity by burdening the child with premature fear of loss of
the object. We have seen this in the history of borderline adults who,
at this early developmental subphase, were subjected to as common
an experience as being left alone in the backyard all day because that
made it easier for the mother to proceed with her household tasks un-
impeded by the child's continuing need for her availability within the
context of his own explorations of the wider world. If the child matures precociously, matters can become even worse. For example, if he
walks well, he can walk too far.

At about eighteen months of age, coinciding with the establishment of the third organizer of the psyche, gradual internalization
through ego identification begins. This represents a confluence of maturation and development which we wish to highlight here, not simply because it illustrates several points of agreement among the ego
psychologists, arrived at by means of their separate but mutually validating studies, but also because we are thinking continuously, as we
discuss normal development, about potentially pathogenic pitfalls.
These will form the basis of our consideration of pathology and the
techniques for its treatment.

The second eighteen months of life is a period of great vulnerability. With increasing awareness of physical separateness, pleasure in
autonomous functioning, capacity for semantic communication, repre-
sentational thought which leads to object constancy, "the relative
obliviousness to his mother's presence, which prevailed during the
practicing period, wanes." [12] It is replaced by active approach behavior, the *rapprochement* subphase. The pitfalls of this subphase are
great because so many otherwise adequate mothers fail to respond to
it. One can readily see how it might be regarded as regressive behavior and an imposition on the mother's freedom just when she is begin-

12 *Ibid.*, p. 24.

ning to enjoy the child's independence from her. Maternal rebuff, in the rapprochement phase, and as we shall note when we discuss depression, can be so disappointing that it contains within it seeds for depression later in life. If the symbiotic phase and the subphases of separation-individuation are experienced adequately, the child reaches the point of true identity—that of differentiation between self and object representations, and the capacity to retain the representation of the object independent of the state of need. Structuralization proceeds to normalcy or, at worst, neurosis; borderline pathology is averted.

We shall show in clinical description why we find Mahler's theories so particularly relevant to treatment of adult borderline phenomena. Her description of the normal progression from autism to symbiosis, through the subphases of separation-individuation and toward the establishment of object constancy and identity, provides invaluable information about both normal development and the pathological consequences of developmental failure. Mahler, as the Twentieth Freud Anniversary Lecturer of the New York Psychoanalytical Society, placed particular emphasis on the rapprochement subphase as crucial to normal development. In many instances, the progressive forces of the growing ego tend to even out most of the discrepancies and minor deviations in development. But when deficiencies of integration and internalization leave residua, these may manifest themselves in borderline mechanisms; the synthetic function of the ego has failed.

. . . in those children with less than optimal development, the ambivalence conflict is discernible during the rapprochement subphase in rapidly alternating clinging and increased negativistic behaviors. This may be in some cases a reflection of the fact that the child has split the object world, more permanently than is optimal, into "good" and "bad." By means of this splitting, the "good" object is defended against the derivatives of the aggressive drive.

These mechanisms, coercion and splitting of the object world, are characteristic in most cases of borderline transference.[13]

She presents two propositions thought to be relevant to the understanding of borderline phenomena: "One is the importance of reconciliation and thus of integration of the image of the erstwhile "good"

[13] M. S. Mahler, "A Study of the Separation-Individuation Process: And its Possible Application to Borderline Phenomena in the Psychoanalytic Situation," p. 413.

symbiotic mother, whom we long for 'from the cradle on to the grave,' this image to become blended with the representation of the ambivalently loved—dangerous because potentially re-engulfing —'mother after separation'." [14]

The second proposition relates to the suffusion of the body image with narcissistic cathexis: "This seems to be due to a disturbed cathectic balance of libido distribution between the self and the object." [15]

During the first three subphases of separation-individuation, gender identity is normally established. The potential borderline child who is unable to establish clear gender identity, ". . . might not have taken autonomous, representationally clearly separated possession of his or her own bodily self . . ." [16]

The broad concept that borderline phenomena have their origin in failures in development in the separation-individuation phase is central to precise diagnosis and treatment of these problems.

Although the crucial places in development where the most damaging pathogenic possibilities exist have been delineated, it is impossible to describe the myriad and minute details of every combination of mother-child interaction that make for less-than-adequate structuralization. This is because there are as many combinations as there are mother-child pairs. In the main, there is some reassurance in the knowledge that, if the less-than-adequate experience in one phase or subphase is not continued throughout all the developmental phases, it is corrected in the subsequent phase. But our main purpose in presenting Mahler's scheme of normal development is to point out where the etiology of the borderline pathologies lies. Knowing this has been of inestimable value in our clinical work. It opens one's mind, in listening to the adult patient's life history, to diagnostic hypotheses concerning failures in the primary relationship which may account for the pathology. These hypotheses are often confirmed or corrected in the transferential phenomena. The technical procedures for dealing with these failures therapeutically is, of course, the central theme of our book.

[14] *Ibid.*, p. 416.   [15] *Ibid.*   [16] *Ibid.*

⪧ 5 ⪦

THE CONTRIBUTIONS OF
EDITH JACOBSON

J ACOBSON CHOSE TO BEGIN her theory building by enlarging upon
the concept of the undifferentiated matrix. She proposed that not
only ego and id, but the two kinds of drive as well, are at first undifferentiated. They are contained within a psychosomatic matrix which
Jacobson calls the primal psychophysiological self. She revises Freud's
concepts of primary narcissism and primary masochism (death instinct) on the ground that, before discovery of the self and the object
world, the as yet undifferentiated drive energy can only be discharged
physiologically to the inside. From birth on, this instinctual energy
develops into the two kinds of drive under the influence of external
stimulation. At the same time, increasing pathways for discharge to
the outside open up as the result of maturation.

Jacobson also disagrees with Freud's formulations regarding secondary narcissism and masochism. She clarifies the distinctions among
ego, which is a structure, *self,* which is the totality of the psychic and
bodily person, and *self representations,* which are "the unconscious,
preconscious and conscious endopsychic representations of the bodily
and mental self in the system ego." [1]

It is interesting to consider why Jacobson uses the term representations. She means to distinguish the self and object *as experienced*
from the self and object *in reality,* pointing out that theoretical precision often suffers from failure to make clear distinction between external objects and their endopsychic representations. The infant acquires

---

[1] E. Jacobson, *The Self and the Object World,* p. 19.

self images which accord with the pleasurable or unpleasurable quality of his experience at the same time as he establishes object images which are determined by how he views the object at the moment. The broad dimensions of the object world do not come within the range of the infant's perception until later. This formulation about *representations* is consistent with what we already know about the "good" object being the one who gratifies and the "bad" object being the one who frustrates, although these are, of course, the same person at different moments. It is not until he is approximately six months of age that he becomes aware that the "good" and "bad" objects are one person. When he thus fuses the two representations, there is simultaneous fusion of the drives with the aggressive drive becoming subsumed under the libidinal in normal development. This, Freud had already taught us. Jacobson's contributions have largely to do with the early months before fusion.

That our capacity to form realistic self representations is limited is illustrated by the ubiquitous unconscious fantasy of female castration which exists in men as well as in women. Self awareness, introspection, capacity for realistic perception, discrimination, and evaluation are capacities which arise gradually, later in life. Conversely, in the early stages, our view of the outside world is colored by inadequate perception which makes for distortions. Infantile images are transferred onto other persons and onto the inanimate world; distortions are created because of subjective reactions, empathy founded on primitive affective identifications, and projections. ". . . the establishment of the system ego sets in with the discovery of the object world and the growing distinction between it and one's own physical and mental self." [2]

Jacobson proceeds to clarify why Freud's 1914 concept of narcissism [3] is incompatible with the structural theory. In the course of ego formation, the mental representations of the self become cathected with libido and aggression. This is not the same as libidinal cathexis of the ego, as Freud thought secondary narcissism to be, or aggressive cathexis of the ego, as Freud thought secondary masochism to be. To sum up Jacobson's revision of Freud regarding primary and

[2] *Ibid.*   [3] S. Freud, *On Narcissism: An Introduction.*

secondary narcissism and masochism: She argues that, in the early months of life, before the ego has developed and before there is a distinction between the self and the object world, both drives are as yet undifferentiated and are discharged silently through physiological channels. In this relatively undeveloped state, turning libido toward or aggression upon the not-yet-differentiated ego has no meaning. Thus the concepts of primary narcissism and masochism are eliminated. To understand secondary narcissism and masochism, confusion among the constructs *ego, self,* and *self representation* must first be eliminated. Again, it is not the ego that becomes cathected with libido and aggression but—since the phenomena which Freud viewed as primary and secondary narcissism occur at a stage when the self and the object world begin to become distinguished—the mental representations of the self are thought to become cathected with libido and aggression and thus acquire the status of an object for purposes of drive discharge. This is not a secondary phenomenon but a developmental one. "From the ever-increasing memory traces of pleasurable and unpleasurable instinctual, emotional, ideational and functional experiences and of perceptions with which they become associated, images of the love objects as well as those of the bodily and psychic self emerge. Vague and variable at first, they gradually expand and develop into consistent and more or less realistic endopsychic representations of the object world and of the self." [4]

Adding the ego psychological considerations which provide broader dimension to the otherwise narrow psychosexual aspect of the oral phase, Jacobson describes the impact of maternal care upon infantile ego development. Neonatal experiences, in ego psychological thought, are not limited as was thought in earlier Freudian theory to the feeding experience alone, but they ". . . extend to a broad variety of stimulating, gratifying, and frustrating experiences, to which the infant reacts with psychobiologically prepatterned (instinctive) responses. . . ." [5] Engrams of experience are laid down long before the infant becomes aware of the mother as a person. The psychophysiological equilibrium depends upon the whole mother, not simply the

---

[4] E. Jacobson, *The Self and the Object World*, p. 19.   [5] *Ibid.*, p. 33.

breast, even before she becomes a distinct person to the infant. The symbiotic unit of infant and mother, elaborated upon by Mahler in exquisite detail, is thought by Jacobson to consist of attunement of the infant's and mother's drive discharge patterns. In agreement with Spitz as well as with Mahler, Jacobson emphasizes the importance of the combined oral-visual experience which equates mother and breast and makes for the earliest image of the gratifying mother. This is illustrative of how the three major post-Hartmann ego psychological theorists, all studying different facets of development, nevertheless complement each other at those points where their theorizing converges.

Self and object images begin to build by means of libidinally stimulating experiences and of depriving ones, making for accumulation of memory traces. Until the perceptual apparatus matures, the infant is unable to identify the source of experience. The tendency, traces of which remain throughout life, is to merge with the object in search of the gratifying experiences which emanate from her. Again, Mahler's elaboration of ego-building factors in the normal symbiotic phase dovetails with Jacobson. This pleasurable merger forms the basis for future object relations and identifications. There are, at this stage, constant cathectic shifts, with libido and aggression continuously turning from object to self with, as yet, weak boundaries between them. The mother, by her own affective expression, is able to induce similar affect in the infant who, because of his maturing motor apparatus, is able also to begin some imitative movements in the attempt to maintain symbiotic merger. Jacobson regards this as an empathic state which results in the establishment of *primitive affective identifications.* We referred to this almost intangible capacity for empathy as essential in the equipment of the therapist for his work. It derives, according to Jacobson, Mahler, and Spitz, from early experience with the maternal object through which the capacity for empathy is established. In later life, it imparts an essential quality to good parents, good therapists, good lovers. The earliest identifications are magical, founded on primitive mechanisms of introjection and projection in disregard of realistic differences between self and object.

The maturational spurt which ensues at the beginning of the second year employs aggressive energy for ambitious strivings. The child's desire to remain part of his love objects recedes and is replaced by the wish to be like them. Mechanisms of partial introjection enable *selective identifications* to be made. Thus, a compromise is reached between dependency and symbiotic wish, on the one hand, and aggressive, independent ego functioning, on the other. Admired traits of the object are introjected into the child's wishful self images. The feeling of sameness in the midst of continuous changes is essential to the establishment of identity and is maintained by distinguishing wishful self images from realistic self representations. The wishful self images give direction to potential in the future while the realistic self representations retain the continuity of past and present.

Parental love combined with tolerable degrees of frustration and prohibition promote the establishment of stable, enduring libidinal cathexes of the self and objects and make for normal ego and superego formation and for independence. Necessary frustration teaches the child to relinquish infantile magical expectations as well as preoedipal and oedipal sexual strivings. It arouses ambivalence toward the frustrators, resulting in accumulation of aggression toward them and of libido toward the self, which in turn stimulates progressive forms of identification with the parents and promotes ego autonomy by enhancing narcissistic endowment. Overgratification and severe frustration induce regressive fantasies and reunion of self and object and thereby delay development.

At approximately eight months, the infant becomes able to recognize familiar persons and to distinguish among them. Spitz verified this feature in his observational studies and noted it as an important stage in the capacity of the ego to attain higher levels of organization. Jacobson notes that the ability to distinguish objects develops more rapidly than the ability to distinguish self from object. The child does not need to fuse with other objects as much as with the mother, and so differentiation from mother is impeded. Also, perception of the external world is easier than self perception.

A contribution of major significance is made by all the ego psychologists in their view of the growth-promoting features of the aggressive drive. Jacobson points out that, by the end of the first year, the child experiences not only frustration but also ambition, possessiveness, envy, rivalry, disappointment, failure. Through these, he learns to distinguish his own feelings and the feelings of others. "Thus, not only the loving but also the hostile components of the infantile self- and object-directed strivings furnish the fuel that enables the child to develop his feeling of identity and the testing of external and inner reality, and on this basis to build up his identifications and object relations." [6]

The child projects envious, hostile impulses—resulting from maternal fustrations—onto his rivals. He wants to acquire what they have and seeks to attain it by becoming like them. Envy and rivalry force sharper delineation of self and others. Although the mother-child relationship is the matrix of identity formation, individuation is promoted by the discovery of differences and gains more momentum from ambivalence toward rivals than from intimacy with mother. Identifications, to become enduring, depend upon a proper balance of libido and aggression.

Object relations grow as the child acquires identity. For these developments to proceed, libido must prevail over aggression. This builds up the libidinal endowment of the self images (narcissism) which enhances self-esteem and the formation of the unified concept of the self. Selective identifications become enduring and consistent parts of the ego, permanently modifying it to the point where the child becomes aware of having a coherent, continuous self.

Sexual identity is a significant component of personal identity. Because the female genital is less visible than the male and because it is perceived as a damaged male organ, the boy establishes his sexual identity more readily than the girl. But the child's experience of sexual identity does not rest exclusively on genital comparisons. His curiosity extends to the sexual behavior of others and to physical and mental behavior in addition to the anatomical. Thus, sexual identity becomes one facet of identity as a whole. Discovery and acceptance of sex difference furthers renunciation of symbiotic wishes because heterosexuality and oedipal strivings become dominant and induce identifications with the rival. By means of such identifications, object libido is transformed into narcissistic libido; this joins forces with libido withdrawn from erogenous zones to further the building of self repre-

[6] *Ibid.,* p. 61.

sentations and the expansion of ego functions. In this way, Jacobson reformulates and updates the concept of sublimation by phrasing it in ego psychological terms.

In the weeks after birth something like the following may be described as the first steps in structuralization: the drives have separated out and display two different characteristics, libidinal and aggressive; neutralization has begun and therefore the ego begins to assume its functions—particularly does the function of object relations begin to evolve; representations of the self and the object world are built up; in consonance with increasing neutralization and higher levels of object relations, the infant begins gradually to distinguish between those representations which refer to the self and those which refer to the object.

In the early months of life, these as yet relatively undifferentiated self and object representations impart, almost by definition, a fused identity whereby the self, insofar as it is experienced at all, is felt to be part of the larger world. Although we are, at this point, mainly concerned with normal development, it is pertinent to mention that the concept of undifferentiated self and object representations forms the basis of Jacobson's theory of psychosis. In psychosis, self and object representations that had differentiated in infancy as a normal developmental process, merge again regressively to form an undifferentiated self-object bringing distortions which adhere to it. The psychotic thus lacks the identity that exists when there is a clear self image and distinction between that image and the object world.

Superego formation, by definition, involves internalization. Jacobson borrows from Hartmann and Loewenstein, who define *internalization* as the process whereby regulations which had taken place in interaction with the outside world are substituted for by inner regulations.[7] The superego is a functional unit which regulates behavior in accordance with internalized ethical principles. It is the last agency to be completed in the process of structuralization. With its formation, developmental processes gain impetus because large amounts of psychic energy are liberated; the sexual, aggressive and narcissistic strivings become neutralized, thus freeing energy to serve the building

[7] H. Hartmann and R. M. Loewenstein, "Notes on the Superego."

of ego and superego aim-inhibited pursuits. To the already-known regulatory functions of the superego, Jacobson adds that the superego maintains identity; provides a stable balance in the proportions of libidinal, aggressive, and neutralized energy; regulates self esteem by maintaining harmony between the moral codes and the ego manifestations. The matter of self esteem has interesting implications for technique because the degree of self esteem is an important determinant in the degree to which rejection, failure, physical illness, and the like, all of which tend to impair self esteem, can be tolerated. The extent of impairment depends upon the regulatory capacity of the superego. For the therapist, it is desirable to make some appraisal of this capacity. The extent to which a given life experience is traumatic depends upon many factors and varies from one individual to the other. In addition to capacity to regulate self esteem, the developmental phase when the traumatic event is experienced is of central importance in understanding what it has meant to the individual. A child hospitalized for a tonsillectomy, for example, will experience it as castration if he has reached the phallic phase; a younger child still in the symbiotic phase will experience it more strongly as separation, as loss of the symbiotic object who is part of himself. One addresses oneself therapeutically to the patient in terms of what the experience has meant to him, a factor which may not be readily discernible to the observer who hears only the description of the external event. The impact of the experience upon the individual may be largely unconscious and can only be surmised by the therapist if he takes into account such factors as phase specificity, capacity of the ego to integrate the experience, and capacity of the regulatory mechanisms of the superego to maintain self esteem.

The superego also governs moods and is an indicator and regulator of the entire ego state. Finally, Jacobson assigns a function to the superego which is more traditionally attributed to the ego—the development of a coherent, consistent defense organization. The special identifications which lead to superego formation consist principally of pregenital reaction-formations by means of which aggression turns from the object to the self, altering attitudes toward the self and the object world.

Superego formation begins with incorporation of the first value imposed from the outside—cleanliness. But toilet training contributes also to ego development. The body becomes more strongly cathected, making the child more aware of himself and paving the way toward acquisition of identity. Instead of passive receiver, he becomes an active giver. Disgust, as the affective aspect of reaction-formation, is added to the growing repertory of affects. Because of the child's psychobiological dependency upon the parents, he needs powerful parental images with whom to identify. The value system begins to center around strength, control, cleanliness, instead of pleasure.

Disillusionment sets in when the child becomes aware that the parents are not omnipotent. In normal development, disillusionment is replaced by idealization. Neither one must occur too early, however. Disillusionment, when self and object representations are not yet clearly differentiated, devalues the self as it devalues the object. Too early idealization leads to narcissistic identifications, again because self and object representations have not differentiated. If development proceeds normally, however, idealization takes the infant a long way toward ultimate superego formation. In that direction, the reality-testing function of the ego enables the infant next to distinguish the real parents from the idealized images. The latter become gradually transformed into the ego ideal. At the same time, neutralization proceeds, providing neutralized libido for idealization; neutralized aggression provides the motive force for the direction-giving, self-critical, restraining, and enforcing functions of the superego.

For the very young child, ego and superego identifications derive largely from identification with the mother. Somewhat later, these become combined with identifications with the powerful, phallic father. In this simple but compellingly convincing way, Jacobson adds to the theory of superego formation. To the already known aspect of this theory, that the superego derives from incorporation of paternal prohibitions, she proposes also that the motive for superego formation is not only fear of the father's prohibitory behavior, but identification first with the mother and then with the father. The resultant superego, therefore, is not simply the precipitate of aggressively tinged internalization but consists of libidinally cathected identifications as well. This changes the theory of superego formation into one that provides for benign, loving aspects of the relationship with both parents and leads also to a logical revision of the theory of the resolution of the oedipal conflict.

From the age of approximately two years until the establishment of the superego as the heir to the oedipus, the developmental paths of boy and girl diverge. This divergence is prompted by the discovery of sex difference. For the girl, reality testing will not sustain continuing identification with the father. The boy's superego, built in the early months of life on maternal identification, proceeds in later childhood to acquire identifications derived from the father's strength and power, values which Jacobson says are acquired in the anal phase. Jacobson questions Freud's reliance on the threat of castration by the father as the compelling force which brings about resolution of the oedipal conflict by forcing relinquishment of incestuous wishes. She points out that the benign, loving father does not, in reality, threaten his son with castration. Nevertheless, the boy's own cruelty and castration wishes toward the father cause him to fear retaliation in kind. This, Jacobson emphasizes, is an internal matter and not reactive to the external reality. In her theory, renunciation of incestuous wishes is aided by the idealizations which will ultimately develop into the ego ideal. This process furthers superego development because rivalry does not thrive well in the climate of idealization.

Freud's postulate regarding resolution of the oedipal conflict and the establishment of the superego leaves in question the manner in which these are accomplished by the girl. If the castration threat compels such development in the boy, what is there to provide propulsive force for the girl's development? Some of the logical conclusions are unsatisfactory. One is that the girl, lacking such "incentive," does not ever resolve the oedipal conflict. It also followed, in early Freudian theory, that the superego of the woman is not as strong as is that of the man. Some of Freud's erroneous ideas about women derived from his belief in the castration threat as motivation for development. Jacobson rescues Freudian theory from one of its most egregious errors, first by showing that love, not fear, supports development in both sexes; second, by describing superego development in the girl.

As in the development of the boy, the girl in the anal phase also identifies with the father's strength. With the recognition of sex difference, both boy and girl experience severe shock. The boy recovers more easily than the girl if the preoedipal mother has not been too disappointing, because his oedipal love provides him with reward in the capacity to love. If the preoedipal mother has been disappointing, however, there may be too rapid disillusionment and turning to the father as a love object, resulting in a fairly common form of male homosexuality. The girl does not recover so readily from the castration shock. She devalues the self and the maternal object because of it, resorts to denial, and shifts narcissistic libido in the entire body in compensation for the realization that she lacks a penis. In its place, she establishes an early ego ideal using the value system laid down in the anal phase. This ego ideal consists of an unaggressive, asexual, clean and neat little girl and it combines with the feminine narcissistic goal of physical attractiveness. By this means the female ego ideal acquires high moral values in place of a penis. Devaluation of the mother causes the girl to turn to the father as a love object, thus establishing her heterosexuality.

Jacobson agrees with Freud that the superego as a functional entity is established with the resolution of the oedipal conflict. She provides more detail than did Freud about the developmental processes which make for superego formation. She describes these largely in terms of ego and superego identifications which enhance the development of both agencies. She also believes that eventual resolution of the oedipal conflict in both sexes involves affection for rather than fear of the parent of the same sex, making for abandonment of incestuous, matricidal, and patricidal wishes.

Pathology is defined as deviation from normal development. Understood in this way, Jacobson's theory of normality helps us designate the deviations that lead to pathological development and to elaborate techniques that address themselves to these deviations. Those which do not derive from constitutional factors or from too early trauma are often accessible to therapeutic interventions which correct the developmental defect and allow impeded development to proceed. Jacobson's theory of psychosis, the refusion of self and object representations, is elaborated in her papers on melancholic depression, normal and pathological moods, and psychotic identifications.

In simple psychotic depression there is an intrasystemic conflict

—between the wishful self image and the image of the failing self. In agreement with Mahler, Jacobson proposes that a basic depressive affect may arise through failure of maternal response in the rapprochement subphase, resulting in reduction of self esteem. This disappointment is all the more severe because it follows the elation of the practicing subphase. But this only illustrates the more fundamental theory that depression is the affective consequence of the primitive ego's inability to mourn and to resolve narcissistic and ambivalence conflicts when there is early object loss. Disillusionment and abandonment at an early age, when boundaries between self and object representations are not yet firmly established, may lead to depression, pathology in object relations, and narcissism. Objects become overvalued and overidealized. The wishful self images (ego ideal) cannot be realized. A brittle equilibrium may be reached but is all too readily disturbed by later disappointment, leading to denigration of both self and object.

In agreement with Hartmann, Jacobson holds that insufficient neutralization predisposes to psychosis. The already (probably constitutional) defective ego is thus deprived of the energy that, in normality, accrues to it and contributes to the defensive and adaptive functions. Therefore, the prepsychotic ego is unable to employ neurotic defenses to deal with conflict. It resorts, instead, to back-and-forth shifts in libidinal and aggressive cathexes among object, thing, and self representations. At the same time, there is defusion (of "good" and "bad" object representations) and of the drives accompanied by deneutralization of the already inadequately neutralized drive energy.

The psychotic process *per se* is precipitated by reactivation of infantile conflicts, first around parental objects, then spreading to the entire object world. Cathectic shifts, defusion, and deneutralization, unconsciously intended as defense, fail in their purpose. Attempts to recathect objects result in increased dedifferentiation of self and object representations and in severe distortions of them. Finally, the distorted, undifferentiated self and object representations are split into primitive images. Ego and superego identifications, to the extent that they evolved developmentally in the prepsychotic ego, disintegrate in the psychotic process proper and are replaced by dedifferentiated superego, self, and object images which Jacobson terms *narcissistic iden-*

tifications. Kohut developed this further and elaborated treatment techniques, not for psychosis, but for the personality with *narcissistic identifications.*[8]

In psychosis, object relations deteriorate, secondary process thinking and reality testing are lost, resulting in misinterpretations of and inadequate responses to the object world. The psychotic then attempts to restore his object world in the restitutional process and attempts to use the outside world to buttress his ego. However, he has available largely projective and introjective mechanisms and so he borrows the ego and superego of others and projects parts of the self. Failing this, delusional self and object representations are built up, using distorted fragments of reality; the object world is lost.

[8] H. Kohut, *The Analysis of the Self.*

≫ 6 ≪

EXPLORATION OF THE
SEVERE PATHOLOGIES

TWO CONTEMPORARY INVESTIGATORS, Otto F. Kernberg and Heinz Kohut, are exploring the vast, heretofore relatively unknown territory that lies between the transference neuroses and the psychoses. Kernberg, in conformance with generally accepted usage, designates this as the area of the borderline states and proceeds to examine the construction of these pathologies in fine detail. Kohut, on the other hand, restricts his investigation to the area of pathology which he designates as *narcissistic personality disturbance* and regards this problem not as a borderline phenomenon, but as lying within the realm of analyzability, although differing from the transference neuroses proper. Thus, Kernberg's work extends diagnosis and technique of borderline structures, whereas Kohut's remains within the philosophy of the widening scope of indications for psychoanalysis.

Kernberg's position is that varying types of psychopathology are determined by an abnormal development of internalized object relations. In this regard, he is in accord with our own view, derived from Hartmann, that before the attainment of object constancy, pathology is in its essence the result of impaired object relations; abnormality in the internalization of object relations impedes and disrupts ego integration. With this as his point of departure, Kernberg presents a conceptualization which attempts to integrate psychoanalytic instinct theory with ego psychology. He suggests that instincts are first expressed as inborn behavior patterns and that later, mothering functions and interpersonal interactions lead to internalization of object relations which organizes structuralization. He proposes that there are four stages of development in this process. The earliest stage precedes the establishment of the undifferentiated self-object. Here he is in accord with the ego psychologists who have designated this phase variously as the stage of primary narcissism, nondifferentiation, autism, and the like. A pathological arrest or cessation here would render impossible the attainment of the second stage in that a good self-object image, and therefore an ego core which determines basic trust, would be lacking. Such severe developmental impairment at the beginning of life leads, of course, to psychosis and is attributed to faulty perceptual input, whether innate or environmental (low stimulus barrier or overstimulation). Such impairment further restricts opportunity to attain the coenesthetic constellation of stimuli which leads to a good self-object core. It is possible that, in the context of such severe deprivation, psychosis is averted in some instances when sufficient development of self and object differentiation has occurred and permits superficial adaptation to reality. This can come about, Kernberg suggests, when cognition compensates for lack of opportunity for internalization of object relations; however, it cannot compensate as well for the incapacity to establish interpersonal and intrapsychic object relations. Thus, the individual will develop without capacity for empathy, love, guilt, or pity.

At the second stage, consolidation of the undifferentiated self-object image takes place and is normally libidinally gratifying. This leads to the establishment of a primary intrapsychic structure with memory traces carrying a positive affective charge. Simultaneously, out of the painful and frustrating psychophysiological experiences, a separate structure is built, representing an undifferentiated, "all bad" self-object representation. Thus there arises an "all good" self-object separate from the "all bad" self-object with, as yet, no separation between self and nonself and only rudimentary ego boundaries. Pathological fixation at or regression to this stage of development consists, in the main, of an imbalance on the side of the "all bad," aggressively cathected self-object images and promotes defensive refusion [1] of the

---

[1] The term *fusion* is used in various ways. Kernberg's usage corresponds to the literal definition. Greater precision is attained if *fusion* is reserved for fusion of the drives and *merger* is used to indicate the symbiotic state in which self and object representations are undifferentiated.

primitive "all good" self and object images as a protection against excessive frustration and rage. Such defensive refusion, if carried beyond the early infantile stages, constitutes a psychotic identification. Reality testing is lost by blurring the limits between self and object images, with subsequent loss of ego boundaries. Here, Kernberg is referring to psychosis proper and to the threat of ego dissolution. In schizophrenia, this phenomenon is clinically observable in the defensive flight into a mystical, ecstatic, primitive, idealized self-object fusion. Secondarily, additional primitive defensive operations are triggered, particularly the use of primitive projective mechanisms. These are designed to expel the "all bad" internalized object and this process leads to paranoid distortion. Splitting, which Kernberg defines as pathological dissociation of polar opposite ego states, is brought into play for the defensive purpose of preventing all-pervasive anxiety and fear of destruction. Kernberg believes that, prognostically, schizophrenic psychosis is treatable if the patient attains capacity to establish object relations in the present. Here again, he is in accord with our own view that the technical procedure in the treatment of the very severely disturbed patient involves the use of the therapist as a real object for the purpose of building object relations.

At the third stage of development, from approximately six to eighteen months, potential for borderline pathology is the developmental hazard. Primitive idealization of the mothering person as "all good" is employed in defense against contamination of this image by the "all bad" object image. Kernberg suggests that the stranger-anxiety described by Spitz as occurring at approximately eight months of age may be caused by projection onto the stranger of the "bad" self and object image, dissociated from the "good" one. Such dissociation constitutes the mechanism of splitting which, if persistent, interferes with further integration of self and object representations. While normal splitting keeps the good relationship with the mother intact in the face of frustration and protects the self against overwhelming contamination of love by hatred, pathological splitting divides others into "all good" or "all bad" and is the central defensive mechanism of the borderline personality organization. Thus Kernberg presents his principal theoretical contribution to the understanding of borderline pathology; he designates failure at this third stage of the development of internalized object relations as the determining factor in *borderline personality organization.* Included within this category are several types of severe character pathology; addictions, narcissistic personalities, infantile personalities, antisocial personality structures, the "as if," and other types of personality disorders. Kernberg defines his designation of borderline personality organization as attainment of, developmentally, differentiation of self images from object images to a degree sufficient to permit the establishment of integrated ego boundaries and differentiation between self and others. However, primitive aggression prevents development to the fourth stage in which the "all good" and "all bad" self and object images are integrated into a concept of self and objects. Borderline patients fail to attain this fourth level and such failure is attributable, in the main, to the predominance of primitive aggression. Aggressively determined self and object images, defensively split from idealized "good" self and object images, prevents integration, because that would trigger unbearable anxiety and guilt. That is why, he reasons, that active defensive separation of the "all good" images from the "all bad" constitutes the major defensive mechanism in these borderline states. Distinguishing defense in the borderline states from that in psychosis, Kernberg asserts that, while in both, this actively (unconsciously) employed splitting mechanism is reinforced by primitive idealizations and projective identifications, in the borderline conditions the purpose is to separate love and aggression, while in the psychoses the purpose of defense is against engulfment and annihilation.

Furthering his distinction between borderline states and psychoses, Kernberg points out that borderline patients preserve reality testing but retain serious difficulties in interpersonal relationships and in their subjective experience of reality, in addition to contradictory character traits, chaotic coexistence of defenses against expression of primitive impulses, lack of empathy, and identity defusion. Ego weakness is manifest in lack of impulse control, lack of anxiety tolerance, and lack of capacity to sublimate. In addition, one finds pathological condensation of pregenital and genital aims, with pregenital aggressive strivings dominating. Superego integration, too, is defective because of absence of an integrated self-concept and of integrated object representations; this further interferes with overall ego integration.

Kernberg interprets Hartmann's concept of neutralization as the integration of loving and hateful feelings in the context of internalized relationships with others. The patients with borderline personality organization lack such neutralizing capacity, thus depriving the ego of subliminatory potential and subjecting it to persistence of primitivization of emotions concomitant with lack of impulse control. His discussion of borderline pathology leads, logically, to consideration of self-destructive patterns. Normally, the direction of aggression inward is elaborated into stable internalized object relations that guarantee successful neutralization of aggression. The tendency in the borderline personality organization to self-destructiveness is attributable to failure of this mechanism. Also to be considered is contamination of sexual with aggressive drive derivatives resulting, in such patients, in premature sexualization of relationships with incestuous figures accompanied by aggressive contamination of these relationships as well as of the later sexual life of such persons. Finally, in describing the borderline personality organization, Kernberg stresses that the absence of an adequately developed superego deprives the patient of those superego functions which operate as internalized guidance systems. This leads to overdependency on external sources of reassurance, praise, and punishment.

At the fourth stage in the development of internalized object relations, pathological development is represented by the neuroses. These patients have identity, a well-integrated ego, and stable self and object representations. Defensive mechanisms center around repression rather than splitting. In normality, as contrasted with neurotic development, a benign superego and realistic superego demands, ego ideals and ego goals make for harmony in dealing with the external world and with instinctual needs. Repression successfully bars residual infantile instinctual demands. There is a large sector of conflict-free functioning in conjunction with capacity to repress and suppress ungratifiable needs without excessive stress.

In presenting his schema, Kernberg has provided a spectrum of the development of object relations in both normality and pathology which contributes particularly to our understanding of the borderline states, treatment of which will be the main thrust of our consideration of technique. While Kernberg has also written extensively on the technique of the treatment of borderline and narcissistic personalities, we have restricted ourselves here to the summary of his conceptualizations of the *borderline personality organization.*

Kohut introduces a new diagnostic entity, neither psychosis, borderline state, character neurosis, nor symptom neurosis (transference neurosis). He terms this *narcissistic personality disturbance,* referring it, etiologically, to an arrest in development at a point where a cohesive, grandiose self and cohesive (albeit archaic) idealized objects have come into existence. Because of the cohesion, a stable narcissistic transference is possible; but despite it, there is danger of regressive fragmentation which is defended against by avoidance, dissociation, isolation. On the affective side, shame and low self-esteem predominate. In the therapeutic situation, the narcissistic personality engages in either of two types of transference—the *idealizing transference* or the *mirror transference.* In the former, the therapist represents the idealized self-object and, in the latter the grandiose self is revived. Actually, these are two facets of the same developmental process, revived in the transference.

He deals quite directly with the issue of whether idealizing and mirror transference may correctly be designated as transference. Neurotic transference and transference neurosis revive the repressed state of the neurotic conflict around differentiated, largely incestuous objects. In narcissistic personality disturbance, whether the phenomenon that unfolds in the therapeutic situation is true transference in the technical sense, or is transference-like, is less important to Kohut than the fact that certain aspects of narcissistic structuralization do become mobilized and reactivated. He thinks that, if such phenomena occur, they are to be used for therapeutic purposes. Here he is following the pioneering courage that led Freud to the discovery and use of the transference in the treatment of neurosis.

Kohut's contribution is an exposition and extension of psychoanalytic theory and technique to narcissistic structures, suggesting that these are analyzable because structure exists. He postulates that there are horizontal or vertical splits in the egos of such patients and, therefore, it is only the infantile, narcissistic, split-off part of the personality that calls for technical procedures different from the ordinary psychoanalytic ones. That is because the remainder of the personality has continued to develop, separate from the split-off part, and thus, Kohut reasons, psychoanalysis as a treatment modality may be used effectively in such cases. He would but add to the psychoanalytic technique that the essential task involves dissolution of the pathogenic nucleus as it has become reactivated and enters into the transference relationship. Where this reactivation fails to take place and where transference regression might precipitate severe fragmentation, a different, nonanalytic treatment modality must be used.

Kohut's theoretical postulate rests on his delineation of two separate and largely independent developmental lines: (1) from autoerotism to narcissism to object love, and (2) from autoerotism to narcissism to higher forms and transformations of narcissism. Clearly, he regards narcissism as a line of development and defines it: "Narcissism, within my general outlook, is defined not by the target of the instinctual investment (i.e., whether it is the subject himself or other people), but by the nature or quality of an instinctual charge." [2]

He contrasts the central psychopathology of the narcissistic personality disorders with the psychoses and borderline states. Narcissistic personality disorders, he maintains, concern psychologically elaborated, cohesive, stable configurations which belong to the stage of narcissism, that is, that stage which follows autoerotism. He chooses to designate this stage of development as the "stage of the cohesive self," [3] and he proceeds to describe the normal line of narcissistic development from the early equilibrium of primary narcissism. This equilibrium is disturbed by frustration. In an attempt to reinstate it, the infant establishes a grandiose, exhibitionistic imago of the self and gives over the wish for perfection to an admired, omnipotent self-object. In normal development, the archaic grandiosity is absorbed and integrated into the adult personality and the idealized parent imago becomes internalized as part of the superego.

Kohut's language, as well as aspects of his theoretical formulations, are in pre-ego psychological terms and concepts because he thinks developmentally along the line of progress from autoerotism to narcissism. To attempt to bring this into coincidence with the lines of devel-

[2] H. Kohut, *The Analysis of the Self,* p. 26.   [3] *Ibid.,* p. 32.

opment postulated by Hartmann, Kris, Loewenstein, Spitz, Jacobson, and Mahler would be to resort to reductionism. For the sake of clarity, we may remind ourselves here that the first stage of life in the neonate has been variously termed autoerotism, primary narcissism, nondifferentiation, undifferentiation, the objectless stage, autism. Whatever the term, it is agreed that this is the stage of life when there is no awareness of an outside. Autoerotism, by virtue of its priority in the literature, is legitimately employed by Kohut in its classical meaning. Escalona and Spitz define and use the term in a different sense, as representing the infant's discovery of his own resources in the service of development. To them, therefore, autoerotism represents an *activity,* engaged in at a higher level of development; to the classicists it is a *state of being.*

Similarly, the term *narcissism,* as Kohut employs it, derives from the pre-ego psychological literature and thus does not accord, for example, with Jacobson's view of narcissism as libidinal cathexis of the self representations. Neither is it in agreement with the description of narcissism as a pathological process described by Hartmann and Loewenstein earlier. They anticipated by some ten years Kohut's consideration of the idealized self-object and of the grandiose self which, to them, normally survives in the ego ideal:

In the development of the ego ideal both self-idealization and the idealization of the parents play a role. . . . The degree to which the ego ideal is determined more by early self-idealization or more by idealization of the object later becomes more important for both normal and pathological development. Of significance for future pathological development might also be the persistence of early forms of self-aggrandizement or of overvaluation of parents that may stand in the way of the formation of later types of idealizations.[4]

Hartmann and Loewenstein deal also with the pathological development which ensues upon disillusionment with the parents, if that happens before differentiation has taken place. Jacobson, too, has elaborated upon that theme. The Hartmann position regarding narcissism necessarily revolves around whether it exists in the instinctualized or neutralized mode. This, we believe, obviates obscurities as to whether narcissism is pathological or is a normal developmental

[4] H. Hartmann and R. M. Loewenstein, "Notes on the Superego," p. 61.

phase. Kohut's concept of *self* also differs from that of Hartmann and Loewenstein. They say: ". . . we do not, as some analysts do, consider the 'self' as a separate psychic system, to be conceptualized in the same way as ego, id, and superego." [5] Kohut argues about the self that, while it is not an agency of the mind, it is a structure within the mind, since (*a*) it is cathected with instinctual energy, and (*b*) it has continuity in time—that is, it is enduring. Being a psychic structure, the self has, furthermore, also a psychic location.

Proceeding to psychopathology, Kohut describes the impaired development which results when severe narcissistic trauma intervenes: ". . . the grandiose self does not merge into the relevant ego content but is retained in its unaltered form and strives for the fulfillment of his archaic aims." [6] If the disappointment is in the admired parent, there results failure of the idealized self-object to become transformed into an internalized, self-regulating aspect of structure. Such developmental failure is fostered largely by the shortcomings of the maternal person. Traumatic disappointment results from her impaired capacity to empathize with the infant, to act as an auxiliary stimulus barrier, to be a tension-relieving regulator, and to provide the kind of stimulation and gratification that enables the infant to begin to recognize himself as a person. Therefore, a general structural weakness ensues, one which is unable to maintain basic narcissistic homeostasis. Later developmental phases may be further impaired because of this basic weakness. For example, massive oedipal trauma may destroy the idealized external counterpart of the internalized object and may thus become one of these threats to homeostasis by precipitating regressive search for an external ideal figure. Obviously, superego development is also impaired.

One of Kohut's most valuable formulations is that of the self as a tension regulator. This capacity comes about by means of what Kohut terms *transmuting internalizations*. He describes three steps in the process of their formation, presupposing that traumatic disappointments do not intervene: (1) The psyche must reach a state of preformed receptivity for specific introjects. (2) Withdrawal of cathexis from the idealized object must take place fractionally, that is, grad-

---

[5] *Ibid.*, p. 59.   [6] H. Kohut, *The Analysis of the Self*, p. 28.

ually and in parts, to avert sudden, severe, and traumatic disappointment in the whole object. (3) There must be a shift in emphasis
from the total personality of the object to certain of its specific functions. "The internal structure, in other words, now performs the functions which the object used to perform for the child." [7]

When there is failure in internalization, the individual does not acquire soothing mechanisms, such as those which aid sleep. In
illustration, Kohut mentions the psychopathology of drug addiction;
he contends that the psychological facet of the craving for drugs is
not, as is usually believed, object seeking, but is a distorted attempt at
creating structure in the absence of the partner in the dyad whose
role it is to provide opportunity for transmuting internalizations.
Kohut distinguishes among archaic (undifferentiated) self-object; internalized structures which take over drive-regulating functions formerly performed by the object; and the true external object. He cites, as
illustrations of the first, the addict's feeling of depletion in the absence
of the soothing therapist, and those types of patients who, in the
transference, reactivate the need for an archaic, narcissistically experienced self-object.

Cathexis of the cohesive self, he asserts, is critical for development.
For the developing child, there is a period when grandiosity is age
appropriate. In the patient suffering from failure of cohesion, the pathology lies in the fact that the archaic, grandiose self has become dissociated defensively to avert fragmentation. Thereby, the grandiose
self fails to become integrated gradually into the reality-oriented organization of the ego. There are three forms of the grandiose self, representing three developmental levels. The most archaic form is the one
in which the grandiose self absorbs the object; the second, termed
twinship or alter ego, is somewhat less archaic in that it admits of the
existence of an object, although still one that is part of the self; the
third, still less archaic, seeks affirmation of existence from the object.
Kohut describes this last type of development as relating to the time
of life when the mother's response to the child, her calling him by
name and her enjoyment of him, support development.

Kohut is at his technical best when he advises that the analyst (in

7 *Ibid.*, p. 50.

our frame of reference, the therapist) must employ the transference
(or its equivalent) and must adjust his empathic capacity to the patient's requirements. In the type of patient with which Kohut is concerned, the original archaic condition is reinstated in the therapy, and
so it is to this level that the analyst must address himself. The reason
for Kohut's theoretical delineation of the line of narcissistic development comes into focus as he elaborates his technical precepts. His
treatment goal is to provide access to the ego of split-off or repressed
narcissistic cathexes of the prestructured, idealized self-object and
grandiose self. To aid this process, the analyst must constitute an object, as distinguished from the therapeutic stance in the treatment of
neurosis in which the analyst is the recipient of purely transferential
ideation. A major part of the therapeutic work, in Kohut's scheme, is
devoted to the patient's reaction to loss of the narcissistically experienced object. Interventions must be designed to permit inclusion into
the adult personality of the unintegrated aspects of development. In
the mirror transference, for example, the infantile fantasies of exhibitionistic grandeur must be revived. In the idealizing transference, the
therapist must be able to tolerate the patient's realistically excessive
admiration: "The patient learns first to recognize these forms of narcissism in their therapeutic activation—and he must first be able to
accept them as maturationally healthy and necessary!—before he
can undertake the task of gradually transforming them and of building them into the higher organization of the adult personality and of
harnessing them to his mature goals and purposes." [8]

The pitfalls of countertransference in dealing with such types of
transference phenomena are particularly great. (We are reminded
here of Freud's admonition that the analyst must forebear attributing
the patient's admiration of him to the charms of his person.) Kohut
stresses empathy and acceptance. The narcissistic personality is particularly vulnerable to rejection and therefore, rather than point out his
lack of realism, the analyst must be patient in allowing the synthetic
function of the ego to achieve spontaneous, gradual dominance over
the narcissistic portions of the personality as they unfold. Such patients may cause particular frustration to the analyst who finds it difficult to tolerate therapeutic impotence.

[8] *Ibid.,* p. 213.

Therapeutic results involve, structurally, the integration of archaic aspects of either the idealized parent imago or the grandiose exhibitionistic self within the ego. As a secondary result of treatment, object love becomes possible because, behind the wall of regressive narcissism, lie object-libidinal affective ties. Kohut does not hold that such result is indicative that a change from narcissism to object love has taken place, but rather that, because of the narcissistic personality disorder, object love already in existence nevertheless remains bound to incestuous objects—a sort of secondary pathology. With treatment, the greater availability of libido makes for emotional deepening of object strivings, and the greater cohesiveness of the self increases capacity for object love. Also, as a by-product of therapy, highly valued sociocultural attributes are attained. The individual becomes capable of empathy, creativity, humor, and wisdom—qualities which are now autonomous because removed from their narcissistic origins. Thus Kohut's theoretical differences with the ego psychologists is marked. Nevertheless, some of his technical procedures are exceptionally valuable because of his superb empathic capacity to deal with the patient's need for repair of early traumatic object relations.

Both Kohut and Kernberg propose that pathology can be stable. Indeed, it is upon this proposition that their diagnostic conclusions rest. Kernberg refers to "a rather specific and remarkably stable form of pathological ego structure." [9] Their positions on this matter highlight the existence of two diverging pathways in theory building and consequently in elaboration of technique. Kohut, in particular, follows in the tradition of some of the most brilliant theorists in the history of psychoanalysis—such as Nunberg and Waelder—who, although never departing from classical theory, have been able to encompass and explain ego psychological phenomena within the confines of that theoretical frame of reference without the constructs of ego psychology. Fundamental in ego psychological as well as pre-ego psychological theory is the metapsychological aspect of forces, their interaction, and the vectors they produce, and it is this dynamic concept which these classicists employ with such brilliant virtuosity. However, it was Freud himself, foremost among classicists, whose work was so seminal that it also provided another direction—that

[9] O. F. Kernberg, "Borderline Personality Organization," p. 641.

taken by Hartmann and those who have elaborated upon his work. Perusal of Freud's actual therapeutic techniques discloses how thoroughly he understood the ego and the concept of developmental lines long before they were defined and described. We shall refer later to Sharpe as another brilliant clinician who, before the advent of ego psychology as theory, nonetheless understood and used ego psychological techniques.

It fell to Hartmann to carry this aspect of Freud's work further and to inspire the theoretical formulations of ego psychology and of psychoanalytic developmental psychology. In his work on adaptation, Hartmann discussed the attainment of equilibrium as basic to the process of adaptation. How interdependent are equilibrium and adaptation is illuminated by their definitions. Webster [10] defines adaptation as the modification of an organism or of its parts or organs to fit it more perfectly for existence under the conditions of its environment. Equilibrium is defined as a state of adjustment between or among opposing or divergent elements. Hartmann discussed the relationship of adaptation to fitting together, postulating the four forms of regulatory processes described on page 30. The ego, however, is the specific organ of adaptation, and its "synthetic function is . . . a specific organ of equilibrium at the disposal of the person." [11]

In pursuing Hartmann's theoretical pathway, it can be seen that ego development, the actual process of psychic structuring, integration of these structures within the personality, and the consequent adaptation of the individual to his environment are both processes and results of development. We may view the individual's inner stability, as well as his capacity to remain stable in his environment, as the consequence of the processes which take place along the several developmental lines described, and upon which we elaborate in chapter 7. Thus, stability, equilibrium, fitting together, and adaptation become the goals of structuralization of the psyche. This leads us to regard stability as the end result of growth processes. The postulate of a stable pathology is incompatible with this view inasmuch as stability, to whatever extent attained, results from the functioning of the ego. We present two analogies: (1) Let us consider the stability of an airplane.

[10] *Webster's Third New International Dictionary.*
[11] H. Hartmann, *Ego Psychology and the Problem of Adaptation,* p. 39.

The automatic pilot, which we suppose includes some form of gyroscopic apparatus, responds to changes in external air pressures by making necessary alterations in the wing flaps or trim tabs. Where the pressures cannot be totally compensated for, the degree to which they are *met* (achievement of stability) is a consequence of the apparatus, not of the pressure or of the pathology. (2) The ocean liner, equipped with stabilizing fins and gyroscopes, uses those apparatuses to maintain equilibrium. If, from internal or external causes, the ship develops a list, the fact that such disturbed equilibrium becomes stabilized is a consequence of the apparatuses for maintaining equilibrium and does not constitute a pathology. We find, therefore, that to view stability as the result of structuralization, and pathology as the result of failure of structuralization, enables the therapist to apply theory and technique to the problem with precision not hitherto available.

We have presented the views of Kernberg and Kohut as ventures into the realm of the treatment of certain heretofore confusing pathologies which are neither neurotic nor psychotic. Many gifted therapists have treated and continue to treat such very disturbed patients empathically and intuitively without, however, attempting conceptualizations proffered by these two authors. Kernberg and Kohut are to be credited with having made bold forays into relatively unknown territory. It is our own opinion, nevertheless, that, at our present state of knowledge, it is premature to attempt to delineate specific diagnostic entities for which specific courses of treatment may be prescribed. The general direction taken by investigators into these deeper pathologies is that their origins are to be sought in the developmental period of life before and during the process of differentiation of self from object. As we study the many-faceted aspects of mother-child interaction in these critical months, unfortunate opportunities for pathological development appear infinite. Currently, there is theoretical controversy regarding the therapeutic possibility of reconstructing preverbal experience. We believe that it is possible to make such reconstructions and that, out of these, as well as out of continuing infant observation, new and more refined information will become available. Kris, addressing himself to the work of reconstruction in psychoanalysis, noted the complexities caused by telescoped memories and combinations of defenses. He said of reconstruction, "In one sense one may say it is a hopeless task," [12] adding that the purpose of reconstruction, while limited in relation to factual events, is really more vast in that it seeks to find the repetitive processes which are integrated into the structure of personality and may be discerned both in patterns relived in the present and in the transference. In this regard, Kris would seem to support Kohut's use of the reactivation in the transference, as well as Mahler's work in direct infant observation. Kohut prefers his own observational position, believing that to speculate about object love in the infantile era "rests on retrospective falsifications and on adultomorphic errors in empathy." [13] We think that continued investigation of the pathologies based in early developmental failure and accumulated experience in treating them will continue also to refine more and more distinct configurations which appear like diagnostic entities. Nevertheless, neat categorization, while alluring, is at this stage in our knowledge of theory best avoided in describing the pathological consequences of myriad combinations of failure in development on the way to object constancy.

[12] E. Kris, "The Recovery of Childhood Memories in Psychoanalysis," p. 76.
[13] H. Kohut, *The Analysis of the Self*, p. 220.

2

TECHNIQUE

❧ 7 ❧

DESCRIPTIVE
DEVELOPMENTAL DIAGNOSIS

PSYCHOANALYSTS HAVE LONG FELT that the psychiatric classification of mental illness, bound and constricted by the medical diagnostic model, does not transpose satisfactorily to diagnosis of emotional
problems.[1] Especially does it fail in dictating appropriate treatment
procedures because of the now well-known clinical fact that similar
symptoms may appear in otherwise different diagnostic entities. In
the practice of medicine, those diseases which are well understood are
diagnosed by means of an orderly sequence of physical examination
accompanied by appropriate laboratory procedures; when diagnosis is
established, the form of treatment is indicated. Those diseases which
are still not understood are being investigated with a view toward
bringing diagnosis and treatment into the same order as the known
disease entities. Beginning with Kraepelin, and to this very day, psychiatric nosology tends to follow the medical model. Standard psychiatric nomenclature suffers, thereby, from the attempt to squeeze psychological data, which are of a different order from the physical, into
the medical mold. Psychotherapists, confronted with standard nomenclature such as *depressive neurosis, schizoid personality, passive aggressive personality,* and the like, do not always know even whether
the patient has either a neurotic (and therefore intact) ego, has an
ego which has developed to the degree that there is an admixture of
both neurotic and psychotic features, or has a frankly psychotic structure.

[1] E. Glover, "A Psycho-Analytic Approach to the Classification of Mental Disorders," in *On the Early Development of the Mind;* N. Ross, "An Examination of
Nosology According to Psychoanalytic Concepts."

The diagnostic scheme which we present is consistent with the view that diagnosis is to be made, not from the symptom or symptom cluster, but from appraisal of the structure of the ego in which the symptom is embedded.[2] In psychoanalytic treatment, diagnosis is built around the distinction between the *transference neuroses* and the *narcissistic neuroses.* The latter term, no longer in use, referred to the less-structured personalities which, in Freud's time, were little understood. It was left to the ego psychologists to elaborate that persons suffering from transference neuroses had reached a level of ego development which makes transference possible because self and object representations are differentiated, facilitating the use of the analyst for displacement and projection of feelings and attitudes toward objects from the past; also, because reality testing is intact, the danger that the analyst will be mistaken for the real object is averted. It is interesting that Freud, with less developmental theory available to him than we now have, nevertheless diagnosed from the way in which the ego functioned in the therapeutic situation, that is, from the structure of the ego. Although we now better understand the process of structuralization and thereby the less-structured personalities, there are many unresolved questions about them, such as whether they are capable of transference and transference neurosis. These questions we shall attempt to answer. We think that the avenue along which to search for answers about diagnosis (as well as for treatment) of these types of structures is the wider one of assuming qualitative difference between the transference neuroses and the narcissistic neuroses. To deal diagnostically (and therapeutically) with the less-structured personalities as though the differences are in degree only, as is sometimes attempted, is in our opinion erroneous. With less structuralization than the neurotic, the so-called modified egos cannot be treated on a simple continuum ranging from near neurosis through the severe borderline states to psychosis.

The term *ego modification* is generic and subsumes four specific types of impairment: ego defect, ego deviation, ego distortion, ego regression. Some of these terms are used interchangeably in the literature, but greater clarity is attained if we distinguish among them. We

[2] K. R. Eissler, "The Effect of the Structure of the Ego on Psychoanalytic Technique."

reserve the term *ego defect* for those impairments in the ego that are contained within the apparatuses of primary autonomy and that are therefore constitutional, so far as is presently known. *Ego deviations* result from those aspects of development that depart too early from the normal. We may consider as an example Spitz' description of the succession of organizers of the psyche. If the first organizer develops in a less than optimal fashion, it burdens the even development of the second, and the end result of these combined deviations in development will in turn prevent the normal emergence of the third organizer. Another example is that of premature ego development. Quantitatively, a deviation may be so slight that development is not impaired substantially on the one extreme, or it may be so great that subsequent development is severely hampered on the other with, of course, many falling in between. An *ego distortion* is an impairment of the ego which results from internalization of faulty perceptions of self and object representations. An *ego regression* is the result of a backward movement of an ego function from a higher level of development to a lower one, usually manifesting itself in loss or diminution of function. Some of the more blatant ego regressions are loss of speech, of locomotion, of sphincter control.

The development of levels of anxiety proceeds from fear of annihilation in the early weeks of life to fear of loss of the object in the symbiotic, need-gratifying phase; to fear of loss of the object's love when differentiation has progressed to the point where the infant can experience love; and, finally, to fear of the superego when processes of internalization have reached that relative state of completion. Capacity to deal with anxiety reveals an aspect of ego development illuminating for diagnosis. The intact ego of the normal or neurotic has, somewhere in the second year of life, acquired the capacity to regard anxiety as a signal; it no longer threatens to annihilate and can be defended against in response to the signal. If such development has not come about, however, traumatic anxiety can overwhelm the ego just as an invading army can seize a country incapable of defending itself.

In adult borderline and psychotic structures, it is always essential to be aware that rarely, if ever, is the situation the stagnant one of simple arrest at a point in development. In addition to modification (usually ego distortion), regression is always to be considered, both ego regression and psychosexual. Therefore, diagnosis includes consideration of degree of modification; of the highest level reached; and of where regression exists at the time of diagnostic evaluation. The more intact egos are better able to reverse regression. The neurotic regresses along psychosexual lines, but not in lasting ego regression. Finally dictating our diagnostic philosophy is the clinical fact that all sorts of symptoms, even those traditionally regarded as psychotic, are found in normal and neurotic structures as well. An example of this is depersonalization, found by Jacobson[3] to have been used by normal women in the particularly trying situation of being noncriminal political prisoners. Another example is that of loss of an ego function in neurotic structure. The everyday comment, "It left me speechless," is sometimes more than a metaphor. If the stress is great enough, one can lose speech, or memory, and the like. Lawyers know that witnesses to the same scene perceive and remember it differently.

These are some of the reasons we think that a descriptive rather than a classificatory scheme is more accurate and, as we have said, directs the therapist to the developmental lesion. Since the lesion leaves the adult patient with an ego structure so different in quality from that of the neurotic, we have also contended that the technique of psychotherapy is not simply an extension of psychoanalytic technique. We have said also that it is probably not possible, but certainly now premature, to try to establish distinct diagnostic entities from some clinical clusters manifest in borderline structures.

Psychoanalytic diagnosis is briefly reviewed: Freud established that neurosis is the result of failure to resolve the oedipal conflict. Anxiety arises from conflict between ego and id, or ego and superego, or id and superego, and, because of the neurotic ego's capability, is responded to as a signal for the employment of defense. Compromise between the conflicting agencies is effected by symptom formation, which provides gratification in disguised form to each agency. The model neurosis, hysteria, is the result of repression of incestuous wishes and of compromise in the form of conversion symptoms if there is somatic compliance, or of phobic formations, employing

[3] E. Jacobson, "Depersonalization."

the mechanism of displacement in addition to repression, if the soma is not involved. Obsessional neurosis involves one step beyond the hysterias in the process of defending against the core oedipal conflict. Unable to deal with the anxiety adequately by means of repression alone, the obsessional neurotic regresses from the phallic-oedipal position to the anal, where already existing fixation predisposes the individual to obsessional neurosis. At that regressed level, additional defense mechanisms, particularly reaction formation, isolation, and undoing are employed. Freud derived these theories largely from analyses of "Dora," [4] "Little Hans," [5] and "The Rat Man." [6] There exist also neurotic structures in which symptom formation is not a prominent feature. These are the so-called character neuroses; there the ego joins forces with the pathology, resulting in ego syntonicity with less suffering to the individual and therefore with less motivation to change.

All neurotic structures have in common that the ego is well developed and intact. Regression is along psychosexual lines mainly. Ego regressions are temporary, reversible, and usually occur in the service of the ego.[7] A few of these formulations have been somewhat reconsidered in recent years. The clinical facts failed to bear out, in every instance, that conversion symptoms and phobias existed in structures always at the phallic-oedipal level. Rangell showed that conversion and hysteria are not necessarily wedded; Wangh, in a similar vein, demonstrated that phobic symptoms exist in other than hysterical structures. Ross amplified and extended theoretical concepts concerning phobias, emphasizing the importance of ego structure. He proposed a classification based upon the nature of object relations, and of the defenses against aggression. By drawing attention to these developmental features, indices of the level of psychic structuralization, opportunity was provided for more precise classification. Thus Ross reflected not only the general dissatisfaction with nosology, but illuminated the pathway toward a more useful clinical understanding of the phobias. Those which are altogether psychic, he argued, differ from

[4] S. Freud, *Fragment of an Analysis of a Case of Hysteria.*
[5] S. Freud, *Analysis of a Phobia in a Five-Year-Old Boy.*
[6] S. Freud, *Notes upon a Case of Obsessional Neurosis.*
[7] E. Kris, *Psychoanalytic Explorations in Art.*

those which involve somatic illness in that higher levels of ego functioning, especially symbolization, are operative in the former.

Psychosomatic medicine, a subspecialty of medicine, developed in a direction different from the psychoanalytic. Adherents of Alexander attribute psychosomatic illnesses to transmission of psychic events to the autonomic nervous system, thereby employing consideration of the two different nervous systems in explanation of the "mysterious leap" [8] from psyche to soma. This theory dominates psychosomatic medicine to this day, although psychoanalysts find that clinical observation does not bear it out. The logical conclusion from the premise that psychic phenomena are transmitted to the nervous system is that the nervous system can be influenced by medical procedures such as surgery, which is little used these days for that purpose, and drugs, which are used profusely. While there is no room to doubt that drugs do act upon the nervous system, they cannot affect the psychological causes of the illness, nor do most advocates of chemotherapy so claim. Drugs do alter behavior. The easy availability of such drugs, the facts that they can be prescribed by a physician regardless of his knowledge of psychology and that they are far less expensive and time-consuming than psychotherapy, places chemotherapy in the position of providing symptom alleviation for the masses. This augurs dangers for the future, some of which already exist in the present. As insurance plans, whether private or government sponsored, tend to take over more and more of the financial burden of therapy, the tendency is to be persuaded that the least expensive method is the best. We are likely to have a drugged population whose psychological problems are obscured by symptom management, with fundamental cure available only to the wealthy.

The psychoanalytic direction of psychosomatic thinking was established by Schur, a scientific descendant of Freud, Hartmann, and Jacobson. Using the concept of silent physiological discharge to the interior as the neonate's normal pathway for discharge of undifferentiated drive energy, Schur proceeded to construct his theory of *somatization*. It is the result, he proposed, of deneutralization of

[8] F. Deutsch (ed.), *On the Mysterious Leap, from the Mind to the Body: A Workshop Study on the Theory of Conversion.*

the drives and of dedifferentiation of self and object representations. In this regressive process the pathways established in infancy are retraced. According to Schur, psychophysiological rather than strictly anatomical phenomena prevail. He used a case of dermatoses to demonstrate the regressive process and its resultant reversion to the infantile use of the skin for discharge of affect. His suggested technical procedure whereby this process may be reversed is verbalization as the vehicle for promoting neutralized discharge of aggressive and libidinal drive energies.

Modern thinking about diagnosis was stimulated by Anna Freud and her collaborators, who presented an adult profile detailing criteria for personality assessment.[9] The "adult profile," as it is called, departs radically from traditional psychiatric diagnosis, especially from expectation that complete diagnosis can be made in a few sessions. Now, psychoanalytic diagnosis is thought of as being complete only with completion of treatment. While this hardly appears to be useful as a guide to treatment, it is no cause for dismay because diagnosis in psychotherapy, unlike much in medicine, is a process continuing throughout the course of treatment. Diagnosis changes during treatment because ego-building techniques have as their goal alteration in ego structure. In fact, one way of describing the purpose of treatment is to change the diagnosis.

The first approach to diagnosis is tentative appraisal of ego development from its functioning in the present and in the life history, especially in those areas as love and work and in how successfully developmental milestones—separation-individuation, the oedipal conflict, and the like—have been passed. From such rough data, a tentative decision is reached about whether the patient falls into one of the three broad categories—neurotic, borderline, or psychotic structure. From that point on, if treatment is decided upon, it proceeds hand in hand with diagnosis. Diagnostic hypotheses are tested, altered, discarded, reformulated, as new information dictates. Treatment is undertaken concurrently with refinement of diagnosis. In this inexact science, we have to be content to work, initially, with the rough and tentative diagnostic hypotheses that our early impressions provide. If we are fairly well content that the structure is neurotic, psychoanalysis is indicated whenever possible; for the borderline structure, psychoanalytically oriented psychotherapy is the treatment of choice; for the psychotic structure, decision has to be made about whether ambulatory or in-patient treatment is more desirable. Never is there constraint upon the therapist to make decisions quickly. One may need one, two, or ten or more sessions to arrive at even broad diagnostic conclusions.

One of the most frequently asked questions is, "What does one do during prolonged diagnostic exploration?" The best procedure is to think, while the patient unfolds his story. Questions designed to elicit information about the way the ego has functioned in life situations are always in order. For example, a thread in the patient's life history may give the therapist the tentative thought that separation anxiety is present. There may have been phobic or other strong reaction to the first day of school; there may have been anxiety when the family moved to another apartment or to another city; the patient may be, let us say, thirty years old and still living at home; he may have remained in the same job despite opportunities elsewhere. When some such direction shapes up in the therapist's mind, he may ask, "Is it always hard for you to leave something?" Such a question is designed to elicit more information and elaboration, *and* to interest the patient's ego in his developmental problems. How competently the ego becomes involved in this task tests prognosis as well as diagnosis. If the patient can become actively involved in working in his behalf, it augurs well for the future therapeutic alliance. We shall continuously stress the patient's capacity and willingness to work in the therapeutic partnership. If work is expected of him at the outset, treatment, if undertaken, will be in the context of having already taught him how to conduct his part in the endeavor. Patients are able to perform in varying degrees which often correlate with ego strength. We do not demand that a patient try to work beyond his capacity, but the very encouragement to try to work is a therapeutic device which tends to increase that capacity. In the early stages of diagnosis, then, how the ego performs is an indicator of its strength and capability. Before arrival at a fairly reliable, albeit tentative diagnostic decision, the therapist is under no constraint to undertake to treat. The patient is to be informed in some way such as, "We will look into your problem to-gether and we will decide what to do when we understand it better." This lets him know that the commitment is not yet made and enlists his ego in exploring the problem.

Beginning therapists, in particular, are apt to make hasty commit-ments which they later regret. Miss Andrews was an eighteen-year-old girl, depressed and suicidal. She proposed to the therapist that she attend once-a-week sessions because that was all she could afford. Her parents, in fairly good circumstances, did not know much about her condition and the patient was adamant, in the first session, that she did not wish to involve them. The therapist deemed it undesirable to undertake treatment of a rather serious problem on the patient's terms. While we never want to impair autonomy, it is not a contra-diction to consider that patients' judgment may be faulty. Decision as to the form and frequency of treatment is usually made by the thera-pist. This therapist decided that no commitment could be made under the conditions the patient prescribed; that if the therapist could not have the opportunity to keep in close touch with her during her de-pression, treatment could not be carried out responsibly. Out of this, the patient got in touch with her parents, who agreed to provide the intensive treatment that such a case requires.[10]

In addition to the tentative decision as to whether a patient has an essentially neurotic, borderline, or psychotic structure, one scans the entire range of development to arrive at appraisal of its evenness. A neurotic or normal ego develops in a more or less consistent and even fashion. Drive attenuation, psychosexual maturation, and ego growth have been kept apace by maternal guidance. Particularly does the competent mother guard against the danger that one aspect of the child's development will too far outpace another. As an example, psy-chosexual maturation, which is biologically dictated and therefore less subject to environmental influence, may proceed according to its own timetable regardless of whether ego development has kept pace. This can be traumatic because the ego is then forced to cope with a matu-rational demand for which it has not developed competence. Com-monly, such unevenness is seen in the borderline structures and in

[10] Material provided by Leonora Tint.

psychotics who maturationally have reached perhaps the phallic level while the ego has remained relatively undeveloped, lacking defenses which would enable it to cope with anxiety aroused by instinctual demands. Whether development has been relatively even or chaotic can usually be determined in a few sessions by noting the highest psychosexual and ego development attained; the extent of regression; the kinds of defenses available and whether they prevent traumatic anxiety; whether productions are mainly in the secondary process or whether primary process intrudes; how the therapist and other important persons are dealt with—a clue to the level of object relations.

There are cases in which severe pathology is obvious. Overt psychosis, accompanied by hallucinations, delusions, depersonalization, excessive mood swings, suicidal depression, and the like is less a problem of diagnosis than of management and treatment. The suicide attempt that has failed because of accidental external intervention presents a more morbid sign than the one that has failed because there was, even in the very act of attempting to take one's life, also some will to live. Some consultations occur at the point where decompensation is proceeding at a rapid pace and the breakdown occurs in full view of the therapist. In one such initial consultation, for example, a patient felt anxiety beyond endurance because the venetian blinds were not straight. She had to be hospitalized. The level of anxiety had regressed to that of fear of annihilation. This bears comparison with the obsessional neurotic who may also become anxious because the blinds are uneven, but whose anxiety is at the level of fear of the superego. In the first instance, obsessional defenses give way; in the second, the defenses remain intact despite anxiety. A patient whose defenses are still holding may straighten the blinds or ask the therapist to do so, may flick dust off the table, may arrange the articles on the desk. The decompensating patient is so overwhelmed that, like the infant, no power to alter the situation is available.

Some less obvious but equally morbid signs of approaching or potential breakdown may also be detected in the initial consultation. Blatantly inappropriate social behavior is an example. A woman came for a consultation with a male therapist dressed in the shortest of miniskirts and seated herself in a way designed to ensure maximum exposure. To term this seductive behavior would violate diagnostic accuracy by blurring the distinction between levels of development. The true hysteric may act out incestuous wishes by seductive behavior. She is not likely to do so before a transference neurosis is established, a sign that the seduction is object related. The less-structured patient, whose behavior is immediately bizarre, has developed more chaotically, and so the ego does not know how to deal with the sexual drives, nor is there truly an object in the sense of object constancy. Any stranger will do because there is no *object* independent of the state of need, but *only* a state of need. Behavior of persons with such structures is often erroneously described as sexual acting out. True acting out is motivated by unconscious fantasy, while casual sexual behavior is more often than not simply the gratification of a need without the existence of an object-related fantasy. In the less-structured personality, therefore, the technical problem is not to make the unconscious conscious, but to make the ego capable of coping with the drives by means of neutralizing libido and aggression, thereby making them available for the building of higher levels of object relations. Detection of the difference between *acting* and *acting out* is not difficult if the diagnosing therapist bears in mind that a central feature in severe pathology is pathology of object relations. *Acting out* refers to behavior motivated by unconscious, object-related fantasies repressed by an ego capable of employing such high-level defense. These fantasies, in the treatment process, center around the therapist as the representative, in the transference neurosis, of the primary objects. When they are interpreted and worked through, acting out ceases. *Acting,* on the other hand, may be the result of direct drive discharge because the ego's capacity for delay is minimal, or it may represent reproduction of preverbal experience.

We offer an extended clinical illustration of how diagnosis and treatment proceed hand in hand, describing and explaining both these processes. Figure 1 (at the end of this chapter) charts the aspects of development to be taken into consideration in diagnosis. In no case will all of these diagnostic criteria be satisfied.

Mr. Baker began to experience anxiety attacks of unbearable severity upon graduation from college. As soon as he found employment he sought treatment. He was the oldest of four children. His next sibling, a sister, was born when he was four years old. He said, at the beginning, that his relationship with his mother had always been good. The therapist wondered at this, because the patient exhibited intense anxiety and inability, at moments of stress, to erect competent defenses against it. This raised a question in the therapist's mind about the adequacy of the mother-child relationship. Later, in the course of treatment, it was found that the patient thought the relationship was good because it had not been troublesome. He had no comparative way of realizing that his mother was cold, aloof, and insensitive to his feelings, because he had never experienced maternal warmth. It was only after he found that the therapist was different that appreciation of the ingredient missing in his childhood became highlighted. His mother had always been there, a life situation providing a sort of consistency which has its assets, but which makes it difficult for the child to appraise the quality of her presence. Blatant abandonment, by contrast, is an acute trauma difficult to deny. Mr. Baker suffered the chronic trauma of unattunement.

It is not useful to challenge the patient's convictions about important relationships too early because object relations, even cathexis of a negative object, must be maintained. Only gradually, within the context of a good working alliance, can a patient begin to accept and tolerate interpretation of distorted object representations. There does arrive a time in treatment when it is helpful for the patient to know that his aggression toward the negative object was justified, but this time is never in the initial stages of diagnosis. In the case of Mr. Baker, the therapist chose, instead, to seek details with questions such as, "Can you give an example of how she treated you?" In thinking about the answer, the ego sometimes arrives at its own realization that perhaps she was not as good as his need for an object-at-any-cost forced him to maintain. If such awareness comes about, the ego corrects its own distortion without heavy-handed therapeutic intervention.

Mr. Baker described his father quite differently, as a tyrant who supervised his every activity. As the details unfolded, the patient's resentful compliance stood out. There was much quarreling, but never did father and son come to terms or alter their daily interchanges. Tentatively, at first, the therapist thought about the possibility that the aggressive drive was employed to perpetuate libidinal ties. (This form of quarreling without end is more often seen in marital relationships where closeness is unconsciously desired but is so feared that it is defended against aggressively, a form of defense which at the same time gratifies the wish with angry closeness.) Mr. Baker's father often forgot the boy's name, calling him by the names of several of his own brothers and of the other children in the family. This suggested that, despite the apparent interest in this son, the father's object cathexes were unstable. He had neither awareness of the boy's individuality nor parental interest in promoting it. The therapist thought, still tentatively, that Mr. Baker had a borderline structure, basing this on the hypothesis that separation-individuation could not have been attained successfully in this parental climate. On the prognostically favorable side, Mr. Baker impressed the therapist as having good innate endowment which probably had prevented more severe developmental failure and which promised to be an ally in treatment. This is not yet enough basis for a firm diagnosis. We need to know more about the maternal side of the picture and about early childhood. We need also to know about the endopsychic aspects. These, the patient is unable to volunteer, because they are unconscious. In general, patients are more likely to emphasize the interpersonal than the internal features of their life experience.

In the diagnostic evaluation, one can only learn about early childhood that which is consciously remembered. The major events that Mr. Baker told the therapist were of fear of starting school, and the following: at about age three (evidently shortly before the birth of his sister), his mother left him to wait outside a store. She seemed to him to be taking an inordinately long time and he became anxious. He entered the store to look for her and got hopelessly lost. Another memory that did not come spontaneously but responded to a little questioning was that he felt altogether ignored when his siblings were born. The therapist also thought, but reserved for later in treatment, that there must have been observation of the sister's "castrated" state, which would have made a deep impression on a boy at the height of the phallic phase. A presumptive fact which the therapist elicited by asking about the sleeping arrangements was that the patient was witness to the primal scene. This, too, was held in reserve with the knowledge that fantasies now unconscious would emerge in the course of treatment.

The internal structure could be ascertained to some degree from Mr. Baker's behavior and attitudes toward the therapist and the therapeutic arrangements. He was seen, in this initial period, on a three-times-a-week schedule. Before, we described a case for which we advocated that the therapist not accept the patient's dictum about frequency. That was in a situation of danger because of suicidal depression. In this case, it was wiser to begin on the patient's terms. The therapist, in making this decision, had in mind the father's drastic impairment of autonomy. This illustrates another feature of how treatment begins even in the exploratory, diagnostic stage. The therapeutic climate must not repeat the pathogenic one. Apparently simple acceptance of the patient's terms, for this case, began the ego-building process.

Mr. Baker desperately wanted to feel better, which to him meant relief from anxiety. He expressed longing for some quick and magical cure—a drug, an injection, hypnosis, and the like, an indication of passive, symbiotic longings. A keystone of diagnosis is determination of whether the symbiotic phase was adequate, deprived, or overindulged. Putting together these passive longings, the mother's presumptive coldness, the patient's capacity to function in secondary thought processes, the therapist further hypothesized that the symbiotic phase had been barely adequate at the appropriate time; there had been a taste of symbiotic gratification, enough to have prevented psychosis, but not enough to have prevented hunger for more. That gratification came in the form of the father's encroachment when symbiosis was no longer phase specific.

Gratification out of phase further impaired development. This is not only because it reinforced fixation, but because it also deflected from development which should, normally, have taken place at that later period of life. It was hypothesized that separation-individuation processes had begun but had not reached completion. This was derived from the initiative he exhibited in entering the store to search for mother, thus dealing with anxiety actively rather than enduring it passively; from aborted attempts to free himself from his father's intrusions; from ventures in independent assertion with the therapist, showing that there was some neutralized aggression available for the expression of difference, although not enough to complete the separation-individuation process. The therapist, here, thought of the vicious cycle described by Mahler, in which insufficient neutralization of aggressive energy prevents employment of aggression in the service of separation-individuation, and the accumulation of such aggression at the threshold of separation-individuation becomes so great that, in the unconscious, self and object are endangered by independent moves. Separation anxiety reinforces regressive pull to the haven of symbiosis and there joins forces with already existing fixation.

Defense against symbiotic longings is, as is true of any defense, more favorable diagnostically and prognostically than is yielding. At least there is anxiety about irreversible regression. Such anxiety feels to the patient like fear of loss of identity and manifests itself, in the relationship with the therapist, as fear of engulfment. If the therapist is careful to establish a climate of guardianship of autonomy at the outset, the further course of treatment reduces opportunity for projection of symbiotic wishes upon the therapist. The patient then comes to realize that the therapist is not, in reality, threatening to engulf him, but that this fear arises endopsychically. Thus, even in the early stages of diagnosis, the therapeutic manner paves the way for later opportunity to interpret the symbiotic wish. Again, as we said about the possibility that the patient might correct distorted object representations without the therapist, here there exists a similar possibility that he might himself interpret his symbiotic longings in the therapeutic climate where they do not attain reinforcement from the therapist's side. We think of this kind of technique as illustrative of employment of the much misunderstood abstinence rule in its most positive sense.

In the presence of mildly depressive features, one may speculate, even though the patient cannot provide evidence from memory, that an unattuned mother might have been unresponsive in the rapprochement subphase. It is all too easy for mothers, who themselves do not enjoy their symbiotic union with the infant at the phase-specific time, to welcome the differentiation and practicing subphases as freedom from the demand of the infant's closeness and thus to fail to respond to the rapprochement subphase. For the toddler who has explored his world for a while and then seeks his mother again, failure in return to home base is disappointing and constitutes a form of object loss accompanied by frustration and depression because the as-yet relatively undifferentiated self and object representations become cathected with aggression. This promotes the vicious cycle of inability to separate and individuate for fear of destroying self and object.

There were evidences of castration anxiety in Mr. Baker's guarded description of his sexual functioning. While we need, eventually, to know all about this, it is never desirable to insist upon details before a trusting, therapeutic alliance is attained. In fact, that the patient is guarded at the outset is indicative of a defensive stance which connotes a modicum of ego strength. In psychiatric clinics and other like situations where a quick diagnosis has to be made, often by a psychiatrist who will not be doing the treatment, the patient is subjected to sharp questioning, without regard for his defenses, for purposes of testing his anxiety tolerance. This kind of stress interview provides diagnostic information far more quickly than the leisurely way that we are advocating. We do not want diagnostic information for its own sake, at the expense of the patient and at the sacrifice of a therapeutic alliance. Therefore, we have to be content with less information at the outset and with a tentative rather than a firm diagnosis. In this case, castration anxiety combined with and burdened by separation anxiety was assumed from the patient's brief mention of premature ejaculation and from the life history, especially from the fact of the sister's arrival at the height of the phallic phase and the patient's undoubted observation of her genitalia. Ubiquitously, children of both sexes tend to assume that the girl's or woman's genitals are damaged. It was speculated also that this insensitive mother, in the child's preschool days when he was at home alone with her, probably was not too careful about her attire, toilet habits, and the like in the presence of the boy. Psychologically unattuned parents tend to assume that a young child has no perception. Comparing the layering of separation and castration anxiety in this case with a hypothetical neurotic structure, in the latter identity would have been clearly established with conquest of the separation-individuation crisis and there would be castration anxiety, to be sure, but at the phallic level relatively unencumbered by severe separation anxiety as well.

On the positive side was evidence of a not-too-shaky gender identity. Although there was fear of homosexuality, there was no history of overt acting out of homosexual wishes. Rather, the fear of it was indicative of a strong desire to maintain masculinity in the face of the symbiotic wishes which represent, in this regard, regression to the stage of life when discovery of one's gender has not yet been made. The therapist reasoned that, if masculinity is insisted upon, then it is logical to assume that it had been attained and that the problem lies in retaining it.

Passive, submissive features were very much in evidence on the anal level as well. For the sake of getting well quickly, the patient expressed willingness to pour out everything, to reveal what was dirty and nasty in him, to get rid of it. The therapeutic position is that so much sacrifice is not required to effect cure. The details of the bitter struggle around toilet training were revealed. His mother wanted him to be clean very early. He adamantly refused and there were severe scoldings over his deliberate soiling in defiance of her. While it remains correct to view this as the negativism of the anal phase, the ego psychological therapist regards it as a positive sign that, in this respect, the ego had developed to the point of some differentiation to the ability to say, "no," and to insistence upon retention of that which feels like one's own body part. The therapist also kept in mind that, since toilet training was demanded so early, the child was unable to distinguish the anal product from the rest of his body, and especially from his penis. All the more reason for the therapist, in joining Mr. Baker's desire to protect his masculinity as well as his autonomy, to remain undemanding of material for its own sake. To the fact that much that we need to know is unconscious at the beginning of treatment may be added this kind of therapeutic restraint in explanation of why we never acquire complete diagnostic information at the outset.

The defensive function is to be appraised diagnostically. Here, Mr. Baker's capacity to tolerate anxiety fluctuated. It could operate competently, but in stress was less than optimal. Defense against symbiotic merger has already been described as has the tendency to project the underlying wishes. In addition to projection, displacement was used in mild phobic arrangements; reaction formation and other such middle-range defenses clustered around the anal features. From his heterosexual behavior, it was surmised that the oedipal level had been reached, probably too tenuously and heavily burdened by submission to the father, with its homosexual implications, and by the father's role in gratifying symbiotic longings. The good secondary-process functioning implied that repression was employed to some extent. Signal anxiety was operative but could be lost.

The level of object relations is not always easy to ascertain at the beginning diagnostic evaluation unless the patient has ongoing relationships which he can describe—for example, if he is married, the marriage inevitably enters the description of the life situation. Mr. Baker had sporadic dates with various girls but no meaningful attachments. It could be speculated that he was at the need-gratifying level, but that remained to be confirmed later. Patients at that level usually have no awareness of the therapist as a person and no curiosity. In fact, it becomes a milestone in treatment when the patient at the need-gratifying level begins to notice the therapist as a person, to ask personal questions, or even ordinarily polite ones such as, "How are you?" Before such progress these patients do not notice minor matters such as when the therapist has a cold, looks tired, looks well, and so on. In comparison, neurotic patients are usually much interested in the therapist's personal life. Technically, the beginning interest in the therapist as a person by the former borderline patient who is developing a higher level of object relations should always be acknowledged and his questions answered if they are not too intimate. By contrast, the stronger ego of the neurotic patient can tolerate not being answered for the sake of encouraging his fantasies.

The therapist concluded that, in Kernberg's terms, this was a "higher level" [11] borderline state. By this is meant that there were borderline as well as neurotic features. A "lower level" [12] borderline state would be much closer to psychosis, with absence of the neurotic defenses and relatively advanced ego development apparent in this

[11] O. F. Kernberg, "A Psychoanalytic Classification of Character Pathology," p. 802.
[12] Ibid., p. 803.

case. The prognosis, in terms of bringing the patient, Mr. Baker, to the resolution of the separation-individuation crisis and establishment of a distinct identity, seemed favorable.

It is often possible, much later, if the patient is willing to undertake long-term analysis after identity is established, to make a transition to traditional psychoanalytic technique and to cure the neurosis which becomes more patent once the borderline features are resolved.

Figure 2 illustrates how this case may be traced on figure 1 and may be plotted on a graph. (Figures 2 and 3 follow figure 1 at the end of this chapter.) Instead of the static psychiatric label, the graph itself represents the descriptive developmental diagnosis. It guides the therapist toward those aspects of development to which treatment is to be addressed. After plotting the salient developmental features, the first matter to be noted is the irregularity of the graph. A hypothetical neurotic tracing is illustrated in figure 3 for contrast. In neurotic or normal structures, the almost straight-line tracing is indicative of more favorable development. Some points to be noted are the following:

1. That Mr. Baker had reached the phallic level and approached the oedipal conflict is consistent with the fact that maturation of psychosexuality is relatively unaffected by the parental climate unless the parents are so severely damaging as to cripple even that aspect of growth. In this case, the good conflict-free endowment and the fact that the parents were moderately unattuned rather than severely damaging assured psychosexual maturation.

2. Neutralization had proceeded to some extent, but was insufficient.

3. The objects were sometimes split in order to protect the "good" object from aggression.

4. Object relations were on a need-gratification level. Need for the object had not become superseded by regard for the object as a person.

5. Fear of castration, of object loss (because of unneutralized aggression), and of loss of parts of the prephallic self (feces) blended together.

6. The defenses had developed to the middle range, but higher level defenses were weak.

7. Separation-individuation was not completed.

8. Some minimal selective identifications had been made, especially with regard to gender identity. Excessive amounts of unneutralized aggression prevented positive ego and superego identifications to
proceed to higher levels of internalization. The level of sphincter mo-
rality (fear of loss of love) was reached.

The treatment plan is now clear. The therapist is aware of each of
these aspects of development and will be alerted to material which
will provide opportunity for development therapeutically. Some of
the beginning therapeutic attitudes were explained in the description
of the case. Some aspects of the therapy will be described here, and
will be further elaborated in chapter 12.

1. Fear of symbiotic merger had to be attenuated before the therapeutic alliance could be well established. In the climate of guardianship of autonomy, the patient himself reached his own interpretation
of symbiotic longings. At first he expressed fears of envelopment, engulfment, that he would not know who he is (loss of identity). The
therapist was supportive, "I will not let you lose yourself." This is a
therapeutic statement analogous to the position of the "good enough
mother" [13] who provides optimal symbiotic gratification at the phase-
specific time, but who is also the guardian of the child's development
and therefore remains alert to the next phase when the child, closer
to acquisition of identity, needs a mother who gives up her symbiotic
tie to him for the sake of furthering his development. With a more
symbiotically deprived patient, the therapist would have provided
some symbiotic gratification after the fear of it diminished. In this
case, it was deemed not necessary because there had been some in infancy, but also because there had been too much in the later relationship with the father.

2. Self-interpretation was encouraged. This builds the ego by exercise of function.

3. The highest level of psychosexual maturation, the phallic, was
supported, interrelated interpretively with attainment of gender identity. This helped the patient to appreciate his developmental accomplishments and provided a more solid base for further development to

13 D. W. Winnicott, "Transitional Objects and Transitional Phenomena," p. 94.

proceed. The highest levels of ego development were similarly supported—the courage to disagree, to say "no," and the like.

The anal struggle with the mother was dwelt on as a positive aspect of development rather than as anal stubbornness, withholding, and negativism. Such comments as, "Already, at that age you had a mind of your own and wanted to retain what was yours," were helpful.

4. Disagreement with the therapist was welcomed also as occasion to discuss employment of aggression in the service of separation and to further neutralization. Here was involved one of the major therapeutic aims, to aid the separation-individuation process. Neutralization was furthered as the therapist maintained that verbalization replace action. When Mr. Baker's roommate annoyed him, he was encouraged to talk it out with him rather than to "bash his head in." Neutralization of libido was also promoted. When Mr. Baker began to respond positively to the therapist's helpfulness, he expressed fear that he would feel sexual desire for her. The therapist said, "Well, it would be natural if that should happen and we will understand it as an expression of your love and masculinity. We will not do anything about it, so that you will be able to use it with girls of your own choosing."

5. With neutralization of both drives, the therapist became more meaningful to the patient. This first became manifest around the therapist's vacation time. At first, the patient clung desperately and experienced severe separation anxiety around the therapist's vacation. As neutralization reinforced fusion of "good" and "bad" objects, splitting diminished.[14] Object representations became more constant and the patient became aware of his own and the therapist's continuous existence regardless of whether they were physically together. When subsequent vacations came about, the patient was able to wish the therapist a good time. Capacity to delay and to value the object had developed. Tendency to split the object under stress of separation anxiety had to be interpreted, including the purpose

[14] Generally used terminology such as "good" and "bad" is prevalent in the literature despite its judgmental connotation. While we believe that "libidinally" or "aggressively" cathected would be more objective and therefore more desirable terms, we yield to general usage in order to remain consistent with the literature.

behind it, to maintain the "good" object. When higher levels of
thought process were operative, in moments of less anxiety, Mr.
Baker knew that the object was one person.

6. The intactness of the body was a prominent therapeutic theme.
The adult, reasonable ego became the therapist's ally in interpreting
misconceptions from the past. These were always presented to the patient as understandable and even intelligent surmises and conclusions
formulated by the young child, but now subject to correction by the
adult intellect. That the feces are, at first, thought to be essential body
parts was clarified. That the penis does not fall off as feces do was discussed. That his sister was not born damaged but as a girl should be
was stressed. These corrections of the child's misperceptions are commonplace, even in cases with more intact egos. However, in those
cases there is no danger of fragmentation. With Mr. Baker, at moments of stress, rapid ego regression threatened to lead him to the
state where his thought processes and body parts had insufficient
cohesion. The therapeutic stance supported to the utmost the wavering synthetic function.

7. Defenses were not assailed. We are sometimes told to aid repression, but if repression is weak, then material from childhood which
normally would be repressed is conscious. Mr. Baker could remember his mother's disregard of his interest in her inadequately clad
body and the sexual feelings that were aroused. We deliberately avoid
calling this seduction because we think it more accurate to regard it
as insensitivity to the child's perceptions and feelings. The more intact
ego of the normal or neurotic is able to repress incestuous wishes.
Since these wishes were conscious to Mr. Baker, they were dealt with
directly. Fear of sexual arousal in relation to the therapist has been
mentioned. When memories of incestuous wishes were presented, the
therapist explained that this is a welcome sign of masculinity. Other
ways of supporting masculinity were comments such as, "Isn't it good
that you developed to the point where you knew you were a boy and
would become a man?" The homosexual wish was explained as feelings of love toward his father. It was connected, interpretively, with
the symbiotic wish to merge and to regress to the state before gender
identity had acquired meaning.

8. Because the main developmental lesion lay in the separation-in-

dividuation phase, all aspects of the patient's attempts at independence were examined, encouraged in the present and in the transference, and distinguished from the past. For example, much use was made of the experience of being lost while searching for his mother. As already mentioned, the attempt to do something about the anxiety was supported. The initiative of this was pointed up. The goal of finding his mother was supported and separated from the unfortunate fact that it failed. There was discussion of what a victory it would have been had it succeeded, this to encourage further efforts with the implication that they are not always doomed to failure.

We have described the interweaving of diagnosis and treatment in a borderline structure, following the guidelines of psychoanalytic developmental psychology. In day-to-day treatment, many themes unfold concurrently and it can be confusing for the therapist to know which one to pursue. Especially is this so in cases which are chaotic because of uneven development. Diagnosis in the form of the descriptive developmental graph should help the therapist in selection of theme by indicating the points of lesion. Usually, building object relations introduces order into the otherwise hopeless morass of data. When we discuss beginning treatment, how this is done will be made specific. The point to be made here is that any of a number of developmental failures may be selected for therapeutic pursuit. We tend to prefer object relations because the implications for working within a transference facilitate treatment and because building object relations proceeds hand in hand with neutralization, which in turn strengthens the ego. It never ceases to be a surprise that, when such selectivity is exercised, the patient begins to work in a more orderly fashion, too, so that both patient and therapist know more securely what they are doing from day to day. However, we do not want to leave the impression that this becomes simple progression from one topic to another. The patient still begins the sessions with his own theme, or, more usually, introduces many themes. Like a skillful weaver, the therapist deals first with one, then with another, all the while keeping the overall pattern in mind.

The diagnosing therapist who becomes familiar with psychoanalytic developmental theory, with those developmental features charted in figure 1, will, by exercise of function, attain competence in clinical

PSYCHO-SEXUAL MATURA-TION	DRIVE TAMING PROCESSES	OBJECT RELATIONS	ADAPTIVE FUNCTION	ANXIETY LEVEL
Genital	Ambivalence resolved	Postoedipal	Fitting together	Fear of superego
	Neutralized libido serves narcissism and also the capacity to maintain constant relations with an object	Object constancy	Synthetic and integrative functions	S e c o n d a r y P r o c e s s
Phallic	Cathexis of object representations with value		Abstract thought	Fear of castration
Anal	Neutralized aggression serves identity formation	Beginning endowment of object representations with value	Speech Object comprehension	Fear of loss of love of the object
	Neutralization of aggressive drive serves establishment of defense mechanisms	Diacritic perception brings awareness of need-fulfilling function of object	Semantic communication, a new level of object relations Eight-month anxiety	Locomotion	Signal anxiety achieved
	Libido and aggression fuse	Fusion of "good" and "bad" object representations	Reality testing Intentionality	Fear of loss of the object
	Drives differentiate into libido and aggression	Awareness of need gratification	Smiling response, beginning of psychological relations	Motility Perception	P r i m a r y
Oral	Neutralization begins	Coenesthetic receptivity	Nondifferentiated stage, biological need gratification, objectless stage	Delay Memory traces	P r o c e s s Fear of annihilation

U N D I F F E R E N T I A T E D

Birth	Undifferentiated Drives and Apparatuses of Primary Autonomy including Motility, Memory, Intentionality,

ID   E G O

Figure 1

DEFENSIVE FUNCTION	IDENTITY FORMATION			PROCESSES OF INTERNALIZATION			
Secondary autonomy. Defenses change in function and become adaptive	Constant cathexis of differentiated self and object representations			Superego is structured			
Repression	Increasing internalization by means of ego and superego identifications lead to establishment of identity			Resolution of oedipus by means of identification with parent of the same sex		Ego ideal	
Regression		S e p a r a t i o n / i n d i v i d u a t i o n					
Intellectualization	Separation-individuation completed, object constancy attained			Identification with phallic prowess			
Isolation	Gender identity						
Reaction formation	Rapprochement subphase			Toilet training initiates identification with strength and cleanliness	i d e a l i z e d		G r a n d i o s e
Undoing	Practicing subphase		S y m b i o s i s			Gradual disillusionment with omnipotent objects	
Identification Displacement Reversal Turning against the self	Differentiation subphase		m b i o s i s	Selective identifications begin	o b j e c t ,		S e l f
Projection Introjection Denial	Merged self and object representations			Imitation			
	Autistic stage			Primary narcissism			

M A T R I X

Intelligence, Perception, Thinking, and Others	

S U P E R E G O

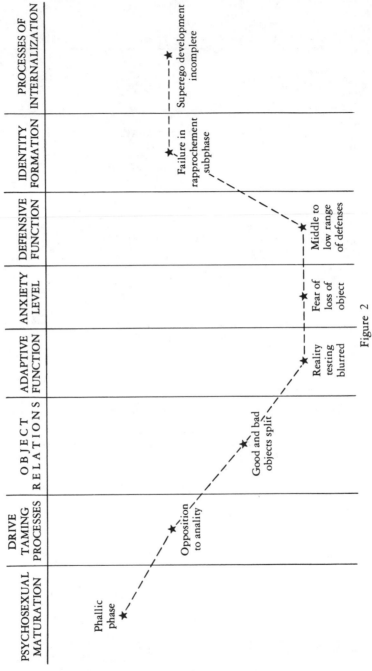

Figure 2

PSYCHOSEXUAL MATURATION	DRIVE TAMING PROCESSES	O B J E C T R E L A T I O N S	ADAPTIVE FUNCTION	ANXIETY LEVEL	DEFENSIVE FUNCTION	IDENTITY FORMATION	PROCESSES OF INTERNALIZATION
★ Genital phase	★ Drives tamed	★ Capacity to maintain constant relations with an object. Oedipus resolved.	★ Adaptation secure	★ Anxiety response to superego	★ High level, mainly repression	★ Identity secure	★ Superego nearly discrete

Figure 3

diagnosis. Nevertheless, diagnosis will probably never be an exact science, even with the extensive progress in theory building that has been made in the last twenty years and that promises to continue. Therefore, even the most skillful diagnosticians are subject to error.

⇗ 8 ⇖

DIFFERENCES BETWEEN PSYCHOANALYSIS AND PSYCHOTHERAPY

F REUD FORESAW THAT SOME DAY "the large scale application of our therapy will compel us to alloy the pure gold of analysis with the copper of direct suggestion" [1] and even that there would be reversion to hypnosis. In the same vein, Glover asserted that all therapy that is not correctly and exactly applied psychoanalysis is nothing but suggestion. Such fears arose because, at a point in theory building when little was known about ego development, one could only conceive of treatment for the unanalyzable patient in the form of bypassing the ego or taking over its functions. Nevertheless, analysts of that era, such as Freud, Glover, and Sharpe, knew intuitively that which was to be conceptualized much later—namely, that autonomy is to be protected and preserved. Technically they knew how to do this in working only with an intact ego. It remained for Greenacre, with the advances in ego psychological theory available at the time of her writing, to give conceptual form to a technique which had become common practice in the hands of the skilled psychoanalyst. Greenacre, we must remind ourselves, was still writing about the technique of psychoanalysis. How to deal effectively with the psychotherapy patient was not yet clear. While Freud had maintained that the "ingredients" of psychotherapy would have to be borrowed from psychoanalysis, it is likely that he meant technique. It took some thirty-five years more before Rangell could suggest that psychoanalysis,

[1] S. Freud, *Lines of Advance in Psycho-Analytic Therapy,* p. 168.

not as a technique but as a body of knowledge, might be used to evolve a technique of psychotherapy. Bandler [2] pointed out the important diagnostic consideration that psychotherapy addresses itself to a psychological terrain different from that of classical psychoanalysis. Our position, strikingly similar to that of Rangell and Bandler, extends classical psychoanalytic theory to include the contributions of Hartmann, Kris, Loewenstein, Jacobson, Mahler, and Spitz. From these conceptualizations can be extrapolated techniques for ego building which are not essential for the psychoanalysis of the intact egos, but which constitute the essence of the psychotherapy of the modified structures.

There have been innumerable suggestions for variation of classical psychoanalytic technique, beginning with Freud's recommendation that the phobic patient be instructed, at a certain point in his analysis, to face that which had been avoided in order to begin to cope with the anxiety it aroused. Eissler sounded the keynote for disciplined departure from psychoanalytic technique by defining and delimiting the *parameter*. He said:

We formulate tentatively the following general criteria of a parameter if it is to fulfill the conditions which are fundamental to psychoanalysis: (1) A parameter must be introduced only when it is proved that the basic model technique does not suffice; (2) the parameter must never transgress the unavoidable minimum; (3) a parameter is to be used only when it finally leads to its self-elimination; that is to say, the final phase of the treatment must always proceed with a parameter of zero.[3]

To these he added a fourth requisite: ". . . in order to delineate the conditions which a parameter must fulfill *if the technique is to remain within the scope of psychoanalysis* [italics added]: The effect of the parameter on the transference relationship must never be such that it cannot be abolished by interpretation." [4]

Eissler was striving, by this means, to extend the technique of psychoanalysis to the treatment of those structures which required

[2] See O. S. English, "The Essentials of Psychotherapy as Viewed by the Psychoanalyst."
[3] K. R. Eissler, "The Effect of the Structure of the Ego on Psychoanalytic Theory," p. 111.
[4] *Ibid.*, p. 113.

"stretching" the technique. It is not clear, however, that he intended thereby to encompass treatment of certain types of borderline structures within the confines of psychoanalysis proper. Essential to his purpose is that the parameter be eliminated because only then could the transference neurosis be resolved. This leaves a central question in treatment of the unintact ego—what if the parameter cannot be eliminated? It is the experience of many psychoanalysts and psychotherapists who have treated psychotic and borderline structures that departure from strict psychoanalytic technique is essential to treatment, but, if they choose to think of those departures as parameters in Eissler's sense, then they are unable to arrange one that will meet his last requirement. Despairing of being able to eliminate the departure from strict analytic technique, therapists tended to yield resignedly to that fact and to do whatever seemed feasible, abandoning all four of Eissler's requisites. There ensued many therapeutic maneuvers that disregarded the strictures that the departure be minimal and that it be dictated by diagnosis—that is, by the structure of the ego. Thus arose a dangerous pragmatism that, in psychotherapy, anything goes.

We think a better solution to this important technical problem is provided by maintaining sharp division between psychoanalysis and psychotherapy. Instead of stretching psychoanalysis beyond its boundaries, preservation of its identity as a therapy for the neuroses leaves scope for elaboration of techniques for the borderline and psychotic structures designed specifically for them. This alters the commonly held belief that psychoanalytically oriented psychotherapy differs from psychoanalysis in a quantitative direction only. At a point in the process of structuralization, acquisition of an intact ego represents qualitative change in the personality. Technique follows an analogous course; at a certain point, the difference between psychoanalysis and psychotherapy becomes qualitative. This resolves the problem of the parameter, allowing for its retention within the confines of the technique of psychoanalysis—in the treatment of those structures for which all requisites of the parameter, including its elimination, can be fulfilled.

Differences in structure between the neurotic and borderline egos dictate not only differences in technique but also in goals. Rarely, if

ever, can psychotherapy attain the goal of psychoanalysis—
particularly that of resolving the oedipal conflict. An apparent paradox is that structural change can be greater in psychotherapy than in
psychoanalysis. This is because, in psychotherapy, structure building is
the very purpose of treatment. Therefore, in the qualitative sense of
acquiring identity, structure undergoes profound change. In conjunction with building the ego to the point of attainment of object constancy and identity, much psychotherapeutic effort must be expended
in the problems of drive attenuation and correction of distortions and
deviations, and so the psychotherapist devotes attention to aspects of
structure which the psychoanalyst may comfortably take for granted
as already existing in neurosis.

The neurotic, although he suffers severely, enters the treatment situation equipped with a level of development that makes it possible
for him to engage in the psychoanalytic endeavor. His sense of identity, derived from differentiation between self and object representations, enables him to regard the analyst as another person, not part of
himself. Because he possesses frustration tolerance, he can work in the
analysis without immediate reward. Neutralization and the capacity
to interpose thought before action facilitates verbalization and maintenance of drive discharge within the control of the ego. His level of
object relations makes transference and transference neurosis possible
and useful as therapeutic tools, while his capacity for reality testing
prevents his really believing that the analyst is a true object from the
past. Although psychoanalysis is the treatment of choice for neurosis,
there are times when, for reality reasons, this is not possible. The patient may live at too great a distance from the analyst to be able to
attend sessions frequently enough. He may be experiencing one of the
crises of life which, for their duration, render him temporarily
unanalyzable—the state of mourning, for example. Some psychoanalysts think that a person entering marriage does not have libido
available for an analytic endeavor at the same time. Psychotherapy
for the person whose structure could tolerate psychoanalysis is used
also to deal with immediate reality problems, such as job, marriage,
children, illness, and the like. A most valid and often-used form of
psychotherapy is preparation of an unmotivated patient for psychoanalysis.

The individual with a less-than-intact ego cannot tolerate psychoanalytic technique, especially abstinence and the so-called uncovering techniques. The modified ego is usually unequal to the task of coping with the drives. Often, one of the most pressing problems in the psychotic or borderline psychotic is the failure of repression. The technical problems that come into focus are strengthening the ego so it can contend with the drives, and taming the drives to make them less formidable to the ego. We refer to ego-building devices, such as sharpening differentiation between self and object representations, aiding neutralization, building object relations, furthering the defensive capacity, and the like. If early experiences, despite trauma, have provided a modicum of good-enough self and object representations, psychotherapy for structure building may lead to psychoanalysis after identity is established. These become very long-term cases, but if patient and therapist have the necessary endurance, their work together can be exceptionally rewarding.

Miss Carroll began her twelve years of treatment with a borderline structure. The treatment of choice, based upon the diagnostic features of dedifferentiation of self and object representations and failure of repression, was psychotherapy. The first few years of treatment were devoted to the purpose dictated by these factors. The patient had grown up in an intact family with infantile parents who had problems in gender identity and who actively furthered "togetherness" at the expense of separation-individuation. Much therapeutic time and attention were applied to helping Miss Carroll maintain her shaky identity by devices such as showing her that the therapist could not read her mind, which she very much feared. Underneath this fear, of course, was the symbiotic wish, which was interpreted after the defense was understood and the patient had become thoroughly convinced that not only was mind reading not the therapist's intention, but was not even possible. This kind of case warns against the danger of so-called intuitive interpretation because intuitive work on the part of the therapist increases the patient's conviction that the symbiotic wish is realizable and that, thereby, identity will be lost. The therapist also made use of the natural developmental thrust toward separation-individuation which had been thwarted by the mother.

When the child had begun to expand her object relations to

include the father, the mother had become jealous and had openly suggested that the child had incestuous wishes, thus tacitly both encouraging and prohibiting them. The oedipal wish had barely begun to develop before the mother prevented its repression. Since repression is essential for progress into latency, neurosis in the psychoanalytic sense of defense and symptom formation could not develop full-blown, although there was a faint spark of such development. The consequences of this experience had to be reversed in therapy by encouraging expansion of the object world, including object relations with the father, no longer in reality but in relation to the father of childhood. Before the oedipal problem could be dealt with therapeutically, however, there had to be much ego building in the direction of encouraging defense, separation-individuation, and acquisition of secure identity. The matter of gender identity proved to be particularly important in this case because, as a child, the patient had been deprived of full opportunity to make selective identifications with either parent. She found her father interesting and to a large degree more loving than her mother, yet realistically and in fantasy feared the mother's wrath as well as her own aggression, which she projected. Aggression toward the mother precluded separation-individuation and adequate feminine identification.

The therapist did not provide new opportunity for identification but did much to interpret first the positive and later the negative identifications and their distortions in the self and object representations. The importance of first emphasizing positive identifications is stressed continuously in our case material. The rationale, already explained in the case of Mr. Baker, is that object representations should not be destroyed, lest the patient become totally bereft; negative and distorted self and object representations can be dealt with therapeutically only after a solid foundation of positive self and object representations is provided. One never assures the patient that the parents were better and more loving than they really were, but one does seek out those areas, no matter how minimal, in which they did function as good parents, thus providing the patient with a base that will make tolerable knowing also where they failed.

Miss Carroll had good-enough self and object representations and positive identifications to have developed the modicum of optimism and ambition essential for long and arduous treatment. After several years of ego building, as described, identity became more secure and it was appropriate to give her an opportunity to terminate. She chose, rather, to continue. Because the ego was stronger, conflict tolerance was greater, and the capacity to form a therapeutic rather than a symbiotic alliance had come into existence. The further course of treatment took a more classical psychoanalytic form. The patient was then able to say, "I no longer come out of desperate need for *you,* but because I need treatment."

Mr. Dickens had identity that was too easily lost regressively, because separation-individuation had not been securely attained. He was an unsuccessful businessman until two years of therapy gave him the courage to face refusal by a customer. Before that, every sale was a test of his adequacy as a person and, therefore, he had to succeed in every attempt. This stance restricted the number of risks he took in venturing to make a sale. Shortly after treatment began, feelings of adequacy increased because the therapy focused on the tendency to dedifferentiation as the regressive pathway in times of stress. Mr. Dickens became able to accept with equanimity that a certain percentage of prospective customers would not place orders with him for reasons which did not reflect upon him as a person. His need was constantly to find external proof of his existence, founded on incomplete differentiation. Anxiety brought on rapid regression to the state of merged self and object representations. This was his sanctuary because, in early childhood, his mother had stressed that he was part of her and that he could always rely on this when he was in distress. She took him to her bosom, literally and psychologically, long after the nursing period was over. Thus, when faced with the usual boyhood competition with his contemporaries, he was encouraged by an absorbing mother and a passive father to come home to mother rather than to find his own resources. He regressed to the symbiotic mode.

When there was no stress and anxiety, Mr. Dickens knew clearly who he was. But identity had a fluctuating quality. Some sessions were characterized by competent free association and ego mastery by means of elaborating self interpretations; some were dominated by primary process thinking. The therapist refrained from using uncovering techniques when the regression to the undifferentiated, symbiotic phase was so dominant that Mr. Dickens could not distinguish himself from the therapist and expected that the therapist would understand what he was saying no matter how garbled. But refraining does not, in and of itself, build the ego; it protects it from further regression. The therapist interpreted actively to help him understand that he was dedifferentiating under the stress of anxiety. It is usually exhilarating for the patient who has had identity to experience reestablishing it. But characteristic forms of defense, such as regression, are not permanently reversed with a single interpretation. Mr. Dickens had to reexperience and reinterpret many times before each successful reestablishment of identity became more gratifying than the regressive dedifferentiation. But, after initial interpretation in the transference and genetically, the therapist needed to say less and less to encourage the burgeoning ego to work on its own task. When the garbling presented itself later, the therapist could ask, "What is making you unclear this time?," to which he could reply, "Oh, I'm blending in with you [his term] because I got frightened again."

We shall proceed now to discuss the specific techniques of psychoanalysis and to compare them with psychotherapy. These specific techniques are: free association; use of the couch; abstinence; use of the transference and transference neurosis; frequency of sessions; use of interpretation and auxiliary techniques; noting the degree of anxiety that can be tolerated; use of regression. Use of dreams is discussed in chapter 12.

Freud's introduction of the tool of free association, as is well known, followed his realization that hypnosis bypassed the ego. It is characteristic of his genius that, in this regard, too, he anticipated theory that developed years later. At the time of the introduction of free association, he had not yet arrived at the structural theory and thus knew less about the ego than he was later to learn, but he did know that it is the vehicle through which enduring change can be attained. With hypnosis, material is produced but the synthetic and integrative functions of the ego cannot make therapeutic use of it. Full description of the process of and rationale for free association is available in the standard texts on the technique of psychoanalysis by Freud, Sharpe, Fenichel, Glover, Menninger, and Greenson. We shall restrict ourselves to discussion of whether and how it is to be used in psychotherapy.

Free association may be used in psychotherapy when the ego, even though not as intact as the ego of the psychoanalytic patient, nevertheless functions largely in the secondary process and requires some loosening of cathexis for uncovering purposes. We prefer to follow Freud's philosophical position that recommendations, rather than rules, are desirable for the therapist. A recommendation presents itself here—namely that the greater the foothold in secondary process thought, the more safety in free association. This leaves a preponderance of psychotherapy cases in which free association is to be used most sparingly or not at all. Especially in cases in which the synthetic function is not in command, free association is contraindicated.

Beginning therapists often make the error of following too literally the recommendation that the patient determine the material of the hour. Even for the psychoanalytic patient, Freud did not mean that the analyst may not deal with latent material after he has listened to the manifest content with which the patient chooses to begin. The analyst may always select that which is to be worked on. If that were not so, resistance, for example, could not be dealt with because the patient would not bring it up. The analyst is also required to point out—if he knows of them—when there are omissions. For the psychotherapist, there is even greater scope. The patient who speaks largely in the primary process is not free associating, and there, it is necessary to move in to help him firm up instead of to loosen cathexis of secondary thought process. It is a technical error to remain inactive while the patient literally wanders in the wilderness of his incoherent, primary process thoughts. We step in when we have built object relations to the point where the patient wants to communicate. "Wouldn't you like to explain that so I can follow it?" usually meets response after the therapist has become meaningful enough. Similarly, one curbs the tendency of patients to use the session for purposes of discharge.

Miss Epstein came to her once-a-week psychotherapy session from her office, usually full of anger about the last thing that happened at work before she left. If the therapist were to hear her out, a valuable session would be lost in discharge of unneutralized aggression with no therapeutic gain. The therapist interrupted freely. "Is this really how you want to spend the session?" Miss Epstein, for many sessions, went on nevertheless. She said that she had to finish her story. At another time she said that she could not let go of whatever happened at work. Gradually, by varying the question and noting the patient's varied responses, the therapist learned that Miss Epstein's object cathexes were meager, and so she had to cling to the last person she saw, lest she have no one. This information became therapeutically usable; the therapist could then work on providing opportunities for internalization of constant object representations. This was done by first ascertaining the genetic situation which prevented progress toward object constancy.

Miss Epstein was the sixth of eight children of borderline psychotic parents. The children were conceived planlessly and received only minimal care in the form of food and housing. The parents were unable, out of their own paucity of object relations, to provide emotional or even much physical contact beyond the first few months of life. Thereafter, the children fended for themselves, as Miss Epstein put it, like animals. Concerning object relations, she was on the need-gratification level where anyone would do. The therapist, in trying to help her understand this, constituted more of a real object for this patient than would be desirable for a more structured patient. Miss Epstein said that she did not know how people live, so some such questions about the therapist were answered. These should not be too revealing lest they make the patient feel too different from the therapist and his life style, and lest the therapist's privacy be invaded, which would violate ego boundaries. But answers about various things in the office —for example, where a vase was purchased—helps the patient realize that the therapist has to acquire possessions in the same way as all persons do. The neurotic patient takes that for granted.

Continuing with the theme of free association, the recommendation becomes clear. Free association is useful when there is uncovering to be done by an ego that is capable of adequate defense and that operates in the secondary process most of the time. It is contraindicated when incoherence emanating from the primary process and when drive discharge signify that the integrative function is weak. After a while, Miss Epstein appreciated the therapist's interruptions. Her way of putting it was that no one had ever before disciplined her. She did not mean that she took the therapist's keeping her to her task as a superego prohibition, but rather as a helping, guiding force which could result in gaining ego and superego identifications in conjunction with encouraging synthetic and integrative functions to develop. No one had cared enough before.

The use of the couch has been much misunderstood because of Freud's superficial remark that he did not like to be stared at by his patients. However, there are more cogent and profound reasons for using the couch, such as that it promotes regression and fantasy, if those are desirable for the treatment, and that it restricts motor activity so that verbalization will replace action. There is no contraindication to the use of the couch in psychotherapy if its purpose is clear. For some psychotherapy patients regression and fantasying are undesirable, and if patients are found to be subject to these on the couch, they are better treated sitting up. Depending on the nature of the case, some patients also need to see the therapist to know he is there. For others, it is more desirable to learn that the object exists even if he is not in sight.

We do not recommend the overanxious procedure in which the patient is asked to sit up the moment his productions on the couch begin to sound psychotic-like to the therapist. There is no magic cure for psychosis in the simple process of sitting up. Ego-building work can be done in the recumbent position, if that is where the patient happens to be, and it can be more alarming than reassuring to him to be commanded suddenly to sit up. If the therapist finds that he regresses too much and that primary process predominates, he can introduce reality while the patient is on the couch just as well as he can when the patient is in any other position. While we ourselves prefer to have our psychotherapy patients sit, especially if object representations are blurred, some of them prefer to lie down and there is usually no reason to deprive them of this status symbol. The psychoanalytically sophisticated patient, in particular, is likely to think that he is psychotic unless he is lying down. Rather than debate the diagnosis with him, we allow him the couch.

There are many patients who fear the couch. They are defending against powerful symbiotic wishes, loss of identity and of regression, which may not be reversible. Such patients should never be forced to lie down. Often they choose to do so after their symbiotic fears are understood as wishes and are no longer projected upon the therapist as *his* need to envelop. On his part, of course, the therapist has to be very certain that his regard for the patient's autonomy and ego growth is such that he will usually not gratify these symbiotic longings, although it is his task to interpret them. Many borderline patients have lived in too much parasitic symbiosis and need therapeutic help in reaching and resolving the separation-individuation crisis. The rule of thumb here is that, where there has been too much gratification, abstinence and interpretation of the wish is in order; where there has been too much deprivation, some gratification is necessary. This corrects the oft-heard statement of the psychotherapist that, since he is not doing psychoanalytic treatment, he is at liberty to gratify. In psychotherapy no less than in psychoanalysis, gratification of infantile wishes, especially if they have been too indulged and have created fixations, is contraindicated.

The word *abstinence* has an unpleasant connotation and is not well suited to psychoanalytic thought in which acceptance of instinctual demand by a benign superego is fundamental to its philosophy. A better word, perhaps, would be *restraint.* However, abstinence is so thoroughly engrained in the literature that we can only propose here to explain its use rather than attempt to change it. Many therapists tend to equate abstinence with silence. Of course, this rule has no such simple connotation. The therapist may, and is even obliged to, say much that will be helpful to the patient as long as he is working toward interpretation and not toward gratification of infantile wishes. In psychoanalysis, infantile gratifications are never in order. In psychotherapy, there are diagnostic indications for providing *measured* gratification in those instances in which there has been deprivation severe enough to have impeded ego growth. Never is so much gratification provided that it becomes a fixation in the therapy itself. It must always be in symbolic form, usually in words and not in touching, feeding, and other real acts that will keep the patient from proceeding further in his development. The only exception is with psychotic patients who are not treatable as outpatients but who may, in a hospital setting, respond to basic physical care such as being fed.

Differing radically from psychoanalysis is regression as a technical device. In psychoanalysis, it is the deliberate purpose to promote regression. The structure of the analysand is such that regression is along psychosexual lines only, the ego remaining intact. Regression is in the service of the ego, therefore reversible. A psychoanalytic patient can, for example, function at a regressed level in the transference neurosis, but confine this to his analytic session; he can leave the couch and go about his business. Such elasticity is not to be relied upon in the borderline structures. There, regression is likely to be along lines of ego regression, which is not to be encouraged. It runs counter to the purpose of ego building. Borderline structures have potential for irreversible, or, at best, difficult-to-reverse regression, and often this is in itself a diagnostic sign. The ego is to be kept as intact as possible in psychoanalysis as well as in psychotherapy, but the analyst has less cause to be concerned if he has diagnosed correctly.

Were it not for the recurrent fads which masquerade as therapy, we would hardly think it necessary to mention that it is never desirable to act on libidinous or aggressive feelings toward the patient, whether these emanate from the patient, the therapist, or both. The stance of the therapist with regard to abstinence is analogous to that of the good parent who respects the generation gap and does not entwine the child in libidinal or aggressive ties that prevent his eventual partnership with a contemporary. This is true regardless of the actual ages of patient and therapist; they may be contemporaries in reality, but that is of no moment. The psychotherapist follows the same rule as the psychoanalyst that the patient is not to be touched. The exception is that one shakes hands when this form of physical contact is appropriate. Otherwise, the patient's corporeal intactness is not to be intruded upon.

Mr. Fisher, age twenty-six, was over six feet tall and broadly built. He was in treatment with a female therapist of slight stature. He had had a very close relationship with his nurse, who bathed him until he was eleven years old, after which, for other reasons, she was abruptly dismissed. Mr. Fisher never saw her again. His loyalty to his mother prevented his even mentioning how much he missed the nurse, or even asking where she had gone. He cried like a baby in his therapy sessions, wanting to be held, bathed, fed, and the like. He especially wanted to be held in the therapist's lap, disregarding altogether the reality that this would have been physically impossible. The therapist empathized consistently with his feeling of need and refrained from

interpreting too quickly that he had had too much gratification, to
the detriment of his development. The delay in interpreting was decided upon because of the object loss (nurse) and the therapist's caution lest the "good" object be attacked before the patient had been
enabled to mourn for her. However, there was the immediate technical problem of how to deal with his insistence upon physical care.
This was handled rather successfully by acknowledging the validity of
the desire, always with the preface, "If you were a baby, I would."
Another illustration of the use of abstinence in arriving at the deeper
meaning of the need for physical contact and of using it for growth-
promoting purposes is to be found in a dream of Mr. Baker, in chapter 12.

In psychoanalytically oriented psychotherapy, transference is used
—if it exists. Tarachow regarded transference as a resistance to be
dealt with only in psychoanalysis proper. He believed that, in psychotherapy, the therapist's intrusion into the patient's life is permanent and cannot be dissolved at the end of treatment. Murphy is reluctant about the use of transference, but acknowledges that
psychoanalysts who are performing psychotherapy tend to use it. The
crux of the issue, it seems to us, is resolved not by ambivalence about
whether and to what degree to employ transference, but by relying
upon the very definition of transference itself. The interpersonal
schools speak of using the transference, but they mean the real relationship between therapist and patient. This Greenson would regard
as the working alliance and Zetzel as the therapeutic alliance, which
both authors, we think correctly, distinguish from transference.
Strictly defined, transference is powered by the repetition compulsion
and refers to those feelings and attitudes which belong to past objects
but which are displaced and projected upon the therapist. Fenichel
abbreviated this definiation without losing its precision; he defined
transference as mistaking the present for the past. By so defining
transference, we are in a better position to decide whether to use it in
psychotherapy on the basis of whether the patient is capable of transferring from past to present. Those with established object representations can and do transfer to the therapist. Those whose object representations are undifferentiated from self representations are less
capable of transference. The matter is settled, therefore, not by hesita-

tion and indecision about whether transference belongs in psychotherapy or only in psychoanalysis, but by the degree of differentiation and level of object relations. Often, interpretation of transference and transference-like phenomena is therapeutic as an aid in furthering the distinction between self and object representations.

We think it the greater evil to fail to employ transference when it exists, and so we are not deterred by Tarachow's reasoning that it is not to be employed in psychotherapy because it cannot be resolved. Granted, a resolved transference is always more desirable. But considering the usefulness of the phenomenon as a therapeutic tool, the risk of leaving the patient with some degree of unresolved transference is worth the gains that can be attained in psychotherapy by using it. Certainly, there can be no structural change without it. Tarachow's position derives from the early psychiatric goal of psychotherapy—symptom alleviation rather than structural change. We now aim higher.

A valuable addition to the classical concept of transference is provided by Greenacre. She regards the mother-child dyad as containing the roots of transference, and this view accords well with developmental theory. To Greenacre, transference is not uniform, but fluctuates with the varying unconscious factors that exert pressure on the reality alignment of the ego. Hence "active transference-neurotic manifestations," [5] a term which keeps the therapist alert to the fluctuating quality of the transference, is particularly pertinent to the use of transference as a tool in psychotherapy because the psychotherapy patient is even more likely than the psychoanalytic patient to exhibit wide divergencies in his feelings, behavior, and attitudes toward the therapist, these being factors of his more distorted self and object representations.

In the borderline structure, self and object representations are not only relatively undifferentiated, split, and distorted, but are tinged with unneutralized drive energy, often aggressive. This makes for distortions which can result in low self-esteem because the object has to be maintained defensively as "good" regardless of the negative cathexis of self and object representations. It is correct, but not always

[5] P. Greenacre, "Certain Technical Problems in the Transference Relationship," p. 486.

timely, to say to such a patient, "You see me as so powerful and even omnipotent because you saw yourself as small and inconsequential in comparison with your mother. Even when she treated you cruelly, you needed her, and so you believed that you deserved this treatment." This is an interpretation of the past displaced upon the present and is directly designed to correct distortions, not of the present, as the interpersonal approach would have it, but of split self and object representations established before full differentiation.

The work of Jacobson and Kohut suggest that the timing of such intervention has to be carefully considered. There are cases in which rapid termination of the idealized transference may serve the therapist's superego better than it would the patient's need to participate in the omnipotence and grandiosity of the therapist for a while. Miss Garcia was a secretary in a large office where she was usually given the poorest equipment. She worked at a shaky typewriter table while a good one lay idle. The therapist did not know this, but had worked for several weeks on the general matter of self-esteem. In one session, Miss Garcia reported that she had demanded that the office manager give her the good table, and she was very pleased at how easy it had been to accomplish this. She said to the therapist, "You were there with me asking for it." It would have been an error in timing for the therapist to have rushed in with the reality, "No, I was not." Recognizing Miss Garcia's need to participate in the therapist's omnipotence, and that this constituted a way-station toward future identification, the therapist said, "It was good that you could think of me that way." Thus, the therapist recognized a stage in development that had been approached but had not been experienced fully in early life. It is important, however, to provide such union only as long as the patient needs it, remaining alert to indications that the next level of differentiation is approaching. Then, the interpretation, "It was you, not I," becomes correct in both content and timing.

In cases with higher levels of internalization, there is less room for benign experience with a good object, such as the therapist, until the distortions are corrected. Such work has to be carried on to the conclusion of establishing differentiation. Only when the aggresivized and libidinized self and object representations become endowed with more neutralized energy is the patient able to distinguish well enough between the two types of representations to acquire a distinct identity. When such a milestone in the treatment of the borderline structure is attained, the patient reaches a capacity to form new and more realistic object relations in the present. Then he is ready for new ego and superego identifications.

We have said that, at times, the therapist does use himself as a real object; these are when he is treating psychosis proper. But here we are no longer discussing transference. We are referring to those situations, usually in the restitutive phase, when the patient does indeed deal with the therapist, not as he really is, but as some dimly perceived object who is part of the distortions of the restitution. This is not to be confused with transference. The therapist acquires value, not from the past and not because he is appreciated as a real person, but because the patient is in desperate need of an object world no matter who or what it may be. In such cases, the therapist may act as a good object for the purpose of helping the patient acquire a libidinal object proper. He may, for example, use his own ego to aid reality testing and the synthetic function. He may, as we have mentioned, feed the patient or perform other acts of personal care, in a hospital setting, in the direction of becoming a good object. These acts are valid in the treatment of psychosis because they lead the patient toward acquisition of good self and object representations. When such a patient values the therapist as distinguished from all other persons in the hospital, a long step has been taken.

We return to discussion of treatment of the usual out-patient psychotherapy cases. Another and most valuable use of transference is in the attempt to reconstruct preverbal experience. Most often, however, transference is employed in psychotherapy, much as it is in psychoanalysis, for those patients who are capable of entering into it. Of greater importance than in psychoanalysis is the positive transference. Active work must be undertaken toward increasing its intensity as the need-gratifying-level patient yields to capacity for object love. Negative transference manifestations are also to be dealt with, but always against the backdrop of first having built up positive self and object representations so that the relatively unneutralized aggression of the more disturbed patient does not threaten him with destruction of self and object.

If transference is used when it exists, and if the capacity to form object relations is built, there are many opportunities in psychotherapy for the therapist, as a transference figure, to be eliminated as the treatment proceeds to termination. This is done through interpretation, as in psychoanalysis. When the ego recognizes and sorts out the confusion between past and present, transference dissolves. We do agree that there are many more instances of unresolved transference in psychotherapy than in psychoanalysis, but this is because the goals of psychotherapy are so much more diverse. While it may be possible and therefore desirable to resolve the transference in one case, it may be just as desirable to remain as a real object in the patient's life in another case.

In psychotherapy, but hardly ever in psychoanalysis, there is danger that the transference may become too real. The psychoanalytic patient has competent reality testing and, therefore, even in the throes of an intense transference, would not so mistake present for past that he would be unable to distinguish. He might say, for example, "You are just *like* my mother!" The ego always "knows" that the analyst is someone else. The more disturbed patient, however, longing for a mother and less able to test reality, may say, "You *are* my mother." Such phenomena probably do not truly represent transference. If they are, as described, fulfillment of a wish, they are definitely not transference. So-called transference phenomena, devoid of reality testing and of capacity to make distinction between present and past, can only be termed psychotic transference, if one wishes to apply the concept of transference at all. If a psychotic transference should come about, despite the therapist's best effort to help the ego distinguish in anticipation of such an occurrence, then the therapist must devote full effort in coming to the aid of the ego after the fact. It appears almost too simple to state that one of the best tools for this purpose is the word really. "Do you really think so?" "Are you *sure* I am your mother?" "Is it not that you want me to be even though *really* I am not?" Used artistically, such simple-sounding attempts to improve reality testing are usually effective.

Transference neurosis is to be distinguished from transference. While it may appear that, by definition, only the neurotic patient is capable of forming a transference neurosis, the classification *border-*

line means that there are neurotic features even in these less-developed structures. Again, we refer to the standard texts on the technique of psychoanalysis for complete definition of transference neurosis and its distinction from transference. Glover is particularly explicit about this phenomenon, not only defining it but indicating how it can be recognized. Transference neurosis is thought of as more extensive than transference in that the totality of the infantile neurosis is repeated in the analytic situation, with the person of the analyst representing the primary figures. Transference neurosis develops less frequently in psychotherapy than in psychoanalysis; often not at all. There are several reasons for this. First, by virtue of their lesser level of object relations and absence of conflict, the majority of psychotherapy patients are less capable of neurotic solutions and therefore of transference neurosis. Second, if treatment is to be restricted either in length or by decision to treat a circumscribed area only, then it is not desirable that the therapist encourage development of a transference neurosis even when one is possible; third, with transference that a transference psychosis will develop if the neurotic features of the borderline structure appear in transference manifestations that are subject to poor reality testing.

In some psychotherapy cases, despite all the above, transference neurosis does develop spontaneously. If that should occur, it is not desirable to sidestep it. It may be dealt with by the usual techniques prescribed for psychoanalytic treatment, including analysis of transference resistance. In two important papers on transference, Greenacre stressed that caution should be used in guarding the patient's autonomy within the paradoxical situation of dependency and transference. This technique accords with proposals by Kris, who advocated that the patient be encouraged to engage in self-interpretation in order to gain true independence from the therapist. Out of this, G. Blanck suggested that the intensity of the transference neurosis may be attenuated by careful and consistent effort in encouraging the patient to do his own therapeutic work whenever possible. An overintense transference neurosis is easily avoided by a therapist who avoids taking over the patient's part in the therapeutic alliance. The therapist has his own work to do—he must especially think about what is going on. The act of making interpretations to the patient which he is able to

make for himself militates toward a dependent, awesome, and therefore intense transference neurosis. We have said that transference neurosis, if it should come about, is not to be feared, but in the interest of
the patient's autonomy it is desirable to keep it minimal.

Frequency of sessions cannot be determined by a simple rule of
thumb in psychotherapy. This is one of the arrangements about
which, in psychoanalysis, there is no equivocation. Ideally, psychoanalysis is conducted on a four- or five-session-per-week basis. Psychotherapy, more often than not, is conducted on a once-a-week basis,
but the rationale for this is hazy. We often hear that this is because
the patient wishes to come once a week, or can only afford that much.
This is so flimsy a reason that it is not to be considered a technical
one. We do think that once-a-week attendance at psychotherapy sessions may be technically indicated, but the reasons should be based
upon diagnosis and goal rather than upon the patient's whim. We
are advocating a professional stance; the person best equipped to
make the decision does so. Insofar as the diagnosis and treatment plan
are concerned, there is no question but that the therapist decides.
This does not contradict that the patient may not be ready to comply
with the therapist's decision and that it may, therefore, be desirable
to go along with what the patient can accept without struggling with
him. When motivation and transference become stronger there will
be no struggle. Neither does a professional stance impair the patient's
autonomy, as is often feared, because autonomous decisions do not extend to areas where knowledge and judgment are absent. Only the
therapist knows the diagnostic and technical aspects of the problem.
We strongly advocate good working conditions for therapist and patient. We sometimes use the rather ridiculous analogy of the surgical
patient who asks that the operation be performed on the kitchen
table because he prefers not going to the hospital. Just as no surgeon
would consider this request, so is it undesirable for the therapist to
treat a patient under conditions which he imposes if they are not in
his best interest. Rarely does a patient reject reasonable conditions if
they are explained to him.

The frequency of attendance at psychotherapy sessions may be once
a month in so-called maintenance cases, once a week, or two, three,
four, or five times per week. It sometimes takes a bit of trial and error

to determine the frequency with which the given patient works best. We have seen outstanding results on a twice-a-week schedule and rather draggy ones on three- and four-times-a-week treatment. Sometimes the very infrequency spurs the patient on to use the sessions more productively. But this, too, is a spurious reason for diminishing the number of sessions, one which we prefer to deal with interpretively rather than by manipulation. We think the usual borderline psychotherapy patient works best if he attends twice or three times per week. He sits up and deals now with reality and now with transference manifestations, at different moments in treatment. There are many exceptions to this state of affairs. The depressed and potentially suicidal patient is best seen more frequently during periods of crisis. The psychotic patient may be treated intensively five times per week on an out patient basis if the home environment is supportive enough so that hospitalization can be averted. Generally, frequency of attendance is not to be varied to manipulate transference manifestations and dependency, but it may be necessary to see the very disturbed patient more frequently during periods of crisis and less so when the crisis abates.

Termination of psychoanalysis approaches with the resolution of the oedipal confict. It announces itself in the transference, if ego psychological measures have been followed, by the patient's increasing independence from the analyst, manifested by his ability to do his own analytic work. Kris described how independence and autonomy may be recognized in the "good hour" [6] as the patient begins the hour with a slightly negative attitude, consistent with Spitz' and Mahler's observations that neutralized aggression is operative in the service of separation and ego growth. The "good hour" proceeds, perhaps with a dream, or with other material, which the patient works on himself and finally interprets. This signals the approach of the time when the patient will be able to continue his analytic work without the physical presence and interventions of the analyst. The transference neurosis, never too intense if maximum independence has been assured throughout the analysis, dissolves; the analyst becomes more of a real object, no longer overvalued and idealized, and the pa-

[6] E. Kris, "On Some Vicissitudes of Insight in Psychoanalysis."

tient is encouraged to set a date for termination. During this final subphase of the terminal phase, one observes carefully whether "good hours" continue, heralding true readiness for termination. Kris compared the "good hour" with the "pseudo-good hour" in which the patient, defensively and with unneutralized aggression, tries to dispense with or compete with the analyst out of fear of dependency. And so the ego psychological considerations in the technique of psychoanalysis help the analyst know when the time for termination is approaching. G. Blanck says:

. . . If the patient's autonomy has been so respected and promoted that he becomes increasingly independent as analysis proceeds, the terminal phase tends to develop naturally.

The apparent contradiction, of course, is that in the process of analysis, we wish to elicit the full force of the patient's dependency, often even having to analyze defenses against it. However, it is precisely because we do this in an atmosphere of simultaneous guardianship of autonomy that the full intensity of transference, no matter what its form, need not be feared. The drama can be played out to the fullest extent because the analyst does not participate in it as a real figure and does not do too much for the patient. Such regard for autonomy obviates the need for some of the desperate devices sometimes advocated. Thorough understanding of the process of separation replaces such measures as enforced time-limits, tapering off, altering the frequency of the sessions, etc. The separation process is best accomplished via interpretation rather than devices. If devices *do* have to be used to augment interpretation, then they should be tailored to the individual separation conflict which has been understood in the course of the analysis. Only then can the arrangement avoid constricting the ego, because it will necessarily be devised to undo the original blockage and to release the patient to live in as much freedom as is possible in the human condition.[7]

For termination, as for so many other aspects of technical management, the psychotherapist has fewer guidelines. In most psychotherapy cases, the goal is not resolution of the oedipal confict. This, of course, may be accomplished, but usually there are more urgent goals. We agree with Mahler that the core problem of the borderline structure is failure to have completed the separation-individuation crisis and to have attained object constancy. For the majority of borderline structures, therefore, attainment of identity, a stronger and better-

[7] G. Blanck, "Some Technical Implications of Ego Psychology," p. 13.

functioning ego, object relations at or approaching object constancy, neutralization of the drives, and other developmental accomplishments are goals of therapy, successfully attained in varying degrees. Many experience identity for the first time. This is often approached with fear as well as with pleasure. Sometimes there is exhilaration; the patient experiences dramatic success. He usually, then, wishes to terminate.

It is even more crucial for the psychotherapy patient than for the psychoanalytic that the therapist be alert to manifestations of independence and do nothing to retard them. Timing is critical. Hesitation on the part of the therapist is noted by these unusually sensitive patients, inured as they are to symbiotic longings and, some, to what Mahler has termed "parasitic symbiosis," [8] one in which the parent needs the child for the gratification of his own symbiotic needs. It is desirable for the therapist to listen without hasty opposition to the first verbalizations of wish to terminate. If the therapist believes this is premature, he has the responsibility to protect the patient. How this is done, however, can make all the difference between helping the patient attain independence and discouraging him so thoroughly that valuable ground is lost, sometimes irrevocably. The specific techniques for termination in psychotherapy are discussed in chapter 17.

The differences between psychoanalysis and psychotherapy cannot be discussed here as finite because they will be subject to addition and correction as theory building adds to our body of knowledge. Wallerstein [9] raises nine points which can be answered with the knowledge we now have.

"1. Is there a scientific psychotherapy apart from psychoanalysis?" This we have answered in asserting that there is no difference in the theoretical base, but there are differences in technique, some slight, some moderate, and some vast.

"2. What are the similarities and differences between psychoanalysis and dynamic psychotherapy?" Here we reiterate that the similarities are in theory and the differences are factors of the structure of the ego.

"3. How important are the differences (or the similarities)? Should

[8] M. S. Mahler, *On Human Symbiosis and the Vicissitudes of Individuation,* p. 148.
[9] R. S. Wallerstein, "Psychoanalysis and Psychotherapy."

they be blurred or should they be sharpened?" We have suggested
that the differences in technique be sharpened.

"4. What are the proper boundaries of each therapeutic modality?
Or when does 'modified' psychoanalysis or psychoanalysis with parameters become psychotherapy?" Our answer is that, unless the parameter can remain within the confines that Eissler proposed, the technique is psychotherapy, not psychoanalysis. It remains psychoanalysis
only when the parameter can be eliminated.

"5. How are differential treatment indications determined? Is the
patient fitted to the treatment or the treatment fitted to the patient?"
We see no room for other than fitting the treatment to the patient.
Therefore, we have stressed versatility on the part of the therapist.
Procrustean treatment cannot be of benefit to the patient.

"6. What are the proper dividing lines across the range of psychotherapies conceptualized within the framework of psychoanalytic
theory? Is the major dividing line between the expressive-uncovering
therapeutic modalities (of which psychoanalysis is one) and the suppressive-supportive modalities? Which divisions are meaningful, in
theory and in practice?" Here we think Wallerstein is posing a question about a division long held in psychiatry, based, in essence, upon
the fact that where the ego is weak repression is incompetent, and
that therefore "suppressive-supportive" techniques are indicated. That
view neglects psychoanalytic developmental theory altogether. It does
not consider ego growth as a possibility; it regards suppression as
competent to replace repression; it does not view support as ego support in the sense that ego building can, in many cases, follow support.
We propose that the psychiatric "suppressive-supportive" techniques
are now outdated. As for the line of cleavage described in this question, we think the correct dividing line is between analyzable and
nonanalyzable structures. This answer implies that diagnostic considerations are paramount in decision as to form of treatment. Uncovering is not contraindicated in psychotherapy if the first therapeutic attention is to strengthening the ego to the point where it can tolerate
"expressive-uncovering" techniques.

"7. What is the relation to non-psychoanalytic therapy? Can a
theory of psychoanalytic therapy extend to a (non) psychoanalytic
theory of therapy?" We think that there can be only one science of

human behavior. Either psychoanalytic theory (and therefore techniques derived from it) is correct, or another theory is correct.

"8. Can derivative conflicts, can any conflicts, be substantially resolved by means of short analysis?" This question presumes that conflict is neurotic with which we agree in essence. It seems to us that the question arises out of the outmoded attempts at "brief psychotherapy" and "sector analysis" of several decades ago. Neurotic conflict can only be resolved by psychoanalysis. Neurotic problems, as we have said in our Introduction, may be alleviated by psychotherapeutic measures which are decided upon because the reality situation is not conducive to a psychoanalytic endeavor at that time. Is there nonneurotic conflict and can it be resolved by psychotherapy? We believe so. But a different view of conflict than the intersystemic is involved. A nonneurotic or borderline conflict is more likely to be intrasystemic, within an ego that cannot cope adequately with either type of conflict. Again, ego-building devices can strengthen the ego to deal with both kinds of conflict.

"9. What are our problems as psychoanalysts in doing psychotherapy?" These cannot be enumerated briefly. We shall dwell on the main problem, which is that of versatility and flexibility. Psychoanalysts are ideally prepared to do psychotherapy by virtue of their thorough theoretical training, but they are hampered by a constricting technique which was designed for the psychoanalysis of neurosis and which cannot be usefully stretched, modified, or expanded. The technique of psychotherapy should be added to their repertory.

⨎ 9 ⨎

ON BEGINNING TREATMENT

THE TITLE OF THIS CHAPTER deliberately paraphrases Freud's 1913 paper. He said, succinctly: "What the material is with which one starts the treatment is on the whole a matter of indifference—whether it is the patient's life-history or the history of his illness or his recollections of childhood. But in any case the patient must be left to do the talking and must be free to choose at what point he shall begin." [1] The reason for this latitude is given by Freud earlier in the same paper: "The extraordinary diversity of the psychical constellations concerned, the plasticity of all mental processes and the wealth of determining factors oppose any mechanization of the technique. . . ." [2]

Since then, the tasks of beginning therapy have been detailed many times. Attempts at enumeration include: establishing a working alliance (Wolberg), assessing readiness (Glover), determining diagnosis (Alexander and French; Tarachow; Bellak and Small), and facilitating communication (Mullahy). Most if not all authors agree that the therapist must present himself as a helpful person, but Tarachow makes a point of insisting that the first interview is not of itself a therapeutic one, but is only for clarification as to whether therapy is to be sought. This seems consistent with Menninger's analogy with law of a contractual relationship between the parties which perforce must be agreed to in advance.

While these opinions vary in importance as parts of the beginning process, they are secondary to the obligation incurred by the therapist

[1] S. Freud, *On Beginning Treatment,* p. 134.   [2] *Ibid.,* p. 123.

when he arranges an initial appointment. By the time an individual has made and kept this appointment, he has conveyed the message that he needs help. He may "walk in backwards" as though he were leaving, he may be ambivalent, he may have been coerced into coming, he may present the most ingenious and least identifiable form of resistance; nonetheless, the therapist carries the responsibility for applying himself to the patient's purpose. This is a professional stance behind which lies a body of knowledge and experience which makes it possible to offer something quite different from the help of a friend or a loved one. The therapist professes knowledge of growth processes, familiarity with the kinds of failures which frequently take place in development, awareness of features of arrest, fixation, regression, defense, and transference, to mention a few of the main aspects of theory and technique. With such a base, he can apply himself to whatever line of inquiry seems appropriate almost regardless, at this point, of the patient's capacity to cooperate. Such capacity determines how the therapist applies himself initially in the patient's behalf. A true professional stance expresses interest in the patient and his problem, offers great leeway in the forms in which the patient may describe it, affirms his autonomy, but reserves for the therapist the method and direction of therapy. No contradiction exists between respecting the patient's autonomy regarding his own life and yet not yielding to false concepts of equality or democracy with regard to decisions as to what constitutes proper therapeutic activity. The therapist is more knowledgeable about the latter and this is indeed why the patient consults him.

When the patient arrives for the initial consultation his ambivalence with respect to therapy has been decided momentarily. One may compare the therapist's task here with the problems facing the men who sailed the seas before the advent of steam power. They depended upon the movement of the seas and the wind; the therapist depends upon the patient's motivation, and must learn to put every ebb and flow to therapeutic use. By the time the therapist is constrained to ask the frequently posed question, "Why have you come?" communication has failed. The fact that the patient has come suffices, for the time being, as proof that his irresolution is temporarily tilted in favor of the therapy, and it is not useful at such a point for the therapist to

do anything which may move the patient to the other side of his ambivalence. Ambivalence may be turned, technically, into an asset by
seizing the opportunity to go with the tide, thereby making sufficient
headway to assure the therapeutic journey a better chance of proceeding when ambivalence, like the tide, shifts. To ask the patient why he
has come does not provide the welcome which is always essential. It
all too readily presents him with an opportunity to regret the action
which brought him to the consultation.

Frequently the child who is brought for treatment because his behavior is disturbing to others will say, if asked, that he does not know
why his parents brought him or will parrot what they have told him.
Similar defensive maneuvers are seen in adults who are coerced into
consultation by others. It is not at all difficult to understand the defensiveness of the husband who accepted an appointment in order to
appease his distressed wife and who could be quite happy to report
back to her that the therapist found "nothing wrong." Such an unwilling patient will not easily unburden himself of whatever he, himself, may be feeling as the deeper reason for his having come. Especially if he feels, as is frequent, that his masculinity is compromised in
his obedience to his wife, it is of critical importance to avoid entering
such highly charged areas in the first session lest defense and resistance thicken. It is far less threatening to him to have his premise accepted, namely that he came to help his wife, and then to explore
what he thinks the trouble comes from and what *he* can do about it.
This describes a way of staying with the defense to avoid creating too
wide a gap between therapist and patient at the outset. The therapist
is not thereby abandoning his role of therapeutic leadership. On the
contrary, by asking the patient how he sees the problem, the therapist
is leading him one step at a time until transference and therapeutic
alliance make possible a faster pace.

For the borderline and psychotic structures the matter of challenge
to the patient is even more delicate. The neurotic patient is capable of
secondary process thinking with less danger of ego regression and can
often consider question and challenge in that part of the ego which is
relatively uninvolved in conflict. Borderline and psychotic personalities, on the other hand, cannot be counted on consistently to have the
capacity to use reason to arrive at an answer. One has to expect

blankness and sometimes momentary loss of the capacity to think in the secondary process as ego regression ensues from traumatic anxiety. Also, the more disturbed patient may have to resort to derealization more often than the neurotic and for the same reason—namely, inability to employ signal anxiety, and weakness of the defensive function of the ego. For a therapist to be so out of tune with the patient as to challenge him inappropriately does not augur well since it forces a confrontation without due regard for the diagnosis and therefore for the capacity of the ego to deal with challenge. With such patients it is necessary to support the thinking processes which brought them to the therapist's office as the way toward further exploration of the problem. One might say, "It is so frightening to be here that it may seem at the moment as though it would be better to live with your problem. But you will feel better and it will help you more if you appreciate how much you have done for yourself already by having come."

After more than twenty years of marriage Mrs. Hartley learned that her husband was having an affair with his secretary and she was understandably upset. The form her distress took manifested itself in an explosive torrent of words. Within the process of her ventilation the therapist discerned much confusion in content. There were several neologisms that slipped in almost imperceptibly and, while formal sentence structure was maintained, meanings became obscure. She assumed knowledge on the part of the therapist which he could not possibly have had, such as the first names of her husband and the secretary. As the consultation proceeded, the unconscious purpose of her visit became clear to the therapist. Although she was still capable of formulating the words which stated that she wanted help with the marriage, that was really a lever. It was, of course, a more benign diagnostic sign that she was able to present a rational rather than an amorphous request for help and one would not want to challenge that. But the therapist detected that the unconscious need was to have someone; she was making a plea to the therapist to be available, even if only to listen to her. Her distress resembled that of a terrified child who must have the mother's presence almost regardless of the content of the interaction. It may be said that this patient did not really will to come, but was forced into it by separation anxiety which prevented

her from taking a more realistic view of what might be expected from
the therapist.

Where "volition" derives from terror, the act is not really voluntary. Mrs. Hartley therefore needed the therapist's welcome in a form
that provided no more than her ego could tolerate at the moment,
but no less than the almost total support that she needed. A statement such as, "It is plain that you are suffering and are in some sort
of shock. Perhaps if we continue to talk about your situation we will
be able to find a way to help you cope with your fears a little better,"
is deceptively simple in external appearance. That it contains support
is evident. Less evident is the tailoring of the comment to meet the
underlying need without challenge to the manifest request and yet
without opening up more than is appropriate at the outset. It informed Mrs. Hartley that she was welcome, that she was understood,
that she had done something useful for herself in coming, that while
the therapist would listen to more than the manifest content and try
to understand her better, he was not a magician. Sometimes beginning therapists, out of their uncertainty, suggest to the patient that
talking about the problem on an ongoing basis is indicated. This is
not incorrect for, if the therapist does not understand the situation, it
is far wiser to continue to study it than to proceed hastily. However,
in the case of Mrs. Hartley the procedure we suggest is not based on
the therapeutic need to gain time and information, but on an in-
depth assessment of her problem which tells us that she, not the therapist, needs to proceed more slowly—that the manifest content of
her verbalizations is not to be taken at face value because the underlying pathology is more urgent. Thus, a therapeutic decision to go
slowly may have to be made out of the therapist's need to know
more—and this does often pertain—or out of the necessity dictated by the patient's internal structure which takes precedence, technically, over the manifest presenting problem.

Rapport, it may be seen from the foregoing, results from application of professional purpose as though the therapist were saying, "You
are here because you are in trouble and I am a mental troubleshooter,
so we have a common purpose, albeit different roles." Nothing more
is required—no "gimmicks," coffee, excessive warmth, or effusive
behavior of any sort. Courtesy, on the other hand, is always in order.
We are here discussing an application of the psychoanalytic rule of

abstinence. The patient's wish for infantile gratification is not to be met lest it reinforce the fixation; but appropriate gratification in the form of considering ways and means of solving his difficulties is the raison d'être for the therapy.

We have thus far discussed the beginning phase as though it were a definable stage of the therapeutic process. It is usually not so clear-cut. It is true that the introductory period has the quality of a phase of therapy, but it would be an error to separate it too sharply from the remainder of the ongoing process. While in one sense it represents the beginning in establishment of a therapeutic transference, shifts and turnings in the transference are a constant feature of psychotherapy. Greenacre refers to these as "active transference-neurotic manifestations," [3] thus emphasizing that a consistent positive or negative transference is a myth.

All the tools so essential to beginning are necessary to the ongoing therapy as well and are especially pertinent to the terminal phase. It is sometimes thought that the initial phase is brought to a close with the establishment of transference neurosis. Glover, Fenichel, Menninger, and Greenson refer to psychoanalysis. In psychotherapy, there is not always a transference neurosis, not only because so many psychotherapy patients are not neurotic, but because the very nature of the treatment process in not intrinsically conducive to the establishment of a transference neurosis. There is usually transference, and it may be considered that the opening phase ends and the middle phase ensues when transference manifestations are evident, when an ongoing working alliance is established and when motivation is assured. Such compartmentalization of the therapeutic process is, however, undesirable; it contains misunderstanding of the nature of the unconscious and assumes that resistance may once and for all be conquered. In reality, every time a new level of unconscious is tapped we are entering a new beginning. As Freud put it, the therapist becomes a stranger when,

During the work on the resistances the ego withdraws—with a greater or less degree of seriousness—from the agreement on which the analytic situation is founded. The ego ceases to support our efforts at uncovering the id; it opposes them, disobeys the fundamental rule of analysis, and

[3] P. Greenacre, "Certain Technical Problems in the Transference Relationship," p. 486.

allows no further derivatives of the repressed to emerge . . . and he be-
haves towards him exactly like a child who does not like the stranger and
does not believe anything he says.[4]

Nevertheless, there are special tasks in beginning, and illustrations
of these may be cited in all diagnostic categories, but the borderline
structures lend themselves best to this purpose. For example, Mr. In-
gram overcame his initial terror at the first consultation, recognizing
that his fear of the therapist was similar to his fear of his boss. He
was able to use this partial insight to ease his work situation slightly.
The resulting wave of confidence and pleasure in working with the
therapist lasted only as long as the same subject was being discussed.
When material about his wife entered the discussion, as he recounted
something about their relationship, the terror returned in full force.
The therapist need not feel disappointed over this because no other
development is to be expected. When one considers the developmental tasks involved in achieving what Erikson calls "basic trust," [5]
which arises out of having had a "good enough" [6] mother as part of
an "average expectable environment," [7] a satisfactory symbiotic phase
and gradual and untraumatic movement toward separation-individuation, and an establishment of identity, expectation of quick rapport in
the psychotherapy patient who, by our definition, has been impeded
in some of these developmental areas, is inappropriate.

That growth proceeds along specific developmental lines carries
with it a technical corollary. Each new step in growth in treatment
brings its own beginning. This is because each new stage of development brings about an alteration in the level of object relations. Mahler shows this in her delineation of the several subphases of the
separation-individuation phase. At the *practicing* subphase the toddler moves away from his mother; at the *rapprochement* subphase he
moves toward her again, and so on. In an analogous way, the adult
psychotherapy patient whose separation-individuation experiences in
childhood were not satisfactory enough for him to complete that
phase may, in the course of proper treatment, approach separation-

[4] S. Freud, *Analysis Terminable and Interminable,* p. 239.
[5] E. H. Erikson, "On the Sense of Inner Identity," p. 352.
[6] D. W. Winnicott, "Transitional Objects and Transitional Phenomena," p. 94.
[7] H. Hartmann, *Ego Psychology and the Problem of Adaptation,* p. 23.

individuation. As he does so, he employs neutralized aggression in the process of establishing individual identity. And so symbiotic wishes give way to delineation between self and object representations; the patient whose mode of relating was dominated by search for closeness begins to create distance. If the therapist fails to appreciate such shifts the danger of his becoming a stranger increases. Therefore, while there is a crucial aspect in the very first beginning—because, there, determination is made of whether the case is to continue and thus whether there will be subsequent beginnings—all is not won after that beginning. The many prematurely terminated cases attest to that.

Having shown the relationship of the opening phase to ongoing processes of therapy, it is useful also to consider some of the tasks that are more specific to the first beginning. Above all, there is the absolute requirement that the patient feel welcome. Concretely, this means that the patient is not to be given any indication or even implication that his behavior is "wrong, bad, stupid." At this stage it is not even useful to convey the sense that his behavior is pathological, although the therapist who thinks it is not would have to explain his rationale for undertaking treatment. But the difference between telling the patient that he is "sick" and recognizing that he is troubled is the difference between whether one becomes a stranger or whether one joins him in the therapeutic search for the cause of his problems. Ella Freeman Sharpe belonged to an earlier generation of psychoanalysts but much of her technical advice, because it was so concerned with not becoming a stranger to the patient, holds up remarkably well today. She wrote: "Have not many of us had the experience in early stages of our analysis of an immediate conviction of sin if we have been told 'that is anal sadism, that is narcissism'?" [8]

It is sufficient, at the outset, to convey recognition that the problem is troublesome. It may even be necessary to accept the patient's premise, for the time being, that it is another person's behavior that causes the difficulty, provided that the therapist keeps in mind that it is the patient who experiences the discomfort and has to cope with it. This is the way to avoid the pitfall of arguing with the patient or of pursuing the fruitless course of stating or even implying that the pa-

[8] E. F. Sharpe, *Collected Papers on Psycho-Analysis*, pp. 24–25.

tient has no right to feel as he does. The basic premise—indeed, conviction—must be that he has every right to his feelings. Again, we do not mean at all that one abandons the role of therapeutic leadership. The therapist retains his knowledge that, whatever these feelings, they derive not only from the present but from sources of which the patient is not aware at the outset. To try to force such knowledge upon him prematurely would only drive him away. The therapist needs to regard the patient as in some way right, not to seduce him into treatment but to begin treatment with the fact that there *is* a point of view from which he is right. This paves the way for joint inquiry into the deeper sources of the problem.

Mrs. Jackson came for treatment because her overt expressions of aggression threatened her marriage and upset her children. She began by saying she was very hostile and wanted treatment for that. The therapist was in somewhat of a dilemma here. If he attempted to reassure her, then her goal would be lost sight of and he would have contradicted her as well, thus losing the opportunity to help her feel understood. If he accepted her statement about her hostility as an objective fact, his difficulty would be even greater because the ensuing work would fall into the realm of the superego and value judgments would prevail; the therapist would be in the position of having to make a better person of her. But the statement, "It is obvious that these feelings trouble you because they bring you here," leaves room for the development of the necessary and unpunishing working alliance. It enlists the patient's participation in the inquiry without prejudgment. No "condemned" individual should be expected voluntarily to join an inquiry into his "crime." Not that some patients do not willingly enough accept such condemnation, but in those cases there is a problem of masochism which the therapist must avoid gratifying.

Continuing with the theme that the patient needs to be made welcome, it is essential to counteract any suggestion that he is imposing. "I know how busy you are, Doctor," is a gambit easily understood as expressing doubt as to whether the therapist considers him worth time and trouble. One needs generally to avoid, "I'm so glad you came," which may carry the wish-fulfilling implication that the patient is loved. While capacity to love in its broadest sense has to be part of the therapist's personality in that a misanthrope cannot be a therapist, it is excessive and artificial to attempt to convey anything of this sort directly. The patient can only feel uneasy about such effusiveness, much as he might like to believe it. Nor is there anything to be gained from an attempt to interpret such wishes in the opening phase. When the therapist evidences interest in the patient by listening carefully, the implicit assumption that he is worth listening to will get across and will carry far more reassurance than any direct statement of the patient's worth. Notes of falseness are to be avoided always; their absence distinguishes professional interest from overpoliteness, excessive concern, excessive warmth, and the like, all of which would be problems of countertransference.

As the therapist demonstrates that he understands what he is being told, the patient is drawn more closely into the transference with a concomitant movement toward the establishment of a working alliance. Traditional diagnostic goals are sacrificed in the service of establishing a connection with the patient. Out of the concept of developmental lines, diagnosis acquires an emphasis somewhat different from that of other approaches to it. Traditionally, one thinks of diagnosis as a process apart from treatment, usually made upon initial contact and having the goal of deciding upon a definite designation in accordance with preestablished diagnostic categories. The developmental approach is determined by purposes which take precedence over rapid categorization; principal among these purposes is development of the therapeutic alliance.

In the early phase, as lines of inquiry into the patient's growth processes are opened up, the therapist has the dual intention of enlisting the patient's curiosity, interest, and ultimately his strong participation, while at the same time formulating tentative diagnostic hypotheses in his own mind long before diagnostic knowledge can lend itself to interpretation as part of the process of resolution of the problem. While this resembles the opening phase of psychoanalysis in that the analyst listens attentively, for psychotherapy it is not necessarily true that his responses are minimal. It is assumed that the analysand is capable of enduring the frustration of limited response from the analyst, whereas the psychotherapy patient usually requires more participation from the therapist precisely because his development has not reached the level of structuralization where his ego can tolerate psychoanalytic procedure.

The case of Mrs. Hartley illustrates the kind of diagnostic task the therapist faces. One cannot know whether her behavior is dictated by a punishing superego such as might exist in a well-structured neurosis or whether it represents identity problems in which object representations are not sufficiently differentiated from self representations. In the latter event, what she hears from others and what she feels herself to be would be merged. If that is so, her confusion can be recognized and acknowledged as a way of meeting her where her problem really lies without burdening her with more information about herself than she can tolerate. It is of crucial importance to determine which diagnostic thought is correct, since it will make a vast difference in the treatment plan. But the therapist must develop the capacity to let the material carry the message clearly before he commits himself one way or the other. Nevertheless, such patients do require some conviction that therapeutic work is going on and so the therapist cannot remain totally inactive while he does his diagnostic thinking. He remains aware of the necessity for following the main diagnostic highway, but at the same time travels a service road parallel to the main highway. Described in this way, beginning treatment may be seen as a process in which the therapist uses his growing knowledge to deepen and extend his connection with the patient. This serves to keep therapist and patient traveling in the same direction until the parallels converge. When present behavior and historical determinants meet, developmental diagnosis is established. Often this is the optimal moment for interpretation as well. Here is an instance where timing is difficult but not impossible to teach. When the genetic determinants of present behavior come together in the patient's preconscious, the moment for interpretation has arrived.

To say that it is essential that the patient feel understood is, after all, only another way of stating that the ongoing process of exploring diagnostic lines is in continuous progress. Understanding cannot proceed without diagnostic conceptualization of the material received from the patient. Tentative as they may be at first, at least some hypotheses are to be formed which provide guidelines to paths of inquiry. By tentative we mean that, when a patient states that he has come for consultation because his wife threatens to leave him otherwise, we can draw some conclusions definitely, while other aspects remain open for further elaboration and construction. What is definite is that he fears his wife's threat; what is not definite is whether this fear is based on love, on separation anxiety, on guilt. Nor is it definite yet how much fear is felt. These conclusions depend very much upon the level of development that was reached along lines of levels of anxiety and of object relations, and upon how much regression has taken place. And so the therapist, like the archeologist, may only know, at first, where to explore, but not exactly what he will find.

To return now to consideration of the tools the therapist must have, there is no better literature than Freud's papers on technique.[9] Fulfilling the expectation that basic truths endure, Freud's specific detailing of the daily aspects of the therapeutic attitude retain their pertinence. Although written fifty-five to sixty years ago, they remain relevant today, particularly in relation to the opening phase. Especially impressive are his "Recommendations" [10] and "Further Recommendations." [11] Indeed, the metapsychological base for many of his techniques was confirmed by direct infant observation long after his death. Freud provided the analogy of a French surgeon whose response to praise for his skill was, "I dressed his wounds, God cured him." [12] Freud thus stressed that the analyst is to be an investigator who continuously inquires into whatever loopholes may be found in the patient's rationalizations of his problem, at the same time affirming that the analyst does not "cure" but propels the patient in a healing direction.

This is the essence of the applicability of modern ego psychology to technique. It takes into account that there is a natural tendency toward development which, in pathology, is hampered by arrest or regression. The task of the therapist is to show the patient where his developmental impediments lie and how they came about. Then growth can proceed. It is important to note here that the first part of the task—designation and demonstration—is relatively simple and is often performed by the astute layman in the form of "confronta-

---

[9] S. Freud, *Papers on Technique.*   [10] *Ibid.*, pp. 111–20.
[11] *Ibid.*, pp. 122–44.   [12] *Ibid.*, p. 115.

tion." However, growth is furthered only when the genetic base for the current behavior is found jointly by therapist and patient within the confines of a therapeutic alliance. This explains why the sometimes well-intentioned and sometimes malicious confrontation often stirs up resentment or compliance or a variety of other responses but does not promote healing. Here again, the rare opportunity to teach timing or tact presents itself. Confrontation from without, for lasting therapeutic result, is no match for the convergence of past and present *intrasystemically,* as the observing ego confronts the experiencing ego. At such points it matters little whether therapist or patient makes the interpretation. Whenever possible it is more desirable if the patient can arrive at it. In either event, however, this type of interpretive work serves to confront the reasonable ego with the influence of past upon present. In psychoanalysis and often in psychotherapy the past refers to an id wish that remains alive in the present. In psychotherapy always, and in psychoanalysis much of the time, the past is the time of most severe developmental trauma. Interpretation enables development to proceed.

Mr. Dickens spent the better part of a session to good advantage describing the lengths to which he would go to keep people in a good mood. Usually, in his business relationships, he was aware that he talked obliquely around a subject until he had won his listener. Thus, he avoided clashes. Both patient and therapist knew from previous sessions that Mr. Dickens had never been able to oppose his mother directly and that he always feared that even his wish to do so would be read by her and cause her displeasure. It would have been correct but untimely to have helped Mr. Dickens put these two facts together at that moment. The therapist waited for the supporting evidence to arrive in the transference. Toward the end of the session, after having discussed his silent wish to oppose, he began to praise and thank the therapist for the excellent work that had been done in this session. In a way, this was the truth and at another time the therapist might have responded with a simple, "You're welcome," to such thanks. But such a response would have been inappropriate at this time because the praise was being used to cover over the emerging aggression which Mr. Dickens sorely needed to learn to appreciate as the road to freedom out of the symbiotic bond. Accepting praise would have served the therapist's narcissism but would have kept the patient from taking a long step in his development. Instead, therefore, the therapist used the material as an ideal opportunity to connect past with immediate present (transference manifestations) and, simultaneously, to provide support toward greater independence. The therapist asked, "Are you trying to ensure that I will be in a good mood next time?" This has to be said very graciously lest the gift of praise be denigrated. Mr. Dickens responded, "Wow, that's what I do all the time with everyone." The session ended with this insight, leaving the interim between sessions for Mr. Dickens' ego to integrate the newness of it. The therapeutic expectation was that he would begin to venture differing more with the therapist in future sessions. In that way, the steps toward separation-individuation and establishment of identity could be encouraged simply by the therapist's providing an atmosphere of welcome for them, but never permitting overt expressions of unneutralized aggression. The latter would not be useful in supporting development. This illustrates, also, the difference between encouraging the use of neutralized aggression for growth, on the one hand, and ventilation which goes nowhere, on the other.

Such developmental concepts cannot but be of inestimable relief to the therapist. The beginning of treatment is doubly burdened if the therapist is oppressed by having to arrive at a diagnosis and to find the cure single-handedly. How differently one can approach the patient if the task is to inquire and to learn about his development, enlisting his cooperation in the diagnostic and therapeutic task, including the search for where, why, and how he is getting in his own way!

The metapsychological base for Freud's concept of cure was not elaborated until Greenacre conceptualized the necessity for reinforcing the patient's autonomy and Mahler had worked out the steps in separation-individuation. Now it can be stated with precision that so long as cure is vested in the therapist it will tend to affirm the patient's wishes for omnipotence which are so much a part of the symbiotic phase of development, and this militates against establishing whatever autonomy the individual might otherwise be capable of reaching by means of growth processes catalyzed by the therapy. To conduct a therapeutic campaign on the basis that the task of the patient is to use therapeutic insight for purposes of continuing development is the best assurance that such growth will indeed take place. Therefore, therapy founded upon the philosophy of "dressing wounds" provides a milieu in which the patient's healing capacities flourish.

Since Freud's own papers on technique remain the best text, and are readily available, they will be summarized only briefly here. The emphasis will be upon the smaller details of the conduct of the sessions themselves. While the details are small, the concepts are not.

Continuing with the task of the therapist in the beginning of treatment, Freud used the phrase "evenly suspended attention," [13] which he described as the therapist's counterpart to the patient's task to say everything that comes to mind. This is of special relevance in beginning consultations because of the pressure upon the therapist to form some understanding of what it is that he is hearing and to place it within a diagnostic frame of reference. Yet Freud warned against this; not against the ideas which may form in the therapist's mind, but against seizing upon familiar concepts too quickly. A firm decision would deafen the therapist to other material which might also emerge. Here is another example of the kind of discipline essential for the conduct of therapy. The therapist has to be free of entanglements of his own needs so that he can make himself available to the patient's productions. Otherwise, "he, the therapist, will be following his expectations or inclinations." [14] Freud discouraged any procedure which might hamper full attention, such as note-taking during the session. So strong was Freud's insistence upon this point that he even disclaimed the usefulness of note-taking for scientific purposes. The therapist is to be free from presuppositions so that the unconscious of the patient has the best chance of stimulating threads of thought in the unconscious of the therapist which may be followed productively. One of the most frequently quoted statements of Freud appears in this same paper: "I cannot advise my colleagues too urgently to model themselves during psycho-analytic treatment on the surgeon, who puts aside all his feelings, even his human sympathy, and concentrates his mental forces on the single aim of performing the operation as skillfully as possible." [15]

---

[13] *Ibid.*, p. 111.   [14] *Ibid.*, p. 112.   [15] *Ibid.*, p. 115.

This is sometimes quoted as evidence that Freud thought little of the immediate relationship between patient and therapist, but it has far more relevance to the issue of countertransference. Freud was insisting that the therapist not burden the patient with his own feelings but, instead, keep the therapy room as free from contamination as would the surgeon in the operating room. Although Freud refers to putting "aside even his human sympathy," once again this is to be understood as his way of emphasizing that the therapist follow a professional role instead of a personally sympathetic one. Freud's intent was to emphasize the obligation to abstain from personal gratification. He said: "The justification for requiring this emotional coldness in the analyst is that it creates the most advantageous conditions for both parties: for the doctor a desirable protection for his own emotional life and for the patient the largest amount of help that we can give him to-day." [16]

He was careful to separate out the patient's capacities from the therapist's wishes or ambitions. The course of therapy is kept closely to those goals that the patient may want for himself and is capable of attaining. Freud was doubtful that educative methods can help, but it is essential to keep in mind here that he referred not to education per se, but to therapy. He thus also decried asking for intellectual cooperation.

Freud made quite a number of recommendations in regard to the relationship between patient and therapist. The simple statement that he lets his time for a fee is an example of the clarity with which he delineated his own ego boundaries from those of the patient. Pretension of omnipotence is avoided in the simple acknowledgment that the therapist makes his living by his fees. This offers the patient an opportunity to identify with the self-regard of the therapist. Special problems of acquaintanceship and friendship inevitably cause difficulties. Broken appointments are to be paid for; hours are to be regularly scheduled. The therapist and patient are not on an equal footing in that the therapist is constrained from disclosing any part of his own life to the patient because it would be damaging to the transference to do so. It is surprising that this suggestion is so often misunderstood

[16] *Ibid.*

since it represents no more than clarification of the difference between the professional stance and the attitude a layman might have toward the patient. It is contraindicated for the therapist to attempt to form the patient in his own image; this obviates the narcissistic temptation to offer oneself as a model. Greenacre adds clarity to this matter by counterposing the therapist's narcissistic needs against regard for the patient's autonomy.

Some elaboration is essential to clarify an apparent contradiction. That the therapist is a potential model for identification is implicit in the therapeutic situation and provides growth space. This is quite different from setting oneself up as a model for behavior. As a model for identification the therapist demonstrates to the patient's preconscious that with growth and continued development he can find means to cope with difficulties which now overpower him. Specifically, by defining ego boundaries, differentiating between self representations and object representations, clarifying realistic and attainable goals from unattainable ones, the therapist provides self-regard from which the patient will borrow until he can make it on his own. Thereby, structural growth by internalization is promoted without presuming to offer value judgments about behavior.

Freud also mentioned, about beginning therapy, that a trial period of two weeks is useful. It must be remembered that two weeks of Freud's time represented twelve sessions, or the equivalent of three months at once a week, the frequency prevalent in psychotherapy clinics today. He stressed that the patient does not have to trust the process, although some trust in the therapist had to have been present for the patient to have come in the first place. Demands for trust cannot be imposed by a therapist who understands the unconscious, resistance, and respects autonomy. One cannot speak of trust in relation to matters that are as yet unknown to both patient and therapist. As long as therapy is not interrupted, the patient's "ostensible" cooperation is not of great value; if, however, the therapist notes that the patient's overt cooperation conceals intense antipathy to the therapy, this is to be taken up without delay lest the patient act on the underlying feeling by failing to return for the next session. He is to be encouraged, in such instances, to verbalize the negative feeling before he "talks" with his feet by leaving.

When Freud stated to the patient, "Never forget that you have promised to be absolutely honest," [17] he had not lost sight of the fact that resistance obscures honesty, but he proceeded, in that manner, to establish a guidepost, deviation from which would alert therapist and patient to areas of conflict. Freud made these comments in relation to the famous fundamental rule that the patient is to say whatever comes to mind. In psychotherapy, this rule is still a useful tool but its application cannot be as widespread as in psychoanalysis. The more varied structures of psychotherapy patients require greater flexibility, especially in situations where the diagnosis may preclude the usefulness of free association because too much primary process thinking already predominates. Loosened cathexis by free association is only effective when the secondary process is secure. Also, borderline and psychotic egos require more anchoring to reality than do the better-structured egos of neurotics. Therefore, free association in psychotherapy, while still potentially useful, must be employed selectively in accordance with the diagnostic impression. The patient's goals for himself must also be taken into account because many persons come for psychotherapy without the clear-cut goals of the "ideal" analysand.

Discussion of the method of free association invariably brings to mind Freud's early use of catharsis. It is noteworthy that Freud tried and discarded this method almost a century ago. It is by now well proven that any method which fails to include consideration of the ego and its further structuralization will not endure. Thus, catharsis produced the same limited results as hypnosis. Free association, on the other hand, does directly involve the ego in the therapeutic task and is therefore desirable for those psychotherapy patients who do not thereby regress too much.

It is notable that Freud did not attempt to mete out justice, that his patient's "crimes" (neurotic behavior) were not seen as morally wrong, but rather as symptoms to be regarded with a nonjudgmental therapeutic attitude. Freud was aware that there is no such thing as psychological surgery; an offensive aspect of personality cannot be excised even with the patient's cooperation. Instead, he spoke of the ne-

[17] *Ibid.*, p. 135.

cessity for the patient to consider his problem as an "enemy worthy of his mettle." [18]

It is pertinent here to make one further observation about a matter on which Freud is frequently misquoted and misunderstood. "Freudian" technique is thought of as "deep" therapy, a process in which the dynamic present is often ignored in favor of uncovering the unconscious and the past. It is, therefore, of more than passing interest to note what Freud actually said. In *Remembering, Repeating and Working-Through,* he wrote, ". . . We must treat his illness not as an event of the past, but as a present day force." [19] The statement deals with the phenomenon of transference as it appears by means of the repetition compulsion, ensuring that the patient will bring his conflicts into the consultation room displaced and projected upon the person of the therapist. The patient thereby relives the original conflict. The therapist must be prepared for a perpetual struggle to keep in the psychical sphere all those impulses which the patient would like to direct into the motor sphere. This, of course, is very different from many forms of therapy today, which seem to permit and even to encourage acting out. These other modes of therapy rely rather heavily upon catharsis and, indeed, sometimes do result in temporary relief for the patient. In psychoanalytic psychotherapy, where the goal transcends immediacy, more lasting results are assured by helping the ego strengthen itself by means of verbalizing rather than acting out. Verbalization is a complex of ego functions including such major ones as symbolization, delay, interposition of thought before action and of object relations. As the ego is encouraged to exercise, its functioning improves and structuralization proceeds.

Nowhere else in the literature can one find as clearly described the appropriate attitude toward the patient's needs as in the writings of Ella Freeman Sharpe. Since Miss Sharpe wrote in English, there is the added advantage for English-speaking therapists that her work does not lose in translation. She makes an important and, at the same time, very human contribution to the technique of beginning in describing the purpose of the sessions as ". . . not to find out his com-

[18] *Ibid.,* p. 152.
[19] S. Freud, *Remembering, Repeating and Working-Through,* p. 151.

plexes, but to help him to find out why he *feels* like this, why he *does* that, what *prevents* him from accomplishing this task, why he has this symptom." [20]

Elaborating Freud's themes on countertransference and value judgments, she further states:

The person on the couch has his own problems, and it is not for us to envisage any result out of the analysis in accordance with our particular sense of values and desirabilities. I would here search the analyst's conscience with regard to the use of the word "normal." Do we hope that our patient will be so analyzed as to emerge a *normal* person, or do we hope that by analyzing resistances to resolve anxiety the patient's own potentialities may be realizable? The first is to set one's *own* goal in front of the patient; the second is to set oneself the *patient's* unknown goal. Only as we can bear the unknown, only as we are not "hot for certainties," shall we be able to let the patient alone.[21]

Of course, Sharpe does not mean "alone" in the sense of abandonment. On the contrary, she advocates being very much "with" the patient in the sense that one so respects autonomy that the patient is never intruded upon.

The overall purpose of the beginning phase is to pave the way toward termination. After all, the patient comes for treatment so that eventually he will be free of his problem and no longer in need of the therapist. In the course of the therapeutic endeavor his problems will incur involvement with and dependency upon the therapist. This is inevitable and can be put to therapeutic use. But much that is done in the beginning will influence the middle and end. The stage is sometimes set in the opening sessions for a very "sticky" termination if the end goal is not clearly in the therapist's mind. Of major concern are the patient's magical omnipotent fantasies about the therapist. One does not crudely dispel them, nor are they resolved in the opening phase by any other means, but the therapist neither harbors such attitudes toward himself nor accepts the patient's endowing him with unreal qualities. This has the immeasurable advantage of allowing room for the patient to develop, experience, and enjoy his own realistic power as more desirable than merging with the fantasied power of

---

[20] E. F. Sharpe, *Collected Papers on Psycho-Analysis*, p. 25.
[21] *Ibid.*, pp. 25–26.

the therapist. One way to reduce omnipotent wishes is to use caution in making promises. When the patient says, "I know you must have had a lot of experience with such problems and I know you will be able to help me," it can be flattering, but it is dangerously overloaded with great expectations and great dependence. Even if it does not appear in words, the act of seeking help acknowledges that help exists, but all too often it is misperceived as residing in the therapist instead of in the mutual work. It is, therefore, of utmost importance that the therapist clarify that he will work toward helping the patient find his own way; this serves to define the method and ultimately to enable the patient to terminate.

The last lesson to be drawn here from Sharpe is her attitude toward prohibitions. Everyone is familiar with the old admonition that important changes in the life situation are not to be made while the patient is in therapy. Such rules were more tenable in the days when analyses were of three months' to one year's duration. They are less suitable today when therapy may take much longer. On the other hand, there is always the danger that change of profession, spouse, and other major aspects of living may constitute much more acting out of unconscious fantasy than is realized at the time. So one is in a dilemma as to whether the change the patient seeks to make in his life situation represents an eruption of unconscious conflict and a search for symptomatic resolution, or whether it represents a normal and desirable shift in his life forces. With the advent of ego psychology, a new factor is introduced, namely the deleterious effect upon the patient's autonomy of directives by the therapist. Sharpe antedated ego psychology by a decade, yet found her own solution to the problem of prohibition versus autonomy. She felt that prohibition, ". . . even if it seems it might be an added leverage in analysis, always means that we are strengthening our role as super-ego, the prohibiting parent." [22] That prohibitions infantilize is confirmed by the belief that many patients express, namely that all decisions may be postponed until "after the analysis" (read: "When I grow up"). Avoiding prohibition and direction affirms the present adult status of the patient and helps him realize the degree to which he is able to live up to it.

[22] *Ibid.*, p. 30.

If he finds that he is not able, he knows better than before the definition of his therapeutic task.

Knight [23] was one of the early psychoanalysts who applied concepts derived from ego psychology to psychotherapy. He warned against Procrustean therapy which would fit the patient into the particular method of the therapist, even if such method should be classical psychoanalysis. The desirability of versatility on the part of the therapist cannot be overstressed; the ego structure of the patient, rather than restricted capacity on the part of the therapist, should determine the type of treatment. Knight also emphasized the importance of defenses and warned against attacking them. Anna Freud had already pointed out that defenses enable the patient to continue to function rather than surrender to his conflicts. She said:

. . . our study of these mechanisms [defenses] impresses us with the magnitude of its achievement. The existence of neurotic symptoms in itself indicates that the ego has been overpowered, and every return of repressed impulses, with its sequel in compromise formation, shows that some plan for defense has miscarried and the ego has suffered a defeat. But the ego is victorious when its defensive measures effect their purpose, i.e., when they enable it to restrict the development of anxiety and unpleasure and so to transform the instincts that, even in difficult circumstances, some measure of gratification is secured, thereby establishing the most harmonious relations possible between the id, the superego, and the forces of the outside world.[24]

Knight elaborated. He distinguished between supportive therapy, on the one hand, and tactics of exploration and confrontation. To this we would add that all therapy is supportive which encourages growth and improved functioning of the ego. In this regard, one would even, in some psychotherapy cases, not only support defenses but strengthen them because inadequacy of the signal function exposes the patient to too much anxiety. In the light of metapsychological developments that have been proposed since Knight, we would expand the concept of support to include ego building, not only in support of its defensive function but also in support of those aspects of

[23] R. P. Knight, in R. P. Knight and C. Friedman (eds.), *Psychoanalytic Psychiatry and Psychology.*
[24] A. Freud, *The Writings of Anna Freud, Vol. II,* pp. 175–76.

ego development other than the defensive, such as adaptive. We shall elaborate and illustrate shortly. First, however, we present a case to show how to support defense at the outset of treatment in a border-line structure.

Mr. Kenneth had been in group therapy for a number of years and appeared to have begun to cope with some of his social impedi-ments. Originally a "loner" and transvestite, terrified of women, he became able to court and marry a young woman who had been a member of the same therapy group. He was still in the group when the marriage began to fail. This resurrected his anxiety to full force and, together with it, outbursts of rage. At that point his therapist suggested that they had gone as far as possible in the group and re-ferred him elsewhere. The patient "accepted" the referral and the stated reasons for it, and began individual treatment with another therapist. His behavior in the early months of individual treatment had several clearly defined qualities. While generally almost obse-quious during the sessions, this did not prevent frequent outbursts of rage at the therapist. Any small event would serve his aggression. He referred constantly to the way in which his former therapist would have responded. In any crisis he would telephone that therapist who, for reasons best known to himself, would discuss the crisis over the telephone regardless of the lateness of the hour and of the fact that another therapist was now responsible. Inquiry as to whether this did not cause some confusion brought denial and anger. He was happy that Dr. X. was still so interested in his welfare and followed this with unfavorable observations about his present therapist.

He was not aware how precisely this repeated his parental relation-ships. His mother and father preserved the unity of the family in the physical sense, but fought continuously with each other. The patient recalled the kind of anxiety he experienced when he looked at his mother's face upon returning from school to see if the usual frown was present. His father teased him unmercifully about his ineptness, frequently demonstrating how much better he, the father, could per-form. The patient and his younger sister learned to live within an at-mosphere of alternating hostility and competition from the parents as well as the withdrawal of the parents into total involvement with each other to the exclusion of the children. Mr. Kenneth's continued clinging to the positive relationship with his former therapist was seen as an essential defense. To have confronted him with the fact that that therapist had given him up would have exposed him prematurely to the terror of rejection he had lived with throughout his childhood. It would have left him totally without objects, since the current therapist had not as yet assumed sufficient importance to him. This would have been an unthinkable risk. The only course open for the therapist was to limit himself to recognition of the former therapist's importance to the patient, of how much he felt he had gained from the group therapy (even though by that time it had all been lost), and to try to enlist Mr. Kenneth's efforts in an attempt to understand what had helped him feel better in order to see whether this could be attained again.

Greenacre's contribution to understanding the beginning phase has already been mentioned. Her technical papers on transference offer concepts of great value in understanding the patient's needs of the therapist and therefore lend themselves well to application in the early stage of therapy. Of greatest importance, in our opinion, is the safeguarding of autonomy expressed and inherent in her work. It was she who recognized so clearly the paradoxical situation involved in therapy, that dependency has to exist side by side with the therapeutic goal of enabling the patient to become less dependent. Since insight can only be attained by the patient's ego, careful safeguarding of autonomy is essential. This rules out so-called supportive measures such as direct encouragement, advice, manipulation of the environment, all of which inevitably weaken the patient's capacity to cope with his own reality problems. Especially in the beginning phase, when the patient is most likely to be seeking a cure from external sources, does the temptation arise to present him with solutions. But understanding of transference phenomena assures the therapist that the patient's own solutions will inevitably emerge in the therapeutic climate if the therapist will wait. Greenacre's technical suggestions were made with the analyzable patient in mind and therefore are to be applied selectively in psychotherapy cases. Where there is not sufficient ego structure to draw upon there is less hope that meticulous safeguarding will be productive until ego building has proceeded.

Much therapy becomes interminable because the therapist was not sufficiently alert to the undesirable development of what Greenacre calls a "narcissistic alliance" [25] as distinguished from a therapeutic alliance. Careful safeguarding of autonomy requires that the therapist have the capacity to forego gratification of his own narcissistic needs in dealing with patients.

A valuable technical point is stressed by Greenacre's preference for the phrase "active transference-neurotic manifestations" [26] as distinguished from the more classical phrase *transference neurosis.* By this she means that the transference manifestations are not of uniform "thickness" [27] but tend to vary according to the vagaries of the patient's inner life. This is especially useful in psychotherapy where there is not usually the frequency of daily sessions nor the degree of object relations to facilitate establishment of the transference neurosis per se. Knowledge that transference distortions cannot be uniform makes for increased flexibility on the part of the therapist in that he has to be more continuously alert to the productions of the immediate session, relying less upon prediction from behavior in past sessions. Such flexibility is well suited to the treatment of the borderline patient whose ego structure is such that there may be marked fluctuation between minimal and optimal functioning, for example, in reality testing and levels of object relations. The usual borderline ego is capable of functioning on a reality-oriented basis except when stress causes a regression of such magnitude that much of that functioning level is lost. It is this kind of flux, reflected in the transference, that Greenacre's phrase "active transference-neurotic manifestations" [28] describes so well. With regard to object relations, understanding such variability in the relationship of the patient to the therapist defines more sharply than heretofore the therapist's task in involving the patient's ego in a working alliance. This is particularly pertinent in those psychotherapy cases in which transference manifestations threaten to obscure reality to the point where a transference psychosis might ensue.

The following case is presented here not necessarily as an illustration of beginning treatment, but because it shows in fine detail how

[25] P. Greenacre, "Certain Technical Problems in the Transference Relationship," p. 487.
[26] *Ibid.,* p. 486.   [27] *Ibid.,* p. 485.   [28] *Ibid.,* p. 486.

Greenacre's concept of active transference manifestations are even more patent in borderline structures than in neurosis. Not always, in these deeper pathologies, are they even correctly designated as transference phenomena. More accurately, they are to be described as occurring within the therapeutic situation.

Miss Loran became frequently and unpredictably angry at the therapist, sometimes because of the content of his verbalizations or the manner in which they were delivered, sometimes because he took a holiday, and the like. As an example of the unimportance of the content itself, she once became enraged because she did not like the tie he wore. Her rage was so intense that she was moved to denigrate him completely. Yet this was not the sum total of her feelings. At other times she appreciated his helpfulness and was aware that she had profited from therapy. But whenever she became disappointed or angry, differentiation between self and object representations became blurred. In these moods the transference manifestations, colored by traumatic early experiences of severe disappointment and rage at her mother, dominated. Upon recovery she was usually puzzled by her regressed behavior and wondered that her reactions had been so intense that she could retain so little of her otherwise positive feelings. The therapist had to determine from each day's productions whether the past would dominate the session or whether the reasonable ego was in control. This pattern of behavior provided diagnostic clues. Outwardly, it resembled the volatility observable in infants who, frustrated at one moment, become enraged, and, pleased at the next moment, smile and are happy. In developmental terms, regression in Miss Loran was to the point where object representations became merged with self representations, losing the evenly distributed cathexis which, at other times, enabled her to experience her separate identity more fully; diminished sense of identity led to displeasure at the therapist's not being exactly like her and sharing her taste; deneutralization of aggression, combined with loss of frustration tolerance, made for the uncontrolled outbursts of rage; "good" and "bad" objects were split, so that she could not retain positive feelings about the therapist even if his tie were in inexecrable taste; diminished reality testing permitted license to complain about the tie without regard for the social reality that its choice was his prerogative; object relations reverted to the need-gratification level where the other person's needs have no meaning.

It is not prudent, technically, to attempt to force a patient in the throes of such a regressive episode to function at levels above those to which she has regressed. It is of immeasurable value, however, to know that this is a temporary and reversible regression. If it were a fixation, the diagnosis and prognosis would be less favorable. When the patient recovers her higher level of functioning and begins to ask, as this patient did, why she has such outbursts, one can enter the therapeutic alliance thus proffered and join the ego in its search for genetic causes. Then the case may be said to enter a new beginning phase.

Our discussion of the beginning phases of treatment has highlighted the fact that there is no single beginning, but rather that each step in the progress of therapy leads to a new beginning at a new level. Thus, we may speak of the first telephone call when diagnosis and treatment begin with the approach on the telephone and the manner in which this is handled by the therapist. By the time the patient arrives for his appointment, the therapist might already have learned that the patient is compliant from, "My wife said I should see you"; that he is defiant from, "I don't think therapy is much good, but I'll try it"; that he is dependent or desperate from, "I must see you right away"; that he is ambivalent or frightened from, "I've carried your phone number for months, but couldn't get myself to call until now." The therapist's response, such as, "We will talk about it when we meet," sets the stage for the first session, which is another beginning. After that, the initial resistance is handled and then there is still another beginning when the transference and therapeutic alliance become firm. And so one might describe a series of beginnings which even include the beginning of the end. We have already described how to recognize the beginning of the terminal phase.

We have also emphasized that the therapist begins with a method for addressing himself to the patient on two levels—to the manifest request and to the underlying problem—and with techniques for drawing the patient's ego into the treatment process. It is no more correct to proceed directly to the underlying problems which only the therapist perceives at first, thus overriding the patient's beginning defense and resistance, than it is to accept only the manifest request at face value. We have shown how to go with the patient, to begin where he is, which is with the problem as he sees it, defenses and all, and then to proceed into greater depth by leading him step by step away from his projections, denials, rationalizations, and the like to an introspective working alliance.

❧ 10 ❧

ON BEGINNING TREATMENT: PRACTICAL CONSIDERATIONS

THE OPENING PHASE is logically the time when decisions regarding sessions and fees are made and when rules about missed appointments, vacations, and the like are promulgated. Frequency of sessions was discussed in chapter 8. Freud's rules regarding attendance and responsibility for fee were established with the neurotic patient in mind. Although he did not have the language of modern ego psychology available to him, he had considerable understanding of the capacity of the well-structured ego to tolerate frustration and especially to function at that level of object relations which automatically allows for awareness of reality and for the needs of the other person. Thus, when he advocated acknowledging that the therapist expects a fee, he was relying upon the neurotic's possession of object constancy, including appreciation for the therapist's need to earn a living. We can make no such broad assumptions in deciding upon practical arrangements for the treatment of more disturbed patients. Some can abide as well as the neurotic patient can by the terms of agreement between patient and therapist as Freud stated them; some are at such a regressed level of object relations and have such poor reality testing that we speak another language if we hold rigidly to these demands; some begin treatment so unable to fulfill such ordinary requirements as fee payment and regularity of attendance that it becomes a high-water mark in treatment when they become able to abide by some of these requirements. In no other aspect of therapy is the versatility and flexibility of the therapist put more to the test than in determining how demanding to be, for it is as detrimental to the patient to ask for less than he can do as it is to ask for more. Development is best prompted within a consistent, positive, reliable therapeutic climate which contains tolerable doses of frustration. It is the experience of frustration that promotes differentiation of self and object representations. The therapist who holds out implied promise of gratification risks not only disappointing the patient because one can never do enough, but also implies that differentiation is unnecessary. The best guideline we can offer is to keep the requirements just slightly ahead of what the patient can fulfill, without insisting upon immediate compliance. This has the advantage of flexibility in relation to level of object relations and, at the same time, proposes that the goal of the therapy itself is the attainment of higher levels.

Beginning therapists sometimes tend to be self-abnegating about the fee. It is useful for them to know that the fee is the only part of the therapy that is legitimately for the therapist. If one is clear about this and establishes an adequate fee, there is less temptation to desire other compensations from the patient. The therapist who is adequately paid for his services is less likely to need positive transference manifestations, gifts, and other tokens of love. It is for this reason and its corollary of representing a self-respecting figure for purposes of identification that we do not advocate the low fees and other forms of self-abnegation sometimes demanded of therapists. We are not unaware of the urgent need for low-cost therapy. We believe, however, that obligation to provide for community needs does not rest upon the therapist as an individual, but that, as a citizen, he shares the same obligation as others. Most therapists are not wealthy and should not be asked to make philanthropic contributions in the form of service. If a therapist in a clinic or similar facility accepts minimal fees in exchange for supervision or other learning experience, then that constitutes compensation in another form. In most other instances, inadequate fees not only denigrate the therapist but fail to contribute to the patient's feeling of worth. This is not to be construed, however, as agreement with the oft-heard philosophy that it is good for the patient to pay because only then will he be well-enough motivated. Motivation is more profoundly promoted by other means. It is not usually detrimental to the treatment, for example, if a relative pays. Like motivation, independence is not attained by simplistic external devices.

There is one more consideration related to establishment of fees which involves calculation of what the therapist's time is worth. Some would include retroactive compensation for his entire education. This seems unreasonable to us. More realistic calculation, we believe, is based upon the actual number of hours per week that the therapist works and upon consideration of what constitutes a fair income for a professional person in the economy as a whole. The conscientious therapist does not work a given number of patient hours only. He reads the literature; consults; attends seminars, professional meetings, study groups; travels to national and international conferences. Even professional writing is an activity from which the therapist learns and which therefore benefits the patient. If this time is added to the number of patient hours, it may very well reveal that the fee to the individual patient for his therapy hour is lower than appears. These considerations are relevant to the therapist's determination of the fee, but the patient is not to be involved in such elaborate explanation. That would only reflect defensiveness on the part of the therapist.

If the patient has the means, but his level of object relations does not encompass consideration of the needs of the therapist, one may, if one wishes to accept the case, say, "This is my fee, but if it feels like too much for you now we can make an adjustment later." It happens more often than one might expect that, regardless of the initial arrangement, as the therapy proceeds helpfully and a higher level of object relations is attained, the patient volunteers that he would like to compensate the therapist more adequately. We do not imply that fees are to be escalated open-endedly. The therapist should have a maximum fee no matter how wealthy the patient is or becomes during treatment. Patients whose functioning improves are usually able to increase their income when the economy is favorable. They should not be penalized for getting a raise as a result of better functioning, nor should the therapist continue to accept a reduced fee under such circumstances. Fair compromises are possible. The most desirable arrangement is for the therapist to have a fee range that has lower and upper limits within which he can function best.

It is also, by now, rather generally known and accepted that the patient pays for broken appointments. Those with object constancy accept without question that they have contracted for the therapist's time, which is set aside for them. Some patients will argue that dentists, lawyers, hairdressers, do not charge for broken appointments. Psychotherapy is not comparable to any other profession or vocation. Time set aside for a patient on an ongoing basis cannot be filled on short, or even long, notice. Some therapists, if they happen to be able to fill time for short-range purposes, such as a consultation, will not charge the patient who has canceled that session. It seems only right not to charge the patient if the time is otherwise filled. However, there is a problem here because it burdens the patient with the issue of whether the therapist can fill his time, a matter which we believe should not be the patient's concern. It even happens rather frequently that the patient prefers not to have his time taken by someone else. In cases in which the primary object did not distinguish the patient sufficiently from others, it is not desirable to give the impression that the patient is easily replaceable. While it is true from the therapist's position that patients can be replaced when their therapy is completed, that is quite different from failure to maintain an attitude *during* therapy that the patient is a distinct and important individual. For these reasons, it is best for the patient to pay for the time that he misses without involvement in what the therapist does with that time.

The patient on a need-gratifying level of object relations finds it difficult to pay for time he does not use. This is part of the larger whole of his inability to consider that the therapist has needs of his own or even exists except to serve the patient. It is one of the rare instances when the patient is required to function beyond his psychological capacity. However, the situation may be used to highlight that he is troubled by this as part of his illness. Thus, greater regard for the object is held out, not by lecturing the patient on what he should or could do if he were better, but that *when* he is better he will also understand and be able to tolerate the requirements of life. The same patient, for example, may not be capable of working. He may offer analogous arguments, such as "Why should I work?" We deal with these regressed or arrested levels of development with understanding, but not with acceptance that regression is a way of life. Therefore, with respect to the only thing the patient must give the therapist— the fee—the patient has to know that it is required; that if he cannot bear it, such problem is grist for the therapeutic mill.

Another aspect of missed appointments is becoming more and more an issue in these days of extensive travel. Many types of businesses and professions require travel on regular or irregular bases. In general, the rule that the time must be paid for still holds. In exceptional circumstances, an individual arrangement may be made. Whether for business, illness, vacation, or the like, it is always useful to raise the question with a patient who is reluctant to pay, "Who, then, should pay?" [1] This is not an answerable question, but it is not meant to be altogether rhetorical either. Its purpose is to raise in the patient's mind the question that he himself has failed to consider. The therapist earns his living by setting aside a given number of patient hours per day. If the patient refuses to pay for his time, who indeed does pay? Patients on a need-gratifying level cannot answer such a question because, in their unconscious, therapy is equated with mothering. It is unheard of to pay for mothering. But, in therapy, there is, in this misunderstanding, a fine opportunity to clarify the therapist's role and the purpose of therapy. Even though we do not advocate lecturing the patient, it should be clear in the therapist's mind that he is there to treat and not to offer himself as a better mother. For many borderline structures and for most psychotics, transference psychosis can sometimes be averted if the therapist has such distinction always in mind.

It is not unusual for a patient who desperately needs the therapist to refuse, nevertheless, to pay for a missed session. He may even prefer to terminate treatment rather than to have to give the therapist the fee which, in the patient's mind, he has not earned. While the therapist remains firm that the fee is due him, it is not usually necessary to get into a head-on clash, especially if the patient will really terminate to his own detriment. The therapist can say, "You are obviously not able to deal with this now except by doing yourself the disservice of terminating treatment, so we will defer the fee for that particular session until you can bear to pay it." This solves the immediate crisis and, at the same time, holds out the long-range view that, in a more developed state, the patient will want to reimburse the therapist fairly. It states in another form that the level of object relations at

[1] This technical point was first proposed by Martin S. Bergmann.

which the patient is functioning is not the level he will be able to attain when treatment has proceeded further.

It is more traditional to think of unwillingness to pay as having its roots in stinginess and withholding, character problems arising from the anal level of psychosexual maturation. We agree with this fundamental feature of psychoanalytic theory. However, the dimension added by psychoanalytic developmental psychology explains more fully that the anal level is also the stage of development when identity formation has made good headway, when the child has begun to say "no," in employment of the aggressive drive in the service of separation and for the establishment of a new level of object relations which includes semantic communication. In adulthood, money might be the symbolic representation of the anal product. The right to withhold is not under full control of the ego as long as one can only withhold. Only when it is a matter of choice can one truly decide whether to withhold or to give. Ego expansion provides choice and volition. And so we hope to convey that the problems of payment of fee offer many ego-building opportunities in the therapy if the therapist will understand them as such and not as offenses against him. We must not behave like the mother who is personally deprived if the child is constipated. The anal product does indeed belong to the child alone and he learns to "give" it when he appreciates that it is not an essential part of his body ego.

Raising fees is also not difficult if one maintains an ego-building philosophy. Even if the patient has agreed to the therapist's maximum fee at the outset, therapy takes many years and inflation can outpace fees that seemed high when therapy started. The therapist has the right to increase even his maximum fee in accord with the general economic climate. When fees are at less than maximum, increases are always part of the ongoing process. This has to be accomplished in a reasonable, flexible, and dignified way. Above all, the patient is not to be left on tenterhooks about frequent fee increases. The ideal way to increase fees (and it has happened more frequently than one would expect) is to have the patient who has experienced radical changes in his life because of therapy offer to increase his payment. Sometimes such offers contain dangers as well, if they are made at too great a sacrifice as propitiation or as bribe. Offers detrimental to the patient's best interests, those that pander to the therapist's narcissism, are to be politely refused and interpreted. Offers which genuinely reflect attainment of a higher level of object relations and consideration of both self and object are to be accepted graciously and not interpreted to the point where the generosity of the patient is put to shame. If the patient cannot afford the offered increase, it should be declined. There are left to consider some patients who will not offer to increase the fee no matter what their improved financial circumstances. Here the therapist must step in because it is good for neither party to have the therapist exploited. If the patient attempts to deceive the therapist about his income, again this is not to be met with a judgmental attitude, but with an attempt to understand and interpret the distrust or superego defect. The patient with a competent ego and superego knows that he does himself no service if he "fools the doctor."

When the therapist decides that it is appropriate to increase the fee in an ongoing case, it is desirable to do so early in the month so that there will be ample opportunity for the patient to discuss his feelings before billing time. If the therapist is convinced that the fee increase is warranted but the issue is still not resolved by the end of the month, the increase may have to go into effect nevertheless, with room for the patient's continued airing of his feelings until enough material for interpretive purposes is accumulated. Sometimes the increase is deferred while the discussion continues, with the understanding that it may be retroactive when mutual understanding is reached.

We can think of no occasion when it is appropriate for the patient to be in debt to the therapist. For ongoing cases, fees for the preceding month are payable during the first week of the new month. There are exceptions to this traditional billing rhythm. If the patient is so disturbed that he cannot manage his finances competently then the therapist might, for the sake of not having to interrupt the treatment, suggest weekly or even daily payment. This has nothing to do with the wealth or poverty of the patient. We have known wealthy psychotics who write bad checks because the therapist asks for a check and, in primary process thinking, the abstract complexities of having to have a bank balance to cover it do not exist in the patient's mind. We think it a mistake in most, if not all, cases for the therapist to extend credit. What may be intended as generosity may often involve the therapist in an aspect of transference psychosis in which the patient considers the therapist as the good, all-giving parent. It is preferable to be firm about credit and to allow room for the aggression that this firmness might arouse. The overgenerous therapist ultimately becomes one from whom the patient can never separate. There are rather simple techniques for dealing with requests for credit. If the patient has the prospect of being able to repay a debt, then he can borrow from relatives, friends, a bank, and so on. The therapy is thereby freed of becoming a credit institution. If it should happen, and it sometimes does, that credit extended by the therapist is not repaid, it brings the therapy to a negative impasse. Unless the therapist is exceptionally masochistic, he is bound to begin to feel resentful for having given too much. "It is better to be in debt to someone else in order not to add a complexity to the therapy," is usually accepted by the patient as reasonable. It is essential to maintain clarity about the therapeutic situation since it does become the repository of many of the patient's distortions about himself and his objects. Extending credit, like other aspects of a relationship with the patient which are extraneous to the therapeutic purpose, runs great risk of distorted comprehension by the patient.

Need for money from the therapist can represent less tangible need and is to be interpreted, but it can also be realistic. Some years ago, when a subway token in New York City cost fifteen cents, a patient arrived with thirteen cents and needed to borrow two cents from the therapist. The patient lived thirty blocks from the therapist's office and it was snowing. Adhering rigidly to his mistaken interpretation of the abstinence rule, the therapist refused to lend two cents. Inhumane and doggedly rigid behavior does not help the therapy.

Gifts in psychotherapy are to be handled differently from the classical psychoanalytic techniques which recommend analyzing why the gift is given and the symbolic meaning of the gift itself. That is well and good for the neurotic structures. But the borderline structures are to be treated as in any other facet of treatment, in accordance with diagnostic evaluation of the level of development. We do not wish to inflict narcissistic injury by refusing something that the patient has himself created, such as a painting. Expensive gifts are as much a problem with the psychotherapy patient as with the psychoanalytic patient, especially if the cost of the gift exceeds the patient's financial means. But gifts, if they are to be refused, can be refused graciously. Sometimes this involves accepting one with the understanding that the therapist will enjoy it temporarily and then return it. That, of course, depends on how perishable it is and whether it can be refunded at the store after a given period. The major consideration in this delicate problem is, as always, to promote ego growth. The patient who began therapy on a need-gratifying level may, after a year or more, notice that the therapist needs something. He may bring flowers for an empty vase, for example. The temptation to analyze the symbolism of filling the vase should be postponed in favor of giving adequate recognition to the ego growth. It can be a devastating setback to the patient who, for the first time in his life wants to give to another person, to be told, "You want to give me a gift of feces" (or a baby, or whatever else the gift may correctly symbolize). This would be an example of an interpretation correct in content that is altogether incorrect in timing. The correct statement is, "Isn't it nice that you thought of what I would like?" Such statements are to be made with great caution, however. Never should they represent demand or value judgment. It is good for the patient to be considerate and thoughtful of another person when his level of object relations is such that consideration and thoughtfulness come naturally to him. It is painful for him to be chided for being unable to function on a level that he has not reached.

Sometimes the therapist does have personal needs which inevitably impinge upon the therapeutic rhythm. We are referring to those events in every person's life such as illness, or business or family matters which require attention. The patient is not to be burdened with these. "I have to be away next Thursday," is all that is necessary, unless the patient asks further questions, which are to be answered truthfully, but sparingly. Often, "It will be better for your therapy if we do not get you involved in that," can be accepted as the therapist's conscientious desire to reserve the relationship for the patient's problems. The rule is that one always tells the truth, but the whole truth is often more than the therapeutic situation requires or can tolerate.

The therapist's vacation is almost always stressful for the patient.

Ideally, the therapist should have a stable vacation and holiday schedule with which the patient becomes familiar after the first year of treatment. Not only for stability is this desirable; it also allows the patient to plan his own vacation to coincide with that of the therapist. When the patient's vacation does not coincide, the time is to be paid for. Vacations should be announced well enough in advance to provide opportunity for working on the feelings engendered. Patients on a need-gratifying level see no reason for the therapist to take a vacation and initially this should not be argued on the level of the therapist's need. The first therapeutic step in dealing with feelings about the therapist's vacation is always to ascertain what it means in terms of separation anxiety and repetition of traumatic separation in the past. One woman in her early thirties grew up in a fairly well-to-do household where the parents spoke openly about taking weekends and vacations *away from the children.* For this patient, as for many whose parents left or threatened to leave, the therapist's vacation meant, "You need a vacation from me." Variations on that theme are, "I must wear you out," or "You need a rest from me," and the like. The therapist should make it very clear that he is not leaving the person. If his libidinal reservoir is adequate for this demanding profession, that is always the truth.

The extent of further explanation depends upon the capacity of the ego to tolerate more knowledge. Sometimes it stretches the ego toward object constancy by explaining that one leaves to preserve one's health, to change from the daily routine of city life, and so on. Again, one must exercise caution lest the patient be overburdened with even this much detail. The best preparation for the therapist's vacation still consists of interpretation of separation anxiety, of narcissistic injury, and of the aggression which causes the patient to think that he is driving the therapist away. A moderately competent ego is able to use interpretation of whichever of these is applicable. A good test of where the level of object relations lies is, "Would you want me to have a good vacation?" We recommend that this be done with extreme caution and only when there is good reason to believe that the patient is one small step below this level and can take the next step with this kind of encouragement. The question, therefore, is designed to stimulate the ego to reach out to the next level. If, however, that patient's ego is far below this level, then the leap is too great for him and he should not be tantalized with a question that can only represent an expectation that he fails to meet. It is never ego building to shame the patient with those developmental lesions that he cannot yet help. It is the task of therapy to bring him to higher levels and this cannot be accomplished in an atmosphere that deals repeated narcissistic injury. We stress this because, contrasted with the ego psychological approach, there are "confrontation" techniques which barrage the patient with his deficiencies as though he can mend them if they are pointed out to him. In all but the most ego syntonic kinds of situations, the patient is already painfully aware of his incapacity to live up to levels of behavior which would make him better liked by himself and by others.

Often patients threaten to leave treatment when the therapist takes a vacation. It even happens that they return for one session after the therapist's vacation only to announce, then, that they are leaving. It is inexact to interpret this as the wish to retaliate in kind, although that element is certainly present. More usefully, one can say, "You want to leave me because you felt so bad when you were left" (an interpretation of separation anxiety) "and the best way of letting me know how it feels is to have me experience it" (an interpretation of preverbal affect).

The neurotic patient need not know where the therapist goes on vacation. His intact ego encompasses continuous existence of stable object representations. The decision about whether and how much to tell other patients has to be made, again, upon appraisal of the level of development and of the ego's capacity to sustain constant object representations. The seriously depressed patient should be able to reach the therapist. The psychotic patient needs to know at least that the therapist still exists on earth. For the borderline structure, it is often sufficient to mention the geographical area where the therapist will be; it helps him tolerate the therapist's absence if he can refer to a map or to his knowledge of geography to reinforce his uncertain and shaky knowledge that the therapist exists in absentia.

Usually the sex of the therapist does not matter. Different themes may emerge in a different order depending upon whether the therapist is a man or a woman but, on the whole, the same ground will be covered. We see no reason to begin a case under a handicap, however, if the patient has strong feelings about it. Some women's liberation persons these days do not trust a male therapist. If a competent female therapist can be found, there is no reason to refuse this. On the other hand, these kinds of problems are worked out rather easily once a transference is established. In a few cases of homosexual panic, the patient is afraid to enter treatment with a therapist of the same sex. Again, when this can be worked out better, if the beginning is less encumbered by such fears with a therapist of the opposite sex, there is no reason to do it the hard way. In the long pull, it is best to have a competent therapist regardless of sex.

The etiquette of the therapeutic atmosphere is important. The patient is a special kind of guest in the therapist's office and is to be treated courteously at all times. However, he is not a social guest, and that fact delimits certain common courtesies. We always address the patient politely, which means that an adult is not addressed by his first name. He may protest about this, but the therapist is not there to help him remain a child. If the patient is a woman, she precedes the therapist into the room; a male patient is not comfortable preceding a female therapist, so she greets him in the waiting room and precedes him until they are both seated. Handshaking is not as common in the United States as in Europe so, in this country, one shakes hands on the first meeting, if that is not awkward for the patient, on leaving for vacation, and on other occasions similar to those in everyday life.

There are certain courtesies that are antitherapeutic and it is desirable, at the outset, to set a tone which does not lead the patient to expect all that would be expected on a social call. Food, cigarettes, coffee, or other refreshments are never served. Many patients bring their own cigarettes and some bring containers of coffee and even sandwiches. We do not accept the patient's offer to share these, but we refuse politely. At the outset of treatment it is usually untimely to raise much question about why the patient needs to fortify himself with oral supplies when he comes for treatment. Later, it is of central importance to discuss and interpret this. The most common reason is that the patient does not expect to get much from the therapist. In the context of promoting the capacity to postpone, feeding oneself may be postponed later in treatment. It is often asked what is wrong with serving such things as coffee. The only answer is the psychoanalytic one. We are there to reverse regression, not to reinforce fixation. The therapist regards all psychosexual phases without value judgment. It is no more valid to permit the patient oral gratification than it is to permit him anal and phallic gratifications. The therapist has appropriate reaction formation against anality, but that is not the reason for or against its being acted on in treatment. About verbalization of these kinds of desires, however, there must be no taboo.

Cigarettes are not offered. Many patients bring their own. The more disturbed patient is permitted to smoke because his frustration tolerance would be overtaxed by prohibiting this. The neurotic patient who smokes can be "weaned" by suggesting that, when he feels the urge to smoke, he verbalize the feelings that necessitate it. Ultimately, this is the goal with all patients, but the less-developed ego has to be brought to the kind of working alliance that makes such a suggestion seems sensible to him; the neurotic ego is already there in most instances.

Traditionally, therapy sessions are fifty minutes long. This is giving way rapidly to the forty-five minute "hour." Probably as much can be accomplished in forty-five minutes as in fifty. The patient becomes accustomed to the rhythm of the session and works within it. Some patients cannot leave, no matter how long the session. It is not desirable to prolong the time habitually, but it should be done flexibly in times of crisis. The patient who lingers, who has to say one more thing, who makes the most important statement of the session at the door, is to be asked next time to help search for what this serves him. This always provides valuable material that is lost if the therapist simply yields to the lingering. The most usual reason, of course, is that separation is difficult, but this needs to be understood in terms of the specific past, and worked through. Sometimes the same problem manifests itself in the opposite way—that is, defensively. Such patients watch the time and prefer to leave before the therapist announces that the time is up. They deal with the trauma of separation through active mastery rather than through passivity. We allow this until material for interpretation enters the therapy naturally.

Emergency sessions are in most cases to be granted freely if the therapist is able. We think of only one exception, and that is the already overindulged patient whose frustration tolerance has not developed because he was never required to endure even moderate waiting. But in other instances, it is, after all, a triumph of the transference, of level of object relations, of therapeutic alliance and trust in the therapist if the patient calls on him in states of intense anxiety, depression, or other emotional crises. More often than we would like, the therapist with a busy schedule is not able to meet every request for an extra session. Then one may say, "I'm sorry I am unable to do it today, but it is good that you tried." Such a welcoming attitude not only encourages the patient to try again next time, when he might be more successful, but it makes him feel immediately better about having had the courage to call.

Most patients find it hard to telephone the therapist and we have not found, in our experience, that the telephone is much abused. More often than the telephone call, one hears in the session itself, "I thought of calling you yesterday, but I didn't." "Why didn't you?" has too much the connotation of a scolding. But much can be learned if one asks, "What was the thought that deterred you after you had the thought of calling?" The most frequent answer is, "I didn't want to disturb you." Then one can ask, "What is your fantasy about how it would disturb me?" In this way, one learns a great deal which would otherwise not emerge spontaneously. In the rare instances when telephone calls are excessively frequent or excessively long, one can consider legitimately charging for the time. In our own experience, we have not had to do this, but we can conceive of its needing to be done in some instances. More usually, if the calls are truly excessive, the reasons for them can be discussed during the sessions. If the patient tends to remain on the phone longer than his real need requires, it is up to the therapist to deal with the business at hand briefly, courteously, but firmly. Only in the most rare and unusual circumstances is it desirable to use the telephone as though it is a face-to-face session. We have heard of some instances when this is done, but we see few reasons for it. If the patient is ill and cannot come, he will sometimes want to use his time with the therapist on the telephone. This is not to be encouraged because a telephone "session" is a poor substitute for the real one. Life-saving measures are always excepted from hard and fast rules.

In this electronic age, machines are available which seem to be useful for teaching and research, and are even regarded as useful for therapy by playing sessions back to the patient. The rationale (or rationalization) is that tape recordings and even video tapes reproduce the sessions more accurately and objectively than the therapist's memory; that the patient can improve by means of this sort of self-confrontation; that supervision and research are enhanced. It is argued that, following initial sessions, both therapist and patient forget the presence of the machine and proceed as usual. We maintain that object relations cannot be promoted by mechanical devices. The process of structuralization takes place within a dyadic relationship which resembles the primary dyad. Introduction of machinery tends to diminish reliance on the relationship. As technology adds more and more devices, it is important for the therapist to be aware that there are as yet none which record the subtle feeling tones, the empathy in the silences, and, above all, the unconscious. In many tape recordings, the silences which, to the empathic therapist, might be the most important parts of the session, are edited out because they are "boring" to the listener. As for the unconscious, the burden of proof is on those enthusiasts who maintain that both patient and therapist truly "forget" that the device is present. We cannot see how such intrusions can fail to have an impact, even if they are "forgotten" after a few sessions by denial. Every beginning therapist knows the influence upon his therapeutic behavior of having to report to his supervisor. Many sensitive patients, even though they have not been told that the therapist is in supervision, feel its effects. No matter how rapidly technology develops, we are not now able to foresee that there will be machines that match human empathy. In the patient with paranoid tendencies, a machine can promote panic. The passive patient may feel relieved of his ego task of having to remember and synthesize past sessions. The deeply disturbed patient's belief in magic can be promoted by the presence of a machine. Although we value teaching and research, we think that, on balance, the price of using machines for those purposes is too high.

The matter of extratherapeutic contact is always a delicate one. Because the still-valid guideline of avoiding such contacts whenever possible has been applied by some therapists with excessive rigidity, there is now a backlash school of thought which advocates socializing with patients. Especially in group therapies do some therapists believe in sharing their personal lives on a par with the patients. But the therapeutic situation is not equal. The therapist, as we have made quite clear, respects the patient. But this does not mean that he abandons his role. In no situation wherein one person seeks the specialized expertise of another is the situation equal. So we do not think the therapist should vitiate his role as expert and leader, nor should he burden the patient with his problems, nor hold out his personal solutions as though these are useful examples of how to live. It is an accepted tenet of psychoanalytic and psychotherapeutic technique that extratherapeutic contact "contaminates" the treatment. But many therapists are mystified about what is meant by "contamination." It means simply that, if the patient knows too many details of the therapist's life, opportunity for fantasy and for transferences from the past are lost. Fantasy, distortion, and repetition in the transference are vital therapeutic tools and, if lost, are often not retrievable. It is essential to avoid turning oneself into a real object unnecessarily. We have said that there are structures which call for the therapeutic availability of a real object, but such therapeutic decisions are always to be made on a diagnostic basis. All but the most disturbed patients need more to correct their distortions than they need a real object in the therapist.

There is no other reason for the therapist's life to be secret, but this one reason is of overriding importance. We believe that the therapist should be well-enough adjusted so that his personal life could stand the closest scrutiny, but this does not dictate that he open it up to the patient's curiosity. Especially if doing so gratifies the therapist's exhibitionism is it contraindicated. Greenacre has even pointed out that the therapist has to forego publicity if he is to preserve his value as a transference figure. That does not mean that he may not make scientific contributions to his field and receive the reward of recognition by his colleagues. It may mean, however, that he avoids running for political office and similar activities if he wishes to continue in practice.

But there are extratherapeutic contacts that cannot be avoided and, on those occasions, natural courtesy is the only sensible rule. If the therapist and patient meet in the elevator, in the subway, in the theatre, in a department store, or even at a party, a polite, natural greeting is in order, but not prolonged and intimate social conversation. A patient can always understand that the purpose is to preserve the therapeutic relationship. He especially understands this if it is pointed out at some appropriate time that, for the sake of the therapy, the therapist, too, is depriving himself of the gratification of the patient's social company.

When therapists-in-training are themselves in therapy, it is inevitable that they will encounter their therapists at scientific meetings and the like. The same rules of unstilted cordiality but preservation of the transference apply. If the therapist is invited to a small dinner party, it is socially awkward to ask the hostess who the other guests will be. But if the therapist knows that a patient is one of the hostess's acquaintances, he must take this precaution, with explanation that therapeutic reasons prevail. It is a fact often overlooked by therapists who are comfortable with their patients, as they should be, that the patient is not equally comfortable with the therapist. In addition, when there is a good therapeutic alliance and good motivation, a patient never wants to allow a social event to impair his treatment, and so he will easily forego it.

Neither, we have said, do psychoanalytically oriented therapists treat the husbands, wives, children, or siblings of patients concurrently. This is one of the aspects of technique which differs markedly from treatment not psychoanalytically oriented. The principal and, in our opinion overriding, reason for this rule is, again, transference as a prime tool in treatment; a relationship with any other member of the patient's family will inevitably impair it. There are arguments on the other side. One of the most convincing is that the therapist who sees both spouses learns much about the interaction. This cannot be disputed. We are concerned, however, with what one does with such knowledge. One can confront the patient, in the presence of the spouse or at another time, with his behavior and its impact on the other person. But the ego psychological approach observes that confrontation from without informs the patient of something which, unless it is ego syntonic, the patient already knows—namely that his behavior is unacceptable to others. The painfulness of such knowledge is increased by the fact that the change that is demanded is usually beyond the patient's developmental level. If he could behave otherwise, he would. And so we prefer that confrontation be intrasystemic, when the ego is capable of observing and altering its own behavior because development has proceeded. "You have no consideration for your husband," is meaningless to the woman on a need-gratification level of object relations. When her object relations begin to encompass regard for the object independent of her state of need, she will become more considerate without having suffered a scolding for what she had not yet been able to do.

The chief argument against concurrent treatment remains preservative of the therapeutic alliance. It is essential that the patient feel that the therapist is there altogether for him. There are therapists who believe sincerely in their own objectivity. But if they believe also in the subtle, unconscious operation of the repetition compulsion, they will be cautious about undertaking arrangements that contain inherent danger to the therapy. For example, a patient may unconsciously induce attitudes in the therapist that repeat a parent's preference for a sibling. The therapist would, of course, consciously want to remain impartial. But victory of the repetition compulsion can be indiscernible and so detrimental to treatment that the most objective of therapists may find that he has been drawn into a situation which is all but impossible to repair.

These considerations are, nevertheless, to be applied flexibly and to be related to the capacity of the patient's ego to operate within them. For example, married couples often ask to be seen together. If the reason is only that they think that this is the preferred method of marital counseling, then it is usually easy for them to accept the suggestion that they come separately. Particularly are those couples who are symbiotically bound together, however, unable to accept any arrangement that separates them. These situations are the ones that have to be handled with flexibility at the outset. One might ask, "Do you think you will be able to talk freely with your wife present?" If the answer is something like, "Oh, yes, we always share everything," then there is little to be gained by trying to treat the symbiosis mechanically by refusing to see the couple together initially. There will be time, later in the therapy, when such a joint problem can be treated interpretively with a view toward proposing individual treatment, preferably with different therapists.

Professional courtesy and professional ethics are often neglected aspects of one's behavior toward colleagues and patients. We are sometimes surprised at the absence of communication with colleagues on matters of mutual interest. Most therapists rely on referrals of cases by colleagues. The most courteous way of functioning is to telephone and ask the colleague to whom one wishes to refer a case whether he has time and whether he would be interested in the particular case. This is good for the patient, too, because it saves him the trouble, and often pain, of getting in touch with a therapist who has to tell him that he does not have room in his schedule. When the patient has been seen, it is proper to inform the referring therapist of this fact and of the disposition of the case. A therapist may refer a patient, but the patient may not follow through on the referral. The referring therapist would like to know this, as he would also like to know if the case has been taken on for treatment. We do not refer on a case that has been referred to us without the courtesy of asking the referring therapist whether he wants us to do that or would prefer to have the patient turned back to him for his own action on it. The referring therapist may have selected a particular therapist for a case and may not want that case sent around the therapeutic community. If a case is taken on for treatment, or otherwise disposed of, it is desirable to write a brief note to the referring therapist thanking him for the referral and informing him of the disposition. Unless one knows the therapist and his schedule very well, telephone calls are likely to be intrusive.

Ethics are not well enough spelled out by professional societies. While there are strictures against advertising and similar commercial kinds of behavior that are generally frowned upon by all professions, it is not sufficiently emphasized that ethics have value only if they are designed for the protection of the patient. A physician will not knowingly treat the patient of another physician. But this ethical tenet is not, as some suppose, to protect the practice of the physician from "stealing" by his colleagues. It is designed to protect the patient from conflicting simultaneous treatment. In psychotherapy, too, we do not "steal" patients from another therapist. If a patient consults us about his treatment with another therapist, we prefer that that therapist be informed of it. But it is never ethical or desirable to protect a therapist who is mistreating the patient. If the patient is in treatment with a therapist who works within a theoretical frame of reference similar to ours, that therapist would welcome having a mistake or oversight pointed out so he can correct it. Transference is always a consideration in dealing with a patient who is still in treatment with another therapist or who has just terminated. If the patient is acting against his best interest, as might be so in a negative transference, then this is to be interpreted to him so that he will understand what he is doing and return to his therapist to work it out.

There is one very delicate aspect of interprofessional relationship which applies more to psychotherapy than to medicine, law, or other professions. In those professions, accepted procedures are more or less firmly established and are taught fundamentally in the same way in all professional schools. Deviations from certain standard practices by a physician, for example, are usually not debatable. Psychotherapy is a field in which there is more diversity than agreement on crucial features of professional practice—on theory and technique. One therapist's conviction may appear as irregular practice to a therapist of another orientation. There are many therapies today which reject the psychoanalytic developmental point of view—often, we regret, without understanding it. And so we think that it is not only ethical, but an obligation to the patient, to express an opinion if we find that the therapy to which he has been exposed is damaging. Ethics, we repeat, are not for the protection of the therapist, but for that of the patient.

In fact, protection of the treatment is the guiding consideration in all the arrangements surrounding the therapy. Therefore, while some of the reserved behavior of the psychoanalytically oriented psychotherapist has been criticized as unnecessary and rigid in these days of increasing informality, we have tried to convey that the arrangements

can be made flexibly and naturally. Again, if the ego-building purposes are understood within the context of psychoanalytic developmental psychology, the otherwise inexplicable behavior of the therapist is also understood.

❧ 11 ❧

THE UNMOTIVATED PATIENT

THE "UNMOTIVATED PATIENT" is a contradiction in terms admirably suited in its paradoxical quality to the unconscious in which contradiction is well tolerated. Insofar as an individual presents himself to the therapist for consultation, he desires help; insofar as his defenses may be operating with mechanisms of projection and displacement, producing a conscious reluctance on his part to enter the therapeutic situation, he is described as unmotivated. Individuals with "poor motivation" for treatment constitute a large segment of the patient population of many psychotherapists. Probably most children, for example, fit this category, brought to treatment as they are by their parents. We have shown elsewhere [1] that marital relations also lend themselves to projection and displacement, bringing individuals to the consultation rooms who are in effect seeking self-justification rather than insight into their own developmental disturbances. Those schools of thought that locate psychic problems in the transactions and interactions between people tend to affirm the defensive projections and displacements. Legally required treatment for offenders and for the addict population, and divorce laws that demand predivorce marital consultations, all contribute to the ranks of the unmotivated or poorly motivated patient population. We think that these are useful attempts to bring into treatment the person who would not seek it voluntarily. Precisely because we agree with these attempts, however, we wish to contribute techniques for the baffling problem of engaging the unwilling person to the point where he becomes a willing participant in the treatment process.

[1] R. Blanck and G. Blanck, *Marriage and Personal Development*.

Unwittingly, and against their conscious professional self-images, therapists tend to have value judgments about motivation. This is understandable because of the difficulties involved in working with an unmotivated patient. How much easier to have the patient announce firmly his wish to be treated and then delve into the more familiar unconsciously determined resistances that psychoanalysts and psychotherapists have long known how to treat. Perhaps prejudice against the unmotivated patient is instilled by the training process. Beginning with the ubiquitous anxiety of the training period, aided and abetted by the usual search, in training institutes, for cooperative, well-motivated candidates, a high premium is placed upon the initial attitudes and verbalizations of the applicant. It is striking that once the patient affirms his wish to get help, his resistances are met with a far more benign response from the therapist. At such points one hears of unconscious factors, the defenses which lie behind the resistances; challenge to professional skill replaces the often found negative response to absence of motivation. When the therapist no longer views the resistance implicit in the unmotivated aspect as opposition to him, his professional training produces the necessary objectivity so essential to the ongoing work. We see no reason to regard lack of motivation in any way different from resistance in general. While it is an obvious fact that one cannot deal with the resistance of the patient who does not present himself, so many individuals are brought to treatment rooms more or less involuntarily that it begs the issue to focus on those who never arrive. For many individuals, the life situation makes the need for help abundantly clear to others close to them, and theirs are opinions the unmotivated patient cannot successfully continue to ignore.

Resistance has been traditionally defined as the expression of defense, unconsciously instituted, against anxiety arising out of conflict. Thus there arises the typical blocking of memory, words, and so forth, as the patient approaches conflict areas which were not satisfactorily resolved during growth. This definition, based as it is on drive theory and intersystemic conflict, no longer does justice to the present state of knowledge about structuralization. Development, as we now know it, is not altogether conflict-borne. Consideration of the processes of formation and preservation of identity provides a different view of resistance. Oppositionalism and negativism, so often viewed solely as resistance based upon the defense of reaction formation, can also represent a struggle to establish and maintain identity. To be sure, this, too, may be a defense, in this instance against symbiotic wishes; on the other hand it may also be seen as a normal step toward separation-individuation. When resistance is viewed as ". . . a part of a patient's wishing, part of his hope, part of his identity, as well as part of his handicap," [2] then it is obvious that technical means must be found to affirm that part of the resistance which expresses the patient's wish, hope, and identity.

It is of some interest to trace the development of attitudes of therapists toward resistance because to do so provides historical perspective for the surprising degree to which superseded formulations are still held. Freud's earlier attempts to eliminate resistance as a bar to recovery quite naturally led to such statements as ". . . the defensive ego [is] our enemy," [3] or, "Resistance means opposition . . . operating against the progress of the analysis, the analyst, and the analyst's procedures and processes." [4] In a similar vein, "The important thing to see is that resistance exists, that it opposes treatment, that it is aggressive, and that it is self-destructive." [5] But Freud himself had moved a long way beyond viewing resistance with "pained astonishment." [6] The very fact that one of his major cases involved a most passive, reluctant patient—the Wolf Man [7]—demonstrated Freud's own capacity to work with, not against resistance. As early as 1917 Freud was noting that "resistances . . . should not be one-sidedly condemned . . . they become some of the best supports of the analysis if a skillful technique knows how to give them the right turn." [8]

It was Glover who stated that resistances in therapy assume forms which accord with the level of object relations reached at the time conflict arose. Applying and extending this concept, that forms of resistance may reflect varying levels and lines of development, the ther-

[2] L. Friedman, "The Therapeutic Alliance," p. 150.
[3] O. Fenichel, Problems of Psychoanalytic Technique, p. 37.
[4] R. R. Greenson, The Technique and Practice of Psychoanalysis, pp. 59–60.
[5] K. Menninger, Theory of Psychoanalytic Technique, p. 119.
[6] S. Freud, Resistance and Repression, p. 288.
[7] S. Freud, From the History of an Infantile Neurosis.
[8] S. Freud, Resistance and Repression, p. 291.

apist can become more precise in his interventions. To cite a few examples:

1. The kinds of defenses available to the ego reflect the extent to
which development has taken place. Where the unwilling spouse arrives for his initial consultation sweating so profusely that he must
take off his misted eyeglasses, and has trouble with his knees jerking,
one may assume that anxiety is not used as a signal; he has become so
anxious that his anxiety falls just short of overwhelming him. This is
the patient who requires the kind of supportive welcome that affirms
that he has already done a good deal for himself by keeping the appointment, painful as it obviously is for him. The task of the therapist
is to do nothing that may make him even more anxious, since such
individuals are likely to walk away from their anxiety because other
coping mechanisms are so weak.

2. Internalizations of object representations play a crucial role. Unmotivated does not mean that the wish to feel better is absent. It has
far more to do with negative (aggressive) internalizations, based upon
distortions of and failure in early experiences, preventing optimistic
anticipation and comprehension of the therapeutic experience as a
dyadic interchange holding out favorable possibilities. For the most
part, such patients view therapy with foreboding, with fears of damage to self and therapist, arising out of the fact that self and object
representations are cathected with aggression.

3. Problems in object relations which impede beginning treatment
can now be restated in terms of the stages of this line of development.
For example, it is obvious that fixation in an early level of need gratification will reflect inability to accept the frustrations of therapeutic
abstinence. For such patients, proper balance of gratification and frustration, missed in initial development, may be fruitfully employed as
a motivating factor. Especially when avoidance attitudes have become
embedded in character structure, technical means must be sought to
overcome the serious misunderstandings of such patients about the object's intentions. The individual who arrives with a typically passive
attitude based upon magical expectations of the therapist is already a
step ahead of the one with negative expectations. His objects, although perceived from an infantile position of omnipotence, are at
least favorable. The more serious developmental failure results in in-

capacity even to *misperceive* the therapist as a need-gratifying object.

The "unmotivated patient" pays a severe penalty for this reluctance. Challenges to the prospective patient's motivations are a frequent part of initial consultations. We have said that therapists tend to have far more tolerance for resistance in its unconscious forms than for resistance which has found conscious rationalization and is displaced upon beginning treatment. Yet it is theoretically inconceivable that there are more and less preferable kinds of resistance. Since the unconscious is always present and may never be overlooked, the therapist may almost always feel secure that the patient's approach behavior will contain both the wish to get help no matter how well it is concealed, as well as defenses against the anxiety which must inevitably militate against that attempt. Glover puts it that "the patient has been unconsciously repenting his temerity ever since he rang the bell." [9] Thus, like the youngsters who jest about getting into a theater by walking in backward so that the ticket-taker will think they are coming out, the prospective patient also walks in backward. Why should more credence be given to the patient who says he wants to be treated than to the one who says that he only needs a "little help"? Freud observed, ". . . his [the patient's] critical faculty is not an independent function, to be respected as such, it is the tool of his emotional attitude and is directed by his resistance." [10] What then is to be done with the young woman who merely wants an opportunity to talk the situation over once and who maintains, despite the paradox of appearing for a consultation, that the proper direction is already clear to her? Or the college student who is all too eager to accept advice, indeed demands direction; or the impotent husband who asserts *to the therapist* that he has no faith in therapy; or the reluctant woman who states, "My husband thinks therapy will do me some good." Or, similarly, the mother who says, "My son has a problem." Would it make an appreciable difference if she had said, "I have a problem with my son"? Or, "My husband wants to leave me and I just want to die"? Are these, or could they be, patients, and, if so, what techniques can be used to deal with the resistance expressed in such lowered motivational attitudes?

[9] E. Glover, *The Technique of Psychoanalysis*, p. 19.
[10] S. Freud, *Resistance and Repression*, p. 293.

Following the rule that we can use only that which the patient presents to us for use, it becomes necessary to recognize the developmental level of the conscious presentation, so that the therapist conveys a sense of connection with that level. This must capture the patient's conviction that he has been heard, and either that he is understood or that an attempt being made to understand him is strong enough to be apparent to him. As Friedman pointed out, an approach to an id connection can be made in a way that presents the analyst as recognizable rather than as a stranger. To his technical suggestion we may now add that it is as important to connect with the developmental level as with the id.

In considering techniques for dealing with resistance as it presents itself on the preliminary level of absence of motivation, classification of resistence as deriving from ego, superego, or id is not of more than academic interest. Since resistances manifest themselves through the ego, they reflect the ego's relative success or failure in processes of structuralization and development. Therefore, it remains the therapeutic task to ascertain the developmental level which has been reached in finding our diagnostic bearings in relation to motivation. This takes direct issue with the concept that resistance ". . . refers to a special manifestation occurring in the interpersonal relationship of a transference situation." [11] That is exactly how the patient would have it, if permitted. Correct technique demands that it not be allowed to remain in that state of projection and displacement. Considerations of diagnosis and tact in timing dictate when it is to be reduced by interpretation. However, it is useful to remember that transference serves only to illuminate, but must not become the ultimate field of struggle in such instances, for only when the patient stops struggling with the therapist can he begin to deal with his intrapsychic and intersystemic conficts and—as this contribution suggests—with his developmental lags as well.

This approach calls for a special quality in the therapeutic alliance, which is usually regarded as restricted to alliance with the patient's intact ego. Two extensions of the concept of therapeutic alliance suggest themselves here. First, the pragmatic one that the therapist ally

[11] E. R. Zetzel (reporter), "Defense Mechanisms and Psychoanalytic Technique," p. 321.

himself with whatever allies are offered, consonant with reality. Few
indeed are the patients who do not expect magical solutions to their
difficulties through alliance with an omnipotent, overidealized figure.
Except for those special situations described by Kohut, it is not desirable to play in with such magical expectations. It need not be disturbing to the therapist to respond with the most gentle humility, reject-
ing the magic attributed to him, but at the same time respecting the
unconscious wishes of the patient for the purpose of finding common
ground. Patients do not want to get better for the "right reasons" and
always, when resistance thickens, it remains a major task to help
them want to get better at all. There need be no fear of a compromise
in temporary alliance with whatever the patient offers initially. The
surgeon does not hesitate to rely on sutures, temporarily, to hold tissue
together until healing takes place. Similarly, the therapist can aid in
the support and sometimes even in the creation of motivation by accepting the resistance as a manifestation of levels of development—
of object relations, anxiety, identity, positive and negative ego identifications, and the like. This position removes the danger of viewing
initial resistance as realistic opposition.

It is also useful to bear in mind that the therapeutic alliance, at its
best, is not reciprocal. From this it follows that the therapist remains
an ally despite the patient's best efforts to dislodge him from this post.
The therapeutic alliance fluctuates markedly, if not wildly, on the patient's side, despite the widely held belief that there can be a steadfast
ego which remains constant in the treatment. It harries a patient to
expect object constancy of him, for example, before therapy has had
the opportunity to help him attain that particular developmental position, if that is his problem. Beginning therapists, in particular, are
burdened with the illusion that one can find the patient who will remain steadfast in the face of beginning errors because of "good motivation." It is not a truism that the "better" the motivation, the less
the resistance. We do not really find it so desirable to have patients
without resistance, even though, when this takes the form of apparent
absence of motivation, it confronts us with difficult technical problems. Since resistance is ubiquitous, the well-motivated patient is not
likely to be any poorer in that commodity than the unmotivated one.

There can be no greater appreciation for the value of resistance in the therapeutic endeavor than that expressed by Freud: "Thus the course of this treatment illustrates a maxim whose truth has long been appreciated in the technique of analysis. The length of the road over which an analysis must travel with the patient, and the quantity of material which must be mastered on the way, are of no importance in comparison with the resistance which is met with in the course of the work, and are only of importance at all in so far as they are necessarily proportional to the resistance." [12]

Returning to the clinical vignettes presented earlier, we now illustrate the technical moves more specifically. The patient who began with the need for "only a little help" was stating his conflict, although its derivation cannot yet be clear. The possibilities extend from fear of the symbiotic wish for merger with the negatively cathected, poorly differentiated self-object, on the one end, to the other diagnostic pole in which a relatively well-structured individual has become baffled by unconscious pressures he cannot understand. A very common example of the latter are those good-enough parents who become confused by the sporadic rages of an adolescent child which alternate with more placid intervals. The therapist's response must therefore leave room for all eventualities—even that only a little help is really what is required. "When I understand your situation more, I will be better able to respond to what you need," does not get the therapist entangled in challenging the form of request. This is a fundamental step in the direction of establishing a therapeutic alliance; it accepts the patient's autonomy in determining his approach behavior, but leaves the way open to introduce the therapist's professional opinion when that is formed.

This technical directive extends to patients such as the man who was so terrified that his request for a "little help" was in blatant disproportion to his anxiety, and to parents who can be helped to understand their adolescent child's behavior in a relatively short time. In the latter instance, even if the parents are evidencing their overinvolvement—such as their own problem with the child's separation-individuation process—it is not always useful to draw them into treatment immediately, even though often this can be done. They

[12] S. Freud, *From the History of an Infantile Neurosis,* pp. 11–12.

may well misconstrue their therapeutic involvement as a means of fending off their own anxieties about separation, and thus begin treatment under a most serious misconception, namely that they can usefully remain excessively involved in the adolescent's confused oscillations and remain participants in it. A more desirable therapeutic goal would be to help them to extricate themselves from the child's arena of conflict, thus protecting both him and them from grinding each other down in the adolescent's developmental struggle.

We have found it heuristically useful to parse this opening sentence in motivational (not grammatical) form: "I only need (a) little help" has five meaningful words. The second and fourth words express the motivational problem caused by the resistance, whereas the first, third, and fifth words spell out clearly, "I need help." This is an excellent example of the use of evenly suspended attention as described by Freud.

The young woman who is already clear about her direction and who wants to talk her situation over once can also be met on the terms of her approach. "Since you have taken the trouble to arrange this consultation, I am of course quite ready to consider your situation with you. I must add that at this point I cannot be certain that we will be able to fulfill your hopes of resolving completely the uncertainty which brought you here, but we can try." Once again, her opening gambit goes unchallenged, but the way is left open to explore the situation further. A therapeutic alliance is thus proffered, for the moment on her terms. As the discussion develops, the therapist can form some professional judgments of what is being defended, and of the state of object relations.

As these aspects of internalizations become clarified in the discussion, opportunities for further therapeutic involvement, if this is indicated, will open up and may be used without challenge. In this particular situation—a proposed separation and divorce—discontent with the spouse manifested itself primarily around their different interests and their difficulty in finding common ground. Since these differences had not prevented their mutual pleasure in the marriage for the first years, during which a wanted child was born, the next question was not only obvious to the therapist, but had relevance and interest to the patient. "What was it that caused this shift?" The possibilities are still quite broad—Is it difficulty in tolerating differences (symbiotic needs) which had been obscured for a while by the sexual needs? Did the arrival of a child and the consequent necessity for ongoing progression to the developmental-phase level of parenthood find them unready? Whatever problem emerges will, of course, be grist for the therapeutic mill.

The college student who demanded direction does not seem at first glance to lack initial motivation. He is included here, however, to illuminate the fact that the problems he will present in treatment will be serious. Where resistance exists, we can be certain that an ego is functioning defensively. The crucial diagnostic issue here is whether this young man's request represents confident expectation of a benign experience, or whether it is the far more morbid expression of total yielding which would mean too great readiness to surrender the prerogatives of identity and autonomy. If the latter is so, then this may be seen as the poorest kind of motivation, since not growth but regressive symbiosis is sought. "Since you are so ready to put yourself in my hands, you must have become totally baffled; perhaps as we talk about your difficulties we will be able to see why your own attempts at problem solving failed." Such an opening response safeguards the patient from rapid regression because of symbiotic wish, or safeguards his autonomy if he is on a higher level of development.

Often deductions are made in attempt to distinguish between phrases such as "My son has a problem" and "I have a problem with my son." The latter statement would seem to indicate that the patient is closer to locating the problem in herself and that she would therefore be better motivated. Once again, this is based on the illusion that there are individuals who resist more, as compared with others who resist less. In either situation, what will really matter is the therapy itself and how the patient is helped toward participating in the therapeutic process. Since there will undoubtedly be defense, unconscious, lags or hindrances in the myriad lines of development, the therapist needs at first only to pursue the path on which the patient is willing to embark. From that point on, the therapist's knowledge can help him find some way of connecting with the resistance rather than of fighting it. "I have no faith in therapy," can be met with, "I'm sure you have very good reasons for your feelings but since you have taken the trouble to come, let us try to see whether there is any way for me to help you. Faith is not a requirement and can even be a hindrance."

The patient whose fear of separation is so intense that she "just wants to die" is evincing a morbid fear of abandonment. While her psychic structure may not necessarily be at the level of fear of annihilation, it is essential to make some determination as to whether her situation is analogous to infantile marasmus, or whether it represents dramatization reflective of higher stages of development. "You are obviously feeling so hopeless about yourself. Let *us* look together at your situation to try to determine what may be causing such intense distress." Here the offer of a therapeutic alliance may provide sufficient, albeit attenuated, symbiotic gratification to enable her to participate in exploration of the impending separation and of previous experiences with separation in order to learn what her responses were then. If this patient is indeed on an early level of need gratification and fear of annihilation, she will require a balance of gratification and frustration in the therapy. Such a patient may be offered more frequent appointments and telephone privileges. On the other hand, should she telephone at 2:00 A.M. and then complain that the therapist sounds sleepy, the therapist may ask, "How did you expect me to sound?" Her needs, which reproduce the early experience of the infant crying for mother, can then be used to help her develop greater frustration tolerance within the benign atmosphere of the therapeutic alliance.

Where motivation is obscured by legal stricture, the task of discovering it is more difficult. A couple referred by a Family Court Justice may resent this step and may arrive for consultation full of their resentment. The therapist may nonetheless offer a useful service in pointing out that they have already performed their legal obligation by arriving, but as long as they have come, perhaps the time could be put to use. Youthful offenders remanded for treatment, while even more difficult, also require some affirmation of their autonomy by giving them choice to use or waste the time, even though they have been deprived of the opportunity to decide volitionally whether to seek treatment. In such manner, the therapist dissociates himself from the legal requirement in an attempt to gain a therapeutic alliance. However, while affirming autonomy, the therapist should not blind himself to the facts of the situation. "It was your own activity that brought you here and it may be useful to you to have some help in figuring out how you got into trouble," pays due respect to the facts and also to the patient's autonomy.

Concept formation in psychoanalytic theory has developed along many different pathways. Here we have offered a small sampling of the history of approach to weak or uncertain motivation. Technical approach was well formulated by Freud, conceptualized in his papers on technique, and illuminated by his case histories, especially that of the Wolf Man. Sharpe, in the period before expansion of ego psychology, intuitively understood that it is well to "go along with" [13] the patient. Hartmann expanded the theoretical rationale, especially in his illumination of the importance of tracing the role of the ego: "It is, however, true and also natural that pure phenomenological description of the details of the *mental superficies* [italics added], which we could disregard previously, is essential for and attains a special importance in ego psychology. But we will probably all agree that these phenomenological details, which nowadays command our interest, serve us merely as points of departure." [14]

Since then, many writers have detailed the application of these concepts and suggested the expansion of them. Thus we are led to a minute examination of the superficies of the presenting request which serves as a point of departure for both diagnostic study and therapeutic intervention.

[13] E. F. Sharpe, *Collected Papers on Psycho-Analysis*, p. 34.
[14] H. Hartmann, *Ego Psychology and the Problem of Adaptation*, pp. 6–7.

≫ 12 ≪

RECONSTRUCTION OF
PREVERBAL EXPERIENCE

T HE EARLY YEARS OF LIFE are spent in a special kind of silence. Before the child begins to speak he vocalizes. Yet vocalization is communication totally inadequate for expression of thought and only to a limited degree does it serve as an avenue for expression of affect. There is, at the beginning of life, no structured ego through which discharge may be channeled. Even when speech is acquired, although structuralization has by then come a long way, much is nonverbally experienced. Even after speech is acquired it takes at least seven years for the child to become capable of abstract thought and to be able to communicate it. For the psychotherapist who is to treat an adult patient years later, it is useful to know that, as an infant and young child, his patient lived in a state in which emotion and complex thought were not cathected to language.

The attuned mother would contend that the infant's vocalizations communicate a great deal and, indeed, it is not at all difficult for a listener to distinguish the infant's sounds of anger or distress from his cooings of contentment. Yet, much goes on internally that cannot be communicated by vocalization. The most fortunate infant—one who is endowed at birth with adequate inborn ego apparatuses and who arrives into an average expectable environment—experiences comfort and frustration within the context of burgeoning object relations. Transfer of libidinous and aggressive energy provides the ego with the motive power to build its functions, including the very complex function of verbalization. But in the early weeks of life before drive differentiation, discharge is largely to the inside. Even vocalization is limited by the time span; mostly the neonate is asleep. As the sleep-waking pattern begins to reverse, ever-increasing opportunity for perception brings wide-eyed wonderment and experimentation with motoric, tactile, auditory, olfactory, and visual capacities. The comfort-discomfort cycle revolves mainly around the gestalt of the feeding experience in which representations of self and object, even while still merged, lead the fortunate child to optimistic expectations. These, although never directly remembered in words, will reflect in later attitudes toward self and others. The importance of self and object representations to motivation for treatment was discussed in chapter 11. These also determine, to a large extent, whether the transference and working alliance will be predominantly positive and cooperative. The person who has had good objects in childhood naturally expects good results from his efforts and that of the therapist. If the therapist trains himself to think in developmental diagnostic terms, he thinks all the time about these kinds of reflections from the past.

In the latter half of the first year of life, as motility and intentionality increase, the ongoing process of gradual differentiation between self and object representations is accelerated by the ability to turn oneself over, crawl, sit, stand, and ultimately to walk and to run. Since crying and other forms of vocalization are in part motoric, they may be included in this consideration of the range of the infant's ability to express himself, to move, to perceive, to think, to feel, and thus to discover differences between self and object representations on the road toward establishment of discrete identity. At this stage of life the needs of the infant are understood by the "good-enough mother" [1] because her willingness to lend herself to these needs is facilitated by their simplicity. Crying may mean "I am hungry, lonely, in pain, cold, frustrated," and not much else. However, there are emotions which are not so simple, such as surprise, pain, fright, dismay, disappointment and, above all, rage. Except for rage, these are not so easily "read." Vocalization other than crying usually expresses feelings of pleasure, including the pleasure of exercising the vocal apparatus in

---

[1] D. W. Winnicott, "Transitional Objects and Transitional Phenomena," p. 94.

preparation for speech. The infant's crying, cooing, and gurgling are, in good circumstances, bent in the service of growing object relations by the mother's tendency to respond in the same "language." The sound of one's own voice and the response of other human voices pave the way to the eventual establishment of speech as the uniquely human form of communication.

Another avenue of preverbal discharge, the psychosomatic, has long been known but little understood. Reference is made to "body language" or "organ language." These phrases are intriguing in their simplicity, but remain more descriptive than enlightening. True, the infant "speaks" with his body before his vocal apparatus matures and before vocabulary is available, and a sort of body language remains with us throughout life in the gestures and postures that sometimes accompany and sometimes substitute for speech. But the process of translating so-called organ language into something communicable is immensely complex. If the body speaks, it speaks to itself. Except for the early weeks of life, when silent physiological discharge to the inside is appropriate, the body distorts itself when organs with specialized functions are misused for purposes for which they are not designed. The three major avenues for drive discharge in the adult are the vocal, genital, and motor apparatuses. They provide optimal relief of instinctual tension when used in the service of the ego. We do not imply that every instance of employment of other organs is necessarily pathological. The gesticulating arm does not become permanently distorted, nor does a momentary grimace remain forever frozen. But repeated automatic use of the *vital* organs as pathways for discharge in lieu of communication through the vocal apparatus can damage these organs sometimes irreversibly, as, for example, the use of the gastrointestinal tract for drive discharge instead of for digestion and elimination. Whether organ use becomes abuse depends upon whether the specialized functions are developed and maintained. When the ego is in control of the organs of speech, other parts of the body may be used to some extent as accessories to verbalization, but never do they constitute the dominant avenue of expression and discharge. Schur's technical procedure for the reversal of somatization takes into account the centrality of object relations in contemporary

ego psychology. By rebuilding object relations, deneutralization is reversed. The ego, thus strengthened, is encouraged to use verbal instead of somatic pathways for discharge.

Schur's contribution to the understanding of somatization extends
Freud's work on acting out versus remembering. Freud recommended,
technically, that what was being expressed in motoric form is to be
verbalized instead. He was referring, however, to verbally cathected
memories which were repressed and which could be retrieved by hy-
percathexis. This technique is applicable to material from late childhood when structuralization, normally, has proceeded. The younger
child experiences much before structuralization, and before he acquires speech. It is widely believed that preverbal experience is irre-
trievable. Greenacre suggests that acting may represent expression of
thought and especially of affect which had never been cathected
to language. And so it is sometimes appropriate in the treatment of
adult patients to encourage verbal cathexis of preverbal experience as
a way of enabling the now-structured ego to gain control retroactively. But acting out, whether in Freud's terms as a resistance in
treatment or in Greenacre's terms as a means of expressing preverbal
trauma, is not the same as somatization. On a continuum, somatization may be thought of as a regression beyond acting out—that is,
discharge upon the soma takes place in a less-structured state than
does motoric discharge, and neither somatization nor acting out is as
much under the control of a well-structured ego as is verbalization.

The impact of these additions to Freud's metapsychological consideration of acting out cannot be overstressed in the treatment of the
nonneurotic patient whose early, and therefore preverbal, life experience was so traumatic that the ego could not develop to organize a
neurosis. Such patients are prone to act. Some therapists hope that an
interpretation will put an end to the action. Disappointed therapists
come to supervision with, "I interpreted and he still acted out." The
technical fallacy is failure to understand that interpretation can reach
the patient only if it is connected with verbally cathected material.
The nonneurotic patient acts on what he cannot remember, not as resistance, but because the action *is* his way of "remembering" preverbal trauma. He "speaks" with his feet when he walks out of a session,
for example. He may be saying, "The thing that hurt me most as a

baby was to be left. As soon as I could walk I made up my mind to show the other person how that feels by doing it to him." Interpretation of this, if it can help the patient cathect the memory and affect, is often effective. The beginning therapist is to be cautioned, however, not to forget the principle of working through lest he be disappointed that one reconstructive interpretation fails to stop the action once and for all.

If the therapist will wait, he can rely upon the repetition compulsion to bring the past into the present. When the therapeutic situation becomes the arena for reliving trauma, it presents the therapist with the unique opportunity to help the ego attain true mastery. Therapy may be described as the place where the compulsion to repeat is brought to an end. This is another reason that the therapist does not join in; interaction more often than not reinforces persistence of the repetition compulsion. Insofar as it influences reconstruction, the fact that preverbal experience repeats itself makes it retrievable if the therapist, unlike the patient, distinguishes accurately between past and present.

In the Eighteenth Freud Anniversary Lecture of the New York Psychoanalytic Society, Anna Freud said that her father had found little or no evidence that it was possible to deal therapeutically with preverbal experience, although he recognized that the preverbal period was an important developmental era. A considerable number of analysts today, she stated, depart from this view and attempt to analyze the first year of life. She said:

Any attempt to carry analysis from the verbal to the preverbal period of development brings with it practical and technical innovations as well as theoretical implications, many of which are controversial.

What strikes the observer first is a change in the type of *psychic material* with which the analysis is dealing. Instead of exploring the disharmonies between the various agencies within a structured personality, the analyst is concerned with the events which lead from the chaotic, undifferentiated state toward the initial building up of a psychic structure. This means going beyond the area of intrapsychic conflict, which had always been the legitimate target for psychoanalysis, and into the darker area of interaction between innate endowment and environmental influence. The implied aim is to undo or to counteract the impact of the very forces on which the rudiments of personality development are based.

Analysts who work for this aim assure us that this can be achieved . . .
I myself cannot help feeling doubtful about trying to advance into the
area of primary repression, i.e., to deal with processes which, by nature,
are totally different from the results of the ego's defensive maneuvers with
which we feel familiar.[2]

Anna Freud went on to discuss the heightened significance of communication through the transference and added:

It is, in fact, this central and unique role given to the transference in the
psychoanalytic process, to the exclusion of all other avenues of communication, which is, to date, one of the points of controversy in the analytic
world. There is, further, the question whether the transference really has
the power to transport the patient back as far as the beginning of life.
Many are convinced that this is the case. Others, myself among them,
raise the point that it is one thing for preformed, object-related fantasies
to return from repression and be redirected from the inner to the outer
world (i.e., to the person of the analyst); but that it is an entirely different, almost magical expectation to have the patient in analysis change
back into the prepsychological, undifferentiated, and unstructured state, in
which no divisions exist between body and mind or self and object.[3]

Brenner disputes not only preverbal interpretation per se, but the
entire area of investigation of the preverbal period of life by means of
direct infant observation. Logically, therefore, if investigation of preverbal life is excluded from acceptable scientific endeavor, then the
data upon which techniques for preverbal interpretation depend are
invalidated and treatment based upon such theory and technique is
unacceptable. Brenner says:

The psychoanalytic method depends on communication, and primarily on
verbal communication, i.e., on language. Its application yields reliable results concerning the mental processes of individuals who are sufficiently
developed to acquire and, in most instances, to use language. . . . The
fact is that we have as yet far less reliable information concerning the psychology of the early period of post-natal life than we should like to have,
despite the several programmes of study that have been conducted in recent years by psychoanalytically trained observers.[4]

---

[2] A. Freud, *Difficulties in the Path of Psychoanalysis: A Confrontation of Past with
Present Viewpoints*, pp. 38–39.
[3] *Ibid.*, pp. 40–41.
[4] C. Brenner, "The Psycho-Analytic Concept of Aggression," p. 140.

The positions of Anna Freud and Brenner are representative of those of a number of psychoanalysts today.

In the Twentieth Freud Anniversary Lecture of the New York Psychoanalytic Society, Mahler took indirect issue with Anna Freud's position in the Eighteenth Anniversary Lecture. Mahler said: "Psychoanalytic observational research of the first years of life touches on the essence of reconstruction and on the problem of coenesthetic empathy, both so essential for the clinical efficiency of psychoanalysis." [5] There is, she continued, a spectrum of opinion. At one end are Melanie Klein and her followers whose *a priori* opinions cannot be refuted by behavioral data.

At the other end of the spectrum stand those among us Freudian analysts who look with favor on stringent verbal and reconstructive evidence. We organize these on the basis of Freud's metapsychological constructs; yet some of us seem to accord preverbal material no right to serve as the basis for even the most cautious and tentative extension of our main body of hypotheses, unless these, too, be supported by reconstruction, that is to say, by clinical and, of course, predominantly verbal material.

Yet Freud's hope was that his fundamental body of theory—that truly monumental basis of clinical and theoretical work—would remain a *living heritage*. Even his genius could not work out every detail in one lifetime; these, added bit by bit, should eventually coalesce to form a general psychology.[6]

Freud himself was somewhat more openminded on this issue than Anna Freud implies. He said: "The direct observation of children has the disadvantage of working upon data which are easily misunderstandable; psycho-analysis is made difficult by the fact that it can only reach its data, as well as its conclusions, after long detours. But by co-operation the two methods can attain a satisfactory degree of certainty in their findings." [7]

Most vexing for therapists are the silent patient and the so-called acting-out patient. Silence, all too often, is regarded, *at least* peevishly and *at worst* judgmentally, as the most blatant violation of free association. It is inconsistent with the concept of the "talking cure." Traditionally, it is regarded as a resistance, usually the withholding of

[5] M. S. Mahler, "A Study of the Separation-Individuation Process: And Its Possible Application to Borderline Phenomena in the Psychoanalytic Situation," p. 404.
[6] *Ibid.*   [7] S. Freud, *Three Essays on the Theory of Sexuality,* p. 201.

negative thoughts in the transference. In 1961, the American Psychoanalytic Association held an all-day symposium on this irksome
problem, and it began to be suggested that there could be more to it
—that perhaps silence could represent the wish to be together with
the mother. There ensued a rash of interpretations of silence as, "I am
your baby-sitter." This was a half-truth because theory and technique
had not developed sufficiently to understand this kind of silence at
that time. At the 1971 meetings of the American Psychoanalytic Association, Ross pointed out that this kind of silence represents the
symbiotic wish. Thus, it took ten years for theory and technique to illuminate an aspect of silence that resonates with preverbal life. By
definition, this kind of silence cannot be verbalized. It is up to the
therapist to help the patient apply words to a wish to be together
without words, to be understood without words, to be one with the
therapist. This is far from the judgmental, "You are withholding."
There are patients who are silent because they are withholding, but
those have neurotic structures and are anally fixated or regressed.
Even in such cases, we have not known this kind of silence to yield to
an accusation disguised as an interpretation.

Mr. Dickens telephoned one evening—an unusual event in
itself—because he was facing a difficult business meeting the next
morning. He did not identify himself by name, but expected that the
therapist would recognize his voice, which he did. Then he said,
"About tomorrow morning," to which the therapist said, still on the
phone, "How can I help you with it?" They had a brief conversation
and Mr. Dickens seemed to feel better. Next session he reported that
the meeting had gone well, but he was depressed. As Mr. Dickens
worked on this, it turned out that he was depressed because the therapist had failed to know the purpose of his call without having to be
told. It did not suffice that the therapist had recognized his voice and
had remembered about his business problem. He should have responded to his telephone call in a totally symbiotic fashion. Although
we have said that the symbiotically deprived patient needs some symbiotic gratification from the therapist, this case illustrates how impossible it is to gratify it all. Nevertheless, the problem can be dealt with
empathically and with helpfulness in providing verbal cathexis to it.
Sometimes it is even desirable to sit with the patient in silence. But

then both patient and therapist have to be comfortable in the situation. We have heard of outrages perpetrated upon patients such as reading a book or tending to one's correspondence because the patient is not talking. A more respectful approach might be, "I am not sure whether you want me to end the silence."

The preverbal child has no sense of time. This manifests itself in a frequently encountered ego regression in the adult patient. G. Blanck said:

. . . a patient is kept waiting by the analyst, or thinks he is. He enters the consultation room in great anxiety. The traditional interpretation would refer to death wishes toward the analyst. This does indeed apply. But exploration of the fantasies that occurred while waiting often brings material that makes for more precise interpretation of the exact experience that led to the aggressive wishes in childhood. It makes possible the reconstruction of preverbal trauma, providing the ego with the possibility of mastery. The technique suggested for this purpose is to solicit the minute details of the fantasy. Thus, whether you were there or absent; whether you had forgotten the patient; whether you were having sexual intercourse; whether you were otherwise engaged and too busy to care about the patient; whether you were angry with him for needing you, etc.; all offer clues which point to the . . . original trauma as revived in the transference. Another patient, who suffers from functional gastritis, clings to predominantly negative object representations. The clinical picture is masochistic-like. The impression is that, while object relations are indeed firmly established, they are connected with unpleasant early experience with an aggressive, unloving mother. The precise nature of this early trauma was clarified when the patient reported that one evening, when depressed, he had wanted to telephone the analyst. However, he decided against it. Detailed questioning about what went into this decision was the technique which led to understanding much about early feeding experiences. The next thought after the wish to telephone was that the analyst would be impatient with him, would rush him, would hang up the telephone if he could not say what was on his mind quickly enough. Here we find the repetition of hurried and unsatisfying feedings. The patient was asked whether he is in the habit of eating quickly. He was not at all surprised at the question and was able to connect his current attitudes with the genetic experience and to understand more about his "loyalty" to the negative primary object.[8]

[8] G. Blanck, "Some Technical Implications of Ego Psychology," p. 12.

The controversy about the therapeutic potential in trying to deal with preverbal experience is well taken at this stage of our knowledge and experience because, it has to be acknowledged, successful reconstruction of preverbal experience is as yet rare. We are here in pioneering territory once more, and only time and experience will make possible such modifications in technique as to assure frequent success. Meanwhile, there is value in understanding a patient's behavior in the light of repetition of his preverbal experience even if it is not used directly with him in the form of a reconstructive interpretation. Such understanding on the part of the therapist can be used diagnostically, as we shall demonstrate, to broaden immeasurably the therapist's grasp of the case. It was Kris's pioneering work that illuminated the therapeutic importance of creating a climate conducive to remembering. While he agreed that anamnestic data itself might not be recoverable, because of the telescoping of events, condensation, distortion, and other defensive vicissitudes, yet he felt there was great value in uncovering the defensive patterns, which in turn could lead to the lifting of defensive countercathexes. Preverbal experiences unquestionably contribute to the establishment of patterns; recognition of the existence of the patterns can provide both patient and therapist with a more profound view of the patient's past.

It is well to raise the question of why verbalization is of such central importance in psychoanalytically oriented psychotherapy, especially while many nonanalytic therapies advocate more primitive forms of expression such as acting out, ventilation, experiencing, encountering, touching, confronting, and so on. We have already mentioned that verbalization is not a simple act, but a complex process. Speech and verbalization are not synonymous. Hartmann shows how the schizophrenic who has learned to speak uses words as things. Without the bridge of distinct self and object representations and acceptance of the reality principle, the psychotic has not acquired (or has lost regressively) secondary process thought; neither does he have a true object with whom to communicate. The major ego functions which enter into the complex function of verbalization are, more or less in order of their development: object comprehension, intentionality, object relations, symbolization, speech, semantic communication —all powered by neutralized drive energy.

Speech, at the outset, consists of global words. Spitz traces in fine detail the complex ego development which paves the way for speech. And yet, the thought or affect behind the first spoken words remains relatively unexpressed. One word, best understood by the attuned mother in the symbiotic union, may contain myriad meanings. Piaget believes that the word "Mama" is formed by jaw and mouth movements which are only one step beyond sucking. The child who utters this global word may be saying, "I am hungry"; "I am afraid"; "I am content"; "Where are you?"; "I see you and remember that it is you who usually brings me comfort," and so on. But he may not even be communicating to that degree; he may be moving his lips and jaw in coordination with the vocal apparatus, thereby unifying these with recognition of the object in the beginning process of symbolization by means of cathecting mental representation with the word.

As the child proceeds in his conquest of language and begins to speak in grammatically constructed sentences, these tend at first to be concrete. "I want my teddy bear." Subject, verb, and predicate contain, but do not convey, "I feel lonely and the texture, odor, and closeness of Teddy Bear comfort me by reminding me of the closeness of Self and Mother that has felt so good in the past." Or take the sentence, "I won't." A sentence, yes, but it does not necessarily mean, "I refuse to do as you say." It may mean, "I begin to feel more like a person in my own right and I have noticed that when I refuse it creates a stir, so I am trying out my newly discovered power—to disconcert the adults." Or, "You have said 'no' to me so many times, which frustrated me and made me angry, and, because I felt so separate from you at such moments, anxiety came from realization that we are no longer one. But it has its compensation because now I can have the same sort of power by imitating your refusal to which I have been subjected so many distressing times, and this will show you how it feels to be on the receiving end of a 'no.' "

It may be remembered that psychoanalysis used to be called the "talking cure." Psychoanalysis and psychoanalytically oriented psychotherapy remain verbal forms of treatment to this day, despite innovative therapies which promote regressive modes of discharge. Fromm even discusses with nostalgia *The Forgotten Language* of the primary process. From the ego psychological point of view, to be able to communicate and to understand the communications of others in the primary process is questionable therapy except for psychotics, because it would make inroads upon identity, autonomy, and would impair many ego functions, particularly the synthetic and integrative functions, but also symbolization, object relations, intentionality, frustration tolerance, reality testing—including ability to distinguish inside from outside—and the defensive function. To put it another way, the ego would be relatively inoperative and structuralization would suffer.

Nor is every experience necessarily therapeutic. We have heard sincere reports of exhilarating experience in encounter groups, for example. To break down inhibition, to encourage closeness, to attack defenses, to ventilate unneutralized libido and aggression, are not ego building. In fact, for the nonneurotic patient, it is a necessary therapeutic goal to help him to acquire distance from the other person as part of the process of acquiring identity. The aloof patient is usually so because he has no objects or, if less disturbed than that, because, by maintaining distance, he is defending against loss of identity through merger. In either type of structure, psychotic or borderline, forcing closeness is harmful; ventilation exposes the ego to more than it can tolerate, exhilarating as such experience may be. Schur clarifies that affect, to be mastered by the ego, must be understood in the light of its genesis; ventilation without such connection can have no therapeutic value. The mechanical principle that a person, like a steam engine, needs to blow off, refutes itself as soon as it is stated.

Verbalization protects identity by guarding privacy. The fact that one has to convey one's thoughts to another person implies differentiation of self and other. Many borderline and psychotic patients come to the therapist with the conviction that their minds can be read. They hold such notions because, relating in the symbiotic mode, they assume that there are no boundaries between themselves and others. Some are quite terrified over this threat to an already-shaky identity and are relieved to know that the therapist cannot know anything not told him. Others, with symbiotic longing, are disappointed when the therapist cannot read their minds. Mrs. Hartley (chapter 9) became enraged because the therapist did not know her husband's and his secretary's first names; the rage arose from the disappointment about separateness and the work involved in having to tell. Some patients say openly that they would like it if the therapist could know all without the patient having to go to the trouble of saying it. Some fear that the therapist will know too much, and such patients resort to interesting defensive devices to prevent this. For example, some try, during their sessions, not to have thoughts, so that there will be nothing for the therapist to read. The best technical procedure for those with so much fear of closeness is to allow them to maintain their distance until they are assured that the danger is diminished. In direct contrast with the basic rule of free association, regarded as a must in the psychoanalytic treatment of neurosis, the borderline patient has to be encouraged not only to respect the defense of keeping his distance, but sometimes he has also to be assured that he need not say everything. This builds his decision-making ability so that eventually, when he feels safer, he will tell everything. But then he will do so out of volition, in alliance with the therapeutic purpose, and not because the therapist wishes to intrude.

Miss Rosenberg was so afraid of losing identity in merging with the therapist that she sat at the far end of the room for more than a year before she could risk moving closer. She said little, carefully guarding her privacy. The arrangements—frequency, time of day of the sessions, and the like—were thought of as being for the therapist. This paranoid tinge was particularly evident in her accusations that whatever she were to tell the therapist would be for him. The therapist said, "If it is for me, do not do it," thus making it possible for Miss Rosenberg eventually to comply with the therapeutic necessities for herself.

It is not difficult to get patients to comply with rules. Why they comply is of central importance in ego building for, if they are obliging the therapist, that will not serve growth. In these sophisticated days, patients have to be assured that their desire for privacy is not "resistance." Such assurance captures the developmental lesion from childhood when the patient reached, let us say, the beginnings of separation-individuation only to be deterred by a residue of unneutralized aggression. Mahler and Spitz show that aggression can only be used for growth in its neutralized mode. Many persons remain fixated in symbiotic union because they fear that separation will destroy both them and the object.

Mr. Sweeney feared the therapist's intrusion. He came for treatment because he could not tolerate his wife's demands that he be with her all the time and tell her everything. She even resented his going to work. He felt guilty about his withdrawal from her and wanted to remedy this. The therapist said that everyone needs privacy sometimes. Mr. Sweeney found this most relieving. The therapist's purpose was not simply to alleviate guilt, but to pave the way for appreciation of where, in childhood, Mr. Sweeney's separation-individuation strivings had reached an impasse. It was discovered that his mother, a manic-depressive, had had to be hospitalized when he was two years old and that his childhood fantasy inevitably connected her disappearance with his aggressive thoughts and feelings. He felt guilty thereafter whenever he ventured to use aggression in the service of proceeding in his impeded development, and so this constituted the point of fixation in his ego development, already shaky because he had a mentally ill mother.

The development of the ego and its functions is seen as the decisive factor in determining whether the form of expression is appropriate to the purpose of treatment. Some patients write notes to the therapist between sessions or keep diaries they want the therapist to read. In many instances, particularly at the outset of treatment, it is ungracious to reject such material out of hand and the therapist has to compromise and accept the written material temporarily. The purpose, always, is to encourage the patient to tell the therapist directly what he wants him to know. Artists sometimes bring their paintings, from which one can sometimes learn a great deal. It has to be decided by the therapist, however, whether circumvention of verbalization in such instances serves the patient's growth. Often, without being rude or injuring these very sensitive patients' narcissism, one can convey the desirability of verbalization. "I read your letter and appreciate the effort you are making to communicate. Won't it be a triumph when you can say all that to me face to face and not have to go to the trouble of writing?"

For purposes of proposing techniques for reconstruction of preverbal material, we extend the preverbal era to include that span of life when verbalization has been acquired as an ego function but is not yet dominant. The duration of this "silent" period of life is longer than we customarily think it to be. Child therapists recognize this in the substitution of play for verbalization because the child cannot convey the complexity of his thought and affect in words. The adult patient has to be helped to acquire or to improve a function which, even in normal childhood, takes many years. In the case material to follow we illustrate how understanding preverbal life deepens diagnosis and, in some instances, makes reconstruction possible.

Mr. Turner, who had been in treatment for nearly a year, came for his session on time. He rang the doorbell and waited to hear the familiar return buzzer which gives him entry. Unknown to the therapist, who had pressed the response button, the mechanism was inoperative and the patient was not admitted. No more than two minutes had elapsed before the therapist, not having found Mr. Turner in the waiting room, went to the front door. He was depressed and this mood was not very quickly dispelled even after the session was well under way. Such a chance event becomes the material of choice for the session unless something of great importance in the patient's life has occurred since the last session. When the therapist voiced recognition of the lowered mood, Mr. Turner commented that he always felt this way when he was kept waiting. The therapist asked whether it felt different to be kept waiting outside the door than at other times. Mr. Turner had described in previous sessions how impatient he got while waiting for traffic lights to change, for service in a restaurant, for his wife to get ready when they were about to do something together, and he had even described his tendency to ejaculate prematurely because managing to wait was not always under good control.[9]

[9] We are not proposing a simple etiology of sex problems. In premature ejaculation, impatience is not the only determinant, but it tends very often to be contributory. Castration anxiety, which is central, is not dealt with here because we are using the case of Mr. Turner to illustrate that psychotherapeutic endeavors sometimes stop short of matters which, in psychoanalysis, would constitute most serious omission. We mean to demonstrate by such illustration that while psychoanalytic procedure would demand addressing oneself to castration anxiety and concomitant problems arising out of the phallic-oedipal phase, the psychotherapy patient with the more severely impaired ego more often than not needs basic work in ego building, particularly on levels of anxiety such as fear of loss of the object, as in Mr. Turner's case, before he can deal with castration anxiety.

At the door, this time, there was no choice. Mr. Turner said that, had it taken much longer, he would have left. The immediate, therapeutic opportunity is to explore what went through his mind. In this manner, the therapist learned that Mr. Turner had no idea how long he had waited; it had seemed a very long time. The therapist did not rush in to say, whether defensively or merely informatively, that it was only two minutes. Rather, the ego regression wherein the ability to judge time is lost was noted in the therapist's mind: is ego regression characteristic for this patient when under stress?

Through continuing exploration of the material, the therapist learned also that Mr. Turner had thought that the therapist was not there at all that day, and probably had forgotten him. Again in the therapist's mind, a historical hypothesis formulated: was Mr. Turner, as an infant, kept waiting too long? One cannot seize on this hypothesis too eagerly. The opposite is also tenable; perhaps his every whim was met at a time when development would better have been furthered if the ego had had opportunity to stretch its frustration tolerance by having to wait a reasonable period. The evidence, however, is in the other direction, because the patient had said he would have gone away if the therapist had not come in another minute or two. This suggests rather strongly that waiting in infancy was not rewarded with gratification. There was no use waiting for the therapist then. Also, Mr. Turner thought that he had been forgotten. This tells the therapist that, very likely, the self and object representations are short of good enough. Mr. Turner does not realize that, to the therapist, he is well-enough cathected so that he cannot be forgotten so carelessly. Thus, the adult's verbalization of the fantasy while waiting (in this instance, "I thought you forgot") voices preverbal experience without direct memory. We say *voices* not *verbalizes* because we reserve the latter term for the process whereby the ego cathects experience with words used for semantic communication.

This case illustrates how understanding in depth is facilitated by listening with a keen ear for reflections of preverbal experience. But how does this help the therapeutic operation? Sometimes by making a reconstruction: "You must have been kept waiting too long before you were able to tolerate it, and thought, even before you could put such thoughts into words, that you had been forgotten." Such reconstruction must carry a great deal of conviction for the patient; it does not matter how thoroughly the therapist is convinced of the beauty of his hypothesis. In this case, as in most, it seemed wiser to keep the hypothesis filed away in the therapist's mind, the purpose being to await accumulation of evidence and better opportunity for the patient himself to make some connections.

It is essential to state that we do not at all advocate contrived situations such as keeping patients waiting; in fact we decry them. For the therapeutic situation to be one of absolute trust, no such arrangements or tricks of any sort are admissible. An untoward happenstance may be used, but usefulness is diminished to the point of no return if it is a contrivance. Some patients will say that these accidents, which do occur in the normal course of any therapist's practice, must have been arranged to test them, but that is another developmental diagnostic problem. Such responses, verging on the paranoid, are always a morbid sign so far as the development of the ego is concerned. They usually connote a degree of narcissism which is pathological if it persists beyond the time of infancy when the child thinks the world revolves around him. The fact that there are adult patients so fixated or regressed is in itself a potent argument against artificial arrangements which would only serve to confirm the self-reference at the expense of reality testing. It is essential to the support and building of realistic self and object representations that the patient be able to trust what is going on.

With Mr. Turner, the therapist waited several sessions while the patient kept more or less to the same theme of his problem about waiting. This consistent pursuit of a theme is the therapeutic reward for the therapist's exploitation of the material in the session already described. The patient realizes the significance of an apparently trivial and easily overlooked event and works on it further. Thus, the case is in less danger of becoming chaotic because he has found a theme that feels right and wants to explore it further. In the next session, therefore, Mr. Turner discussed his impatience at having had to wait for a red light while driving to his session. He nearly tried to jump the light, but he had too many violations already. He could not wait to come to this session. The therapist asked whether it had been easier to wait for other sessions. Mr. Turner thought it had been. He volunteered that this was because he was impatient to work on his impatience. He elaborated with material from the day before. His wife kept him waiting again when they were going to keep a social engagement. The therapist thought, but did not say, that soon Mr. Turner might tie this in with his sex problem. It turned out, however, that he did not do this as readily as the therapist had hoped. The therapist should not have too much stake in immediate outcome. It is the patient's treatment, and he will take his own time about it. It happened in this case (which is not unusual in psychotherapy) that the sex problem per se was not discussed as directly as the therapist had in mind, but his understanding sufficed to help Mr. Turner deal with the general theme of frustration tolerance to the point where his sexual functioning improved somewhat. This came about as Mr. Turner captured the theme and made it his own. In teaching and supervising beginning therapists we sometimes point out that a by-product of the ego psychological approach is that the work of the therapist becomes easier as the patient takes on more and more responsibility for his own treatment. Our true objective is not to relieve the therapist of necessary work, but to help him divide the labor so that, while the patient does his part, the therapist is freed to add developmental diagnostic thinking to the many other silent processes that go on in his mind in the patient's behalf.

As Mr. Turner went on with his therapeutic work he began to raise questions about his impaired ability to wait. The therapist treated them as rhetorical, thus encouraging Mr. Turner to continue in his efforts to answer his own questions. Providing a helping hand here and there, in simulation of the good mother who lends herself to phase specificity and the degree of ability to do for oneself, the therapist nudged Mr. Turner along with questions such as, "Well, try to figure out where and when this problem all started." It would be misleading to promise that this brings immediate and magical results. Mr. Turner's response was, "I can't." The therapist who reads this as, "You do it for me," is correct, but should not oblige. It is better, but not very much so, to say, "Try." The best response is, "Let us work on it together." This bridges the gap between Mr. Turner's limited capabilities and the desirability of having him do as much as possible himself.

It simulates good mothering which imposes just enough frustration to help the ego develop, but no more.

"Let's work on it together," is an offer and does imply that the therapist will make the next move. He must fulfill this lest he disappoint, and yet he must not take over the tasks that are best left to the patient's ego. The therapist said, "There is a time in our lives when it is hard to wait." Mr. Turner responded, "You mean when we are babies?" The therapist ignored the question mark. While a nod of assent would have done no great harm here, it was better to adhere to the principle that not all questions have to be answered. Here, the therapist did not want to interrupt the flow even with a nod, because Mr. Turner was getting as close as is possible to his hazy infancy. He did remember his mother of later years. He said, "Knowing my mother, she probably went by the book and fed me every four hours no matter what." We know that, under the influence of behaviorism, frustration beyond the capacity to endure was imposed upon some infants of the 1920s and 1930s. Mr. Turner's comment about his mother's rigidity rounded out the picture of her that the therapist was trying to construct in his own mind. It was consistent with other material Mr. Turner had presented about his mother—her bookishness and tendency to intellectualize at the expense of affect. To this was now added lack of maternal attunement in favor of the child-rearing fad of the time.

This case illustrates three major technical points: one, apparently trivial incidents sometimes bring to the surface fantasies which, if elicited, reveal much about attitudes that are deeply ingrained from childhood; two, such information may be used, at the very least, to formulate historical diagnostic hypotheses in the therapist's mind for deep understanding of the patient; and three, in optimal therapeutic opportunity, reconstruction of preverbal experience can be made.

Miss Loran's behavior was typical of that of many patients who have acquired speech but still use vocalization or a combination of speech and vocalization in ways that are often bewildering to the listener. She suffered from failure in neutralization of both drives because of callous mothering in infancy. She came to treatment as an adult, full of rage and almost immobilized by it, unable to function in the adult world, to earn a living, or to make meaningful relationships. Although she used words, she screamed them at the therapist and it was impossible to know the cause of her immediate rage. She attached it to real events of the moment, such as the color of the therapist's necktie. But the extent of her displeasure was so disproportionate that the therapist, as he became familiar with this behavior, realized that it was an expression of unneutralized aggression from early infancy, a time when feelings of nongratification were undefinable in words. She was expressing displeasure, projected upon the tie. The therapist did not attempt direct reconstructive interpretation because this would have been too far from where it could reach the patient. He said, "This may be the ugliest tie in the world, but that is not what is causing you to feel so continuously angry." Repeated statements of this sort, with slight variations as the situation dictates, must be made patiently without expectation of dramatic success. It may even be that the damage is so great that the ego will not be able to respond to the attempt to separate present from past, which is the necessary first step. If it should respond, the next move would be to aid neutralization—in this instance by moving on to Miss Loran's feelings about the object as a person, not about his necktie.

The following case illustrates how preverbal experience can be so fundamental to development that one cannot deal successfully with verbal levels until the earlier traumata are worked through.

Mr. Ventnor's presenting complaint suggested conversion, traditionally thought of as a hysterical symptom. Engaged in manual labor, he was on extended sick leave when referred to the therapist because the referring physician, after careful physical investigation, found no cause for severe pain in one leg. Rangell, in distinguishing conversion phenomena from somatization, states that conversion represents a higher level of ego organization and includes symbolization, whereas somatization may proceed by short-circuiting such ego involvement. Differential diagnosis is essential because the ego psychological approach to therapy requires that the therapist address himself precisely to the ego lesions. In Mr. Ventnor's case, exploration of precipitating factors revealed that the onset of pain coincided with his wife's fifth pregnancy. Mrs. Ventnor, however, had not suffered from phlebitis and so the hypothesis of simple hysterical identification was ruled out.

When Mr. Ventnor had been barely fourteen months old, a sibling had been born. The next diagnostic hypothesis, then, became that his mother, pregnant in his infancy, might have had phlebitis and thereby provided a dimly remembered leg problem with which Mr. Ventnor, as a toddler, identified. This is tenable because, at that stage of life, before identity is established, the merged self and object representations make for primitive identification with the object who is perceived as part of the self. Conversion was thus ruled out because the ego, at that stage of development, had not yet had the opportunity to reach full capacity to symbolize. Nor was this true somatization in Schur's sense because the adult symptom was based only in part on deneutralization.

The therapist decided that this was an arrest at a preoedipal stage of maternal identification. Such feminine identification remained and was revived during the wife's pregnancy. But the interesting question then arose: Why during the fifth pregnancy? This was a lower-middle-class Catholic couple, practicing no birth control, and faced, in their early thirties, with the prospect of a larger family than they could tolerate financially and psychologically. Mr. Ventnor's deeply repressed hostile attitude toward his own children had its base in his early years when no such feelings toward siblings were permissible. Educated in parochial schools and devout in his religious adherence, he believed consciously what he had been taught—that he was fulfilling his masculine function in being husband, father, and provider. The conflict erupted at this time and found its solution in regression to nondifferentiation. Then Mr. Ventnor could, without guilt, stop working because of the pain. He could rejoin his mother in the merged ego identifications of that early time of life, with the unconscious objective of regaining some of the gratifications of that merged state instead of the rigorous requirements of the adult masculine role that had been imposed upon him prematurely in that he had experienced too little symbiosis to be able comfortably to accept an adult role.

In addition to the leg symptom, Mr. Ventnor suffered from mild to severe anxiety attacks. His sociocultural position would not have brought him directly to a therapist even though he was suffering severe anxiety. His physician, finding no organic cause for the symptom, referred him first to a psychiatrist who tried to alleviate the anxiety with chemotherapy. After tranquilizers failed, he was referred for psychotherapy. Mr. Ventnor verbalized to the therapist, "You say it will make me feel better, but nothing relieves me. I have friends who feel better on thorazine, but nothing helps me." The therapist might easily have become discouraged after hearing in session after session that nothing helped. Bearing in mind, however, that this might express preverbal affect and attitude, the therapist thought that this referred to the time when the maternal ministrations, especially the feedings, did not provide full emotional gratification. We know that it is not the nourishment alone that is gratifying to the infant, but the gestalt of the feeding milieu. Was Mr. Ventnor saying that the oral administration of drugs alone without love and understanding repeated feeding for nourishment only, and therefore could not relieve the other needs? And about his friends who were helped with tranquilizers, did they represent his sibling who was nursed and comforted while he stood by and watched with envy?

The therapist did not try to enable Mr. Ventnor either to remember or to reconstruct this early period. She decided, rather, to engage in long-term ego building which would help him sort out self from object representations and reestablish more firmly than in childhood his gender identity as distinct from preoedipal maternal identifications. This would also serve to relieve him of homosexual fears. Such a goal is not accomplished quickly because much developmental ground must be retraced in a way that helps the patient understand his arrest without threatening whatever masculine identifications do exist. Thus, Mr. Ventnor's habit of spending the evening drinking three quarts of beer was accepted as being, in very small measure, culturally determined. Of far greater importance was the symbiotic reunion which the alcoholic daze recaptured. Mr. Ventnor consciously thought of himself as a man because he had a father who lent himself to some identification (although not enough to help the boy separate sufficiently from the preoedipal mother). Therefore, this level of development was shaky and should not be shaken further. This illustrates the ego psychological meaning of providing support. In whatever line of development a maximal level has been reached, first support and then furtherance are in order. Here, we are discussing Mr. Ventnor's gender identity, but the same technical rule would apply to any other developmental feature; support first, in order to build upon it. But this procedure requires that the therapist know precisely what to support, because random reassurance is too nonspecific to be of therapeutic value.

There was no sharp line of delineation, for this man as for many, between active and passive. We define passive as largely preoedipal for both boy and girl, referring as it does to the time of life when the separation-individuation process is not completed. Transition from passive to active requires more paternal assistance than Mr. Ventnor had. Greenacre elaborates that, in the second year of life, separation-individuation is aided by the father who begins to be perceived as a glorious, mysterious, idealized figure and who provides his children of both sexes with experiences different from and more alluring than symbiotic union with the mother; thus he accelerates separation-individuation. His masculine musculature gives the child a different sensual and tactile experience. His play has an intriguing quality. He tends to toss, carry, and move the child around differently, providing experience in space and motion. There is beginning identification with his strength and much fantasy about the idealized life the father leads when he is not at home. His appearance nightly and on weekends is greeted by the child with pleasurable relief from waning symbiosis. The boy acquires, as an important facet of his identity, a sense of gender. Then he can move into the oedipal position proper in the atmosphere of continuing benign paternal encouragement and minimal maternal seduction.

For Mr. Ventnor we would have to say that he limped into the oedipal stage. This might be taken almost literally because of the leg problem that emerged so much later in life. We mean it figuratively, however, and shall demonstrate how the therapist arrived at an understanding of the developmental handicaps despite which Mr. Ventnor's conscious masculine image of himself evolved; for he did take on a man's trade, he married, and he lived as a heterosexual. He was able to supply enough remembered history so that one could formulate an outline of some aspects of his development and its lags. We already know that a sibling was born when Mr. Ventnor was fourteen months old. The presenting symptom, then, is at least doubly determined—by the maternal identification and by the probability that fourteen months might be the age when he was ready to walk. It can be painful to a child to have to walk when the baby is being carried. Although the therapist thought that, she delayed conveying such thought to the patient. She thought, further, that his mother was pregnant when Mr. Ventnor was five months old and that this in some way impaired his symbiotic gratification because, whether positively or negatively, the mother was involved with the unborn child. Even if this was an unwanted pregnancy, as is likely, it detracted from the symbiosis which was Mr. Ventnor's phase-specific "right" at that time. Mr. Ventnor's father, a subway motorman, worked irregular shifts and was not much interested in the children when he was at home. When he had to sleep during the day, the main family focus was on keeping the children quiet. His recreation was away from home, with drinking companions. Mr. Ventnor remembered with as much resentment as his suppressive education and upbringing allowed that his father was not much interested in his schoolwork or athletic endeavors and did not offer the companionship that other boys enjoyed with their fathers. This is a considerable deviation from Greenacre's description of the normal role of the father in the second year of life.

Mr. Ventnor had, or was thought to have had, rheumatic fever at the age of seven. He was kept in bed for several months while his father was at work and his siblings were at school. Thus, he had mother to himself and attained a semblance of the longed-for symbiosis at a nonphase-specific time. This arrangement did not, nor can it, have reparative effect. For Mr. Ventnor it set the pattern we see in his adulthood: the graceful way to regress to the still-longed for symbiosis is by illness. This method placates superego, but does not promote ego growth. Mr. Ventnor's attainment of symbiotic gratification at an unsuitable developmental moment was more damaging than growth promoting. This supports our view that, by and large, corrective emotional experience out of phase cannot make up for its absence at the phase-specific time.

Mr. Ventnor's childhood illness reinforced already established regressive pathways and led to a symptom which employs "body language" instead of verbalization. It is an oversimplification, however, to translate the symptom into "I am too little to walk." The translation (which we advocate only for purposes of understanding the patient, not for interpretation) would consist of a biographical statement such as:

First my mother, because of her own emotional deprivation in childhood and the absence of emotional support from an infantile husband during my infancy, gave just about good-enough mothering in the first few months so that drive differentiation and fusion, neutralization, object relations, and other ego functions did proceed. This obviated psychosis. Then, however, she had another unwanted pregnancy and weaned me, probably very abruptly if we consider her cultural orientation. Probably she also felt miserable during the pregnancy, both psychologically and physically, and this deprived me of her interest at a time when I needed her symbiotic closeness for my own development. She might have had phlebitis, and when I was at the walking stage she left for the hospital to deliver my brother.

At that time confinement lasted ten days, which seemed like an eternity. I was taken care of by my mother's sister, who has always been very cool toward me. My older siblings fended for themselves. Mother's absence depressed me and that is why now, when I feel low, I have those beers. Then I don't have to think or feel except to recapture some of the symbiotic goodness from my early months.

When mother returned from the hospital there was this baby and I watched her nurse him while I stood by suffering intense envy. I had just started to walk, but it felt nicer to be a baby and be carried. Then I remembered that, just a short while back, mother had had trouble with her leg. I did nothing about it at the time, but was a good boy, did not show jealousy, went on in my separation-individuation phase with rather inconsistent help from mother. My toddling off was sometimes welcomed as a relief to her, but she also screamed at me if I went off or returned at times that were inconvenient for her. She had the other children to take care of and, when the older ones piled in from school for lunch, she was really too busy to think about me. Again, as when she was in the hospital, I longed for her when she was not there and I felt the panic of being alone.

I had little of my father to myself. When he was at home and in one of his rare good moods, I shared him with the others. I never really got to know him, even when I was an adolescent, but I have images of masculinity. He never seemed to need anything. Now I realize that he had given up trying to get his needs satisfied at home and spent most of his time at bars with his friends. But, at that time, it seemed to me that a man does not need. I had thoughts about sex and heard a lot of talk which I barely understood, but it excited me. No one was very careful about how anything affected me.

In due time I went off to school. The sisters (nuns) were often cruel to the boys who misbehaved, but I tried to be good and even not to have bad thoughts. And so I went on, not developing fully, but toeing the line. There were a few escapades in high school, led by other boys, but they did not amount to much by today's standards. We had a few parties with girls, smoked, and drank beer. I was afraid to touch a girl.

I met my wife when I was nineteen. She came from a good Catholic family, like mine. I got this job and we were married. The responsibilities began to pile up. She got more and more busy with the babies as they came, and it was like my early life all over again. I tried to pitch in like the good father I was taught to be, but I had no internalized model of paternity. It was all duty. By the time the fifth baby came I couldn't stand it any longer, but I had been trained all my life never to acknowledge feelings and needs. They impaired my own image of masculinity. I was afraid of the thoughts I had had all through adolescence that I might have homosexual desires. These began to creep in again, but I brushed them aside. I did not want to think about anything that I would have to confess. When it got to be too much for me it was so much like when my brother had been born, although I did not know that I was "reminded" of that. But I developed this pain in my leg and couldn't work. It was an unconscious attempt to get closer to my mother without impairing my masculine self-image. The doctor was interested and did all these tests. My wife got worried, which made me feel guilty, but I also wanted her to care. So my point of arrest is at the rapprochement and practicing subphases of separation-individuation, with some regression to symbiosis. My masculine identity is shaky because maternal identifica-

tions prevail, but I can never admit this. The doctor said I should see a therapist because there is nothing wrong with my leg. Even as I sit here with you I am afraid of the feelings and dependent longings that are engendered.

This kind of hypothetical "translation" of the patient's preverbal experience is useful because it places him in a diagnostic frame of reference in the therapist's mind, arranging a therapeutic milieu within which Mr. Ventnor will always be understood in historical depth. Almost never in psychotherapy will the patient come to such complete knowledge about himself. Always, his own interpretations take precedence over the therapist's hypotheses. The initial task in this case was not to provide insight, but to deal with Mr. Ventnor's complaint that nothing helps. With deep respect for the tenacity of the repetition compulsion, the therapist avoided reassurance or promise to help, but instead lent herself to the feeling that Mr. Ventnor was expressing through his complaint. The psychic truth is that in Mr. Ventnor's experience nothing from the outside had ever helped.

Combining this knowledge with the desirability of supporting Mr. Ventnor's dearly won masculine position, the therapist said, "You know, you are proud of your accomplishments in life, which are so much to your credit, and since you attained them so completely on your own, it is difficult for you to accept outside help now." This supports without shallow patting on the back; it meets Mr. Ventnor where he is psychologically, thus tightening the therapeutic alliance; it lets him know without guilt-inducing accusation that his defensive independence precludes ready acceptance of help. Implied is that the denial of oral wishes prevents even tranquilizers from relieving his anxiety. It has the objective also of reassuring him by demonstrating that the help the therapist has to offer, with this interpretation of initial resistance as an example, will never undermine his masculine self-image. This will pave the way for increasing receptivity of subsequent interpretations. The equilibrium will shift from defense against dependency to yielding to it, in order to understand it without anxiety and guilt, and thus ultimately conquering it more securely than in childhood. Mr. Ventnor will learn that a man may need and still remain a man. He will come to respect his needs as the therapist, in the context of a solid therapeutic alliance, offers such consistent respect that Mr. Ventnor will begin to identify with it. Gradually, his value system will change, not because of the influence of external authority which has always guided him, but because the superego will become more tolerant. Ego syntonicity will replace guilt as the guide to behavior. The therapist will not make up for all the psychological deprivations of childhood, but she will help Mr. Ventnor to understand some of them. A patient such as this needs to develop self-empathy, not only for his libidinal needs, but for the aggression which has been so much repressed. When aggression is uncovered, understood, and accepted, Mr. Ventnor may be able to envy his children less, thereby becoming a better father to them and enhancing his masculine image, and so the vicious cycle will be broken and replaced by a benign one.[10]

The therapist is well advised to train himself to think in such historical, diagnostic developmental concepts. As these become part of his professional fabric, he will be more sharply attuned to preverbal emanations, whether these appear in the form of action or even, deceptively, in words. It is perhaps most difficult to distinguish whether the patient is expressing himself preverbally when he is actually using the medium of language. Gross disparity between immediate provocation and enormity of affect is one clue, as in the case of Miss Loran. Acting in place of verbalizing is another. Somatization is always an indication that preverbal pathways for discharge are being used.

Mrs. Weber would be traditionally diagnosed as an obsessive character with concomitant tendency to intellectualize at the expense of affect, with evident anal retentive features and with simmering aggression concealed behind a facade of blandness. When displeased, she found nothing to say. Silence retaliated in kind, since the therapist had been silent. No therapist would disagree theoretically about the aggression here, and classical technique dictates that it be interpreted as an anal phenomenon. We find that, correct as this procedure may appear from the theoretical point of view, patients tend to experience such interpretation as a counteraggression, as a superego emanation, as a deadlock in which something is demanded of them and to which they can only respond with more determined withholding—unless

[10] Material provided by Joyce Edward.

ego psychological interpretation precedes the interpretation of resistance as a drive manifestation.

When asked about her silence, Mrs. Weber said, "You didn't say much yesterday and so you didn't relieve me." This seems to confirm the hypothesis of retaliation in kind. Because silence is a special form of retaliation and because the matter of relief became prominent, the therapist suggested, "You must be experiencing feelings you had before you could speak." The patient became interested rather than obstinate. This led to reconstruction of the mother's subtle withholding of libidinal availability in the oral phase, before the patient's adoption of anal retentiveness. It was speculated that the mother had performed efficiently in feeding, bathing, and other mechanical aspects of child care, but in a climate of emotional coldness which Mrs. Weber, at the age of twenty-eight, was repeating in reversal in the transference.

Reconstructive interpretation of the absence of libidinal availability made Mrs. Weber aware, for the first time in her life, that she had felt but had never been able to verbalize that something was missing. The closest she had come to this was her complaint that the therapist had not talked enough in the previous session. If the therapist's own libidinal availability provides him with an attitude of truly listening to the patient, he finds that he will be attuned to the complaint in a way that enables him to dip deeply into the "silent" past. He will not feel tempted to interpret the aggression until he has done full justice to the complaint that something was not gratified. This serves to illustrate that, if we listen carefully enough, there is always an angle from which the patient is right. This "rightness" has to be brought out into the open, verbalized, and acknowledged. After all, how else can preverbal experience be conveyed to the therapist except by silent demonstration? This, in itself, is a communication which the sensitive therapist can help the patient translate into language. When the therapist did not talk in the previous session it reminded the patient of her preverbal days when her mother failed to provide something intangible, wordless, but so very essential to the child's libidinal need. With this kind of therapeutic correction of early libidinal deprivation, the therapist will later be in a far more favorable position to interpret the anal aggression as an understandable and acceptable phenome-

non. The therapist's libidinal availability will have been established
within the confines of the abstinence rule. He will have provided the
most therapeutic of all gratifications, a thoroughly attuned interpretation. A therapist who can do this need never offer the patient pseu-
dogratification such as love, coffee, cigarettes, touching, self-revela-
tions, long telephone conversations, socializing, and the like. How
much more profound to help the patient know that his complaint
that preverbal life lacked an essential quality is indeed correct and
justified!

THE USE OF THE DREAM
IN PSYCHOTHERAPY

THE MYSTERY OF THE DREAM has long been fascinating—to primitive societies, to the ancients, in the Bible, in literature. Yet it remained for Freud to probe this mystery by providing its scientific rationale. His masterpiece, *The Interpretation of Dreams,* was published in 1900. Had he written no further, this work alone would have earned him enduring fame. He used his own dreams to describe the workings of the dream—how day residue and infantile material are intertwined in the dream work; how the manifest content of the dream contains concealed within it the latent meaning; how the dream work is carried out in primary process thought, using condensation and displacement. In sleep the motor apparatus is decathected, leaving only the sensory apparatus which discharges the energies of the repressed in the form of images. Normally, then, there is little or no motor activity. By such means, the dream fulfills the function of protecting sleep. By means of secondary revision, the intact ego organizes the dream thoughts into a coherent, logical sequence. Major distinctions between the dream of the normal or neurotic ego and that of the less-intact structure is that, in the latter, capacity for secondary revision is faulty and the dream of the less-structured personality may not always protect sleep; there may be motor activity, talking in one's sleep, and even waking from anxiety in the dream.

Recently, there have been significant investigations of sleep and dreaming. Modern equipment makes it possible for the investigator to monitor both sleep and dreaming in sleep laboratories. Many aspects of these studies tend to confirm Freud's discoveries; none refutes them.

The studies do, however, add interesting and important information about sleep and dreaming, such as the frequency and duration of the dreams of one person in a given night; that levels of sleep fluctuate; that dreams occur when there are rapid eye movements—generally described as REM sleep.[1]

Freud described the dream as the "royal road" [2] to the unconscious. Although Brenner [3] has argued against the special position of the dream in psychoanalysis, contending that analytic treatment can be conducted without dreams, most analysts do not share his view. Greenson,[4] in a refutation of Brenner, presented the view that there is something unique about the dream. In the treatment situation, however, the usual technical position, reiterated by Waldhorn,[5] is that all material presented by the patient is to be regarded as having equal weight. The dream is still "the royal road," but psychoanalysts and psychotherapists are cautioned against passing up the byways of non-dream material by overvaluation of the dream. Kris, who introduced the ego psychological approach to technique, asserted that rapid uncovering of id content, even in psychoanalysis, is no longer the principal goal. We think that, in many psychotherapy cases, it is not the goal at all.

There are alluring implications, beyond Freud's intent, in the phraseology, "the royal road." It is ubiquitous to wish for a quick, magical cure. Even the well-structured ego retains memory traces of the symbiotic phase when relief from distress seemed to appear magically. In the early period of psychoanalytic theory and technique—the abreaction era—it was thought that cure is effected by lifting repression. Freud revised himself on this as early as 1912–13 when he discovered that the single recovery of a memory, or the single interpretation, was not in itself curative but needed to be followed by the slower process of *working through,* because emotional problems are multifaceted and multidetermined. Each memory, experience, fan-

[1] C. Fisher, "Psychoanalytic Implications of Recent Research on Sleep and Dreaming."
[2] S. Freud, *The Interpretation of Dreams,* p. 608.
[3] E. D. Joseph (ed.), *The Place of the Dream in Clinical Psychoanalysis.*
[4] R. R. Greenson, "The Exceptional Position of the Dream in Psychoanalytic Practice."
[5] E. D. Joseph (ed.), *The Place of the Dream in Clinical Psychoanalysis.*

tasy, and so on must be subjected to interpretation and reinterpretation, now from one angle and now from another, before the symptom begins to yield. Freud used the analogy of a ship tied to the pier by several ropes. The ropes are untied, one by one, but the journey does not get under way until the last rope releases the ship. Freud also noted that it is not the amount of material that determines therapeutic effectiveness; it is, instead, the resistances that are mastered—a simple way of describing structural change. Nevertheless, a popular notion persists that sudden insight produces lasting therapeutic results, in a sense proving an aspect of dream theory to be correct; the strength of the wish to have matters as one would want is formidable.

Freud's work was so thorough that little else has been written about the technique of dream interpretation. Sharpe and Altman are among the few who ventured to elaborate on the technical use of the dream. Freud did not intend his associations to, and interpretations of, his own dreams to represent illustrations of the technique of dream interpretation, but only to demonstrate the nature of the dream work. Nevertheless, students of dream analysis sometimes follow Freud's method as though every element of the dream has immediate relevance to the therapeutic task. Rarely is this correct. More is to be lost in therapy by compulsive insistence upon association to every dream element than by failure to understand the dream altogether. The latent content of an unanalyzed dream remains in the unconscious and will be dreamed again in another manifest form. Strict adherence to the procedure of demanding associations to each element loses sight of ego-building goals and blurs technical differences between psychoanalysis and psychotherapy with regard to the use of the dream. Even in psychoanalysis proper, obsessive concern with each dream element is contrary to relaxed, freely hovering, analytic attention.

A borderline psychotic may tell a dream and may then say that he does not know whether it was a dream or something that really happened. In such a situation, one lets the dream go by the board altogether for the more valuable objective of helping the ego learn to distinguish more sharply between the sleeping and waking states. In psychotherapy, as well as in psychoanalysis, dreams can be used as resistance. Some, fearing the emptiness of their productions, may say that they wished they had had a dream so there would be something to talk about. Others tell a dream with great satisfaction at having re-membered one, but then do no work with it. Such use of dreams is traditionally thought of as bringing a gift to the therapist. This may be so in some instances, but it is certainly not the only explanation and the therapist's response can become stereotyped if he thinks of the anal gift as the sole reason why dreams are "deposited" with him. More often, we think the patient "gives" his dream to the therapist to work on. This is one of the technical opportunities to educate the pa-tient to his part in the therapeutic task by not taking it on for him. We agree with the traditional position, whether in psychoanalysis or psychotherapy, that the analyst or therapist cannot usually understand the dream without associations. There are exceptions, however. The very experienced analyst can often understand a dream, especially if he knows the patient well; some dreams are simple and transparent; some use standard symbols which give clues about their theme even if they do not quite reveal the full meaning. But for ego building, it is better for the therapist to help the patient learn how to work on his own dreams, or at least to find out why he does not, rather than to oblige him with an interpretation even when this is possible.

The royal road is still there to be used when the strength of the ego and the therapeutic alliance are such that interpretation can move the case ahead. But dreams are not to be sought out, demanded by the therapist as something special. That attitude can result in the patient's obedient production of dreams at the therapist's behest, an assault on his autonomy; or in the withholding of dreams if the pa-tient is not so obedient, which, while better than direct compliance, is only oppositional rather than volitional. Most desirably, dreams should come spontaneously within the context of a chain of associa-tions and the patient should take on more and more of the responsi-bility for associating to them and for adding up his associations into interpretations. This implies that there is an intact ego and true inde-pendence which make such work possible. Of course, so competent an ego is not that of the usual psychotherapy patient, and so we shall here suggest techniques for dealing with the dream as well as with other material—techniques that will lead a patient toward greater intactness. Those techniques already touched upon include ignoring the dream altogether in favor of ego strengthening—clarifying the boundaries between the sleeping and waking state and "teaching" the patient how to work on his own dreams. To these we would add that, in psychotherapy far more often than in psychoanalysis, one would also avoid dealing with a dream when the patient's reality is the material of choice. A psychoanalytic patient may more safely be left to deal with his reality without help from the analyst. A psychotherapy patient often needs help with reality, sometimes despite a given therapist's penchant for dreams. At such times, the selection of material for the session still follows the classic rule that the patient determines how he wishes to begin and what he chooses to present, while the therapist decides which material would be most useful in ego building.

Mr. Mason brought a confusion of dreams and reality that told the therapist that faulty ego functions, including misperception of size differences, were part of his borderline structure. He dreamed that he was getting into his car, but could not get his shoes on comfortably because they were too big. The therapist interpreted, "When you were a boy, you thought you would never get to be the size your father was." This, at first glance, appears very much like the oedipal interpretation one might propose for a psychoanalytic patient. It was not intended as such, however, and the patient himself understood it differently. It was designed to help the ego distinguish between past and present, between boyhood and manhood; that is, to gain a sense of time and to indicate continuity to an ego which was too fragmented to have grasped without help that which is taken for granted in the more intact ego—namely, that a boy grows into a man and yet remains the same person. It also informed the patient that he need not be forever fixated in the perceptions of his childhood and with the body image of a young boy. It especially avoided the very tempting but untimely oedipal interpretation of wishing to fill his father's shoes. Because such an interpretation would not seem incorrect to many therapists, we present this case as an interesting and important illustration of how necessary it is to know the diagnosis and level of development in deciding how to phrase an interpretation. Mr. Mason will need many years of ego-building psychotherapy before interpretation of oedipal wishes will be useful. In fact, in many such cases this point is never reached and therapy ends successfully with a stronger ego, higher level of object relations, lessened anxiety, firmer sense of identity, but not necessarily with the uncovering of unconscious fantasies. And so the royal road is sometimes not traveled, but other highways are chosen because they lead to destinations more desirable than direct access to the id.[6]

Dreams are so valued by some patients that they attempt to remember them by writing them down. This procedure is never to be requested by the therapist and is not to be encouraged if the patient chooses it spontaneously. One must be careful, always, however, not to offend the patient who believes that he is making an effort to work hard on his therapy by writing down his dreams. One can say, "Try to tell me without referring to your notes." Often this suffices to eliminate the writing down. If it does not, there is no contraindication to explaining the technical reason—that the forgotten dream is' just as valuable as the remembered one; it provides an opportunity to deal with the reasons for forgetting (the resistance). Anna Freud pointed out that to understand the functioning of the ego in the defensive process is just as valuable as to retrieve the repressed. In psychotherapy, it is even more important to try not to combat the ego in its defensive functioning. Often, in the course of free association, a forgotten dream is remembered in the context of the associations and this is always more pertinent to the therapy than an artificially "remembered" dream—i.e., one that is written down for purposes of neglecting the ego function of remembering or of bypassing a resistance.

We know of instances of therapists accepting written-down dreams, not only the reading of them by the patient, but even accepting the written document itself. After some time, the therapist acquires a file full of dreams. In certain fairly common borderline structures, the patient may feel that he has deposited parts of himself with the therapist. Sometimes the patient will ask for return of his notes with the expressed feeling that they are parts of his person (bodily ego). This does not necessarily imply that the therapist should not have taken them, at first. If the patient needs to deposit himself with the therapist for a while, this might in certain instances have to be accepted,

[6] Material provided by Louis Schneider.

but always with some indication that he will some day be returned to himself. When this is the problem, however, we are not working with dream interpretation, but with a modified ego. To attempt to work on such dreams interpretively is not only futile, but misses the point.

Even with the better-structured ego, a more rewarding approach to the written dream is always to try to learn why the need exists to write it down. What anxiety motivates such need? We know of a case of a stenographer who made a practice of writing her dreams in shorthand. She was never able to read her notes when she came to the session because the resistance prevailed despite the device designed to circumvent it. The therapist did not have to do much to discourage further attempts; the patient got her own message. The therapy proceeded to the more cogent matter of what she feared would be lost if a dream were forgotten. We have already mentioned that there is no cause for concern about loss of the manifest content of the dream. As long as the latent material exists, it will reappear in another manifest form.

When a psychoanalytic patient dreams about authority figures—doctors, teachers, or even the analyst himself—these are indisputably transference dreams and interpretations take that direction. In psychotherapy, such dreams are sometimes similar to the psychoanalytic patient's dream in both content and meaning. Sometimes, however, the content may appear to be the same, but the meaning is not, or should not be so interpreted. For example, a dream which manifests direct aggression against the therapist is often best left uninterpreted or interpreted in such a way that the patient does not become increasingly anxious about his already intolerable unneutralized aggression.

The psychoanalytic patient in the positive oedipal phase may dream of killing the analyst, but it would be in the context of neutralized aggression and libido. He would be capable of gratitude toward the analyst for his help as well as toward the father of his childhood who did not harbor retaliatory death wishes against the son. In such a context, the patient can tolerate knowledge of his death wishes. The borderline psychotic may dream of violent and sadistic acts which he brings to the therapist in great terror. Here the therapeutic task is not to emphasize the aggression, of which the patient is already painfully and anxiously aware, but to help ego building by teaching him the difference between a thought and a deed and by showing him that, if he learns to interpose thought before action, he will not be so terrified of his thoughts and wishes. That these thoughts and wishes happen to be aggressive is not emphasized. The dream is used to build the ego and not to confront it with the powerful and frightening id.

Some psychotherapy patients seldom dream. If they should bring a dream, and especially one which appears like a transference dream in that the therapist is now involved manifestly or in disguised form, this may portend the onset of a new and desirable level of object relations. Miss Epstein (chapter 8) attended her therapy sessions for several years without bringing a dream into the sessions. She had a tight symbiotic relationship with an aging mother from whom she had not been able to separate psychically or even physically. Her sessions were largely occupied with problems in object relations because she could deal with people only in accordance with how much or how little they gratified her. In the latter case, enormous aggression would be generated. She showed no awareness of the therapist as a person, but dealt with him only because of her desperate need. A turning point came when she brought in a dream in which she and the therapist were walking down the street together and she noticed that he loosened his collar because of the heat of the summer's day. Contrary to psychoanalytic procedure, the therapist did not interpret the dream as a wish nor did he concern himself with the symbolism of the heat. He commented, "Isn't it nice that we are together in your dream and you even take notice of my comfort?"

There are three technical purposes involved in this simple-sounding sentence, phrased in the form of a rhetorical question. It is so phrased in order to avoid the semblance of an oracle handing down a dream interpretation from the heights of Delphi and thereby demonstrating skill beyond the burgeoning capabilities of the patient. Since Miss Epstein put herself on "street level" with the therapist, he joined her there in working on the dream. "Isn't it nice" affirms the positive value of the patient's acquisition of the therapist as an object and, therefore, as someone to dream about. This is accomplished without a long, intellectual, and therefore less affective acknowledgment. Particular stress is laid, in the latter part of the therapist's comment, on the patient's growing capacity not only to have him as an object but even to care about his needs. Again, this is done by underlining that the patient noticed (and arranged for) his state of comfort in the dream; this technique is preferable to lecturing on how good it is to notice another person's needs. The appeal is to the ego, not to the superego, and it supports the ego's progress in the therapy.

Bergmann [7] observes that there are patients who, despite infrequent contact with the therapist, use their valuable therapy "hour" to tell a dream, leaving little or no time for other material or even for interpretation. He concludes that the dream has a communicative function and that the patient, therefore, is not really "wasting" the session, but wants to get something across to the therapist that he is not able to say directly. As Bergmann points out, dreams were used for communication throughout the ages, in myths and for prediction. It is rather common for a patient to tell the therapist a dream that he has already told his wife at breakfast. The psychoanalytic rule that telling a dream to anyone but the analyst constitutes resistance, while still correct, calls for modification. It is true that, having been used in one way, the dream cannot be used for analytic purposes. That does not deprive it of all therapeutic value. The very way that it has been used, even as a resistance, is to be understood by the therapist and interpreted, if timely. In the case of telling his wife the dream at breakfast, the therapist might at least understand that the patient had been trying to communicate something to his wife. From this stance, one has a chance to help the patient find out what it was that he was trying to tell her; from the stance of forbidding the telling of dreams outside of treatment, one gets nowhere except perhaps into the undesirable position of constituting a harsh and forbidding superego figure. The patient may obey or defy, but in either event valuable material is lost. Within the same philosophy we are proposing, the patient may even use his entire therapy session to tell a dream that may be unintelligible both to him and to the therapist. One can, if nothing else, know that there must be some purpose to be sought out.

[7] M. S. Bergmann, "The Intrapsychic and Communicative Aspects of the Dream."

A patient with a borderline structure was overly submissive to his wife because of nondifferentiation or, in Spitz' framework, the inability to say "no." He dreamed that "I was shopping with my wife in an expensive department store. She wanted me to buy her an expensive cocktail dress, but I told her I did not have the money, so she asked me to steal it for her. I did not want to do it, but agreed because I could not refuse her. We both ran out of the store, pursued by detectives."

There are many latent elements in this dream that would occur to the therapist as he listens—superego conflict, projection onto his wife, homosexual and transvestite wishes, and so forth. Because of the borderline structure, the therapist did not pursue any of these usual psychoanalytic avenues, but focused on the patient's symbiotic state and inability to say "no," thereby using the dream to illustrate a fundamental failure in ego development in order to enlist the patient's interest in working on it.[8]

Mr. Nelson was in therapy because he was approaching middle age without having been able to attain a satisfactory heterosexual relationship or even an ordinary friendship; neither was he overtly homosexual. He remained locked in an aggressively tinged symbiotic relationship with his mother, whom he overidealized defensively. The main genetic feature was that she had subjected him to brief but frequent traumatic separation in his first three years. He retained intense separation anxiety and the transition to object constancy remained incomplete.

We have described how excessive unneutralized aggression forestalls comfortable use of the aggressive drive in the service of separation. Mr. Nelson dreamed that he was in a restaurant that turned out to be a "clip joint." He was served only the appetizer but was billed for an entire meal. The charges would have been excessive even for a full meal. That the dream is on the oral level is self-evident. It could have been interpreted, without associations, that the therapist was charging an excessive fee for whetting his appetite but failing to satisfy. The therapist did not overlook this classical psychoanalytic interpretation but deemphasized it in favor of highlighting Mr. Nelson's

[8] Material provided by Dr. Rena Shadmi.

courage in venturing so much aggression toward the therapist, albeit in a dream. This prompted Mr. Nelson to compare the current therapy with his former therapy, in which he was exhorted to be "more of a man." In his current therapy, the aggression became attenuated by appreciation for the therapist's capacity to accept it. One has to be cautious about one's narcissism because the sequence suggests an attempt to appease the present therapist with a favorable comparison as a quick coverup of the aggressive dream thoughts. However, that this was only partially so is borne out by the fact that Mr. Nelson then told a dream he had had during his former treatment, and the interpretation by the former therapist.

He had dreamed that he wanted to perform fellatio on the therapist. The interpretation was, "You want to become a man through me." That would have been correct if the therapist had been working knowledgeably on the feature of identification with his masculinity. The patient, however, was not yet at that point in development and so he took the interpretation as a reproach. What the first therapist had overlooked was the oral nature of the dream, a clue to the diagnostic fact that Mr. Nelson was still involved with his preoedipal mother and therefore not ready to become a separate person with a different gender. That the interpretation felt like a reproach (assuming that the therapist had not so intended) is explained by the symbiotic tie to the ungratifying, orally depriving mother. In essence, the interpretation was heard as emanating from the weaner, "You may not be close to me and suck my breast." We give the therapist the benefit of the doubt here. He might have meant to imply that to try to become a man through him was the wrong route. But that would have compounded the error. When the patient resolves his tie to his preoedipal mother, he will most certainly want more wholeheartedly to become a man. The main route will be by means of identification with the therapist, augmented by interpretive reinforcement of genetic masculine identifications. Then, the correct interpretation will be, "You want to become a man through me and that is a good way."

Our discussion of the incorrect and correct interpretations of the dream emphasizes the crucial importance of knowing, in descriptive developmental diagnostic terms, where the lesion lies and how to treat it. The second therapist, in a step designed to correct the interpretation of the first therapist said, "Why not?" We again note here that most of the interpretations we advocate are deceptively simple. Underneath the carefully and economically chosen words lie the profound technical implications we have extracted from psychoanalytic developmental theory. Simple but well-thought-out interpretations, often in the form of a question, use the theory without overburdening the patient with it and without overwhelming him with the therapist's superiority, grandiosity, and omnipotence. As a growth promoter, the therapist leaves room for the patient's wisdom to emerge. While we must be wise indeed in both theory and technique, the patient is there to benefit from our professional skill, not to be awed by it.

Mr. Osborne was in his late forties when he came for treatment after having been in group therapy where his passive behavior was challenged time and again without succeeding in altering it. He had had a rather indifferent mother, a psychotic father, and an older sister who made all his decisions for him throughout life, including choosing a wife for him. The treatment was characterized by an assumption that the therapist, in his greater wisdom, would continue to act in the role of advisor in all matters. The therapy could not have succeeded by abrupt refusal to accept this omnipotent role because, for a while, the patient needed symbiotic closeness. Instead, those ego functions which could be turned over to the patient first and most easily were chosen as the place to start. When Mr. Osborne asked what to do about a problem with one of his children, whether to buy a new car, or even what the subject matter of the therapy session was to be, the therapist always said first, "Let's take a few minutes to see what your ideas about this are." Initially, the patient had no ideas. Gradually, he began to present some. His ego functions were supported even when some of his "decisions" were wrong in the therapist's opinion. For example, he was permitted, for a while, to choose freely the subject matter of the session. This appears to be the simple therapeutic compliance with the rule that the patient determines the content of the session. However, had such a patient been permitted so-called free association, it would have led him into the impasse of always returning to a request, in some form, that the therapist run his life.

The therapist began to break in with questions such as, "Are you sure you want me to take over?" Just enough to create some doubt, but not to dictate another direction. And so the patient became accustomed to working therapeutically by thinking more about what his immediate goal was rather than by plunging ahead in the hope that the therapist, like his sister, would use *his* ego functions to select, decide, advise, interpret, and so on. As this procedure became well established in the therapy, it did not have the magical effect of making Mr. Osborne so self-reliant that he abandoned all attempt to have his ego functions taken over. He accepted having to do things on his own in lesser matters, but still insisted that he needed the therapist's greater wisdom in moderately large decisions. One summer he thought he would like to go abroad and assumed that the therapist, having traveled, would tell him exactly how to go about it. Mr. Osborne did manage to go, but he managed it by his therapist's leaving him to the tender mercy of a travel agent of his own choosing. True, the travel agent took over, but then the therapist could remain the guardian of autonomy.

A turning point came when Mr. Osborne, a teacher, had to prepare a lesson plan. He asked the therapist to help. Yet the patient's education was such that he could be expected to know how to do this better than the therapist could. It seemed timely to try to stretch the ego further by asking whether he could not spend some time in the library working out a bibliography. At first the response was that he would not know how to go about it. He was then asked whether he had ever used card catalogs. Of course he had, but they confused him. It was suggested that he try and then discuss in the next session what specific difficulties he encountered. Mr. Osborne returned to the next session with a dream. "I meet you on the street and inform you that from now on I am going to do as I please." The aggression in the dream is welcome; the therapist took it as employment of the aggressive drive in the service of separation. The interpretation consisted of one word, "Nice." This does indeed override the many other elements in this dream, particularly the resentment and the wish to get rid of the therapist. However, the therapist's choice was deliberate—to make the patient comfortable with his aggression and not allow it to overwhelm him with fear of losing the therapist as the result of his disappointment and destructive wishes. To put it another way, the most neutralizable and growth-promoting aspect of the aggressive wish was chosen for therapeutic use.

The following is the case of a patient who, although possessed of a

neurotic ego structure, is best understood as vacillating, not solely because of the classical ambivalence of the obsessional neurotic, but concomitantly because of prolonged symbiotic overgratification. Cases
like these can be successfully analyzed if the obsessive features are
interpreted in the traditional way. Theoretically, the classical anal-sa-
distic phase coincides with the later subphases of separation-individuation. The technique to be described deals with both facets of maturation and development, the psychosexual and ego growth. In addition
to that advantage, which provides thoroughness that the psychosexual
approach alone lacks, technical approach from the ego side diminishes
the risk of the kind of impasse that is inevitable if the anal feature
alone is tackled; a transference resistance that often leads to stalemate
is avoided.

Mr. Palmer was in therapy because of inability to decide whether
to remain with his wife and children, to live alone, or try to make a
life with his mistress. He had had many extramarital affairs and it
was doubtful whether his involvement with his current mistress was
likely to be any more lasting than the others. Nor was living alone a
solution for him because, whenever he tried it, the loneliness was too
great. Careful examination of his vacillation showed that what at first
appeared to be classical ambivalence suggestive of obsessional neurosis
would be better described (diagnosed) for treatment purposes as failure to have completed separation-individuation. Mr. Palmer complained that his wife wanted to own him, envelop him, absorb him,
and so on. This was understood by the therapist as fear of the patient's own wish for symbiotic reunion. The life history bore this out.
He was an only child who had had a totally devoted mother as well
as a nurse who did everything for him until the age of nine. Then,
because he was a boy, his equally dominating father took over in
order to mold him for a career in the father's business. Separation-individuation was incomplete because overgratification of symbiotic
wishes created arrest. Therefore, whatever natural thrust toward separation-individuation existed nonetheless, could not have been resolved satisfactorily.

As an adult, Mr. Palmer married but found it intolerable to live
peacefully with one woman. His turning from one to another was
repetition of his desperate but futile attempt to complete separation-

individuation within the conflicting longing for the symbiotic state. He brought logical argument to the therapy, weighing the virtues of one woman against the other as though such intellectual stocktaking could lead to a decision. The therapist, for a while, took the course of trying to help him arrive at a decision. Mr. Palmer dreamed that he was commanded by a man to climb over a hill. He obeyed but climbed on all fours. That the man represented his therapist-father is obvious. The therapist commented that perhaps Mr. Palmer was feeling that he was being asked to do too much. Mr. Palmer responded, "Yes, but I do it." The therapist said, "But do you notice that you do it on all fours? Why is that?" To this the patient responded, "Like a baby." The dream illuminated that the vacillating life style represented an attempt at developmental thrust, but that the conflict that made progress so impossible without therapeutic help was clearly depicted by the baby in the dream who tried to go beyond what a baby can do. He failed for that reason as well as because, in attempting to function like a man, he could only do so obediently, not autonomously. Thus, the domination of the object remained the same even though the real objects changed. The interpretation illuminated the conflict by using the dream to help the patient make conscious his developmental lesion, leading him to understand how his current behavior was determined by the unconscious conflict between symbiosis and crossing the separation-individuation threshold.[9]

It used to be thought that the ego, as Freud understood the concept in 1900, was largely eliminated in the sleeping state. Only recently has there been consideration of the ego, as conceptualized in poststructural theory, in the dream. We know, for example, that the defensive function operates in the dream, even though more regressed mechanisms of defense are employed than in the waking state. Consistent with the concept of signal anxiety, the intact ego can tolerate anxiety in a dream, employ defenses, and fulfill the function of preservation of sleep. The less-intact ego is deficient in defensive capacity in sleep as well as in the waking state. Therefore, the borderline structures are more vulnerable to anxiety dreams. The best diagnostic and prognostic signs in dreams are found in the sleepers who can tolerate,

[9] Material provided by Dr. George Bryan.

defend against, and thus sleep through anxiety in the dream. Most
morbid diagnostically and prognostically is the inability to deal with
anxiety at all, such as when the sleeper dreams that he is about to die
and cannot stop it. If the dream proceeds to death, there is cause for
deep concern. Better are those with borderline structures who awaken,
albeit in great anxiety, thereby stopping the dream from proceeding
uncontrolled by the ego. On the road toward building the ego's defensive function, the therapist aids self-preservation in such cases with
comments like, "It is good that at least you could waken yourself before the disaster occurred." The simple phrase "at least" cannot be over-
used in supporting the ego at its optimal level of functioning. In
that way, patient and therapist get together in appreciation of the
development which has been reached, making possible its becoming
the foundation stone for further development. This is the true meaning of "ego support." It addresses itself to the highest level of development the way a builder shores up the last story of a building in
order to proceed to building the next story. It differs from random
support in its precision and specificity, and from praise, which is
therapeutically worthless and is usually perceived by the patient as false.

The next case details sessions in the middle phase of treatment of a
borderline structure, including several dreams. It is presented as illustrative of the nature and content of therapy after approximately two
years of treatment and shows how dreams are used to assist the synthetic function to organize a more neurotic structure.

Mr. Quinn discussed, in one session, the fact that his roommate was
in an encounter group. The group leader suggested to the roommate
that Mr. Quinn was wasting time and money in prolonged Freudian
therapy, and invited him to join the group. The therapist gave free
rein to his ambivalent feelings about the therapy. Mr. Quinn thought
the group was cheaper and quicker; on the other hand, he had experienced enough success in individual therapy to feel that he would not
want to jeopardize his gains. He described some of the group activity.
He was particularly intrigued by the fact that they were encouraged
to touch one another libidinally. On the other hand, he did not like
the fact that they also attacked one another aggressively. He continued on the touching theme, asking why, in a moment of affection, he
could not embrace the therapist (a woman). She asked him whether

he could think of the pros and cons. He thought it would feel good. He was again asked about the cons. It occurred to him that he might have an erection. That would make him feel ashamed. The therapist thought it would be natural, but why make it so difficult for himself. He left the session unconvinced that touching the therapist would be antitherapeutic.

He returned with a dream *which would not have occurred had the wish to touch the therapist been acted upon.* He announced the dream rather angrily. It was, he said, a homosexual dream which should not happen after so many years of therapy. The therapist did not counterreact to the aggression, which was understood as the result of having been frustrated in the last session, but waited to hear the dream. It was that his roommate approached him and stroked his penis. He awoke having had an emission. He began to associate spontaneously, having become accustomed, over the years, to working on his own material. It occurred to him that the roommate represented himself. The therapist nudged gently, "And what would that mean?" "It could be a masturbation dream," he replied. The therapist interpreted, "So you don't always need another person to do everything for you. You can gratify yourself." The session ended with the patient feeling much better and less aggressive than when it began.

Here we have an example of the application of the abstinence rule (no touching) even though the patient had presented his wish to touch in the form of positive feelings for the therapist and the innocent wish to embrace her. While there is nothing wrong with such wishes, acting on them would have had the detrimental result of reinforcing symbiotic fixation. Oedipal desire would also have crept into the picture, exacerbating the symbiotic problem because symbiosis is a safe haven from the raging conflict of the oedipal phase, particularly for an ego not strong enough to tolerate the conflict or to defend in neurotic forms. Frustration of the wish for closeness brought aggression that took the form it would take in normal childhood development—that is, the mother who is attuned to the gradual termination of symbiosis and follows the child in his development through the subphases of separation-individuation does incur the child's aggression, which he is then able to neutralize and use for self-gratification. He turns to himself, in furtherance of his separation, and enters the phallic phase with the capacity to enjoy his newly won ability to gratify himself independently. In a reexamination of the function of autoerotic behavior in the service of separation, Spitz describes the very process developmentally which this patient experienced therapeutically. While it is not our therapeutic goal to encourage adult patients to masturbate, that this is a growth-promoting step in childhood is to be acknowledged. Developmentally, of course, it is superseded by heterosexual interest.

Some weeks later, Mr. Quinn planned a winter vacation, knowing that it would not coincide with that of the therapist, about whose vacation he had already been informed. The therapist recognized this as another venture in the use of aggression in the service of separation and independence. It is useful to be reminded here once again that we refer to Mahler's concept of separation as an internal experience of being a separate person, not to physical separation. While we have said that it is desirable for the patient to plan his vacation to coincide with that of the therapist, that is not always possible and, in this case, was not even desirable. Mr. Quinn presented his plans with some slight trepidation, but the therapist reacted with moderate enthusiasm, designed to dispel feeling that this was a personal affront, and to encourage the independent plan. Here, neutralization was promoted in the context of a transference which revised earlier distortions; the object welcomed the aggression because it was in the service of development.

Two sessions before his vacation, Mr. Quinn began in a gloomy mood. He commented that there was such a short time left before he went. The therapist, wishing to focus around the pain of separation, pointed out that it feels so bad because she will be going away shortly after he returns. He avoided this at first, but the therapist proposed it with the idea that there might be some mild depression around separation unless it could be dealt with before the fact. Mr. Quinn picked it up later. In that same session he mentioned a dream he remembered only vaguely. The dream involved blood. He could not remember clearly. He spoke of fears of dying in a ski accident. The therapist asked about the latter, saying that the usual fear might be of a fracture, but why of dying? Mr. Quinn said that he did not think of an ordinary ski accident, but of falling sixty feet from a ski lift. He enlarged on his phobias of heights and open spaces, then veered away on an intellectual comparision between these kinds of fears and those of his friends who feared the city streets at night. He was never afraid to go out at night, even into the park. The therapist led him away from the defensive intellectualization. Desirable as it is for most borderline structures to have so neurotic a defense as intellectualization, the therapist thought that, because the ego was relatively strong in this respect, Mr. Quinn could tolerate the anxiety in defense of which his phobias were built, and so she asked more about them. He elaborated on his fear of falling, reminded himself of his dream about blood, then thought of having been dimly aware of having had an erection during that dream. He continued in the vein of fearing that things would get out of control. He mentioned, in particular, loss of body parts—blood, feces, even feelings.

The therapist noted to herself that castration fear was conspicuously missing from the list. She saved this for later, allowing him to continue his associations. He described how a snowball at the end of a steel rod would be smashed if hit against a wall; the rod would stand up. The therapist then said, "You think of yourself as the snowball and that your erection will get the better of you. In fact, you feel that all of your parts have independent existence." He agreed, "Yes, and they can be lost."

Mr. Quinn continued on the theme of loss and also return of that which is lost. He spoke of his independent wishes, now picking up the thread presented by the therapist earlier that she would be away from him. To these he added his dependent wishes, and his fear that, once he left, he would want to be back with the therapist. He did not see how he could go away independently unless he smashed the baby wishes. The therapist asked, "Why smash them? Why not sympathize with them?" This was designed to help him tolerate and overcome feelings of loneliness and dependency, not by reunion with the symbiotic object, but by providing opportunity for transmuting internalization and self-empathy. He persisted that he would not be able to go. The therapist said, "I understand it better now. There is no central controlling mechanism for feelings and body parts; they all have wills of their own." He agreed, "They will smash me as though I really am a snowball."

The therapist, deficient in scientific knowledge but knowing that Mr. Quinn was a scientist, said, "We have to go back to the horse-and-buggy days for an analogy that I can use. If you are driving a wagon hitched to a team of horses, they might all want to go in different directions. But if they are hitched up properly and you are holding the reins, they have to go your way." Mr. Quinn agreed with considerable enthusiasm. (It is not necessary for the therapist to be brilliant and knowledgeable in all fields. In fact, it gives the patient more scope if the therapist does not know everything. But there must be no false dissembling.)

The patient said, "I see it now. I want to be here and I want to go away, but I cannot go without the part that wants to be here attacking the independent part." The therapist said, "Let's add to that. Why can't there be one of you that has two or more different feelings at the same time? If you are controlling the team of horses, and if these represent your feelings and body parts, then you would know that they are all parts of *one you.* Your penis does act as though it is independent of you when it erects against your will sometimes, but that is in its nature. Feces are not necessary parts of you, as the penis is, although you equated them when you were a child. And feelings are the most controllable of all—you can have many contradictory ones at once and you do not necessarily have to act on all or even on any of them."

The session ended with the patient feeling very pleased with what had been accomplished. "I want to talk more about that," he said as he left.

This last case was presented in some detail because it so well illustrates that the borderline structure consists of some neurotic and some less-developed features. The therapy shows how the more-developed aspects of the ego are used to bring about growth of the aspects which had been impeded in childhood development. It demonstrates how the highest level of ego development is supported and how the organizing function is brought into play to prevent fragmentation.

Our discussion of the use of dreams in psychotherapy emphasizes that guidelines for technique evolve out of understanding developmental lines. They cannot, therefore, be presented as established rules. A dream arrives at a specific point in the therapeutic process, requiring, therefore, that the therapist understand the interrelatedness between the developmental lesion and the immediate moment. Also, the patient's approach to his dream, his manner of reporting it, how he works on it, are as relevant as the content, manifest and latent, and those matters usually take therapeutic precedence over content. Both approach and content give the therapist material that, skillfully used, may be used to further development.

❧ 14 ❧

DEPRESSION

"What turns us into human beings is, indeed, the organization not only of our thought processes, but also of a wide range of feelings, of complex emotional attitudes and affective states unknown to the animal." [1]

BEING HUMAN MEANS that we are able to enjoy the pleasurable affects—love, joy, sometimes even ecstasy. But these are at the price that there are also unpleasurable affects to be endured— sadness, grief, guilt, disappointment, anxiety, and, perhaps worst of all, depression. More than anxiety, depression is the affect that is of concern to the therapist because of his empathy for the patient who is experiencing such anguish and because of the danger of suicide in some depressive states. The shadings of affects such as sadness, grief, disappointment, and the like reflect response to an external event. Unlike these, depression may or may not be precipitated by external factors, but its etiology is to be found in the structure of the personality, a structure which predisposes the individual to pathological depression. The external event, if there is one, falls upon the fertile ground of an already existing internal readiness for this unhappy affect. As we understand it today, predisposition to depression has its roots in early object loss—that is, object loss at a stage of development when the ego is not yet capable of mourning and of resolving ambivalence and narcissistic injury. Object loss may have been real —the death of the mother, for example—or it may be the consequence of destruction of object representations by aggressive cathexis.

Psychotic depression is now thought to have its origin in the inability of the undifferentiated self-object to cope with disillusionment and

[1] E. Jacobson, *Depression*, p. 32.

abandonment. Coping mechanisms are attempted, consisting in the main of establishing overidealized and overvalued object representations. While neurotic depression, too, can result from overidealization of the object at the expense of the self, in neurotic structure there is a differentiated object. In a psychotic structure, on the other hand, over-idealization and overvaluation of object representations extend to self representations, making for wishful self images which can never be realized. There results a fragile, essentially narcissistic equilibrium subject to dissolution in the face of disappointment or narcissistic injury, loss of the object, or loss of self-esteem.

Thus, depression is to be understood as an affective state which is essentially the consequence of object loss and of superego pathology. We are always in somewhat of a theoretical dilemma when we speak of superego or superego pathology in the unstructured personality when, at the same time, we adhere to the proposition that the superego is the heir to the oedipal conflict and is the last agency to be formed in the process of structuralization. Until this aspect of theory can be described more elegantly, it is useful to bear in mind that the process of superego formation begins early in life—with the first prohibition, which is the weaning—and is powerfully reinforced by the clash between drive and external stricture in the anal phase. Therefore, there are superego components in the unstructured personality, often clumsily termed archaic superego, primitive superego, and so forth. Descriptive of earlier parts which have not yet coalesced into a cohesive structure, we think the term *superego components* most appropriate.[2]

Depression in the more structured personality is roughly described as borderline or neurotic depression. We remind ourselves here that these are not diagnoses proper; they are abbreviated ways of describing that the affect, depression, exists in a given structure. A rather common type of depression consists of simple identification with the affective state of the object—a depressed mother, for example. This is a consequence of merger between self and object representations in the symbiotic state or of defensive retention of the object. While it may seem similar to that which we have already described as the psy-

---

[2] See chapter 2 for a fuller discussion of this issue.

chotic depressive state, it is distinguished from psychosis by the greater degree of differentiation between self and object representations. More often than in psychosis proper, it may consist of regression from a higher degree of differentiation as the result of trauma. This kind of defensive identification may exist even in neurotic structures, but is to be distinguished from identification as a normal developmental process. If such identification as a defense is used by a neurotic ego in an individual who has acquired structure, it is a regression resulting from trauma. One retains the object by retaining the affective state of the object. Regression is partial because, in all other aspects of identity, the neurotic personality is differentiated.

Suicidal depression is most likely in psychotic structures where narcissistic injury is so great that self-esteem is erased and the object world is destroyed by aggressive cathexis. Suicidal risk, however, is not to be ruled out in the more structured personalities. In borderline structures, in particular, the suicide may represent realization of the symbiotic wish. It cannot always be said, therefore, that suicide is the final victory of the aggressive drive alone; it may also represent the fulfillment of largely libidinal wishes.

We consider, also, the milder depressions which are the concomitant affects of the conquest of the developmental phases. Melanie Klein, with a large grain of truth in her otherwise highly improbable theory, gave prominence to this developmental fact by suggesting that the infant becomes normally depressed—in Kleinian terms, arrives at the *depressive position*—at the realization that the former "good" object who gratified and the "bad" object who frustrated, are in reality the same person. We can agree with Klein in the broader philosophical sense that depression is a consequence of the realization that Paradise is lost. Normally, such depression is transient and one soon comes to terms with reality. Mahler, on a firmer base than Melanie Klein because Mahler's conclusions were attained in an experimental setting and not in subjective musings, thinks that a predisposition to depression is established in the rapprochement subphase of separation-individuation if the unattuned mother fails to respond to the needs of that subphase. Even successful conquest of separation-individuation is achieved at the price of a depressive affect because the object as part of the self is lost. Especially in adolescence, when there is another round in the separation-individuation process, depression is a normal, temporary concomitant of that developmental phase. It takes skillful differential diagnosis to distinguish, in adolescence, between normal and pathological depression, among other adolescent phenomena.

There are normal, transient depressions in adult developmental phases. To leave the parental home or to marry may entail some depression. Parenthood as a developmental phase, involving redistribution of libidinal cathexis to include another object, also involves transient object loss and therefore depression. For the mother, the birth process is thought by some to involve a brief depression because of the physical separation of the child. This, of course, is to be distinguished from a true postpartum depression which has its roots in the pathology of early structuralization, especially that aspect of the self-image which includes the bodily ego. We do not find the psychiatric diagnosis, *involutional melancholia,* useful. We have heard of depressive states which are so diagnosed solely on the basis of the patient's age. In such instances, we resort to a heuristic device—we ask our students how they would diagnose the same problem if the patient were twenty years younger. It is more consistent with developmental theory to consider that depression in middle-age is based on a predisposition which makes it difficult to encompass the developmental demands of that age. While this formulation does not seem very different from the involutional concept, it is so if we change the focus slightly. It is not *because* of the disappointments of middle-age that depression ensues, but rather that these disappointments constitute the trauma that connects with an already existing predisposition.

One of Freud's most famous essays is on the subject of depression. For this reason alone, the essay cannot be omitted from a discussion of depression. Interesting and important in its own right, it also provides a theoretical basis for reinvestigation of some of the techniques which are, in our opinion, erroneously based upon it. Freud himself made no technical recommendations. He distinguished between grief as a normal reaction to real loss of the object (the world becomes cold and empty) and depression, in which the ego (self) becomes cold and empty. The normal mourning process consists of gradual withdrawal of cathexis from an object who no longer exists in reality. When this is completed, new object relations can be formed. Normal mourning is limited in time; it comes to an end. Melancholic depression, on the other hand, may or may not succumb to spontaneous remission. It seems to remit in manic-depressive psychosis when the depression is superseded by elation because ego and superego are united. More often than not, however, therapeutic intervention is necessary to terminate a depression.

Much is clarified if we understand the theoretical climate within which Freud worked on his essay. In that era of theory building, Freud and his pupils, in particular Abraham, were thinking about depression (and narcissism) in terms of flux of libido from id to ego to outside world and back to ego. It was not only a prestructural theory which used the term *ego* in place of *self,* but also a libido theory rather than a dual-drive one. Freud and Abraham also thought, at that time, mainly in oral terms. Thus, they regarded the basic mechanism in depression as *introjection,* an oral process. Jacobson, much later, described processes of internalization essential to normal ego and superego development; in Freud's time they were regarded only as defense. Freud described this in one of his most memorable statements, "Thus the shadow of the object fell upon the ego." [3] He meant, of course, that compensation for object loss is attempted by means of internalizing mechanisms. He described how the individual becomes like the lost object (or the object of aggression) in this process. The essential difference between normal mourning (grief) and melancholia (depression) is that, in the first instance the object has been loved and lost and, in the second, love is overriden by aggression. He showed how, in depression, complaints which appear to be leveled at the "poor and empty" [4] self constitute a description of the failings of the object, thereby providing clinical clues to the true object of the aggression. When the ambivalently loved, now internalized object is overcathected with aggression, suicide becomes the extreme of the aggressive intent.

Out of Freud's early formulations, some technicians have evolved a technique which we have termed "the reversible raincoat method." They believe that depression is to be treated by encouraging the pa-

---

[3] S. Freud, *Mourning and Melancholia,* p. 249.   [4] *Ibid.,* p. 246.

tient to externalize the aggression. Based as it is on prestructural and predual-drive theory, it appears now to be too simplistic to be effective. In some instances it is even dangerous. It is no longer tenable to propose that the flux of drive energy can be reversed, especially in relation to contemporary figures, in the instance of this particular technique by ventilation of aggression toward the therapist. We have stressed in several places that object representations are not to be destroyed by eliciting aggression against them before they can be replaced by libidinally cathected self and object representations. Nowhere is that more important than in the treatment of depression. Nor can the past be repaired by ventilation in the present. While we have heard of salutory results with "ventilation," we think these can be explained by the fact that it makes limited discharge possible, affording temporary relief. Why not, then? Because the risk of object loss in aggressive ventilation is too great. Technicians who use such methods have not incorporated the findings of psychoanalytic developmental psychology in their thinking. In more modern terms, we think not only of the imbalance between libido and aggression, but also of the degree to which these drives are neutralized and, above all, the degree to which there exists an object separate from the self.

We summarize the major factors in the etiology of depression. These have to do largely with degree of structuralization and internalization and with distribution and neutralization of aggressive and libidinal cathexes. Thus it matters greatly whether superego formation has remained fixed in the harsh and overcritical component stages before becoming a more benign structure; whether unneutralized aggressive cathexes devalue and destroy the object representations; whether the merged self-object is also destroyed. In borderline and neurotic depression, depressive identifications may be operative, although varying degrees of differentiation have been attained.

TREATMENT OF DEPRESSION

If depression is an affective state, it is theoretically incorrect to speak of treatment *of depression*. We do not treat anxiety, joy, or any other affect as such. Where there is pathological affect, such as anxiety, guilt, depression, and elation, we treat the ego which is experiencing the affect. However, because of the suicidal danger and the intense suffering in depression, it is often necessary to use emergency measures to deal with the crisis. Life-saving devices always take precedence over leisurely technique; we have to preserve the patient in order to have the leisure to treat him.

The cardinal technical rule is that *all* depression is to be taken seriously. We deplore those schools of technique which advocate dealing with depression, and especially suicidal depression, as hostility or attention-getting devices arranged for the benefit or anguish of the therapist. Never is depression a problem of interpersonal relations between patient and therapist (although it can become the therapist's problem if he takes it personally). We have heard the glib statement that counteraggression on the part of the therapist stimulates the patient's overt aggression, thus bringing about sufficient discharge to avert suicide. We have, in fact, heard it often enough so that there is little doubt that, in those therapists' own words, "It works." To such pragmatism, we can only ask, "At what price?" We think with Jacobson that what happens to the already overaggressively cathected self and object representations is that such treatment reinforces negative cathexis and may thus render the situation untreatable. So those therapists succeed in keeping the patient alive, perhaps only temporarily, and doomed to unending misery. We owe the patient the opportunity, if we keep him alive, to enjoy life. And so we prefer to take suicidal threats seriously and to inquire into why there is such desperation. If there is imminent danger, such patients are best treated in a protective setting.

The setting is important. Sometimes the setting is the life situation. We discussed the case of Miss Andrews in which it was deemed inadvisable to treat a depressed patient only once a week without the family's knowledge. Miss Andrews was an adolescent whose final round of separation-individuation was not yet completed. Many severely depressed adolescents have excessive difficulty with separation-individuation because the first round was not completed satisfactorily at the phase-specific time. It seemed worthwhile, in that case, to test whether the setting, represented here by the parents' interest and financial help, could be improved upon from the way in which this young patient had chosen initially to arrange it.

We do not always recommend that, in suicidal depression, the relatives be involved. Each case has to be judged in accordance with the individual circumstances. In many instances, the very familial environment which created and perpetuates the desperate situation is not a useful adjunct to treatment. For example, a suicidal woman's closest relative may be the equally disturbed husband from whom she is separated, or who, even if she still lives with him, does not himself have the kind of object relations that make him a reliable adjunct. A protective setting need not necessarily be a hospital if caring supervision can be arranged, although this is usually difficult because relatives who have not had the capacity to care enough for the patient before the crisis are not likely to begin when the patient is suicidal. Unconscious or even conscious death wishes on the parts of relatives do not make for a favorable environment.

Antidepressive drugs are of some value in getting a patient through the crisis, particularly if out-patient treatment is decided upon. They have had the limitation of taking effect slowly; recently more rapid-acting antidepressive drugs have been developed. Also to be considered is that not every antidepressant is equally effective for every person. Drugs are to be used briefly as life-saving devices. They do not cure depression, but they can keep the patient alive and available for treatment. It is usually more desirable, even if the therapist is a physician who may prescribe drugs, that the prescription be provided by someone else. The reason for such precaution is that the obvious oral gratification which a drug prescription provides, while offering salutory regressive gratification in the depressed state, may also reinforce a fixation to the point where it becomes ineradicable. The most desirable method of procuring antidepressant drugs, or tranquilizers when these are indicated, is first to explore with the patient what his own resources are. If he has a personal physician, the therapist and the physician can cooperate in prescribing whatever is desirable. We do not usually advocate referring a patient to a physician, on the ego psychological ground that it is best if the patient uses his own ingenuity in finding his resources. This, however, does not imply abandoning him to his own devices. It means working with him to encourage him to overcome his helplessness. "I don't know anyone who can help me," can be explored with, "Have you asked your friends which doctors they use?" Rigidity is to be avoided. If the ego is so weak that the therapist's intervention is necessary, then he should step in and refer the patient.

The problem of hospitalization is a difficult one because of the paucity of good psychiatric facilities and because of the medical structure. In psychiatry, as in other branches of medicine, only physicians who hold staff appointments or attending privileges at a given hospital may treat patients there. For the psychotherapy patient, this is undesirable. Although we cannot hope to change the medical structure, we may at least point out that it is difficult to build object relations with changing therapists, even if there are only two—one in and another outside the hospital. In actual practice, with changing hospital staffs, there are usually more than two. Most therapists, whether psychiatrists or not, do not have the kind of hospital affiliation which makes it possible to treat the patient as an inpatient and then to resume with him on an outpatient basis when indicated. Therefore, to the disadvantage of the patient, hospitalization usually means giving up the case. Nevertheless, in life-saving emergencies, this must be done.

Another community problem which we are not hopeful about is the quality of hospital care and treatment. The "therapeutic environment" exists in painfully few, select, and very expensive settings. Most patients who must go to municipal, state, county, or veterans' hospitals are cared for by untrained attendants and few, if any, well-trained psychotherapists. Because of the residency system, the treating therapist might be a beginner in July, or might have to leave the patient regardless of treatment need upon completion of his residency or upon transfer to another ward. In voluntary hospitals, some of which have better physical plants than many public institutions, a procedure is practiced which bears no relation to the needs of the case—the patient is hospitalized for the length of time for which the hospitalization insurance plan will reimburse. These are realities within which the psychotherapist has to wend his way, making professional decisions which are compromises at best. If the risk is not too great or is sufficiently calculated, it is sometimes more desirable to see the patient every day, until the crisis is over, on an out-patient basis, especially if there is a supportive environment and the prognosis is favorable.

This, however, brings up an earlier issue—whether to undertake to treat the case at all. The therapist who accepts a depressed or psychotic patient for treatment must give the matter careful thought. Does he have enough libido to meet the desperate demands of such patients? Can he be on call twenty-four hours a day, seven days a week? (Unlike medical practice, a substitute therapist will not do.) How many other depressed patients does he already have and would an additional one overburden him? Do his life style and family obligations allow him to devote so much libido to patients? These questions should be answered before the commitment to the patient is made. Once the patient is accepted for treatment, there is no going back. The patient, already severely disappointed in his objects, can be irreparably damaged by a therapist who gives up the case in midtreatment. Every therapeutic design must avoid repetition of the traumatic past. This holds true for depression no less than for any other type of pathology.

Before discussing the long-range treatment of chronic depressive states, we shall detail the emergency measures that are designed to deal with suicidal crisis. The suicidal impulse is to be taken seriously and not as idle threat. We take into account that some patients may make such threats to alarm the therapist, but that is because an infantile personality deals with his objects in such a way. Therefore, we believe that the underlying message in such communication is always to be sought. Nor do we feel as secure as some therapists about the abortive suicide attempt. The patient who slashes his wrists superficially, who takes a not-quite-lethal overdose, is also conveying a message. No one, even with considerable knowledge of pharmacology, can, in a depressed state, calculate precisely how much of a given drug is just short of lethal. And it is characteristic of barbiturates and similar drugs that, after the patient has consumed a small amount, he no longer remembers how much he has taken. We cannot know how many successful suicides had been planned to be short of successful —"only for attention." We do know of at least one patient who took an overdose of barbiturates, called a doctor because she had changed her mind, but died before the doctor could be of help. And so we do not advocate the "tough" policy of bluffing it out with the patient. "Let us try to find out what makes you so desperate that you think of killing yourself," is a more helpful and respectful approach than one of taking the patient's words as threat or bluff. "While you feel so desperate, let us make some arrangement for your protection. You will change your mind when you feel better," gives the patient a sense of being protected, of being cared about, and, perhaps most important of all, a sense that there is a brighter future.

We are interested in the method that the patient is contemplating, principally because we would want to know how far the planning has gone. There is some, but not always reliable, diagnostic clue to be found in the method of suicide; one can make a rough estimate of the level of regression. For example, the sleeping pills suggest search for symbiosis; the blood-letting methods suggest castration, and so on. Knowledge of these methods does not always provide precise diagnostic clues. Aggressively tinged self representations, especially when these are undifferentiated from the also aggressively cathected object representations, can lead to random self-mutilation. If the patient has every detail well worked out, it is a morbid sign. We do not ask, "How do you plan to do it?" (a question we have heard asked of a patient), because this joins in with the formulation of a suicidal plan which, by himself, the patient might not have developed too far. But one might, if necessary, ask "Have you gone so far in your desperation that you have thought about what you might do?" The answer to such a question will enlighten the therapist, but the wording is carefully designed to avoid becoming ally to the plan and is meant to indicate that these are desperate, impulsive solutions rather than competent ones. The prognosis is most favorable if the patient, although depressed and contemplating suicide, thinks of those who would suffer from his deed. Here, libidinal object cathexis is the ally of life.

Once the therapist has committed himself to treat the case, he must be available at all times, at all hours. Much can be done on the telephone. The depressed patient who has insomnia is truly lonely at night and his reaching out demands patient response. The therapist's libidinal availability to the patient's loneliness and distress presents an attitude by the object different from that of the original one who was libidinally absent. While we do not believe that the more benign attitude is in and of itself curative, because distorted self and object representations remain, we do propose that a consistent, benign atmosphere will become one the patient can trust when his distortions are corrected; then he will be able to use the therapist's libidinal cathexes to build "good" self and object representations. In the beginning of treatment, the climate is arranged and will be remembered later by the patient. Also, if there is a modicum of libido in the self and object representations, the patient will be able, immediately, to respond to the therapist's kindly interest. If the self and object representations are too aggressively tinged, the prognosis is unfavorable.

An interest in what the patient is trying to convey is always in order, even though not immediately rewarding. The suicidal wish, impulse, or gesture is to be regarded as a form of preverbal communication. Expressing interest in what the patient means will, at the very least, convey to him that we understand that he wishes to communicate something. This will alert the ego to that fact and induce an effort to express the feelings and wishes in words rather than in an irreversible act. Even if verbalization is not immediately successful, encouraging the patient to direct his attention and efforts toward verbalization is ego building. It promotes delay, thought as trial action, symbolization and semantic communication, which involve higher levels of object relations. It is not implied here that all this is accomplished on the telephone in the middle of the night. Usually, merely raising the question gives the patient something to think about, which buys time. He may not have to kill himself immediately while his ego has the unfinished task of finding the answer. If necessary, the therapist should offer to see the patient, but he must be sincere in his offer. Again, if there is a modicum of object libido, the patient will not want the therapist to be disturbed during the night. In many years of practice, giving patients complete freedom to call when necessary, we have had very few night calls. The patient wants to preserve the "good" object.

Availability is more than physical availability or a good telephone answering service. It is an attitude. At the outset of treatment, of course, it is difficult to convey it all at once. It has to be done repeatedly and consistently. Therefore, it is important to arrange the treatment schedule frequently, at first, in critical cases. One becomes a reliable "good" object gradually and this can turn the tide in times of stress. On the telephone, during the night, it is useful to have already built up such a favorable balance. Then one can say, "We will be able to talk more tomorrow." Again, the suicidal impulse may yield to delay if there is something to look forward to. Many depressed patients have a particular bad time of the day. It is frequently difficult, in depression, to get out of bed in the morning. Some depressed persons find dusk difficult. Some find bedtime particularly hard. The therapist should ascertain which is the most difficult time for a given patient and arrange to be available then.

With anorexic patients and even with those more mildly depressed, it is necessary to be interested in their nutrition. For the anorexic patient it can be life-saving to ensure that he is not slowly starving to death and to take strenuous measures if one finds that he is. He might have to be hospitalized to be fed. But short of that, an interest in his food might stimulate his appetite. Again, it might encounter and reinforce whatever modicum of cathexis of the "good" object exists. Even if the patient is well-enough nourished, an interest in what he eats meets him at the primitive, infantile level of concern with bodily need and oral gratification. In our experience, expressions of such interest are usually met with defensive rather than gratifying responses. But the therapist need not be dismayed. The "bad" object and the punitive superego are dominant in depression. One patient jeered repeatedly at the therapist's persistent interest in what she ate. Nevertheless, she looked forward to such sessions with reluctant pleasure. After feeling assured that the therapist would still be interested despite repeated rebuffs, she began her sessions with, "I suppose you are going to ask me what I ate." The therapist's matter-of-fact answer was, "Yes, of course," not responding to but welcoming the aggression in the challenge.

The fact that there is a tomorrow, a future, needs to be stressed. Not only during the desperate telephone call, but throughout, the therapist should phrase his comments to indicate complete conviction about the future. Statements in the future tense, even the near future, are desirable. "When I see you tomorrow, we will try to understand more about that." Such statements are reserved for the depressed patient and are used for the special reason of reminding him of the future. They are contraindicated in all other types of cases as a habitual form of terminating a session.

Some of what is contained in the discussion of emergency measures for dealing with depression apply also to the long pull. In other respects, long-range treatment of the patient who is depressed depends upon the diagnosis—the structure of the ego which is experiencing this affect. In particular, we would assume that there has been object loss and we would search in the life history for its origin as well as for those repetitive experiences which have reinforced it. This explains why, in depression, it is necessary for the therapist to remain a reliable object. The distortions in self and object representations are sought out. The degree of differentiation is important to know. Gradually, as the therapist understands the precise life experiences in which self-esteem was impaired and objects were lost, either in reality or because of aggressive cathexis, early disillusionment, and the like, he begins to build self-esteem by showing the adult ego where these were not the patient's fault and possibly not always the fault of the object either.

Mr. Xavier, thirty years old, was in treatment because his marriage had failed, he was not progressing in his profession, and he was also depressed. He had been hospitalized for pneumonia at the age of twenty months. The therapist engaged him in a joint reconstruction of the event—the pain of separation; being in a strange place; the inevitable rage and regression; disillusionment in his omnipotent objects; the assault upon the self representations as well because, at that age, differentiation is not complete; the wish to regress to an earlier and more blissful state, which in this case, as in many, is represented by the suicidal wish; the actual pain and suffering of the illness and the impairment of the still-hazy body image. All these were understood and the affects relived in painful nights of insomnia. Mr. Xavier would say, "You don't know how bad it feels." The therapist did not protest that he did know. This was the patient's way of verbalizing the feeling of premature separation and loneliness.

When much of this was worked through, the patient's reality testing was enlisted. Unfortunate as this hospitalization had been for him, and much as the infant experienced it as the failure and betrayal of his omnipotent objects, his adult ego could realize that neither he nor his parents were at fault. Caution must be exercised in not pressing such logic too early, lest it become an apologia for the parents against the patient's feeling. Before such realization could be integrated, Mr. Xavier was a discouraging patient. He had adopted, in this infantile trauma, the defense of never trusting or needing another person. This, in essence, was why his marriage had failed. In the transference, he refused to accept the therapist as a "good" object, and often mocked him for his efforts. "You certainly are persistent," he would say. The persistence and consistency were rewarded when the distortions were corrected and the patient began to identify with the therapist, verbalizing that he wanted to be nice and kind like him.

Mr. Young was one of many who suffer from chronic depression because of identification with a depressed parent. Mr. Young's father died suddenly when the patient was three weeks old. That the mother's depression was melancholic, not normal mourning, is attested by the fact that she never remarried, despite opportunities which Mr. Young knew about. He felt that his mother was devoted to the two children. His evidence for this was that she never did anything else. She never went out, and had no friends. From the quality of the transference, however, the therapist knew that her "availability" was only physical. This could be judged from Mr. Young's very limited demands upon the therapist. Brought up in an unresponsive, unattuned atmosphere, he expected no more. He was surprised, but not pleased, to note that the therapist, by his tone and expression, was not depressed. He would have preferred the symbiotic oneness that joining his depressed state would provide. It is simple to realize, however, that after numerous interpretations to the effect that Mr. Young's identification with the only parent he had had kept him depressed, he could begin to loosen this tie somewhat and then the therapist's more normal affective state provided an opportunity for healthier identification.

Jacobson discusses the transference problems in dealing with depression in borderline and psychotic structures. To her, borderline personality structure differs from neurosis in degree: "These patients show ego distortions and superego defects, disturbances in their object relations, and a pathology of affects beyond what we find in ordinary neurotics." [5] And, she continues: ". . . depressives try to recover their

[5] E. Jacobson, *Depression,* p. 285.

lost ability to love and to function by dint of excessive magic love from their love object. As a melancholic patient once put it: 'Love is oxygen to me.' " [6]

Because, in treatment, the therapist inevitably becomes the love object and the center of the depressive conflict, Jacobson regards the prerequisite for psychotherapy as the capacity to form a transference. This coincides with our own position that, for a favorable prognosis, there must be some capacity for libidinal cathexis of the object. Jacobson also advocates frequent sessions during crisis, but she is cautious about prolonging frequent contact beyond the crisis. Daily sessions may be experienced as seductive promises too great to be fulfilled, as an obligation which promotes masochistic submission, and as an opportunity to exacerbate ambivalence conflicts. She therefore advocates three or four times per week rather than five, six, or seven. She says: "I believe that the emotional quality of the analyst's responses is more important than the quantity of sessions." And, "There must be a continuous, subtle, empathic tie between the analyst and his depressive patients; we must be very careful not to let empty silences grow or not to talk too long, too rapidly, and too emphatically; that is, never to give too much or too little." [7] She speaks also of the need from the therapist for spontaneity, flexible adjustment to mood level, warm understanding, and unwavering respect. These are more desirable than overkindness, sympathy, and reassurance.

Another author on techniques for the treatment of depression, Levin,[8] provides an interesting list of emergency devices. We cannot agree wholeheartedly with his approach because it is based on the treatment of depression as though it is a distinct diagnostic entity. That form of treatment disregards developmental diagnosis and constitutes a "blanket" technique for all types of depression. We illustrate our own technical suggestions:

Miss Ziegler, age twenty-one, was referred to the therapist while in a suicidal crisis which her family did not take seriously. She had just been expelled from her home because her stepmother thought she was old enough to be on her own. Her father was a passive man who

[6] *Ibid.*, p. 286.   [7] *Ibid.*, p. 299.
[8] S. Levin, "Some Suggestions for Treating the Depressed Patient."

went along with whatever his second wife wanted. Miss Ziegler's mother had died when the patient was two years old and the father married shortly thereafter. There were two younger children of this second marriage. Although the stepmother had made a home and provided for the patient's minimal physical care, she had never had much emotional interest in her, preferring her own children. The father was very close to Miss Ziegler in her early childhood, latency, and most of her adolescence, only yielding to his wife's jealousy of that closeness when the girl approached early adulthood. When the therapist saw the patient, she was desperate. She was temporarily living with a girl friend and the father was providing living expenses and was willing to pay for the therapy. The patient had tried to begin college but could not sustain it. The therapist saw Miss Ziegler through the immediate crisis by frequent contact, by enlisting the father's libidinal as well as financial support, and by advising more stable and supportive living arrangements. The patient responded well. Although she remained depressed, the suicidal crisis passed. This gave the therapist leisure to diagnose accurately and to address treatment to the traumatic lesions.

We shall use this case to illustrate why ventilation of aggression is undesirable. It would have been no trouble at all to have elicited aggression against the stepmother, a prime representative of the "bad" object in unconscious fantasy and in fairy tales, and against the father who failed to protect sufficiently. However, this patient, as so many depressed patients, was already suffering from unbearable object loss. The therapeutic objective is to build up her "good" self and object representations so that the ego, strengthened, would later be able to tolerate the reality of the "badness" as well. In this case there was reason, in the patient's capacity for positive transference, in her appreciation for the therapist's helpfulness, and in her response to it, to assume that the mother of her infancy was adequate. In this context, an adequate mother is one who had provided gratifying oral and symbiotic experience, had catalyzed ego development, had been available at critical periods to coordinate maturation and ego development, had enabled the child to build up more libidinally than aggressively cathected self and object representations. Unfortunately, the mother died at a stage in the child's development when separation-individuation had not yet been completed, when object loss would feel like loss of part of oneself, when disappointment in the failure of the mother's omnipotence would result in disillusionment, aggression, and loss of self-esteem, when separation anxiety would be severe, when the capacity to mourn and thereby overcome the loss was not yet available.

What we have just described is an early life situation that predisposes to depression. This patient might have gone through latency and adolescence in a state which those close to her might have regarded as "moody" and which we would describe as chronically depressed. The father's closeness provided some continuation of symbiotic gratification, but such a relationship cannot be altogether growth promoting because it is out of phase; it is determined more by the father's need than by the child's; it is imbued with unmanageable oedipal overtones. The suicidal depression ensued at the point when the father's loyalty to his second wife constituted a second object loss for the daughter. The predisposition encountered a precipitating psychic event, remobilizing unneutralized aggression against self and object representations, and resulting in loss of the object and loss of self-esteem. Oedipal guilt also played a role in exacerbation of the depression.

The greater part of the first year of therapy had as its prime objective reinforcement of positively cathected self and object representations—in the present relationships, in the transference, and in the primary objects. This is never done falsely or in a Pollyanna-like manner. The therapist sought out those positive cathexes that actually existed but had been all but destroyed by the aggression. Only when the patient thought better of herself and her objects did the therapist also help her verbalize the aggression she rightfully felt. We do not seek to rid a patient of aggression because it is "wrong" or "negative," but only because, in unneutralized form, it is not available to the ego for purposes that serve the patient. Miss Ziegler, for example, had not been able to continue her studies because neutralized aggression was not available to the ego for that task. Nor could she deal with her father in terms of what he could do for her in a realistic and phase-specific way while she was so excessively angry with him that she remained in the vicious cycle of wishing to destroy him and then fearing further object loss.[9]

The following is a clinical illustration of a technique based on a recognition that the analyst's task with a suicidal patient is to foster separation of the self representations from the negative object representations. A young woman in her early thirties had had a psychotic mother who died when the patient was four. The young woman herself awoke depressed one morning and thought that if she held her breath long enough, she could die. She started to do this, thinking further of smothering herself with a pillow, and then, as she subsequently told the therapist, she thought of her (the therapist) and realized that she would want her to stay alive. So she stopped trying to kill herself. The fact that she was able to think of the therapist as a separate but positive object at such a crucial moment showed that the therapeutic milieu had capitalized on her libidinal impulses, separating them from the negative object representations of the dead mother. This was the fruition of many months of psychotherapy. Lack of response under the guise of benign neutrality would have been experienced by this patient as hostile indifference, a reaction she had often felt from her withdrawn mother. It would have confirmed her fear that nobody had ever cared about her or ever would, and could very well have destroyed the ego growth that had so painfully and precariously taken place. If, at that point, the therapist had attempted to explore the aggression implied in the original suicidal impulse, this patient, addicted to self-blame, would have experienced it as condemnatory criticism and gross misunderstanding. The triumph of the libidinal cathexis of self and object representations would have been lost.[10]

Mrs. Allen was in treatment for two and one-half years as a once-a-week psychotherapy patient. She was fifty-four years old, the mother of two sons. She had been married for twenty-five years. When treatment began she was a moderately obese woman of untidy appearance. Her facial expression was one of chronic, angry discontent and she was never far from tears. Her speech was often coarse and she had difficulty in finding what she considered to be the "right" words to

[9] Material provided by Joyce Edward.
[10] Material provided by Dr. Marjorie T. White.

describe events, and especially feelings. She complained of depression, "bad thoughts," intense fear of serious illness, hatred and contempt for her husband, lack of desire for friends, feelings of inferiority and worthlessness. She had been in treatment several times before, for periods ranging from one to two years, with three different therapists. She had terminated her last treatment about one year before she began this round, as a result of what she regarded as her therapist's lack of interest in her.

She recalled her childhood with tremendous anger and self-pity, describing her mother as an abominable, bitter woman, who took refuge in constant ill health and berated and belittled her miserly, ineffective, unambitious husband. She herself felt neglected, attacked, rejected, and the object of her mother's rages and disparagement. Her father committed suicide some three years after the mother's death from cancer when the patient was thirty years old. She felt that she had suffered unalterable damage at their hands. She had one sibling, a sister, four years her junior, whom she says she raised, and who was a sickly, quiet child. They were close in a covertly hostile way until shortly before Mrs. Allen started therapy, at which time the sister had berated her for what she recalled as mistreatment at her hands as a child.

At the age of twenty-nine, Mrs. Allen married a divorcé. He had one son, with whom Mrs. Allen never countenanced any relationship. She said she never loved her husband but married him because there was no one else. She regarded him as a complete failure as a source of both financial and emotional support, and then he became partially impotent so he could not even give her physical satisfaction. She described her older son as always having had problems, as unhappy and unsettled as far as work was concerned. She described her younger son as intellectually gifted and pursuing an academic career. She herself had held one job as typist-clerk for many years, gave this up because she was bored and despised her boss, and, following that, did not work for some time. When treatment began, she had been working at a similar job for almost two years.

Early in treatment, a diagnostic graph was tentatively drawn: her psychosexual level was primarily oral, with forward thrusts into the anal. Aggressive and libidinal drives were not well neutralized; frustration tolerance was low. Object relations were on the level of need gratification, with some advances toward object constancy, particularly evident in her relationship with her younger son. Differentiation was inadequate. She functioned for the most part in the symbiotic mode. She could not use anxiety as a signal, so she tended to be overwhelmed, could not use defenses well, and feared annihilation. Distinctions between self representations and object representations were blurred. Her preoedipal superego development was harsh and severe. Defenses were primarily projection, denial, turning against the self, and isolation. The therapeutic task was conceptualized as testing out whether there was irreversible ego defect, or ego distortion which might be altered and so enable the patient to begin to use ego functions that existed, but had not been used effectively. If the ego functions of reality testing and judgment could be improved, therapy might proceed beyond the stalemate in which the former treatment had ended. But before progress could be made in this direction, it would be necessary for her to move from symbiosis toward separation-individuation, aggression would have to become neutralized, and her superego would have to become less harsh and overcritical.

Initially she complained that she could not "answer" the therapist's questions or explain herself and that she felt "pushed against a wall" when asked to think about an event. When it became clear that this was connected in her mind with her angry encounters with her mother, with whom she felt helpless and under attack, and to several incidents during her school years when she felt furiously unable to protect herself from teachers by "answering back," she was able to proceed. Since her fear of harming the therapist with her unneutralized aggression seemed to be playing a part, she was assured, when appropriate, that "words could not kill." The therapist was also very careful, in the beginning, not to encourage too much ventilation of aggression because of the patient's powerful belief that she could kill by wishing.

Mrs. Allen announced that the therapist was probably thinking she was a "hopeless case," that no one could help her. It was repeatedly pointed out that this was her conclusion; the therapist did not feel as hopeless or helpless as she did. However, the therapist said that she was not omnipotent, could not read minds, and needed the patient's help to understand her. The job had to be a shared one, although the functions were different. In this way the patient's ego was enlisted so that work could proceed, albeit slowly. The difference between her thoughts and those of the therapist was always pointed out when she started a statement with: "I know what you're thinking. . . ." She regularly made statements like, "Everyone knows that," or "Doesn't everyone feel this way about . . ." These statements were minutely examined so that she could see that what she thought or concluded was not necessarily what others thought or concluded. When she gave the reasons for or probable results of a piece of behavior as if they were facts, it was usually possible to determine with her that she had inferred things from her own beliefs rather than from the facts, which she had not inquired about. There were statements such as, "I know you want me to have friends," or "I can't entertain even though you want me to." The therapist would reply, "Do not do so for me." She spoke about how terrible the elder son must have felt when, at the age of two years, his brother was born and brought home. Inquiry into how she seemed to understand his feelings with such depth elicited the memory that her mother gave birth to a stillborn son when she was two years old.

Opportunities to aid neutralization of aggression came particularly through her relationship with her son. When she felt very angry with him she was encouraged to delay her furious response, if necessary to walk away, to delay words or action. She learned that, most often, it was easier for her to feel angry with him than sad for him, and that her anger masked sadness at the difficult times he experienced. As the therapy proceeded, albeit unevenly and with many setbacks, she began to be able to distinguish between depression, sadness, and anger. On one occasion, her son had broken some dishes; her observation to the therapist was, "You know, I didn't even get angry inside. I helped him clean up the pieces, feeling very sad for him."

Opportunities to work with the harsh superego components came when she described some of her extramarital affairs with great shame and self-blame. They were with most unsuitable partners, and always ended with her feeling rejected and let down. The therapist could say, "How good that you could try to get some pleasure for yourself. But let us look at how you went about it." When she challengingly said that, although the doctor had told her to lose weight, she was not going to diet, the therapist said, "Sometimes in giving yourself pleasure, you tend to have to hurt yourself, too." That she was beginning to feel better began to be reflected in her daily life. She also cried less in the sessions, took pleasure in refurnishing part of her house, led a more active social life, and actually made a relationship which she called a "friendship." However, she could not allow the therapist to feel that she had been helped at all.

She had always maintained that her mother was totally bad. The degree of improvement the patient was showing threw this into question. Careful investigation of this area revealed that the mother was highly unpredictable and inconsistent rather than "bad." There were times when she had indeed been very loving toward the patient. She had called her by a pet name; she had struggled with the father to get money for clothes for the children; she had cooked good food for them. A number of positive memories began to emerge. In talking about her unhappiness at school, one event was described in detail. The therapist asked if her mother had been able to do anything. The patient looked startled and said she had never told her mother what was happening! As she reflected on this, she could admit that her mother could not have helped to relieve pain she did not know about. When asked if her mother had ever intervened on other occasions, she remembered several situations of which she had told her mother, who had indeed tried to help and protect her. The patient liked to hear about other people's misfortunes, especially if they were individuals whom she disliked. Her sister told her that their cousin was having financial trouble because she had so many children and she had heard that their house was a mess. Mrs. Allen reported the following dream: "I went to see my cousin; the house was beautiful and everything was tidy and well organized." The interpretation was: "You seem to have many loving wishes that have to be kept hidden."

Mrs. Allen defended against loving feelings. She had learned to avoid good feelings because their loss was so painful. Instead, she chose to have a consistent object, even though it was a consistently bad one. Positive feelings toward the therapist had to be defended against too; she could not feel gratitude. The object world had to remain distorted. As work on this aspect continued, Mrs. Allen began to correct her distortions. There followed a session in which she reported that she was feeling "pretty good" and described having had some good experiences. She even could laugh, always a sign that the ego is stronger.[11]

In this case, the presenting symptom of depression and the apparent level of ego functioning, self and object differentiation, defensive system, drive attenuation, and so on suggested a more serious diagnosis and prognosis than turned out to be true after a period of treatment. It is described in some detail to show a few of the ego psychological techniques which are to be employed regardless of prognosis. The particular relevance to the discussion of depression is that it illustrates how identification with the reliable facet of the mother's inconsistent behavior toward the patient resulted in aggressively cathected self and object representations. At the outset of treatment it is not possible accurately to appraise the degree of differentiation. Inadequate differentiation suggestive of borderline structure seemed likely here. Ego-building measures, applied at the beginning, set in motion completion of differentiation. Particularly illustrated is how treatment furthers structuralization. It is shown that an affect, depression, can be used as a defense. The last aspect of treatment described demonstrates ego growth in the capacity for humor. In essence, our techniques for treatment of nonsuicidal depression are no different from general growth-promoting measures. The structure of the ego in which the symptom (or affect) is embedded is of greater therapeutic interest than the symptom itself.

The affect, depression, is difficult to treat, not primarily because it is so often a threat to life and because it elicits empathy and concern in the therapist, but because its theoretical aspects and therefore technical implications are, as yet, inadequately understood. We do not yet have a comprehensive affect theory despite the work of some outstanding psychoanalytic theorists. Not only Freud, but Abraham, Bibring, Brierley, Fenichel, Glover, Jacobson, Rapaport, and Zetzel, among others, have applied themselves to evolving a theory of affects. Although some of these contributions are as significant as one would expect of such major theorists, a twofold reason explains why they

---

[11] Material provided by Nathene Ruskin.

have thus far failed to provide as confident a theory as we find in other areas of psychoanalysis. First, affects have been thought to follow the model affect, anxiety. Freud usually proceeded in his lifelong building of theory, rarely returning to revise earlier formulations. His theory of anxiety, however, was one of the few about which he made a major revision. Some contemporary theorists are still working out the problem of anxiety and are considering whether Freud's second theory entirely supersedes his first.

Second, and consequent upon the first reason, is that affect theory has not yet been integrated with ego psychological theory as a whole. Rapaport [12] and Jacobson [13] have attempted to systematize affect theory, but only recently has another contributor, Ross,[14] selected one aspect of it—the relationship between affect and cognition—to consider as part of a larger attempt to unify affect theory and to integrate it with psychoanalytic developmental theory. Along with the post-Hartmann ego psychologists, Ross enlarges the postulate of an undifferentiated matrix. He presumes that, at the beginning of life, there exists an unorganized mass of equilibrial, proprioceptive, thermal, vibratory, tactile, rhythmic, sonal, and tonal phenomena, leading to a diffuse state of affectivity in the neonate. He regards empathy as synonymity of feeling and knowing and shows that, at the outset, affect and cognition are one, becoming differentiated in the course of development. After differentiation, normal affective experiences may follow the pathway of regression in the service of the ego. This direction in theory construction points the way toward an ego psychological, unified theory of affects. It accords particularly well with Spitz' [15] concept that affect and percept form a bond that enables the neonate to bridge the area between soma and psyche. These theoretical explorations promise to solve the mind-body problem—the so-called mysterious leap from soma to psyche—because careful theoretical consideration of affectivity in the early weeks of life can lead to clarification of how this leap is taken.

[12] D. Rapaport, "On the Psycho-Analytic Theory of Affects."
[13] E. Jacobson, *Depression.*   [14] N. Ross, "Affect as Cognition."
[15] R. A. Spitz, "Bridges: On Anticipation, Duration, and Meaning."

⤳ 15 ⤳

SPECIAL FORMS OF EGO MODIFICATION

THIS CHAPTER WILL SHOW how those ego modifications which are manifest through sexual behavior may be understood within the context of psychoanalytic developmental psychology. We refer to aspects of sexuality which are usually categorized as perversions—homosexuality, transvestitism, fetishism, and the like. Normal sexuality is the expression of attainment of genitality, which psychosexual level is extended to include capacity for object love and is most desirably exercised with a nonincestuous partner—that is, upon resolution of the oedipal conflict. It is evident, by such definition, that innumerable pitfalls lie along the complex developmental path to this perhaps ideal state of mature sexuality.

It is difficult, these days, to comprehend fully the storm created some sixty years ago by Freud's discovery of infantile sexuality. More than any other aspect of his psychoanalytic investigations, it was this that led to his virtual excommunication from the scientific community of that era. Obviously, science retained the taint of Victorian hypocrisy; sex could be practiced but not mentioned. In his despair, Freud said that it was his fate to have discovered that which every nursemaid already knew; sex was practiced in the nursery but not mentioned in the drawing room.

But infantile sexuality differs markedly from true adult sexuality. In much popular thought and writing, infantile sex practices are confused with adult sexuality. Most lower animals attain sexual maturity and the physical capacity to employ it simultaneously. Man's sexual maturation is diphasic; it proceeds through the pregenital phases

—oral, anal, and phallic—in the infantile period (birth through five years) and then becomes latent until puberty and adolescence bring resurgence of sexuality, now consistent with physical capability. Normally, genitality is reached in late adolescence. The genital and phallic phases are not the same. The phallic phase is pregenital, often incorrectly confused with the genital phase because the *physical* genital apparatus is involved in both. True genitality, however, involves the combination of physical capability with capacity for object love, thus distinguishing it from the pregenital phases, including the phallic, which is concerned with the physical apparatus more for narcissistic and exhibitionistic purposes than for the expression of love toward an object.

This framework of normal sexual development provides an opportunity to understand sexual deviation of all kinds. The term *perversion* is another psychoanalytic term with negative connotations in popular thought, yet it means nothing more than the persistence of pregenital arrest or regression into the period of life when normally pregenital sexuality is superseded by genitality. That competent sexual functioning depends upon attainment of genital primacy had long been a basic tenet of psychoanalytic theory. Genital primacy is regarded as that level of sexual functioning that results from psychosexual maturation through the oral, anal, and phallic phases to the genital. The term *primacy* is added because pregenitality is never altogether lost; pregenital desires recede, giving way to genitality, but remain available for pleasure—for example, in foreplay—under the dominance of genitality. Hence, genital *primacy*.

Incisive modification of the theory of genital primacy was suggested by Ross, as chairman of a panel discussion, The Theory of Genital Primacy in the Light of Ego Psychology, held in 1968.[1] In his introductory remarks, Ross said, "The concept of genital primacy appears to be one of the most solid bastions in the structure of psychoanalytic theory." [2] He pointed out the apparent paradox that there are patients with severe neurotic and even psychotic symptomatology

---

[1] M. A. Berezin, (reporter), "The Theory of Genital Primacy in the Light of Ego Psychology."
[2] N. Ross, "The Primacy of Genitality in the Light of Ego Psychology: Introductory Remarks," p. 267.

who, nevertheless, are fully orgastic. This led him to suggest that the theory of genital primacy be reexamined. He proposed that, in order to do this, the particular problem of female orgasm be discussed. This matter has been confused by inadequately controlled methods of observation, by confusion between anatomy and psychology, and by nonobjectivity. Ross thought that much that is concluded to be female frigidity is the result of male prematurity and insufficient foreplay. He observed that most women can reach clitoral orgasm in a relatively short time and without too much foreplay; with prolongation of lovemaking, these same women may reach vaginal orgasm.

Returning to the main theme of genital primacy, he spoke of:

. . . the stark clinical fact that many men and women achieve such genital levels without being capable of mature functioning, not only in the realm of object relationships, but in other areas of ego functioning. . . . It is an open question whether it is enough to correlate orgastic potency simply with mature object relationships, or to subsume other ego functions under a broader category of personality than the theory now encompasses.[3]

Another clinical phenomenon was posed, that of the person with higher levels of ego functioning but whose sexual functioning is nevertheless less adequate than that of the less-mature personality. He answers this issue himself by stating that ". . . I am far from unmindful of the fact that the genital apparatus may often be the avenue of discharge for impulses and fantasies of pregenital and nongenital nature." [4]

We think that the paradox of the concept of genital primacy is reconciled by the ego-psychological addendum to psychoanalytic theory—namely, that the psychosexual maturational line is not the sole component in the totality of development. Our own observation concurs with that of Ross; the sexual apparatus can mature biologically while ego development remains severely flawed. Patients with impaired ego functioning credibly report competent sexual functioning, whereas patients with higher levels of ego development appear to be prone to sexual malfunction—usually impotence or frigidity. Especially in women is this disparity noticeable because the female sex-

___

[3] *Ibid.*, pp. 271–72.   [4] *Ibid.*, p. 275.

ual apparatus is more complex than the male. Impotence in the male
ranges from total erectile incapacity, through weak erection, premature ejaculation, delayed ejaculation, ejaculation without orgasm, to
inability to ejaculate. In the female, frigidity ranges from total anesthesia of the sex organs, through vaginal anesthesia with clitoral orgastic capacity, to partial vaginal sensation without orgastic intensity.
Especially pertinent to the problem of perverse sexuality is the observation that gratifying heterosexual discharge in some instances nevertheless does not ensure libidinal gratification. Ross concluded that
"although there appears to be no doubt that sexuality plays a unique
and leading role in psychic development, with the advances in ego
psychology . . . it is no longer possible to maintain that libidinal development and the maturation of the personality are dependent vari-
ables. The theory of genital primacy, as originally stated, assumes that
they are." [5]

This led us to reconsider the concept of genital primacy in the
light of contemporary theory. We believe that Freud always had in
mind the crucial matter of relatedness between self and other and
that it remained for the ego psychologists, beginning with Hartmann,
to define more sharply the development of object relations and of
drive-taming processes. It is evident, for example, that with inadequate neutralization, aggression may dominate and aberrant sexual
behavior, such as sadism, will be the logical consequence. When we
consider the object-relations developmental line, it is obvious that sexuality in conjunction with relatedness to another person consists of a
combination of developmental features. It is developmental failure,
therefore, that makes for difficulty in reaching "genital primacy."

Miss Judson, now thirty-three years old, was told by her manic-
depressive mother that there were approximately twenty-five infant-
nurses in her first two years of life—a "parade" of nurses, the
mother said. Miss Judson can herself remember having had five or
more in the years when continuous memory became possible. The
parents, probably because of the mother's lifelong emotional illness,
secluded themselves from the child. Miss Judson, since adolescence,
has had countless sexual encounters and does function orgastically.

[5] *Ibid.*, p. 281.

She has been married and divorced. She now dates four or five men and enjoys all of them sexually, a matter which she perceives as a problem to be worked out in therapy. Indeed it is a problem in object relations, because, as an infant, Miss Judson had had to learn to extract from the environment (Mahler) that which she needed for development. This saved Miss Judson from psychosis, but left her arrested at the object-relations level of need-gratification; she could respond to anyone who happened to be at hand. But she came for treatment, nevertheless, because she wanted not simply orgastic pleasure but also the capacity to love.

And so it is no longer tenable to think of psychosexual maturation as the sole determinant of sexual functioning, nor do we think that Freud meant to have his theory interpreted so simplistically. Contemporary and past psychoanalytic thought regarding sexuality run counter to the behavioristically based conclusions of a growing number of sexologists, of whom Masters and Johnson are representative. They view sexual functioning in mechanistic terms and have proposed cures for sexual dysfunction which consist of teaching any two persons how to adjust to each other mechanically. For the time being, this form of sexual training is restricted to two persons of opposite sex, but that may change shortly. If any two persons can be taught to provide mutual gratification, regardless of level of object relations, sometimes without having known each other before the training sessions, then homosexual couples might well be treated similarly. But we are unable to predict where the line will then be drawn in such treatment modalities. Will they, for example, match up masochists with sadists so that the partners in such arrangements can attain more gratifying experiences? What can be done to improve the sexual functioning of fetishists? We shall discuss more fully the psychoanalytic view of these sexual problems shortly. Here we want to indicate that nonpsychoanalytically oriented treatment of sexual dysfunction leads to untenable logical conclusions because they are based on shallow conceptualization.

Nevertheless, Masters and Johnson, in their first book,[6] made a few valuable contributions to understanding female sexuality through

---

[6] W. H. Masters and V. E. Johnson, *Human Sexual Reponse.*

having conducted minute investigation into the physiology and functioning of the female sexual apparatus. They are equivocal about Kinsey's erroneous conclusion that, because there are few nerve endings
in the vagina, the Freudian notion of vaginal orgasm is a fiction.
Masters and Johnson think that the vagina and clitoris operate in
concert but that the clitoris remains the organ of discharge. Here they
fall into the same error as Kinsey and his collaborators, who also fail
to relate psychological aspects to the biological. It is also unfortunate
that, not content with investigations into gynecology (which is his
area of competence), Masters ventured, along with Johnson, into the
therapy of sexual dysfunction, as they term it.[7] There they use the
nonpsychoanalytic methods we have discussed.

In psychoanalytically oriented psychotherapy the road to adequate
sexual functioning and especially to genital primacy is far more difficult because here we are interested in more than symptom cure.
While symptom cure may seem desirable in some instances, its dura-
bility is doubtful. But duration is the least of the matter. The most is
that genitality is inextricably interrelated with object constancy, and
so we feel that those who are willing to settle for mechanical orgasm
without love settle for less than life has to offer. This is the problem
with which the Ross panel grappled. Unwilling, as psychoanalysts, to
seize on simplistic solutions, the connections among frigidity, genitality, and object relations were carefully considered and, as scientists,
the panelists raised questions for open-ended research and continuing
investigation. Our own hypothesis regarding the issue the panel
posed—namely, that clinicians often encounter frigid or impotent
persons whose psychic structural development is higher than that of
others who are nevertheless more orgastic—is that precisely because of the higher development, the well-structured personality has
to cope with object relations and unconscious (usually oedipal, incestuous) fantasy. Therefore, to go to the other diagnostic end of the
spectrum, the psychotic woman who is relatively objectless may be
orgastic because she is "unencumbered" by the higher structuralization of the neurotic woman. The lesser structuralization of the psychotic facilitates simple physiological response to stimulus. In borderline structures, one has to consider the innumerable problems in

[7] W. H. Masters and V. E. Johnson, *Human Sexual Inadequacy.*

sexual functioning in terms of such guidelines as failure in gender identity, and fear of irreversible regression in orgasm, because the barely differentiated self and object representations may become undifferentiated. Or, to put these concepts of Jacobson in Mahler's frame of reference, fear of symbiotic merger and loss of identity may inhibit orgastic regression. The more intact ego can better tolerate the momentary regression in orgasm because regression is reversible—in Kris's terms, in the service of the ego. Other problems to be considered in borderline structures are fear of dominance of unneutralized aggression, fear of loss of sphincter control, and, most morbid of all, absence of such fears with resultant decompensation.

The neurotically structured woman may present herself to the analyst as perhaps frigid in some degree, or frigidity may come to light after defensive arrangements, which had made apparently adequate sexual functioning possible, are swept away. While, on the face of it, such temporary frigidity in the course of the psychoanalysis of neurosis has the appearance of having made the patient worse instead of better, defensively determined sexual functioning is later replaced by true genital primacy. In the psychoanalysis of the neurotic woman and in the psychotherapy of the more highly structured borderline personality, the treatment goal in the area of sexual functioning can be that of uncovering unconscious fantasy, resolving oedipal ties, and thus releasing orgastic potential in the context of already-existing capacity to love. Where capacity to love is deficient because of problems in object relations, this important line of development requires therapeutic attention.

Another discussion on problems of female sexuality, also sponsored by the American Psychoanalytic Association, reconsidered the psychoanalytic position on female sexuality in the light of Masters and Johnson's and Sherfey's challenge to the transfer theory.[8] This is the theory that holds that the psychosexual maturation of both boy and girl are similar through the phallic phase but that, with attainment of genitality, the girl transfers cathexis from clitoris to vagina. The panel acknowledged Masters and Johnson's contribution to physiol-

[8] M. Heiman, J. S. Kestenberg, T. Benedek, and S. Keiser, "Discussion of Mary Jane Sherfey: The Evolution and the Nature of Female Sexuality in Relation to Psychoanalytic Theory."

ogy. Kinsey's conclusions as well as his methodology had already been dismissed as naive because he had not taken the unconscious into account.[9] This panel found that vaginal orgastic capacity, unless reflexive, involves the profound matter of feminine identification. Despite paucity of vaginal nerve endings, vaginal orgasm is possible because feminine gender identity, unconscious as well as conscious, promotes cathexis of the vagina as the organ of sexual receptivity. Facilitated by this factor, the entire female sexual apparatus functions in coordination, thereby concentrating sensation in the vagina. Thus, the transfer theory is upheld when the unconscious developmental features in female sexuality are included in consideration of this important subject.

Obviously, the physiological details of the foregoing discussion of sexuality cannot be applicable to male sexual functioning. However, major psychological and especially developmental features are the same—namely psychosexual maturation, ego development with special emphases on gender identity and object relations, drive taming, and so forth. In the more highly structured personalities, the place of unconscious fantasy is central and is unique to psychoanalysis as distinguished from all other theories. Male sexual pathology is no less complex than female, although male physiology is simpler. Of particular importance is the passive-active issue. Much male impotence may be attributed to problems in the subtle shift in object relations—from cathexis of the preoedipal to the oedipal mother as the first sexual object. While these are externally the same person, the passive mode of the boy as receiver of maternal ministration can, if it persists into adulthood, result in impotence of varying degrees. The differences in formation of male and female gender identifications, in oedipal conflicts, and in the vicissitudes of superego formation, are well described by Jacobson (chapter 5). Sexual pathology in men and women can be attributed to failure in any line of development— arrest or fixation in pregenital psychosexual stages, or failures in drive taming, object relations, and the other developmental vicissitudes indicated in figure 1.

With the clarification that sexual behavior can be diverted to purposes other than genital discharge—such as for pregenital needs or

[9] R. P. Knight, "Psychiatric Issues in the Kinsey Report on Males."

for physical contact, the main purpose of which is to gratify symbiotic needs, or for objectless discharge even when another person is overtly involved in the act—we are able to show how sexual pathology, including the perversions, may be understood within the context of psychoanalytic developmental psychology. Since diagnosis is not made on the basis of the symptomatology alone, we cannot regard homosexuality, fetishism, sadism, masochism, exhibitionism, and the like as clinical entities. Nonetheless, there are some structural considerations peculiar to the perversions which call for elaboration beyond emphasizing their place within the totality of developmental considerations.

There is a vast literature, both popular and scientific, on all aspects of sexuality and the perversions. Pioneering works of another era are those of Havelock Ellis and Krafft-Ebing, now obsolete. Review of the most pertinent of the current scientific literature on the perversions must begin with Freud's *Three Essays on the Theory of Sexuality,* where he eliminated the myth that homosexuality can be caused by genetic features. He thought then that the source of all sexuality, including the perversions, was based in universally innate bisexuality. This he concluded from the observation that there exist in both sexes anatomical vestiges of the opposite sex. In extending this physiological fact to the psychological sphere, Freud was influenced by Fliess, who was a physician but not a psychoanalyst. The concept of bisexuality is not upheld by modern genetics, which has demonstrated that, chromosomally, an individual is either male or female. At that time, however, these facts were not known and it was Freud's purpose to bring homosexuality and other sexual pathology into the orbit of psychoanalytic theory, which then tended to regard all pathology as rooted in phallic-oedipal conflict. The vicissitudes of the drives in consideration of source, aim, and object could then be seen as determining that bisexuality could lead to homosexuality, that is, to a manifestation of the negative side of the oedipal conflict—as, in the male, to love for the father rather than rivalry with him.

In that same paper, therefore, and in *The Infant Genital Organization,* in *Fetishism,* and in *The Splitting of the Ego in the Process of Defense,* Freud's emphasis was on the centrality of the castration complex, rooted in the phallic phase, as the basis of sexual deviation. Unique to fetishism is the concept of the split in the ego, by which

Freud meant that a part of the ego can maintain the delusion of the female phallus while, in the remainder of the ego, reality testing can continue intact. Freud speculated that a degree of fetishism persists in normal sexuality. In 1927 he defined the fetish as the "token of triumph over the threat of castration and a protection against it." [10] He also thought of the fetish as a safeguard against homosexuality.

Since Freud's emphasis was on the importance of the castration complex and of phallic and oedipal considerations in the etiology of sexual disorders, he could account in that way for the fetish. Fetishism, however, assumes significance beyond Freud's expectations as investigation of child development reveals that inanimate objects are used ubiquitously in the prephallic period for purposes other than solutions to conflicts on the phallic-oedipal level.

Fetishism per se is rarely seen clinically. As is true of many other perversions as well, a person usually does not present himself for treatment as long as gratification is possible. A fetishist, for example, whose wife will obligingly wear a stocking, garter, or particular pair of panties, does not usually feel impelled to seek treatment because he needs this prelude to the sex act. A masochist who can find a partner who will beat and humiliate him before sexual gratification is possible is usually content, as is his sadistic partner who finds complementary gratification. Often such persons are seen, but because there are other factors troubling their lives, not because of the perversion. Sometimes they even ask the therapist for help with these other matters but also ask that he not disturb the equilibrium of the perversion. (Such requests, of course, cannot be granted.) Some homosexuals are also content. However, homosexuality, more than any other sexual pathology, presents itself clinically with severe suffering from having to go against one's biological destiny even when homosexual partners are available. Therefore, the many who are not content with the assault upon their gender identity which homosexuality imposes, do seek treatment. Although some organized, militant groups insist that their condition is not pathological, they overlook the large number of their kind who would wish to change their status.

We give passing mention to transexualism. It is an amputation

[10] S. Freud, *Fetishism*, p. 154.

performed by surgeons in concert with psychiatrists who are ignorant of psychoanalytic developmental psychology. Although it is a serious matter, the rationale for deliberate surgical deformation is not to be considered seriously in the psychological sense.

We return to fetishism because, even though it is infrequently seen, its structure constitutes the model perversion. As early as 1933, Glover had already called attention to the fact that perversions have as their underlying purpose the patching over of flaws in the development of the sense of reality. These earlier contributions are validated when considered in the context of Mahler's emphasis on the developmental importance of a satisfactory symbiotic phase followed by reasonable separation-individuation, taken in conjunction with Spitz' concept of sequential cumulation and integration leading to next higher stages of cumulation and integration. These new developmental theories also amend a number of previously held views—for example, that female homosexuality is based solely upon penis envy and masculine strivings, a logical correlate of the earlier concept of male homosexuality as determined by vicissitudes of the phallic phase. They also obviate the simplistic notion that a specific incident or trauma can constitute the single determinant in the etiology of such dramatic pathology. Now, fetishism is regarded as resulting from a partial split in the ego which preserves a specific failure in reality testing, with the fetish employed as "the keystone of wavering genitality." [11] Fetishism is the theoretical model for the other perversions because its structure demonstrates most clearly how sexual functioning in the perversions depends upon the prerequisite of a specific, unconscious prop. To the fetishist this prerequisite is an article which represents the illusory female phallus; to the masochist this prerequisite is pain; to the homosexual the prerequisite is the partner who bolsters failing gender identity.

Bak and Greenacre have written extensively about fetishism. Bak emphasizes the etiological factors arising in disturbances in the early mother-child relationship which create separation problems. He believes that the uncertainty of body image in the fetishist is the result

[11] P. Greenacre, "Certain Relationships Between Fetishism and Faulty Development of the Body Image," p. 94.

of a regressive phenomenon in which a part of reality is changed into uncertainty by the reinvestment of the image of the phallic mother. This leads him to state that "castration anxiety and its phase specificity to the phallic phase play the central role in perversion." [12] While Bak also traced the problems of fetishism from castration anxiety to prephallic ego development, he continued to maintain that precursors of the castration complex do not diminish the importance of the phallic phase. Thus, although he emphasizes separation anxiety, and the weakness of ego structure, he maintains that the fetishistic defense must arise in the phallic phase. It constitutes, then, an attempt to identify with the penisless mother. A very useful contribution of Bak is the modification of Freud's thought that the fetish creates independence from the love object. As Bak sees it, the fetish undoes the threat of separation by creating a substitute gadget to which to cling, thus affirming the relationship of the fetish to the transitional object. We shall discuss this further shortly.

Greenacre began her contributions to the theory of fetishism by extending Freud's thought along ego psychological lines. Initially she stressed the body image, that flaws in this pregenital development were patched over by the use of a fetish. She later shifted the emphasis from the castration anxiety of the phallic phase to earlier pregenital experiences which prevented structuralization, thus rendering the child incapable of meeting the demands of the later oedipal crisis. Already, in 1953, Greenacre had located the development problem in either the last half of the first year or the first half of the second year. In 1955, she added:

Severe disturbances in the period from six to eighteen months of life which produce the need for a strengthening of the clinging dependent relationship to the mother, are generally severe, permeating, and sometimes repeating. I believe it is of particular importance that these severe disturbances occur at a time of the gradual transition from dominance of the primary process to that of the secondary process. They constitute an enormous stimulation of aggression (with which the infant is more liberally supplied than at any time later in life) which affects all of the developing

---

[12] R. C. Bak, "The Phallic Woman and the Ubiquitous Fantasy in Perversions," p. 29.

libidinal phases and tends to make for some confluence of discharge routes, or at least the ready availability of alternate routes.[13]

Thus she emphasizes that the serious disturbance in body reality is connected with disturbances of reality testing in general; also, the role of aggression is stressed, especially in the fact that neutralization processes are to some extent disabled with consequent retardation of developing ego functions. This latter theme is developed in 1968 as she stresses the importance of object relations, separation-individuation, developing ego functions, and the role of aggression in all of these. At this point the role of castration anxiety is set in a different frame of reference. The fact that it is so heavily etched in the phallic phase of fetishists is now seen as the result of poor object relations and an increase in narcissistically driven aggressive components. "But this stern obligatory need to believe in the phallic mother must be preceded by disturbances in the first two years of life which drastically affect the progress of separation and individuation (Mahler, 1968) and in consequence interfere with the developing object relationship and the orderly progress of the libidinal phases." [14]

Having earlier proposed that the effect of trauma depends upon the age, and therefore the degree of structuralization at which the trauma is experienced, Greenacre adds that ". . . early castration fear has a different quality from that of its later form as it reaches the phallic phase and is under the pressure and pull of the oedipal conflict." [15] Greenacre proposes, therefore, that conditions which interfere with attainment of separation-individuation serve to intensify genital confusion. Finally, after studying fetishism over several decades, Greenacre arrived at a conceptualization which places it—an abnormality —within a developmental framework. Her paper comparing the fetish with the transitional object, a phenomenon in normal development, indicates how maturational and developmental processes combine to produce either normal or abnormal results.

Both fetishistic and transitional objects have common qualities;

[13] P. Greenacre, "Further Considerations Regarding Fetishism," p. 189.
[14] P. Greenacre, "Perversions: General Considerations Regarding Their Genetic and Dynamic Background," p. 55.
[15] Ibid., p. 51.

they are both inanimate, chosen to achieve or maintain balance under stress. The transitional object appears at the point of discovery of separateness, the physical distancing between mother and infant. Greenacre calls it the "larval representation of the self, arising from already experienced needs of the infant which have been satisfied by the mother." [16] Implicit in this statement is the fact that memory traces of gratification are being used to cope with not-too-severe anxiety problems produced by awareness of mother's absence, at a time when magical solutions are still age-appropriate. The transitional object is then a libidinally cathected object, an inanimate fairy godmother type, which is constantly available, protective, and omnisciently responsive to the infant's needs. Its essentially tactile quality confirms its unique role as a bridge between states of closeness with mother and absence from her. It gradually fades in importance as separation anxiety is eased by a combination of growth factors. Verbal communication and visual perception combine to show that mother may be available, even if not in tactile contact, strengthening the role of the object representation in the mind of the child. In the meantime, the choice of the transitional object and its magical endowment with illusory omnipotence protects the child from excessive separation anxiety. The crucial role of early object relations with the mother in attaining a sense of reality is illuminated by the fact that the magic of the transitional object is gradually given up.

The fetishist is less fortunate. Unlike the transitional object which retains the mother-me illusion while necessary, the fetish becomes an essential aspect contributing to the sense of a body self. It is generally confined to the affirmation of the male genitalia; it therefore requires something more definite and durable and it cannot be given up since body image is essentially flawed and is reconstituted only by the fetish. Thus, a far greater role is played by magic and illusion which contribute to the "successful" operation of the fetish. It contains congealed anger born of unusual castration panic. The appearance of a fetish thereby affirms that object relations have failed to sustain the infant, who has been overcome by traumatic experiences usually involving consistent exposure to female genitalia or an acute experience of witnessing a bloody wound.

[16] P. Greenacre, "The Fetish and the Transitional Object," p. 146.

We would add to Greenacre's presentation of the effect of such trauma the factor of failure of maternal attunement, which exposes the infant to traumatic experiences. Also, a fetish may appear as a magical amulet in otherwise normal individuals under severe stress. We are all familiar with the gallant fighter pilot who must carry his favorite scarf, helmet, or toy with him in order to feel protected.

Transvestitism, while closely allied to homosexuality and often seen in conjunction with it, is also found in attempted heterosexual functioning. In the latter, it makes for even greater suffering because it has to be carried out largely in secret unless the heterosexual partner is willing to tolerate it. The unconscious design of the transvestite is similar to that of the fetishist—to preserve the illusion of the female phallus. Thus the male transvestite, in women's clothing, becomes the living embodiment of the woman with a penis. That this arrangement constitutes search for the symbiotic mother who is exactly like oneself but is more accurately part of oneself is fairly obvious. Denial of sex difference predominates chiefly because there is denial of all difference. Having dressed in women's clothing and thus having proven to himself that the woman has a penis, the transvestite may then achieve discharge either by masturbation (often in front of a mirror) or in heterosexual intercourse which has been bolstered by the transvestite experience.

That the wish for union with the symbiotic partner is at the core of transvestitism was used successfully in beginning interpretation of that developmental feature in the treatment of Mr. Rosen, a thirty-year-old married man who confessed his transvestite tendencies to the therapist with great embarrassment. His wife had left for a week's visit with her parents in another city. During her absence, Mr. Rosen put on his wife's clothes. He remembered that, when he was about eight years old, he had done the same thing while his mother was away. The therapist, in order to begin to work on the symbiotic aspects of the problem, asked simply, "Does it make you less lonely?" This begins the interpretive process with a nonjudgmental approach that helps the patient empathize with his lonely plight. One such interpretation never suffices to unravel all the threads of the symbiotic wish intertwined with denial of maternal "castration." But many such interpretations made from various angles do accomplish that therapeutic purpose. Then the interpretation can be reduced to the genetic—the wish to be part of the symbiotic, noncastrated mother.[17]

How shall we account for the difference between the symbiotic borderline structure without homosexual or transvestite features and those with such symptomatology? We have already pointed to the use of denial as a defense. This suggests that the transvestite and the male homosexual have a tenuous foothold in gender identity. Both seek union with the phallic mother, the transvestite by representing her in himself, the homosexual by seeking a partner to represent the undifferentiated self-object. This leads to consideration of the special techniques that must be used in the treatment of the fetishist because, like the transvestite, the reality of female anatomy is denied. The fetishist, more often than the transvestite, functions heterosexually but needs an article which represents, unconsciously, the female phallus to bolster heterosexual intercourse. Treatment of both transvestitism and fetishism require, therefore, that the mechanism of denial be considered. The method is to seek out the specific "castration shock" that led to denial. It will be found, in such cases, to have been experienced before the child had acquired secure enough structure to be able to tolerate awareness of such dramatic anatomical difference between himself and mother. It is often necessary also to correct the ubiquitously held view that a woman is a castrated man. In every case we have encountered, it becomes sooner or later necessary to point out that this view is fallacious.

While the concept of developmental lines constitutes an integrating factor in the study of the sexual aberrations, it cannot be used simplistically. The most comprehensive study of the personality in such cases includes the kind of reconstruction most difficult to achieve, that of the preverbal era, because that is when the developmental lesion occurs. The importance of a strong therapeutic alliance cannot be overstated, since it becomes especially the task of the patient to find the unique specificity of his own experience in response to what can only be the therapist's broader and more general observations.

---

[17] Material provided by Dr. Edith Ross.

HOMOSEXUALITY

Freud made some profound observations in several of his papers that deal both directly and indirectly with the problem of homosexuality. One of the most outstanding of these was in his analysis of the relationship of homosexuality to paranoia in the Schreber case.[18] There he showed that, by using denial as a defense followed by projection, love of the man for the father figure can be altered from "I love him," to the paranoid formulation, "He loves me," by simple exchange of subject and predicate. In his essay *On Narcissism: An Introduction,* Freud showed the relationship of homosexuality to narcissism. There he proposed that one can love what one once was (a boy), what one is (a man), or what one would like to be (ego ideal). As already discussed, Freud regarded homosexuality as one consequence of failure to resolve the oedipal crisis. He earlier thought of the perversions as the reverse of the neuroses in that perversions permit discharge of pregenital sexuality whereas in the neuroses anxiety is defended against, resulting in symptom formation rather than direct discharge. This formulation is no longer regarded as tenable in the light of the structural theory.

Gillespie, in summarizing his thought about homosexuality at a panel discussion of the International Psycho-Analytic Association in 1955, noted that the defensive function of the ego is no less important for understanding perversion than are the drive vicissitudes. At a later panel (1963), he addressed himself to the question of whether homosexuality is to be regarded as one of the perversions or whether it is to be considered as having a different structure. He ruled out Freud's early assumption that biological bisexuality is a determining factor in homosexuality, this on the basis of advances in genetics which now inform us that Fleiss was mistaken in thinking that chromosomal composition is bisexual. Gillespie also wished to advance theory of homosexuality beyond the point where the etiology of homosexuality is correlated solely with defense against oedipal strivings. As he said: ". . . there have been powerful psycho-analytic arguments

[18] S. Freud, *Psychoanalytic Notes on an Autobiographical Account of a Case of Paranoia (Dementia Paranoides).*

stressing the essential importance of pre-oedipal fantasies. . . . It has
been suggested that there are two types of homosexual activity, the
one based on a pre-oedipal fixation . . . the other arising as a regressive defence in the face of oedipal problems." [19] It would be the
former type of homosexuality that conforms more closely to the category of perversion, that is, infantile sexual discharge as the end pleasure. Gillespie made the then-radical diagnostic point that homosexuality is not a homogeneous category. Pasche, at the same panel,
disagreed with Gillespie, maintaining that homosexuality is both oedipal and pregenital. His purpose was to maintain the pre-ego psychological position that all homosexuality has oedipal etiology. Another panelist, Wiedeman, pointed up the disruption in development
of the homosexual along the lines of drive vicissitudes, object
relations, and ego development, and especially in the establishment of
gender identity. Perhaps exemplifying the reluctance of theorists to
shift from traditional modes of thought, Wiedeman maintained, nevertheless, "I would not try to assign a predominant weight to preoedipal versus oedipal factors in the genesis of overt homosexuality." [20]
Greenson, at the same panel, stated that gender identity arises when
the child becomes aware of his anatomical difference, brought about
by three factors:

(a) awareness of the anatomical and physiological structures in himself;
    this would include sexual sensations and awareness of objects with
    different genitals,
(b) the parental and social figures which label him in accordance with
    his sexual structures and others in accordance with theirs,
(c) a biological force which seems to be present from birth and which
    can be decisive in pushing a child in the direction of a particular
    gender.[21]

   The biological force referred to was drawn from work by Stoller,
who referred to "a congenital, perhaps inherited biological force." [22]
This formulation was subsequently withdrawn.
   While Greenson concludes that different factors are involved in the
preservation of identity at different phases of development, his deline-

[19] "Symposium on Homosexuality."   [20] *Ibid.*, p. 215.
[21] R. R. Greenson, " On Homosexuality and Gender Identity," p. 218.
[22] R. J. Stoller, "A Contribution to the Study of Gender Identity," p. 225.

ation of these phases remains too descriptive—I am me; I am a boy; I, a boy, like to do sexual things with girls. Neither is his observation that the neurotic "reacts as though the gender of his sexual object determines his own gender" [23] useful since it blurs the fact that the crucial aspect lies in the internalizations of gender identity rather than in an interaction, even a sexual one.

Saul and Beck describe some of the psychodynamics involved in male homosexuality. While they refer to developmental deviations in terms of fixations and faulty identifications, their effort is focused on homosexuality serving as a pathway of discharge or as a defense.

Weissman considered psychological bisexuality from the structural point of view. Consistent with Freud's 1914 view of narcissistic object choice, Weissman thought it necessary to consider that factor in determination of the dynamics of the problem. When the object choice is homosexual, sexual continuity with the male predecessor is sought.

Review of the literature to this point shows the flavor of the theoretical struggle, necessarily spanning many years, to bring understanding of homosexuality from the biologically oriented concept of bisexuality, through Freud's formulation of homosexuality as a regressive defense against the positive oedipal conflict, to the ego-psychological view that the vicissitudes of early development play a major role in the etiology of most forms of homosexuality. Although Ferenczi, as early as 1914, had refuted the notion of homosexuality as a homogeneous category, it was only the findings of ego psychology in the late 1940s and 1950s that enabled theorists to define early developmental processes in sufficient detail to delineate the events of that period of life which had been termed simply pregenital or preoedipal. Parenthetically, it may be noted that these terms are vaguely descriptive in the same sense as preadolescent or preadult. Psychoanalytic developmental terminology is now far more precise. This precision led Gillespie to note in 1964 that homosexuality may continue to be included in the general theory of neurosis, as a defense against the oedipal crisis, but that there are homosexuals whose structures are to be understood within the framework of the general theory of the perversions, which includes consideration of ego modifi-

[23] R. R. Greenson, "On Homosexuality and Gender Identity," p. 217.

cation. In our own opinion, these constitute the largest segment of overt homosexuals.

In introducing the Panel on Disturbances of Male and Female Identity, Morgenthaler observed that "the clinical picture of homosexuality is pathogenetically heterogeneous . . . grounded in manifold constellations and configurations." [24] He went on to demonstrate that if ego development has been impeded so that magical thinking prevails beyond its normal phase-specificity, the accelerated drive appropriate to the phallic phase will produce failure of controls in matters of sex and aggression. Integration of maturational advances with psychic structuring thereby becomes impossible.

Socarides refers homosexuality to:

. . . a maturational failure with quantitative variations, characterized by the inability to make the passage through the separation-individuation phase of ego development. It is this failure, total or partial, that is responsible for: (1), the pronounced feminine identification with the mother and subsequent search for masculine identity; (2), the fear of breaking the symbiotic bond with the mother (separation anxiety); (3), the tendency in some individuals to experience a cataclysmic merging and fusing phenomenon with the mother upon approaching other women, or, in any way attempting to leave the mother, the threat of engulfment and loss of self in the undifferentiated phase may ensue.[25]

Although Socarides is quite clear that oedipal-phase conflict is superimposed upon a basic preoedipal nuclear conflict, as quoted above, we find it significant that he prefaces this statement with, "The structure of homosexuality consists of conflicts around the oedipal phase and the greater part of the actual analytic work with any homosexual revolves around the uncovering and resolution of these conflicts." [26]

Our own experience differs. While fear of homosexuality often is presented as a potentially regressive phenomenon in a relatively unmodified ego, much as latent homosexuality appears as a feature in any psychoanalysis, we have found that graver failures in structuralization are more commonplace in overt homosexuality. These reflect ego deviation, especially in the distortion of body image. In such in-

[24] F. Morgenthaler, "Disturbances of Male and Female Identity as Met with in Psychoanalytic Practice," p. 109.
[25] C. W. Socarides, "Psychoanalytic Therapy of a Male Homosexual," pp. 173–74.
[26] Ibid., p. 173.

stances, technical precedence is given to ego building. Persons with perversions which involve splits in the ego—fetishism, tranvestitism, and the like—need help in repairing the damaged structure.

Most writers on problems of preoedipal sexuality refer to strong attachments or fixations to the mother as pathogenic. Spitz and Mahler describe such attachments or fixations with greater precision. Spitz' work on stranger anxiety and Mahler's studies on symbiotic union and the vicissitudes of the separation-individuation phase illuminate the phase-specific or developmental appropriateness of this union. In its age-appropriate stage, attachment to the mother cannot be regarded as pathological. Thus, Spitz and Mahler provide a useful basis for comparison of normal and pathological development. "Strong attachment" now refers to unfulfilled or overindulged symbiotic needs, or to pathogenicity in the separation-individuation process. Hatterer, on the other hand, refers to the interpersonal aspect of homosexuality, such as a boy being branded as a sissy by his peers. The poignancy and depth of the problem is far better understood as related to separation anxiety so strong that it prevents movement out into the world of peers, leaving the child excessively vulnerable to taunts which otherwise would not be so injurious.

Failures in drive control—"excessive" aggression or the "strength" of biological factors—fall into place as manifestations of failures in the development of capacity to neutralize drive energy, which in turn arises out of inadequacies in the mother-infant dyad. Here can be found the failures in neutralization of aggression and of object relations in the etiology of rapists and other sexual psychopaths.

The literature reports also on biological factors that can produce developmental lesions. Bell notes that involuntary testicular contractions can cause feelings of passivity and helplessness, and concludes therefrom that "The development of the male depends, to a greater degree than we have been wont to assume, on his psychological reaction to this biologically induced passive state." [27] Bell's observations are interesting and leave open the unanswered question she poses as

[27] A. I. Bell, "Additional Aspects of Passivity and Feminine Identification in the Male," p. 646.

to whether there is a testicular phase in boys. A more cogent question occurs to us. How do most males escape this ubiquitous danger? Once again we turn to Mahler (reported by Clower) [28] who states that body ego involves dual self representations, toward both inner and outer worlds, and that the symbiotic partner must serve as a buffer against excessive stimuli from within as well as without. Therefore, the sense of helplessness and passivity which may result from these genital sensations in males as reported by Bell can be explained as a failure in the maternal object. The mother, in Bell's cases, we think, was not sufficiently cathected to be useful as a buffer against the anxiety aroused by those contractions.

This same type of failure in the mother-child dyad is a factor in the prevailing problems in relationships so common in those afflicted with perversions.

Absence of a father, actual or emotional, is frequently observed in the history of homosexual males. But if this were the only factor, the absence of a male figure for purposes of affirmation of gender identity would automatically doom all such unfortunate male children to a life of sexual perversion. Once again the vast and often chaotic diversity of the clinical pictures can be organized into an integrated scheme by viewing this feature, too, as a part of the establishment of identity proper. Greenacre (reported by Clower) notes that identity includes a sense of oneness as a unit and a sense of uniqueness, which would be the result of successful symbiosis and separation-individuation. Where progress toward identity formation has been reasonably effected, biological endowment will not be defeated and sexuality will accord with gender. Thus, the absent or passive father may contribute to already formidable identity problems, on the one hand, or constitute "merely" an impeding but encompassable problem.

We have referred to Freud's observations regarding the narcissistic feature in homosexuality. Object choice is based upon what the individual was, is, or would like to be. In contemporary terms, this refers to the persistence of the symbiotic need and to failure in differentiation of self from object representations.

[28] V. L. Clower (reporter), "Panel on the Development of the Child's Sense of His Sexual Identity."

At first, attempts to understand and treat the perversions generally followed the classificatory trend of outlining discrete clusters or structures. When homosexuality was thought of as an entity there ensued growing confusion attendant upon the difficulty of relating castration anxiety and oedipal failure universally to homosexual manifestations in both male and female forms. Fetishism, transvestitism, sadism, masochism, and similar disorders of sexuality had also been thought of as related to such etiological specificity. In ego psychological thought, these phenomena are explained by maintenance of the wish for symbiotic reunion beyond its phase-specific period which militates against seeking an object who is different from the self. The search for a sexual partner is thereby confined to one who will fit the symbiotic (narcissistic) need and is therefore likely to be like oneself in gender. At first glance this may seem paradoxical in male homosexuality although it explains a form of female homosexuality excellently. If the goal of object seeking is reunion with the symbiotic mother, why does the male seek a male partner? The answer, of course, lies in the concept that the symbiotic mother is experienced as part of the self. In seeking to regain that lost part, one seeks a replica of oneself.

In summary, homosexuality may be classified as follows:

1. It may result from regression, in defense against the positive oedipal position, with castration anxiety motivating submission to the parent of the same sex. In structures with intact egos this "negative" oedipal position remains unconscious and constitutes the usual latent homosexuality that is dealt with in the course of psychoanalysis. If there is overt homosexual experimentation, it is transient and occurs usually in early adolescence. Some theorists, Blos in particular, regard homosexuality in early adolescence as a normal developmental phenomenon.

2. It may represent failure in differentiation (separation-individuation) with consequent modifications in ego structure, leading to uncertainty or to outright failure in establishment of gender identity. As part of the diagnostic category of borderline structure proper, these problems may exist on the neurotic border, in the middle range, or on the psychotic border.

3. Perversions are also seen in objectless psychotics where the ego defects or severe modifications permit random discharge of unneutral-

ized drive energy. The criminal sexual perversions such as rape, mo-
lestation of children, or sexual gratification with animals belong in
this category.

Freud was guarded, if not altogether pessimistic, about the outcome
of psychoanalytic treatment of homosexuals. The differences between
psychoanalysis and psychotherapy, however, provide scope for evolving psychotherapeutic techniques that make the prognosis more favorable than Freud thought. Freed from the Procrustean notion that
therapy is most desirably psychoanalysis, we may proceed to apply the
concept of developmental lines to bring order to the host of incidental
symptoms that accompany faulty ego development. The perversions
may then be subsumed under those problems in borderline structures
which arise from developmental failure, with particular attention to
body image, gender identity, and drive taming as aspects of development which retard acquisition of intact structure.

The following case illustrates homosexuality in a borderline structure.

Mrs. Fletcher was a young married woman, separated from her
husband. She had not enjoyed being married, but did what was expected of her socially when she reached marriageable age. There was
no history of overt homosexuality, but also no interest in heterosexual
contact except that she liked being held. Otherwise she was frigid and
had the notion that women ejaculate like men. She had never had orgasm, not even by masturbation. We have discussed that self-gratification at the phallic phase is a transitional phenomenon that aids the
separation-individuation process. It permits discharge, makes for independence from the object, promotes active rather than passive functioning, and leads at least to oedipal and ultimately to nonincestuous
heterosexuality. In our clinical experience, when absence of this transitional phenomenon is reported, we have found that there are problems in resolving the separation-individuation crisis. The exception, of
course, is in those neurotic structures where phase-specific masturbation did take place but is repressed and will be uncovered in the
course of treatment. Obviously, Mrs. Fletcher had not made this transition.

In the second year of treatment, fears of closeness with the therapist had been interpreted in the context of symbiotic need and the

fact that the now-separated husband had failed to gratify this need except when he held Mrs. Fletcher "because he wanted sex." A symbiotically tinged transference developed as is described in the following session with a female therapist:

> *Mrs. Fletcher:*   I was wondering if you are a butch?
>
> *Therapist:*   What makes you think so?
>
> *Mrs. Fletcher:*   Well, you're single and I always wonder about it secretly when I see someone who is attractive and not married.
>
> *Therapist:*   When have you had such thoughts? Do you really mean always?
>
> *Mrs. Fletcher:*   Yes, I always felt attracted to girls but I never did much about it because I thought it was terrible and so I put it out of my mind. Once when I was a teenager, though, I undressed with another girl and we looked at each other.
>
> *Therapist:*   What do you think you were looking for?
>
> *Mrs. Fletcher:*   Well, I felt excited by her breasts. I find myself now always looking at women's breasts if I am not careful.

Evidently the ego is just strong enough to contain the homosexual wishes so that acting out is avoided, but only barely so.

In the next session Mrs. Fletcher's anxiety was great. She expressed fear that the therapist would send her away, not want to treat her anymore. The therapist reminded her of the time when her baby-sitter, whom she liked, rejected her. At age three, the patient ran toward her, arms outstretched. The baby-sitter stepped aside and the child fell.

> *Therapist:*   You probably feel that I will dismiss you because your feelings are so intense. Why would I send you away for that? It would be what your baby-sitter did.

Underneath this, of course, is the experience of rejection by the mother, probably most severely experienced in the rapprochement phase. However, the therapist deals with the cover memory of the baby-sitter's rejection.

> *Mrs. Fletcher:* I always feel unwanted. My husband only wanted me for sex, but he never held me just because he liked me.
>
> *Therapist:* Everyone needs to be held at times, but when do we need it most?
>
> *Mrs. Fletcher:* You mean when we were babies? You seem to be telling me that when I think of a woman, even if sexually, that it really reflects the way I yearned to be held, cuddled, and loved by my mother.
>
> *Therapist:* Do you see now why you asked me whether I am a "butch"?
>
> *Mrs. Fletcher:* Oh, it upsets me. I want a woman.
>
> *Therapist:* But do you understand why?
>
> *Mrs. Fletcher:* I need mothering.

Thus the patient arrives at the realization that her homosexual wishes contain the intense yearning for mothering that was unfulfilled in the age-appropriate symbiotic phase. The prolonged continuation of these needs perforce involves the genital apparatus as this gets increasingly cathected as maturation proceeds.[29]

Discussion of the perversions cannot be concluded without consideration of the active-passive issue. We have already presented our view that passivity coincides with dependence upon the preoedipal mother and that the active mode is attained with the shift from preoedipal to oedipal object relations—to that of giver rather than receiver. Rapaport has shown that activity is related to ego function and is not at all a matter of motility, or of modes such as intrusive or receptive. Many years before, Freud had clearly stated that it would be an error to equate masculinity or masculine mode with activity and feminine mode with passivity. When the ego functions of perception, thought, anticipation, intentionality, and the like have come into play, these constitute activity, although not physical activity. The

---

[29] Material provided by Isabel Sklar.

therapist who sits and thinks, for example, is very active, although also immobile and silent.

The following case illustrates a long-term treatment of homosexuality.

Mr. Howe, a male homosexual, came for treatment because he did not wish to be a homosexual but could not be a heterosexual. He had begun homosexual practices at age fifteen when he joined a group of boys who, at first, engaged in group and mutual masturbation. As they got older, they began to pair off. Changes in partners were frequent. This is because, while some homosexuals manage to maintain stable and even lifetime fidelity to the same partner, most are on the need-gratifying level of object relations and therefore can shift partners easily. Silly arguments, petty jealousies, and changes in partners occurred almost daily in this group of borderline adolescents. As he grew older, Mr. Howe tried to find a permanent partner, but these relationships always terminated when a petty quarrel turned the "good" object into a "bad" one. Eternal quest for the "good" object was resumed with a series of partners. After a while Mr. Howe became more anxious about having to search out partners in bars, men's rooms, Turkish baths, and other homosexual meeting places. He came for treatment because, although he was able to find partners for sexual discharge, the life style was unsatisfactory to him.

Mr. Howe was the younger of two boys. We do not dwell on the issue of whether a child was wanted because we think that conscious wanting before conception and birth is the smallest significant factor among the many unconscious ones which determine the capacity to love a child. Mature parents want children and, even if one should be conceived without having been planned, response to the child can be loving once he arrives, if the parents have the capacity to love. Mr. Howe's mother's wanting of children was so narcissistically determined that, although she would have passed the test of being asked whether her second son was consciously wanted, her unconscious wish was to have a girl, a narcissistic replica of herself. This was never stated to the child in so many words, nor could it have been since it was unconscious. Nevertheless, Mrs. Howe's wish to have a child in her own image was communicated in innumerable subtle ways. For example, he early identified with her mannerisms and found encouragement and reinforcement in her narcissistic approval. He became her companion and confidante. He found great pleasure in having so obviously gained more "love" than his father and brother seemed to have gained from her. In fact, however, it was not love in the growth-promoting sense, but more the lifelong parasitic symbiosis described by Mahler. The mother needed him for her own symbiotic-narcissistic purposes, and so the separation-individuation phase was reached out of a gratifying symbiotic phase, but fixation remained in the separation-individuation subphase of differentiation with retention of a regressive pathway to symbiosis.

Mr. Howe's victory in defeating his father and brother as rivals for maternal love cost him dearly. He learned early in life to cater to his mother's needs on conscious and unconscious levels. He was her nurse when she had her frequent colds, headaches, and other minor illnesses. He learned to bring her tea, aspirin, to rub her back, to lie down with her when she felt lonely. In his preschool years, while his father was at work and his brother at school, he and his mother bathed together. He was early familiar with her body, her menstruation, her preoccupation with clothes, and, unconsciously, began to share her dislike of the male body. We believe that an impelling determinant in seeking transexual surgery is the unconscious wish to have a body like the mother's. Mr. Howe's homosexuality, however, did not reach that extreme of acting out; his took the form of denial of sex difference. It is only when denial becomes inoperative that transexualism follows.

The role of the father in facilitating separation-individuation in the second year of life, as described by Greenacre, is pertinent to Mr. Howe's developmental failure. The elder Mr. Howe was not the usual, obviously passive man with whom a son cannot identify. The older brother did not become a homosexual because he had had better opportunity for paternal identification. The father was an effective and successful businessman who provided well for the family. He had been, especially overtly, an adequate father to his first son. He had engaged in all the usual father-son activities—outings, ball games, and so forth. When the second son needed paternal interference with the engulfing mother-child relationship, the elder Mr. Howe's business interests occupied him to the exclusion of his family. He spent long hours at the office and was away often on prolonged business trips. His preoccupation with his business and obvious preference for his older son intensified the needs of both wife and younger son for each other. The child slept in his father's place with Mrs. Howe while his father was away.

In terms of older psychoanalytic theory, much of the history as we have presented it thus far would suggest hatred of the father, seductive overstimulation by the mother, rivalry with father and brother, resulting in profound oedipal conflict. Ego psychological considerations suggest an altogether different picture and arrive at a different conclusion—namely, that the oedipal conflict is the least important developmental consideration because it was barely attained and, far from being a strong nuclear conflict, is weak and almost altogether overridden by the following factors:

1. Opportunities for neutralization of both libido and aggression were minimal because of the maternal failure in growth promotion.

2. This resulted in apparent closeness with the mother, underneath which raged large quantities of unneutralized aggression. Thus, the clinging, the identification, the service to her narcissistic demands were unconsciously motivated more by aggression than by libido. Separation anxiety kept him close.

3. Related to the above, neutralized aggression was not available in quantities sufficient for growth.

4. Ego functions were relatively intact in the area of primary autonomy because of good endowment in the conflict-free sphere. Many ego functions, however, were deeply involved in conflict.

5. Principal among the conflict-borne and therefore pathological aspects were those involving object relations, gender identity, individual identity (differentiation of self from object representations).

6. Frustration tolerance, capacity to delay, and capacity to employ competent defense mechanisms were weak. Denial predominated in the defensive structure; the haven of symbiosis prevented endurance of tolerable dosages of frustration. All this contributed to the vicious cycle of nondifferentiation of self and object representations.

7. The "castration shock" came too soon. While every child must learn about anatomical differences, the most desirable timing is when identity is secure and the most desirable circumstance is in peer rela-

tionship rather than in the dramatic comparison of the child's with the adult's body. For Mr. Howe, favorable opportunities in this regard were nil. He was exposed to his mother's body, even to her bleeding genital, long before he could assimilate these physiological facts in the psychological security of a body image of his own.

8. Mr. Howe, therefore, lacked a self-image, gender identity, sense of self. He retained frightening and aggressively tinged unconscious fears of blood. He devalued himself, and his own physical and especially genital body ego. Unconsciously he despised the "castrated" female genital. He also feared it as threatening to engulf him. This is why he was totally incapable, although consciously desirous, of heterosexual approach.

9. We have said that the oedipal position, if at all attained, was weak. This is because Mr. Howe remained almost entirely in the passive position of fixation to the preoedipal mother, precluding active oedipal strivings.

10. Opportunity for masculine identification was little provided by father and brother. Their initial exclusion of him gave way to rejection and mockery as his weak masculinity became more and more apparent. This, too, constituted a vicious cycle—desperate need for rescuing masculine identification became more and more unavailable.

11. Nevertheless, Mr. Howe's intact reality testing led him to know that he was a man. He was not an effeminate homosexual. We attribute this feature to the good conflict-free sphere and account also for his conscious heterosexual wish by this fact. Aware of his biological gender, this conscious knowledge could nevertheless not overcome his unconscious failure in acquisition of solid gender identity.

12. On the object relations line, Mr. Howe was clearly fixated on the need-gratification level. Paucity of neutralized libido precluded object love. In large measure, the partner was unconsciously perceived as part of the self, that is, as a participant in the symbiotic union.

We have explained that the presenting (conscious) reasons for seeking treatment were dissatisfaction with life style and wish to be a heterosexual. The unconscious reason was that psychological growth and fulfillment of biological destiny had not been altogether abandoned. We account for these unconscious motivational features by (1) the universal thrust toward growth, especially when it exists in conjunction with good (primary autonomous) endowment; (2) the weak but nevertheless existing identification with the paternal, overtly male functioning. Especially in the father's effective business functioning do we see the factor which led Mr. Howe to a suitable career and moderate success. This, too, brought him into conflict with his homosexuality, not, as many laymen suppose, because he would have been embarrassed at his job, but because he himself unconsciously wished to be like the other men. Thus, the simplistic pseudosociological solution of declaring one's homosexuality to one's employer is ineffective because it leaves the inner conflict untouched.

Mr. Howe approached therapy because he had heard that therapists can make a person happy and accepting of his homosexual fate. Some therapists of different orientations have advocated such growth-retarding "adjustment." Mr. Howe's therapist did not argue with the initial presentation of goal, neither did he controvert it covertly. Rather, he dealt with the other aspects of Mr. Howe's developmental lesions as we have described in the treatment of other borderline structures. Especially was Mr. Howe's wish for symbiotic merger repeatedly interpreted. Mr. Howe, in long-term treatment, came to value and respect the therapist. Neutralization, masculine identification, and object love proceeded in the context of a growth-promoting therapeutic alliance. When differentiation of self from object representations became more marked, gender identity began to be clearer. There were many moments of severe separation anxiety, regression, and even aggressive outbursts. But homosexual acting out diminished without interposition of the therapist's values or prohibitions.

The road to heterosexuality was not smooth. Much interpretive reconstruction of preverbal fears of the female genital had to be undertaken before Mr. Howe could make heterosexual contact without terror. His anger toward women was attenuated with neutralization of aggression and interpretation of its positive value in defense of tenuously held masculinity. The establishment of identity followed a therapeutic course similar to that of Mr. Forrester, to be described in chapter 16.

Mr. Howe did not attain full cure of his structural modification.

This is because we are not yet certain in every case that application of ego psychological techniques always repairs structural damage. The case of Mr. Howe may be compared with the hypothetical one of the neurotic, nonacting-out, latent homosexual whose prognosis is more favorable because his ego structure lends itself to psychoanalytic techniques. It is essential to add, as well, that the oedipal conflict that has not been experienced full-blown in childhood usually cannot be provided retroactively. Therefore, there are three principal reasons why prognosis is unfavorable in many (but not all) borderline structures: (1) constitutional ego defects are not amenable to therapy; (2) early trauma causing developmental lesions may, depending upon timing and extent, be irreversible; and (3) development, such as the oedipal position, if not attained, is difficult to create in adulthood. Identity, on the other hand, even though not attained in childhood, can be promoted therapeutically. We shall illustrate this as well in the case of Mr. Forrester.

Mr. Howe did make a satisfactory marriage—satisfactory in the sense that he had a better self-image, more secure identity, diminished symbiotic wishes, and concomitant diminished fear of being enveloped and destroyed by the formerly aggressively perceived female genital. We are unable to claim that this constitutes a cure in the sense of a psychoanalytic cure. It represents, theoretically, a profound structural change. For the patient, it provides self-fulfillment, the pleasure of experiencing one's psychic and biological identity, and the opportunity to give and receive love.

We have shown that problems in sexuality can exist in intact as well as in modified egos. In the intact structures, however, they are likely to be symptomatic of intersystemic conflict and of unconscious fantasies. Sexual deviations and perversions are more likely to appear in the modified egos and are factors of impaired or undeveloped object relations, inadequate gender identity, fixation in a pregenital phase of psychosexuality, and incomplete differentiation of self representations from object representations. We have not discussed the many forms of sexual contact that have become part of the "sexual revolution"—such as group sex, partner swapping, and other practices which will probably increase with inventiveness in conjunction with the new "freedom." These fall into the general category of perverse sexuality—that is, the acting out of pregenital and preoedipal fantasies and wishes, using the vehicle of the adult sexual apparatus but, in the psychological sense, bearing no relationship to adult sexuality.

≈ 16 ≈

INTERPRETATION

INTERPRETATION HAS ALWAYS occupied a unique position in the technical repertory. In the psychoanalytic literature, tools such as clarification, questioning, and confrontation are regarded as auxiliaries to interpretation. Interpretation is addressed to the ego, that institution of the psyche which is directly accessible to the therapist in the therapeutic alliance. It constitutes intrusion of a new element upon an already existing equilibrium which had been established by the synthetic function, thereby causing a temporary disequilibrium and forcing a new synthesis which then encompasses the added feature. In psychoanalysis, interpretation is nothing more than statement of the preconscious, derived from the patient's associative material. In that sense, interpretation provides nothing new. This fact is of prime importance in the use of interpretation in psychotherapy because it stresses that the role of the therapist is not so much that of interpreter but is, in fact, that of helper to the patient's provision of interpretable material. It is for this reason that, while we yield to the fact that the term and concept *interpretation* is deeply engrained in the literature and therefore must be employed for scientific communication, we prefer the more generic term *intervention* to subsume interpretation as well as the auxiliary devices.

In the literature on psychotherapy, additional auxiliary devices are described: encouragement, support, abreaction, persuasion, exhortation, confrontation, advice-giving, and manipulation. We shall discuss some of these in the next chapter. Many, we believe, are outmoded by recent theoretical discoveries, since these devices were evolved in an era before psychoanalytic developmental psychology provided theoretical rationale for use of more sophisticated techniques. Among the major influences upon modern technique are Greenacre's concept of guardianship of autonomy in the transference, and Kris's contributions: (1) his proposal that, even in psychoanalysis proper, the goal is no longer rapid uncovering of id content, and (2) his description of how the ego functions in the "good hour" [1] when interpretation becomes the function of the patient's ego rather than that of the therapist.

Interpretation, in psychotherapy, is different from the envisioned statement or pronouncement by the therapist. Its main goal is the furthering of impeded development. Id interpretations do belong in psychotherapy, but are to be reserved, if possible, for later stages of treatment when the ego has been strengthened. Sometimes postponement is not possible because both drives are inadequately neutralized and defenses are weak. Not only aggression, but libidinal desires, may be ventilated too soon despite the therapist's best efforts to hold them in abeyance. Then, they should not be sidestepped. For example, the patient may express fear of or wish for sexual contact with the therapist. If the therapist is of the same sex as the patient, these appear like homosexual desires. They may not be so, any more than similar wishes toward a therapist of the opposite sex are necessarily heterosexual. It depends upon the transference role being displaced upon the therapist whether such wishes are toward the preoedipal object from whom maternal gratification is sought, or toward a truly oedipal one. One can say, in order to organize the treatment, "We do not know, really, whether your love for me is truly homosexual. It may be that, insofar as you had a father, you loved him. The fact that sexual wishes appear to get mixed up with that doesn't necessarily make you a homosexual." This is not an evasion. It allays panic while diagnostic decisions are still to be made and before the ego is strong enough to tolerate knowledge of the drives with confidence that it can control them. Freud's analogy of the horse and rider comes to mind here. The horse (id) runs away with the rider (ego) if the rider is a novice. The rider is in control after we teach him good horsemanship. Not only is the suggested partial interpretation one that gains time for the ego, it

[1] E. Kris, "On Some Vicissitudes of Insight in Psychoanalysis."

is also the correct interpretation for the level of ego development, although libidinal development has proceeded beyond. Beginning with the simple interpretation of libidinal cathexis of the object reserves the sexual aspect for more orderly correction of developmental chaos. Later, when the ego has been strengthened, the libidinal aspects of the relationship with the father may be more correctly designated as homosexual and treated as such.

Another way of postponing id interpretation to gain time to build the ego is by choice of material. One might succeed, for example, in postponing aggressive ventilation by saying, "But let's also listen to some of the other things you have said today." As in the instance of libidinal outburst, sometimes aggression cannot be postponed, and then one has to say, "It isn't good for you to shout at me like that while you are unable to listen and understand it." We are here attempting to create an observing ego.

Freud thought in 1912, when he published his papers on technique, that the prospective patient was to be subjected to a trial analysis to ascertain whether his ego was strong enough to tolerate psychoanalytic procedure. By this Freud meant that, if the ego could not withstand abstinence and id interpretation, he was to be dismissed. With the advent of ego psychology, it is no longer necessary to dismiss the patient whose ego is too fragile for strict psychoanalytic procedure. It is only required that, if we have erred in diagnosis or have not yet discovered ego modifications which sometimes cannot be recognized until later in treatment, we change the focus of interpretive work so that the ego, not id content, is given the weight of our interpretive effort. Such a technical position diminishes the much-feared danger that too much uncovering will make manifest a latent psychosis and explains why we have said that it is not necessary to rush the patient off the couch the moment ego modifications begin to reveal themselves. One can simply, and with assurance, make corrective interpretations that will tend to halt the decompensation.

Miss Hollis was in the second year of a classical analysis when some borderline phenomena became prominent and the defenses appeared to be decompensating. Possibly the analyst could have diagnosed the ego modifications earlier and have engaged less strenuously in uncovering the id, working first on strengthening the ego. However, by the time the borderline features became prominent, emergency repair of the ego had to be undertaken. The analyst was alerted to this by a dream in which a person turned into a swan and flew away. This dream suggested problems in object representations which showed a rather tenuous hold on objects as definite persons with continuous existence. Instead of proceeding with uncovering techniques, the analyst turned his attention to the loss of object continuity. Ego interpretations replaced id interpretations and took the direction of, "You are afraid that people can fly away and cease to exist." Many variations of this type of interpretation were necessary in order to present the ego with the idea that object representations can become fixed and permanent. This was an ego interpretation for ego-building purposes. The patient remained on the couch throughout this phase of treatment and when self and object continuity became more secure, id interpretation was safely resumed. It is also to be noted that, in this kind of pathology, interpretation of the sexual symbolism of flying would have been incorrect and premature. Further, dismissal of the patient can, in and of itself, be traumatic. While perhaps it was necessary when we knew of nothing else to do, Freud was humane enough to have made such a decision within two weeks, that is, before transference was well established and before the patient had invested work and hope in a cure. We have encountered unfortunate instances of dismissal after many years of analysis, with the pronouncement that "You are unsuitable for analysis." This is a rigid, unfeeling, and unnecessary move in the present state of ego-psychological theory. Now technique can be diverted from uncovering to ego building.

Interpretation can properly be of the highest developmental level attained in order to support it; of defense and resistance, if these are present in a borderline ego strong enough for defensive functioning; of adaptive functioning; of affect; of preverbal experience. Ego interpretations are usually designed to help the patient understand his lesions so that he can grow from there. They are analogous to, but not the same as, id interpretations, which deal with a derivative in order to designate the unconscious wish and the point of fixation or regression. They produce similar therapeutic results—namely, the most developed aspect of the ego assimilates and synthesizes the interpretation. They differ in content and in the important fact that, in psychotherapy, the very capacity to synthesize sometimes has to be aided. How this is done will be shown shortly in the case of Miss Keller.

Also to be considered in technical decisions around interpretation is whether the situation calls for transference interpretation, genetic interpretation, or whether the therapist is needed as a primary object (in which instance the therapeutic relationship supersedes interpretation as a tool). If possible, revival of the past in the transference is to be interpreted first, later to be reduced to the genetic. This we illustrated in the case of Miss Ellsworth. It represents usual, orderly sequence of interpretation in psychotherapy and resembles most closely the psychoanalytic technique of interpretation. However, if there is paucity of object cathexis to be transferred, then the psychotherapeutic approach cannot be interpretation and certainly not transference interpretation, but must be provision of an object for structure building. This applies in the main to psychosis or borderline structure near psychosis. "After you left on vacation, I could no longer get up in the morning," informs us that the object is lost. Transference and genetic interpretations are not yet in order. The object world has to be restored. "Now that you see me again, you will feel better," is an attempt to restore the lost object. It appears like simple reassurance, but is far more subtle than that if applied properly in the diagnostic sense.

The style of interpretation we prefer is that it be made tentatively and in question form whenever possible. Thus one avoids appearing omniscient, and even saves face sometimes when a decidedly definite interpretation turns out to be an incorrect one. Interpretations that begin, "Don't you think that . . ." or "Isn't it possible that . . ." give the patient room to think, to disagree, or to correct and amend interpretations that may fall short of the mark. Providing an opportunity to participate in the interpretive process also constitutes an ego "stretching" device. Methodologically, interpretation is best made in stages and, as we have said, leaving as much of it to the patient as possible. Always, however, the therapist is at hand to help him along the interpretive path. We illustrate here how to interpret, step by step.

Miss Keller came for treatment because of excessive anxiety about her appearance. In reality, she looked quite well. But her overconcern

with her hair, skin, figure, alerted the therapist to two levels of interrelated, underlying causes for such excessive anxiety. The more classic
hypothesis is that her appearance refers to her "castrated" female self.
We remind ourselves here that Jacobson thinks that the girl, at the
moment of "castration shock," reacts first with denial and then with
transfer of narcissism to the body as a whole in substitution for the
"damaged" genital. The verbalizations presented would be indicative
that Miss Keller's problems were solely on the phallic level. The developmentally oriented psychotherapist would think that, in addition
to unconscious feelings of being castrated, the presenting problem also
encompassed a faulty body image, the etiology of which antedated the
phallic phase. This was indeed the situation in this case because, although Miss Keller developed a fairly undistorted ego structure, a
brother was born when she was only eighteen months old. Awareness
of the brother's different anatomy by an observing toddler at that
stage of development did not result in castration shock at the phallic
level because that level had not yet been reached. It led to persisting
belief in a faulty body image because the brother's arrival occurred at
the phase when the corporeal self was of great interest to the young
child who was becoming increasingly aware of her ego and bodily
boundaries.

We have called the therapist's silent formulations *hypotheses* because a therapist cannot know the correct interpretation without the
patient's ongoing help and confirmation as each step toward the ultimate interpretation is taken. Even when the interpretation is complete, one should be aware that working-through will bring the same
matter into focus again from many varying angles. The technique of
dealing with such a matter in a therapeutically useful way demands
that the therapist not be hasty. He formulates a hypothetical complete interpretation, one he is ready to alter or discard if the patient's
responses fail to confirm it and lead to new hypotheses.

In this case the hypothesis was, "When you were a baby and compared yourself with your brother, you thought you were damaged.
This notion seemed corroborated as you continued to grow and saw
other people who looked different. You proceeded in your development to the point where every girl would prefer to have what a boy
has. The next developmental step was hindered by earlier fears about

the adequacy of your body. You are left with this doubly layered feeling of bodily inadequacy which causes continuous anxiety about your appearance." As we shall demonstrate, this hypothesis was nearly, but not exactly, correct. Also, a patient cannot be expected to understand, accept, absorb, and synthesize the totality of such interpretation. In fact, this particular patient, after two years of working on partial interpretations of this, said, "Had you told me all that when I first came, I would have thought you were crazy!" To illustrate how the interpretation is made from the surface down to increasingly deeper levels, we condense the two-year therapeutic dialogue on this issue. The dialogue was also, of course, interspersed with other themes that will not be introduced here. The therapist was a woman.

> *Miss Keller:* Today I feel that I should see a dermatologist about my skin.
> *Therapist:* You think constantly about your appearance because you are not sure that your body is always as it should be.

This is designed to begin a series of interpretations which does not exclude the phallic but which is broad enough to cover feelings about the more basic issue of body image on the developmental level preceding the phallic.

> *Miss Keller:* Sometimes I think I look better than at other times.
> *Therapist:* You are not always certain that your body is the same.
> *Miss Keller:* I did not know much about my body when I was a child.
> *Therapist:* Where was your curiosity?

This comment is both to encourage curiosity now and also to elicit historical material. Thus the therapist learned that there was no attempt to masturbate. This information supports the diagnostic hypothesis that the phallic phase was inadequately reached. Spitz regards such phallic activity as a necessary step in attaining independence from the primary object. In a contributory study, Escalona has shown how prephallic self-exploration secures the body image.

Miss Keller: I always feel there is something wrong.

This is a classical phallic statement, but the therapist preferred to deal with it slowly in the belief that more prephallic material needed to be interpreted to bring the patient securely to the phallic level.

Therapist: Do you think you noticed your mother's body chang-
                ing when she was pregnant?
Miss Keller: Well, I must have but I don't remember that.

Repression is operative.

Therapist: But you often worry about gaining weight.
Miss Keller: I had a dream last night. I was going on a trip
                abroad. You were the tour director. You divided us
                into two groups—experienced travelers and nov-
                ices. You put all the men in the superior group.
Therapist: You feel I value men more?
Miss Keller: Yes, men are always more admired.
Therapist: They have something more to be looked at.

A dream, presented following an intervention, confirms that the intervention is correct in content and timing. But this dream is more on the phallic than on the broader level of body image. The therapist wants to slow down the interpretive process to get first at the lower developmental level. When the body image improves, the patient will be able to resolve her phallic problems more securely. The therapist, here, wants to lead to the condensation in the primary process of the observation of the mother's enlarged, pregnant body with the broth-er's and possibly father's penis. Compare these interventions with the probably correct but untimely phallic interpretation in which the therapist would seize the same word—admired—and proceed to present to the patient, "You want a penis to show off." That would, indeed, interpret the exhibitionism, but would have the following three disadvantages:

1. It would fail to include the prephallic trauma of the mother's pregnancy, body changes, and birth of the brother, which interrupted the separation-individuation phase.

2. As phrased, the superego might take it as an accusation.

3. This, in turn, would disrupt the therapeutic alliance. The therapist would not, as Sharpe advocates, be going with the patient.

The choice to proceed more slowly and subtly was determined by a twofold consideration: (1) to refrain from going too far from where the patient can follow step by step, and thereby maintain the working alliance, and (2) to look to the patient's ego for confirmation at each step, thus avoiding narcissistic pleasure in one's own capacity to formulate an interpretation at the risk of its remaining untested if incorrect and uncorrected if slightly askew. The steps we are proposing aid the synthetic function by providing opportunity for absorption in graduated stages. The last intervention changed the word *admired* to the broader scoptophilic aspects of *looking at*.

Miss Keller: Oh, you mean a penis.

When the patient says, "You mean," to her own association, it is a projection which represents a last defense against allowing the thought into consciousness. It is an advantage here that the therapist has not ventured such an interpretation because the defensive arrangement is such that the patient would have had to negate it.

Miss Keller: (In a later session) I had a dream that I was involved with a group of newly arrived immigrants. I wonder why?

When patient asks why, she is doing her own therapeutic work well.

Therapist: What are your thoughts about them?
Miss Keller: They are an underprivileged minority.
Therapist: Do you feel yourself to be a member of an underprivileged minority?

An interpretation in question form.

Miss Keller: Yes, of course. All women are.

Here she goes into a sociological discussion of women's lesser role in society. While much of what she says is true, it is not a therapeutic problem and so the therapist leaves social, political, and economic issues to be solved by experts in those fields.

Therapist: Do you think that explains why you feel that there is something wrong with your body?

Miss Keller: You know, I always felt inferior. I'd like to become pregnant, then I'd have something.

Therapist: Something like the others had?

Miss Keller: There must have been a time when my mother was pregnant; my father had his penis, then my brother came along. They all had something.

Therapist: Now you are afraid of gaining weight?

An interpretation of the defense against the pregnancy wish.

Miss Keller: Well, maybe I want something added to me.

She acknowledges the wish for the baby-penis.

Therapist: Would you look better then?

Miss Keller: I would be as good as everyone else.

Therapist: You feel as though you are not good enough as you are.

As you are is stressed because the therapist is beginning to build the body image now that Miss Keller understands some of the genetic features of her impaired self-image and self-esteem.

Miss Keller: I always felt that way. Will it ever feel better?

Therapist: When you were eighteen months old, these terrible feelings of incompleteness were compounded by the fact that your mother held the baby and you had to toddle alongside.

Here the therapist is introducing the loss of symbiotic body closeness which constitutes the prephallic underlay of the phallic wish.

Miss Keller: It does feel terrible to be incomplete.

Patient feels understood at a preverbal level.

Therapist: And so the solution that occurred to you was to ac-
                  quire an additional body part. Then you would feel
                  as good as you once did when your mother held you
                  close. You would feel complete.
Miss Keller: (In a later session) I feel less worried. I went to a
                  party last night and I thought I looked very well.
Therapist: You are beginning to understand that your feelings
                  about your appearance were built on convictions ar-
                  rived at as a baby and these have made you unhappy
                  for a long time.

It now becomes possible to begin to correct the distorted body
image by showing that it is based on the feelings and judgment of an
eighteen-month-old child.

Miss Keller: I would still like what everyone else has. You seem
               to have everything.
Therapist: What is everything?
Miss Keller: Well, your position, career.

Here she goes on at some length about the real and fantasied accomplishments of the therapist.

Therapist: How did I acquire all that?
Miss Keller: Maybe your mother gave you a penis.

The problem is now more on the phallic level.

Therapist: How?
Miss Keller: She fed you more.

Therapist: Do you think you watched your mother nursing your
               brother?
Miss Keller (Excitedly): Yes, yes, that's how I thought he got it!
Therapist: Why didn't you get it that way?
Miss Keller: She loved him more.
Therapist: And so now we get a line on how your feelings
               about your body and about not being loved enough
               got intertwined.
Miss Keller: I get terribly jealous even now if my father gives my
               brother more money than he gives me.

The father is wealthy and gives large gifts to his three children from
time to time. The patient's response touches the genetic experience of
disappointment in her mother which causes the girl to turn in a heterosexual direction.

Therapist: So you think I have more than you, first from my
             mother and then from my father?

This is a synthesizing, partial interpretation. It avoids lecturing
the patient on how one achieves by hard work, but the point is made.

Miss Keller: I'd like to go back to school for my master's degree.

This highly condensed presentation shows how partial interpretations lead a patient with a poor body image to higher levels by remaining close to her responses. Never does the therapist, by brilliant
(exhibitionistic) display go too far beyond the patient. In this case, as
in many, that would have had the added disadvantage of firming up
Miss Keller's belief in the therapist's magical, phallic prowess, thereby
widening the gap to the point where she would feel unable to catch
up. Here, Miss Keller's potential to achieve more came to the fore as
she shifted from the passive mode (the baby who wants to be given)
to the active mode (an adult woman who wants to work to live up to
her potential).

Diagrammatically, graduated interpretation can be envisioned as
a pyramid. The complete interpretation is at the base, which is held

tentatively by the therapist. Unlike an engineer, the therapist builds from the apex. With each response from the patient, the next partial but now slightly broadened interpretation (often in the form of a question that spurs the patient on) is made. The structure is complete when the base interpretation is reached jointly by patient and therapist.

We have mentioned that the aspect of interpretation, which Freud called *tact*, is that of timing.[2] In psychotherapy, timing may be even more difficult to learn than in psychoanalysis because the weaker ego needs more forbearance and smaller dosage than the one that can work psychoanalytically. We teach our students to urge the patient along, from one small step to the next. Timing is often a matter of waiting, even if we think we have a clever thought, until the patient is near it himself. A patient is asked what his material might mean. He says, typically, "I don't know." The therapist says, "Try." Simple, but effective in ego building, this technique may be what Knight meant by encouragement. To urge the patient along, it seems to us, is more than encouragement. It gently refuses to do the therapeutic work for him so that he gains confidence in his own ability instead of remaining fixated in admiration of a brilliant therapist who makes interpretations that he, the patient, could never match.

The following case illustrates a few ego-building interventions in a borderline structure on the verge of decompensation. The danger in this case lay in the power exerted by superego components so aggressively tinged that the ego had no merciful ally in the intersystemic relationships nor were intrasystemic arrangements adequate enough to provide competent defensive functioning.

The patient was an attractive woman in her middle twenties who was a successful actress. She experienced severe separation anxiety upon leaving the parental home, but she overcame this. However, she reexperienced severe anxiety when she moved from a small apartment to a larger one which she shared with a lover. She felt more intact in her one-room apartment than in one which seemed too large to control her fear of expansion and loss of boundaries. She thought she would go out of control. Entering a heterosexual relationship of some

---

[2] S. Freud, *"Wild" Psycho Analysis.*

permanence and commitment seemed also to contribute to anxiety —that is, to fear of loss of the symbiotic tie to the preoedipal mother. Symptoms characteristic of last-ditch borderline defense designed to stave off psychosis became prominent—particularly obsessive mechanisms and preoccupation with her weight. Although she was, in reality, quite slender, she was dieting strenuously with the goal of having no substance so that she could disappear. This was a tantalizing yet terrifying thought, representing the wish for symbiotic merger with concomitant fear of loss of identity. Her success as an actress involved losing herself in the identity of the role, often with difficulty in retrieving her own identity after the performance. The first interventions were designed to maintain the faltering defensive function.

Miss Rose: I can't stop thinking about my weight. I'm constantly worried that I will gain weight, but I love sweets and can't resist them sometimes.

Therapist: But your preoccupation with yourself helps you feel more together.

At the next session Miss Rose felt better, but ten minutes before the end of the hour, she rose to leave. This was the third time she departed early.

Therapist: I notice that you tend to leave your sessions before the time is up.

Miss Rose: It's because I'm tired.

Therapist: Is it possible there could be another reason?

Miss Rose: I don't like to have you tell me the session is over.

Therapist: What does that feel like?

Miss Rose: As though you don't want me anymore.

Therapist: So you leave early so that it won't feel as though I'm leaving you. Being in control makes it more bearable, doesn't it?

Miss Rose: Yes. Then I don't wait helplessly for it to happen. I used to be told that my father [who was sixty years old when the patient was born] was so old he might die any day. I couldn't bear the suspense. I used to wish it would be over with.

At the next session Miss Rose reported having reexperienced feelings of depersonalization, which had been rather frequent before.

Therapist: It is difficult for you to realize that you are the same person all the time. When you become anxious you have to step out of yourself.

Miss Rose: There is a credibility gap. I feel far away.

Therapist: Is that because of what I said?

Miss Rose: The only words that come to mind are "father killer." I don't want to be me. (She begins to sob.) If I am me, I am a murderer.

Therapist: You wanted to be relieved of the tension, not to kill your father.

Miss Rose: I can never really be happy when I'm myself. That's why I like playing roles. I get out of myself, but sometimes it's hard to get back.

Therapist: You could get back if you liked yourself better.

Miss Rose: How can I like myself when I killed my father?

Therapist: You are unfair to yourself. There were times when you were angry with him; then you wanted to be relieved of having to walk on eggs all the time lest he die. You wanted to end the suspense. Those thoughts didn't kill him. He died of natural causes.

Miss Rose: I feel I did it.

Therapist: Sometimes it feels as though you are more in control if you think your wishes can perform deeds. But the price of feeling so omnipotent is that you suffer from having to punish yourself.

Miss Rose: It would be worse to get out of control.

Therapist: Yes. It feels that way. That's why your apartment seems too large. You feel better when you are confined.

Miss Rose: Like being in prison.

Therapist: Maybe so. But I think it is more that you want

someone to police you so that you won't think or wish
anything frightening.

Miss Rose: Okay. That's what it is. I need someone to tell me
what to do. Then I'll never make a mistake.

Therapist: And the way to acquire someone like that is to
lose yourself. Is that why you want to be so thin that
you will fade away?

Miss Rose: I think so. I would be part of someone else that way.
I wouldn't have to worry about being myself.

Therapist: It is so hard for you because you don't feel you
have anyone on your side. But when you were a baby,
there must have been a time when you felt good. You
felt you were part of someone who took care of you.

Miss Rose: (Thoughtfully) Oh. My mother did hold me and it
felt so good I didn't think I was me anymore.

Therapist: Because you never felt you were good as yourself.

Miss Rose: Yes. I want that good feeling back. I get it on the
stage when I'm someone else or, at least, I feel myself
to be a part of that character.

Therapist: We will have to work on giving you that good
feeling while you are still you.

Miss Rose: If we only could.

Here the patient has been brought to understand how her unneutralized aggression impeded development beyond symbiosis. Probably
the symbiotic phase was not adequate to lead to comfortable acquisition of identity. The conjecture is that she was left too early to cope
with aggressive wishes and had to organize oversevere superego components in lieu of neutralization in the attempt to control them. The
therapist leads toward the possibility of providing more benign self and
object representations to replace the oversevere superego component.[3]

We conclude this chapter with a case illustration of how interpretation is carried out in the crucial phase of treatment when the patient with a borderline structure begins to experience identity for the
first time.

[3] Material provided by Dr. Edith Ross.

Mr. Forrester had been in intensive psychotherapy for two years. His presenting complaint had been inability to maintain social, especially heterosexual, relationships. He wanted to marry, but feared women when heterosexual opportunities arose. Diagnostically, this information is suggestive of an unresolved oedipal conflict. The life history might even bear out such hypothesis. Mr. Forrester was the only son of parents who married late in life. His father died when he was ten months old and he lived alone with a lonely, probably depressed, possessive mother in a parasitic symbiosis. He had made several abortive attempts at therapy from the ages of twenty to thirty-five. Then he began a new course of therapy. A former therapist had insisted that he move out of his mother's home. He did so when he was thirty years old, in obedience to the therapist, but with so much pain that he had to seek more treatment. To the last therapist, it illustrated with dramatic clarity Mahler's definition of separation as the psychic experience of one's separateness, not physical separation. Mr. Forrester lived separately from his mother; psychologically, he remained part of her.

We skip description of the intermediate stages of treatment because the therapeutic measures resemble those already described in other cases—designation of the developmental lesion in terms of overindulged symbiosis, encouragement of ego building, self-interpretation, neutralization of the drives.

The following is condensed from approximately twelve sessions. It illustrates the process through which identity begins to be experienced:

> *Mr. Forrester:* I feel as though I hate everyone today, especially all women. (Pause.) You never seem to mind when I say that. (Pause.) You're a cool cookie. I feel sad. Why don't you say something?
>
> *Therapist:* I will. I don't mind when you say what you feel.

The therapist responds to the request for a comment, contrary to psychoanalytic technique. In psychoanalysis, the intact ego can toler-

ate unresponsiveness for the sake of elaborating fantasies. In borderline structures, failure to respond at such a point constitutes abandonment analogous to the unavailability of the mother in the separation-
individuation phase. The therapist responds to the patient's *rapprochement.*

> *Mr. Forrester:* I have said so many nasty things to you and
> you're still here. But I notice lately that I don't
> think about you all the time.

Verbalization of aggression has aided neutralization. The symbiotic tie loosens. Separation is experienced for the first time. Fear of
aggression is diminished. The patient does not need to keep the therapist alive magically by thinking about her all the time. Object constancy approaches.

> *Therapist:*   Does that worry you?
> *Mr. Forrester:* Yes. What will happen if I forget you?
> *Therapist:*   We'll both be all right.

This is designed to help the patient diminish his fear of separateness. It is not simple reassurance, although superficially it appears so.
Reassurance would have been, "*I'll* be all right." The *we* takes into
account the diminishing symbiosis and affirms that both parties can
now survive separately. The deceptively simple phrasing of the interpretation is backed by the profundity of developmental theory. Here,
a single word has a vast technical purpose and effect.

> *Mr. Forrester:* I feel different, apart from you. I used to feel
> that I needed you desperately all the time. I barely
> gave you a thought this weekend. It's strange.
> You're still here, but it feels so different. Sad.
> *Therapist:*   It can feel sad.

This acknowledges that separation contains an element of
mourning.

Mr. Forrester:	But I like it, too. I can't believe that so much could change between us. I used to telephone you when I felt upset. I know I still can but it doesn't feel so necessary.
Therapist:	You know I'm the same.
Mr. Forrester:	But I sure am not! (Describes his improved functioning at work.) It still feels strange that I can continue to come here and talk to you even though I feel distant.
Therapist:	Is it distance or that you are more yourself?
Mr. Forrester:	I'm me. A male. That's why I hated women so much.
Therapist:	It was good, in a way. Hating them was your way of retaining the knowledge that you are different.
Mr. Forrester:	But you never minded.
Therapist:	Why should I mind that you are you?
Mr. Forrester:	My mother did.
Therapist:	Maybe not. We can't know what was on her mind. But we do know that you were more comfortable being exactly like her, as though you were part of her.
Mr. Forrester:	That's the way it felt.
Therapist:	But you always knew you were male.
Mr. Forrester:	I suppose I did. I was afraid she wouldn't like me.
Therapist:	You were afraid to be different, but it hasn't hurt her, or me, and it is certainly best for you to be what you are.
Mr. Forrester:	That feels good. Are you sure you don't mind?
Therapist:	You're still uncertain about it, so you invite me to squelch the whole thing.
Mr. Forrester:	Wow, you really are cool. I would rather be a man. But can I still come? Maybe we should diminish the sessions.
Therapist:	We might talk about that sometime, but right now is not a good time to diminish the sessions.

Here the therapist is preventing too-rapid physical separation. While this is analagous to the role of the mother in the separation-individuation phase, an adult patient does not proceed through these developmental phases anew with the therapist. Only some of the damage caused by early failure can be corrected. There will be scars for most borderline structures because of unsatisfying experience at the phase-specific time.

Mr. Forrester, in another session talks about a situation in the office and becomes upset and angry because the therapist is not familiar with the antecedents of the event. The therapist realized that he returns in this way to the symbiotic mode.

Mr. Forrester: It upsets me to see that you are not perfect.
Therapist: What does *perfect* mean?
Mr. Forrester: Well you should remember what I told you about my co-workers.

Therapist decides it is best to allow the aggression to emerge fully without defending herself.

Therapist: You see that as a flaw in me?
Mr. Forrester: Yes, I used to blame myself when these things happened.
Therapist: So at least now you can blame me.
Mr. Forrester: I'm furious with you about it. (Pause.) But you look as though it doesn't destroy you.
Therapist: Your anger doesn't destroy me.
Mr. Forrester: You make it so easy.
Therapist: But we do now have to look at whether I can know all that you know about what goes on in your office. I have never been there nor seen these people.
Mr. Forrester: I keep overlooking that. I think you know everything that goes on with me.
Therapist: How shall we explain that?
Mr. Forrester: I guess I'm still part of you when I'm that way.

Therapist:	You need to be able to be part of me again after you have felt so separate.
Mr. Forrester:	It's frightening out there all alone.
Therapist:	Yes, it is.
Mr. Forrester:	I feel more self-conscious in the literal sense. I am conscious of myself. I am a man. I am different from you. It's remarkable how calm you can remain through this. I feel such an upheaval.
Therapist:	Is it hard to realize that I am not you and have different feelings?
Mr. Forrester:	Yes. But there is something good about it. You go your own way. You'll be gone for the weekend. I'll be doing separate things. But you won't disappear; you'll be doing what you do.
Therapist:	Our time is up now.
Mr. Forrester:	Have a good weekend. I'll see you Monday.
Mr. Forrester:	(In a subsequent session) How are you?
Therapist:	I'm well, thank you.

Here the therapist responds directly to the first expression of the patient's interest in her as a person. More traditional psychoanalytic procedure would address itself to the aggression underlying the anxiety about the therapist's well-being. This would be discouraging to a patient whose level of object relations is rising and it is therefore postponed in favor of providing an immediate response which meets the libidinal side of the question.

Mr. Forrester:	That's the first time I've ever asked about you. People get colds and things like that at this time of the year. It never occurred to me before that you might get sick, too.
Therapist:	I happen not to have a cold right now.
Mr. Forrester:	It feels so different to think of you as a person.
Therapist:	How does it feel?
Mr. Forrester:	New. I realize that I am going through something I never experienced before.

Therapist:	You're not sure you like it.
Mr. Forrester:	Well, with my intellect I can realize that it represents progress, that it is what I came here for. I even begin to think I can be like everyone else. But the old way is more familiar.
Therapist:	And less worrisome?
Mr. Forrester:	Yes. I wonder whether I ask how you are because I worry about what happens to you when I forget you?

Here the patient begins by himself to recognize the aggressive aspect. Compare this with the results usually obtained by pouncing on the question about one's health with, "Why do you ask?" or "What makes you worry about me?" or the more direct, "You worry about my health because of your wish to destroy me." These can make the patient defensive at best and guilty at worst.

Therapist:	That could be. But what is there to worry about if you forget me?

This simple-sounding intervention supports and promotes the neutralization of the aggressive drive as it begins to be used in the service of separation-individuation.

Mr. Forrester:	I'm just beginning to realize that you still exist even when I stop thinking about you.
Therapist:	So you don't really *forget* me; it's merely that I'm not uppermost in your mind all the time. You recognize me when you see me again.

This intervention informs the patient that he does not destroy the object but rather that the object representations emerge even though they are sometimes relegated to the preconscious.

Mr. Forrester:	(In a later session) I like you so much, yet I've been looking at other women.

Therapist:	Does that bother you?
Mr. Forrester:	I never thought I could be interested in anyone else. It feels disloyal.
Therapist:	That's because you think of love like money in the bank; if you withdraw some, there is less.
Mr. Forrester:	Isn't it like that?
Therapist:	No. Love expands. It doesn't follow the ordinary laws of economics.
Mr. Forrester:	Are you sure it doesn't hurt you if I become interested in women?
Therapist:	Why would it hurt me?
Mr. Forrester:	I always thought it would be disloyal if I didn't love my mother.
Therapist:	But you couldn't love her all the time. You had other feelings, too, didn't you?
Mr. Forrester:	I realize now that I had, but I never allowed myself to know.
Therapist:	So you squelched your desire to go your own way because you thought it would be disloyal.

Here the purpose is to show again that neutralized aggression which serves separation-individuation is not destructive.

Mr. Forrester:	I feel like a twelve-year-old boy beginning to notice girls.
Therapist:	Would your mother have minded?
Mr. Forrester:	No. I only thought she would. And you don't mind either. You think it's good. Well, you're right. I can be a person like anyone else.

Structure building is, of course, the entire burden of our presentation of technique. The foregoing illustrations of how interpretation is used for that purpose demonstrate that interpretive interventions have an overall objective but are made step by step and often so subtly that the manifest wording appears deceptively inconsequential. One goes with the patient and yet exercises gentle leadership, thereby preceding him slightly at times, yielding to his lead at other times, but always

maintaining the shortest possible distance between, so that the therapeutic alliance is upheld. Sometimes we use the analogy of the spark
of electricity that jumps from pole to pole if the poles are at the
proper distance; if they are too far apart, the spark will not jump the
gap; if they are too close, it is not necessary for the jump to be made.
The therapist, by his intervention, provides a pole close enough to
where the patient's ego is at the moment to make it possible for the
patient to jump the gap—not so far that the task is impossible, nor
so close that the ego does not have to work. This illustrates also what
we mean by ego building through exercise of function.

≫ 17 ≪

THE SPECIFIC TECHNIQUES OF PSYCHOTHERAPY

FOR THE APPROACH TO TREATMENT OF borderline structures, there is one organizing feature of human development which can be used technically as the fisherman uses a net that will catch the most fish. Because the development of the human being proceeds within a dyad, pathology in borderline and psychotic structures is, in essence, pathology of object relations. It is to this feature of development that therapy is most usefully addressed, because in the development of object relations are subsumed the processes of neutralization, capacity for delay (frustration tolerance), ego and superego identifications leading to secure and enduring internalizations, and the freedom of the autonomous ego functions to develop outside of conflict. The need for an object is ubiquitous; even the psychotic in the restitutive phase creates for himself an object world, albeit a distorted one. This fact of human development provides the therapist with a central theme around which to pursue his ego-building efforts. Out of this, he is able to organize—at least in his own mind—the therapeutic pathway so that, though he stays with the varying themes that the patient introduces, he is unlikely to be led down byways without bearing in mind the main direction to be taken. Treatment begins, we have said, with diagnosis—that is, with designation of the developmental lesions. Inevitably, in the more severe adult pathologies, there are problems in object relations which interrelate with failure in other aspects of development.

It is not truly possible, although it is necessary for heuristic purposes, to discuss object relations separate from the totality of the developmental process. Therefore, we recapitulate here that neutralization begins shortly after birth within the rhythm of gratification and frustration. Within a few months, neutralization is augmented by fusion of the drives and of the object representations. If these processes fail, flaws in object relations ensue. This is another way of defining pathology of object relations and shows the interrelatedness of the drive-taming processes and the development of object relations.

In the treatment of the adult patient, the unwavering reliability of the therapist is essential to building object relations. The therapist is there, predictable, in the same kindly mood each time. Pressure of need gratification diminishes in such a climate. The energy used in forcing minimal gratification from the object becomes neutralized. The patient does not feel aggressive toward the therapist who does not disappoint him by failing an appointment, but can instead deal interpretively with his now-excessive fear of disappointment because his mother was not always so reliable. It is reassuring to know that, to accomplish this, no excessive gratification is necessary. It is a never-to-be-underestimated fact that patients respond to a benign but not overgratifying therapeutic climate, and that they can begin to internalize self-esteem after distortions have been corrected because they have come to expect courtesy and respect from the therapist.

While this does not appear, at first glance, to be very profound technique, its subtleties lie first in the diagnostic designation of the developmental lesion, and, second, in addressing oneself to precisely the point at which the patient's self and object representations became impaired. At the risk of oversimplifying once again, one might say that the patient responds with relief and gratitude to the profound understanding of his individual problem because the therapist has taken the trouble to seek it out and to lend himself to it. We have seen this most markedly in the current generation of thirty- to forty-year-old patients whom we have designated as "Watsonian babies." These were held to rigid schedules in their infancy and suffered unnecessary frustration because they were the victims of the child-rearing fad dictated by behaviorism and adopted all too eagerly by unattuned mothers. Designating interpretively that frustration was too much and too early begins to alter self-concepts and introduces opportunity for transmuting internalizations. The pressure of need is acknowledged as having been valid at the time. The consequences of inability to develop to levels beyond need gratification are also discussed. The results are slow, but become surely those of a diminishing investment of energy in need, and a concomitant deployment of that energy to object cathexis.

Since all aspects of development are linked together, failure in the drive-taming processes and faulty development of object relations result in the ego modifications discussed in chapters 7 and 9. We review them briefly here:

1. Premature ego development—an unevenness in development characterized by pseudo–self-sufficiency in which part of the ego replaces the symbiotic partner, and by concomitant absence of object cathexis. This is a form of narcissism impervious to alliance with another person. A patient with premature ego development is to be engaged painstakingly in a search for the unconscious, split-off, premature part of his ego. Kramer describes such a patient as having a "little man" inside him. Another patient might refer to a "voice" that directs him; this is not the same as the auditory hallucination of the psychotic. When the premature development becomes conscious, the patient can begin, gradually, to relinquish his self-sufficient arrangement while understanding the failure of the symbiotic experience which made the premature thrust necessary. To the patient, it was a life-saving solution to the alternative of being objectless. And so we gradually intrigue him with the fact that, while it served him well in infancy, it impairs his capacity to live fully as an adult. He will relinquish it gradually in an atmosphere of absolute reliability.

2. Ego distortion—a form of pathology characterized by faulty self and object representations resulting from predominantly aggressive cathexes linked with inadequate drive taming. In Jacobson's terms, these distortions involve, also, too early disillusionment with the object. Complementing this description with Mahler's and Kohut's views, opportunity to participate in the omnipotence of the symbiotic partner at the phase-specific time was meager. The clinical appearance of an ego distortion becomes immediately recognizable if we refer to it as *projection*. This we are reluctant to do. The patient who has been beaten, abused, betrayed, lied to, will of course approach the therapist with aggression and suspicion. Or the patient with low self-

esteem will "project" this by denigrating the therapist. But we prefer to avoid using the term and concept *projection* because, as a mechanism of defense, it is used with the assumption that something from the self is projected onto an external object. Before differentiation, as Jacobson pointed out, there is neither self nor object, but a merger of the two. The patient is in a vicious cycle. Preponderance of negative experience has prevented sufficient libidinal cathexis for progress to differentiation; the merged, aggressively cathected self and object representations cannot be relinquished lest there be none at all. And so, to the patient, the therapist is but an extension of his aggressively cathected self.

Every therapist has had the experience of the unrelenting expectation on the part of the patient that the therapist will be critical of him. Experiences take place in which the absence of value judgments and a friendly, benign supportiveness are forgotten, and the distorted expectation replaces the benign experience. These patients are struggling with internalized past object representations which have not been clearly differentiated and are included in the self representations. Thus, "Your mother's criticism, at a time when her opinion was crucially important to you, has become, so to speak, a part of your own tissue. It is so hard for you to recognize any other kind of response to you because it is not like her or you."

This is the point where we may elaborate on why we do not advocate ventilation of too much aggression in the early part of treatment. The vicious cycle we describe can only be reinforced by aggressive verbalizations which acquire the status of confirmation of the distortions, at best. At worst, the object world may be destroyed. How, then, are distortions corrected? In everyday technique, the word *really* cannot be overworked in this endeavor, because we need to encourage and use reality testing to the utmost. "When your mother's unattuned behavior disappointed and frustrated you, you assumed she hated you altogether." This points up how the infant experiences in totalities and is unable to understand that the other person's behavior is motivated by factors of her own pathology rather than by aggression directly felt toward the child. Again, the wording of the intervention is designed to convey the concept without a lecture. The purpose of such an intervention is the technical one of seeking out past libidinal expe-

rience, no matter how feeble. There might have been, we say exagger-
atedly, only one moment in this person's life when he was well
treated. We need to recapture that moment because it is from there
that we begin to build libidinal object cathexis and self-esteem. This
continues in a therapeutic climate that never wavers in respect and
courtesy. Gradually, as libido increases, distortions from the past may
be corrected in the present as well. "Do you really believe I don't like
you?" can be asked most usefully after libidinal cathexis has accrued
in conjunction with repeated experience that the therapist is a kind
and empathic person. Correction of distortion is a slow but rewarding
process—rewarding because, upon correction, libidinal cathexis of
self and object representations can be enjoyed and differentiation can
safely proceed.

We may also put this same technical precept within the framework
of the concepts of symbiosis and nondifferentiation of self and object
representations. Therapists are baffled about how to provide a good
symbiotic experience retroactively for an adult in compensation for
past failure. To provide such closeness with an adult patient is usually
neither possible nor necessary. What we do provide is a new *intrasystemic* experience. The former preponderance of negative, aggressive
cathexes gives way to libidinal experience of self and object representations, thus substituting for the inadequate symbiosis of childhood.
Following this, differentiation may be promoted. "Did I really say
that, or was it your own thought?" "Did we really do that together,
or does it only seem so because you are not ready to exclude me yet?"
Interventions such as these, designed to promote differentiation, are to
be timed so that they come *after* the libidinal self-object has had its
full measure. Here we extend Kohut to include opportunity for participation in grandiosity and omnipotence and in symbiotic gratification
my means of "bathing" the ego in the libidinal cathexes that we so
painstakingly sought out and emphasized in the exploration of the
life experience. There is also a time for aggression in therapy and we
shall come to this. Here we reiterate that the time is not before the
positive self-object is attained.

Discussion of ego distortion is incomplete without considering distortion of the body image. While that was a central theme in the preceding chapters, we recapitulate here that distortions in sexual iden-

tity, size, strength, beauty, are commonplace. Many patients undergo
futile surgery in the search for a better body image. This is never to
be encouraged. Nor is the man who feels that his penis is too small to
be encouraged to go from doctor to doctor in endless search for reassurance. The correct approach to that ubiquitous problem is, "You
think it is too small because you think of your body as it was when
you were a little boy." This is different from the interpretation in psychoanalysis proper, where the anxiety is on the phallic-oedipal level.
There the interpretation would be related to phallic rivalry, to castration anxiety, and to fear of being too small to be a sex partner for the
oedipal object. In the less-developed structure, we deal first with the
prephallic problem of the body image.

3. Ego deviation—the result of fault in developmental sequence
—is most clearly described by Spitz. He showed how, at critical
periods, development and maturation must converge for development to
proceed favorably. Maternal regulation is essential to ensuring convergence. The following quoted case illustrates the kind of lesion that
results from failure of convergence, leaving vulnerability to ego regression, and indicates the therapeutic approach.

Miss Ellsworth was a doctoral candidate who was in treatment because of inability to complete her dissertation:

When she tries to write she is overtaken by anxiety. Words, in a regressive process, lose their symbolism and become concretized. This patient developed normally, reached the oedipal position and, when not
anxious, is verbal and competent as a writer and speaker. Looking into
her history, she remembers a household with a deteriorating marriage and
much quarreling. During this unstable period, the parents separated and
reconciled several times, and there was much coming and going. She remembers identifying with the aggressive climate by speaking sharply to her
mother, repeating almost exactly what mother had said to father, "I wish
you would go away." About twelve years later, at the age of fifteen, there
was an anxiety attack when mother went out of town for two weeks. Separation anxiety comes immediately to mind, but the patient, as an adult,
functions as though separation-individuation has been adequately trans-
passed in infancy, and the adolescent anxiety is within normal limits if
we consider that adolescence involves another round in the separation-individuation process. The analyst concluded that the onset of speech as
well as the acquisition of identity had occured in a context in which sufficient neutralization was not possible for maximum completion of these

important developments. We see, then, a slightly uneven picture of speech and identity having proceeded normally, but connected in the unconscious with fantasies of precipitating abandonment by mother by verbalizing, "I wish you would go away." The writing of the dissertation may be looked at as still another step in the direction of independence from the object, bringing into play the use of words which in the unconscious are too aggressively tinged for their real purpose.

Employing Spitz' concept of critical periods, we can say that there was failure of convergence of maturation and the ego functions of symbolization and speech in a maternal climate which was not quite adequate at the critical period. That this resulted in a not-too-severe variation in ego development and not in ego modification is borne out by the patient's capacity to use free association and to arrive at insight. It is clear that the ego is intact despite the transient loss of symbolization.

The transference interpretation is, "You cannot complete your dissertation because you would in effect be telling me, 'I wish you would go away.' " The genetic interpretation is, "When you told your mother to go away, she went, and you lost the ability to use words because you thought they were the instruments which brought about her departure." These interpretations are designed to inform an intact ego of the point at which and method whereby development of an ego function became burdened by nonconvergence of maturation, development and appropriate maternal intervention at a critical period. We omit reference to the oedipal determinants of a rather common ego regression for the purpose of highlighting the part played by a critical period in development.[1]

4. Ego regression—results in loss of one or more ego functions which had already been attained developmentally. This is also exemplified in the case of Miss Ellsworth. Deviant ego development left her vulnerable to ego regression, the cause of her "writer's block." Her case illustrates also that, even in neurotic structures, ego regressions can occur. These are usually the normal ones in the service of the ego. But in this case, ego regression resembled that seen in the more pathological structures where it fails to serve the ego. It is to be distinguished from an *inhibition* which results in loss of an ego function because of incursion of the id into the ego's territory. If Miss Ellsworth's "work block" had been an inhibition, we would have seen, as its underlying determinant, invasion by sexualized or aggressivized wishes. This arrangement might obtain and yet be under-

[1] G. Blanck and R. Blanck, "Toward a Psychoanalytic Developmental Psychology," pp. 704–705.

pinned by the developmentally earlier problem of failure in a critical period. The latter, then, would have to be treated first, the better to pave the way for analysis of the inhibition, which is a neurotic arrangement on a higher developmental level.

5. Ego defects—as we have defined them in chapter 7, reside in the undifferentiated matrix. They are constitutional and untreatable by presently known methods. We can only exemplify: the infant's incapacity to engage in the symbiotic experience prevents development, resulting in childhood psychosis. Other defects are known, principally low intelligence (mental retardation) and that ill-defined and elusive learning disability often described as *minimal brain damage.* Treatment methods for ego defects are unknown.

We proceed now to description of the tools of psychotherapy and their use:

1. *Ego support* is probably one of the most mentioned and yet most misunderstood tools in psychotherapy. Some regard it simplistically as a "pat on the back" technique. "You did a good job," "You look well today," "You are a nice person," and the like are amateurish compliments which can be construed as ego support only if one abandons scientific definition of *ego* and uses it as has now become popular among laymen who refer to "ego boost" or "ego trip" when technically they mean narcissistic gratification. Of course, the patient's self-esteem is always to be maintained. But internalized, poor self-images do not yield to compliments. All are familiar with exceedingly beautiful women who regard themselves as ugly despite daily experiences with external reactions to their beauty. Self-esteem is the favorable self-image which results from internalization of parental affection combined with favorable experiences of success in mastery. Kohut's description of the gleam in the eye of the loving mother and its important contribution to the essential narcissism of the child is applicable here. Under favorable circumstances, this becomes an internalized sense of self-worth. Simple reassurance can have no effect upon failure to have an internalized, effective sense of self.

Another less-simplistic construction of ego support is the technique of suppression which persists from an earlier theoretical era. Then it was thought that the impaired ego was not equal to the drives, often because the id was thought to be stronger than the ego. The technical purpose, then, was logically reasoned to be the opposite of "uncovering." Suppressive techniques are now outmoded because of the progress of psychoanalytic developmental theory. While it remains correct that the weak ego is unable to cope with the drives, we can strengthen it with techniques such as correct *ego support.* We can also help attenuate the drives.

The ego is supported by searching out, diagnostically, those areas in which it has reached its highest points of development. The patient is unaware of these achievements and needs to have them pointed out to him. Mr. Baker, who went into the store in search of his mother, had employed the normal initiative of a toddler to lessen separation anxiety by finding the object. He needed to be told this. Many patients report, often guiltily, sexual investigations and explorations in early childhood. They need to hear something like, "Isn't it good that you had curiosity and heterosexual interest!" Very many borderline patients have, at least once in their childhood, ventured to speak or act oppositionally. This is to be sought out and supported by, "At least you had a mind of your own." As the therapist gains experience with this more profound form of *ego support,* he finds his unique ways of carrying it out. Never is it done falsely. But that is less of a technical problem than imprecision. "Blanket" support such as, "You are a courageous person," has little value unless it connects with a specific experience where the therapist can see how the ego functioned and can apprise the patient of it *in relation to that experience.* The purpose of ego support is to provide leverage. It helps the patient appreciate his developmental accomplishment, not primarily for gratification, but so that he will know his own strength. He will use that development again now, encouraged by the therapist's recognition of it. Initiative, reality testing, exercise of curiosity and inquisitiveness, the courage to disagree, can all be resumed from where development ceased when exercise of such ego functions met with failure and discouragement in childhood. The unfortunate results of the childhood developmental venture are separated, by the therapist's intervention, from the victory of the development itself.

2. In psychotherapy, *the defensive function of the ego* often needs to be improved. The foregoing discussion was largely concerned with adaptive functioning. In that form of ego support, the patient's at-

tempts at adaptation are to be sought out in the life history. But the problem of how the ego copes with anxiety is one which calls for equal therapeutic attention in the borderline structures. When dealing with the intact ego of the neurotic, we can assume that signal anxiety is operative. The ego in borderline structures is not always responsive to anxiety as a signal and, even when signal anxiety is present, it often needs strengthening. Again, we revise a time-worn technical precept: often intended synonymously, we have been instructed to "support the ego" and to "support the defenses." This was correct when our lesser theoretical knowledge led us to regard defense as the sole function of the ego requiring therapeutic attention. Even though other functions were known, they were not promoted therapeutically. Now, just as *ego support* has acquired new meaning as the outcome of new theoretical knowledge, support of defense no longer means to impose suppression when repression is weak, for example. It means, in essence, that the therapeutic goal be directed toward enabling the ego to tolerate and cope with anxiety and to bring it to the level of signal anxiety if possible.

In a brilliant integration of Mahler's and Kohut's contributions, Tolpin[2] shows how the transition from reliance on the mother for relief from anxiety in the symbiotic phase is, in the process of separation-individuation, gradually internalized. In this way, such transmuting internalizations build the ego to the point where signal anxiety replaces both traumatic anxiety and reliance upon the external object for regulation. Tolpin regards this development, quite correctly we believe, as leading to separation-individuation and object constancy. We have said that the core problem in the borderline structures is precisely this developmental failure; therefore, technical means are to be sought in the attempt to further these processes. Many borderline patients suffer from severe traumatic anxiety without ego competence to erect defenses. If anxiety-producing fantasies and memories are conscious, we see no point in suppressing them, nor do we feel confident that suppressive measures are at all effective. One might as well face openly the incestuous wish, castration anxiety, fear of loss of the ob-

[2] M. Tolpin, "On the Beginnings of a Cohesive Self: An Application of the Concept of Transmuting Internalization to the Study of the Transitional Object and Signal Anxiety."

ject, and even fear of annihilation, if that is the problem. We do this by providing whatever relief we can by intellectual explanation, by relieving the pressure of oversevere superego components, and so on. For example, one might support awakening from an anxiety dream by saying, "At least you could stop the anxiety by awakening."

These, however, are desperate measures. More enduring, we believe, is the provision of the concept of the *right* to be soothed. Mr. Baker had, at the age of three, excessive fear that wolves would get him when his parents went out at night. He crouched in a corner sweating with anxiety until they returned. Regardless of the symbolism of wolves, it helps for the therapist to agree that he needed soothing before being left. This is done in the context of the therapist's better attunement and availability. Such a patient does need to be able to be in touch with the therapist when anxiety becomes overwhelming. In that way, gradually, transmuting internalizations are built in conjunction with burgeoning object relations. Mr. Baker did, in fact, begin to experience the therapist's desire to help him with intolerable anxiety. Eventually this resulted in his increased capacity to deal with it himself when the enormity of it could be reduced to a signal.

3. *Verbalization* has been particularly stressed as an ego building device. Many borderline patients wish to be understood in the symbiotic mode—that is, without words. Some fear this mode because their symbiotic needs make the wish appear possible of fulfillment and this threatens the slight foothold in identity. Unless the patient is not borderline but frankly psychotic, we do not advocate attempting to understand him wordlessly, nor do we think it possible for most therapists to do so. One can, if symbiotic deprivation has been severe, be together in comfortable silence. If symbiosis has been overindulged, the only proper course is to hold out a kindly expectation that the patient explain himself verbally. But the real technical purpose of verbalization is to bring heretofore unmentioned, often preverbal, material under the aegis of the ego. It is the ego that has to communicate semantically with the therapist, calling into play all the auxiliary ego functions we have mentioned as contributory to the complex process of verbalization—symbolization, intentionality, object relations, and so forth. Particularly does verbalization aid neutralization because the drive energy that might otherwise be discharged motorically or through physiological channels becomes available for transfer

to the ego. In addition, ideation becomes bound in the secondary process when it is put into words. Verbalization also promotes capacity to
delay by building frustration tolerance. The short circuit of impulse
discharge is rewired to go through a central controlling mechanism
—the ego.

4. *Building the ego* by exercise of function is related to interpretation and verbalization. The recommendation is: do not say for the patient that which he can arrive at himself. The therapist who is too
eager to help takes on the patient's task. The therapist's task is to
encourage the patient to try to "add up" the material of the session,
thereby aiding the synthetic function; to urge the patient along when
an interpretation is close at hand with, "What do you make of that?"
Long speeches, lectures, pronouncements and the like on the part of
the therapist only exercise *his* functions. They may intimidate the
patient who would be better served if he were encouraged to exercise
his own interpretive skills. He will become more skillful as therapy
proceeds. It is a triumph of autonomy when the patient is able to say,
"I thought of that without you."

5. *Neutralization* of both drives takes place, in normal development, in conjunction with predictable rhythm of gratification and tolerable frustration. It proceeds, as needs are assuredly gratified, to cathexis of the object. Thus, neutralization is closely related to
development of object relations and to enhancement of other functions,
even those which are already autonomous. In psychotherapy, neutralization is promoted principally by verbalization which replaces, or
at least postpones, action. The therapeutic climate is important because
it must provide the same predictability that is so essential in infancy.
For the adult patient, however, this is not done as though the infantile experience can be duplicated. We do not gratify and frustrate
rhythmically. We provide a predictable, reliable therapeutic context
which usually cannot be used immediately for neutralization, but
which accrues over a period of time. Once assured of the therapist's
unwavering reliability, the patient begins to risk both libidinous and
aggressive expression. This was exemplified in the cases of Mr. Forrester and Mr. Baker, among others. The drives become neutralized
in the intertwined processes of building object relations, encouraging
verbalization in place of action, and promoting autonomy and independence. But perhaps of primary importance among these is that the

patient is thoroughly understood diagnostically so that the treatment addresses his needs with precision. Then, gratification and frustration may be permitted in proper dosage and in accord with diagnostic indications.

We are often asked how to promote neutralization. The foregoing discussion demonstrates that there is not a simple "how to do it." The therapeutic climate as a whole is arranged to afford opportunity to find pathways for need satisfaction which is not reflexive and impulsive. The therapeutic alliance in itself creates possibility for correction of distortions and for use of positive object cathexes for drive attenuation.

6. While *neutralized libido* builds object relations, *neutralized aggression* powers the developmental thrust toward separation-individuation. This is dramatically evident when the eighteen-month-old infant, in identification with the aggressor, begins to say "no." We have described how opposition is to be welcomed and supported as it proceeds further into the neutralized mode. Each step in differing with the object aids differentiation. At the Twenty-seventh International Congress of Psycho-Analysis, the theme of which was *aggression,* R. Blanck said:

1. Even though it awaits validation from biology, it has been postulated that the aggressive drive serves the aim of identity formation by providing the impetus for separation-individuation. This view extends our thinking about the aggressive drive into the area of study of its role in ego development. Thus, aggression may no longer be regarded as stimulating solely hostile, pain-inflicting wishes, but as having the more positive aim of serving ego development as well.
2. One of the connections with biology which Freud proposed, namely that the aggressive drive serves or is involved in the maturation of the musculature, leads logically to the already stated position that the aggressive drive can serve ego development.
3. A similar phenomenon is described by Spitz in that the acquisition of the word "no," a form of identification with the aggressor, denotes a level of ego organization containing a significant contribution to the development and organization of psychic structure. This postulate has been well validated in clinical work.[3]

[3] R. Blanck, Unpublished discussion of Brenner, "The Psycho-Analytic Concept of Aggression," presented to the Twenty-seventh International Congress of Psycho-Analysis.

In that same discussion, E. H. Erikson proposed the term *aggressivity* to connote those aspects of the aggressive drive which are growth promoting and self-assertive rather than hostile and destructive.

Technically, the use of aggression in the service of growth is promoted first by neutralization. This adds to our reasons for discouraging ventilation of aggression in its unneutralized mode. When it is welcomed as serving growth, it acquires its own momentum. For example, Mr. Baker's decision to take a separate vacation was not opposed by the therapist *at that time* because he was beginning to use his aggression assertively in the direction of independence. The timing is stressed because we do not always go along with such moves. When they are resistances or acting out, they are to be interpreted as such. But, in this case at that moment, it would have been a growth-retarding error to have interpreted an independent thrust as a resistance. One must know what is happening with the patient in order to know whether to go along encouragingly or whether he is acting against his therapeutic interest. This policy is technically more difficult than the simple one of interpreting all moves away from the therapist as resistance. One important clue in the case of Mr. Baker was that, although he wanted to go away, he was willing to pay for the missed sessions. This suggested that object relations were on a higher level than that of need satisfaction. Had he wanted the vacation to be "paid for" by the therapist, it would have been a sign that he was not using the separate vacation in the service of a developmental thrust.

When a patient begins to move forward and back and then forward again in self-assertiveness, it is timely, also, to avoid symbiotic gratification. He may have needed some gratification to have reached this next stage in his therapy, but when separation-individuation approaches, his regressions are to be understood but not indulged. These are the moments when one is tempted to provide excessive gratification by extending the time, making up missed sessions, being lenient about the fee, and so on. Being too "good" to the patient at this juncture precludes growth because the growth-promoting use of aggression is suppressed by it. More than one patient has been known to say, "How can I be angry if you are so good to me?" At this time, the patient needs to feel his disappointment and anger that Paradise is lost, that there is no longer an all-giving maternal object, that he has to master frustration and to take over ego functions for himself.

Although we have emphasized that aggression is not to be elicited before it is at least somewhat (1) neutralized and (2) expressed against the backdrop of reliable libidinal object cathexes, sometimes, despite our efforts to postpone ventilation, it occurs. When this happens, it may be necessary to wait it out. If possible, it is to be reduced but not suppressed. The patient is never to be permitted to abuse or physically attack the therapist. Verbal abuse is also to be discouraged as constituting direct discharge outside the control of the ego. Not only is it therapeutically valueless in and of itself, but it places the therapist in a denigrated, masochistic-like role which will preclude positive identifications later on.

We reemphasize that tamed aggression is not hostile if it serves establishment of identity. Neither is aggression to be confused, as laymen often do, with activity. Activity, in our frame of reference, is the changeover from the passive, preoedipal state of receiver of maternal ministrations to the active, oedipal position of giver of love. In that sense, it bears no relationship to hostile aggression.

7. *Confrontation* is a frequently mentioned technique which we regard somewhat differently from the usual conceptualization:

Confrontation consists of presentation from without of glimpses of one's own behavior and attitudes. This may come from friends, spouse, therapist, therapy group members, and others. Since developmental defects are rarely absolute, a function such as object relations is likely to have a fluctuating quality. Although Hartmann did not elaborate upon subphases of the need-gratifying level, it is obvious that none of the maturational or developmental processes is the same at the beginning, middle and end of the phase. If, for example, the patient is fixated in the middle phase of the need-gratification level and has nevertheless made some forward thrust toward object constancy, there is a willingness to please the object. Since the superego is usually not yet an internalized structure, there may be obedience to external stricture. So, a person can be "confronted" with the desirability of changing his behavior in order to retain the object or the object's love. Behavioral change at the behest of another does not become internalized and therefore does not include growth. While behavior can be altered to comply with external duress, its permanence is in doubt. A person can live beyond his psychological capacity for short periods of time because of the beforementioned fluctuation in developmental levels, but this sort of living on borrowed motivation cannot endure. In metapsychological terms, no structural or dynamic alteration takes place; economically, countercathectic energy is expended in defensive effort; this, however, detracts from adaptation; genetic sources remain unidentified.

To continue, in our view,

. . . confrontation has a different technical intent—to help the observing part of the ego "look at" the experiencing part and confront itself intrasystemically. While the most obvious advantage of such internal confrontation is that the patient is less likely to refute and reject internally perceived insight, this is not necessarily the greater advantage. The most valuable aspect of confrontation from within is that it is in and of itself therapeutic because it promotes the ego's capacity *via exercise of function.* Dynamic arrangements fall into alterable position; structural change comes about because the ego comes to occupy a stronger position in relation to id and superego; energy is freed from defensive deployment, resulting in more conflict-free adaptation; the genetic sources can be revealed.[4]

8. *Internalizations* proceed to higher levels in conjunction with neutralization and libidinal cathexis of the object for purposes of ego and superego identifications. We have said that building object relations is central and carries with it concomitant aspects of ego development. We showed how to recognize when the therapist becomes more meaningful than a need gratifier. With attainment of higher levels of object relations, internalization also proceeds. The technique for promoting these processes is delicate because the therapist cannot usefully demand higher regard than the patient's level of object relations permits. The technical situation is analogous to that of the developing transference neurosis in psychoanalysis, where it comes about, not at the analyst's behest, but because the analysand needs the analyst, appreciates his helpfulness, regresses, and makes a libidinal connection. The psychotherapy patient, whose connection is at the need-gratifying level, also experiences being helped, cathects the object, is under less pressure to have needs fulfilled in the climate of therapeutic reliability, neutralizes aggressive energy no longer needed for dealing with frustration by impulse discharge, and thus transfers energy to the ego for object cathexis. He begins to regard the therapist as a person be-

[4] G. Blanck, "Crossroads in the Technique of Psychotherapy," pp. 507–508.

cause his state of need is less urgent. This is why Miss Carroll was able to say, "I no longer come because I *need* you but because I need *treatment.*" Although her problems were far from resolved, the urgency of her need for a gratifying object had yielded to the next higher stage in the development of object relations.

The case of Miss Epstein demonstrates how internalization processes are furthered. She stated that she had felt the therapist's presence when she moved boldly to demand a sturdy typewriter table. Her reality testing was sound. She knew that the therapist had not really been there. It was her way of saying, "I needed to unite with your strength and I found it in libidinal cathexis of your object representation; in that sense, you were there when I needed you." Thus the object representations of the therapist had become a way station toward the next step in internalization when the strength is no longer borrowed but becomes the patient's own. That this was not the final stage in attaining independence from the object by means of more or less complete internalization does not detract from it as a developmental achievement. It is supported as such. Never is it to be regarded as not good enough. When the intermediary stages are acknowledged by the therapist and experienced with pleasure by the patient, they constitute stepping stones to the next higher levels.

9. *Regulatory processes* are, in early life, the function of the stimulus barrier and the maternal adjunct. After the first few weeks of life, regulation becomes more complex. Not only must the child be protected from external and internal excessive stimuli, such as from the unneutralized rages resulting from excessive pain, frustration, and the like but, for homeostasis, the rhythm of gratification and frustration must be predictable. We have discussed, also, the maternal role as tension regulator and soother and how these functions are gradually internalized within the first few years of life. Kohut's theoretical clarification is borne out by some of the observable facts of childhood development. He regards such internalizations not as substitutes for the mothering persons, but as parts of the structure that have taken over her functions. It is in situations where these delicate mechanisms have failed that capacity to maintain homeostasis is faulty. When maintenance mechanisms fail, rapid ego regressions ensue. Signal anxiety and defense may be lost, dedifferentiation of self and object represen-

tations may occur, deneutralization and even defusion of the drives may result, following which the ego suffers loss of function by reduction in available energy. Capacity for self-regulation is lost.

According to Jacobson, it is not until the superego coalesces as a discrete structure out of the several years of acquisition of superego components that the function of maintenance of identity and of regulation of the stability of the defensive structure is assured. This means, practically, that persons with borderline structures who have, by our definition, not reached that state of structuralization, are particularly vulnerable to regressive catastrophe through failure of regulation. This, we believe to be the precise explanation of the phenomenon of decompensation. In chapter 7 we described how decompensation can take place before the therapist's eyes because the patient has waited for such a crisis before seeking help. These are the cases that demand immediate intervention, sometimes in a hospital setting. Wherever the treatment is conducted, the measures to be taken are the same. The therapist and the setting take on the task of auxiliary stimulus barrier and soother. In such extremes, interpretation is of less value than empathic relatedness. This is also one place where the psychoanalytic rule of allowing the patient to select the material does not apply, not simply because the material is likely to be in the primary process, but because the very permissiveness is frightening to a person who has lost his own regulating functions. The therapist lends himself to restoration of those functions and is attuned to relinquishing that role when the patient is capable of resuming his own direction.

This technique is one of the most delicate in timing. It is no simple task to assess exactly where maternal regulation failed, but the therapist must attempt to repair not only the immediate trauma which precipitated the crisis, but the structural lesion which left the patient prone to loss of regulation. Here, again, "blanket" repair is of little avail. In timing the turning back of ego functions to the patient, the therapist must consider that he must neither remain a regulatory adjunct too long nor abandon the patient too soon. Miss Epstein and her typewriter table may again be mentioned, this time to illustrate the problem in timing. The therapist did not immediately say, "I was not there," but allowed for several such transmuting internalizations to accumulate.

Ideally, it will be the patient herself who will inform the therapist that structuralization has taken place when she announces, "I did it myself." To all who have observed young children at this developmental stage, the triumph of doing it oneself is dramatic evidence that a new structure has been attained. In the adult borderline patient who has lost regulatory mechanisms regressively, structure returns more securely because now the therapist is careful and empathic enough to allow it to rebuild more solidly. Where there was not regression, but absence of regulation, the task is more difficult. In both instances, one guards, throughout, against premature independence as well as against prolongation of doing for the patient that which he is able to take over for himself.

10. *Guardianship of autonomy* has been stressed and calls for little recapitulation here. The therapist, as a growth promoter, does not possess magic nor infinite wisdom, nor can he usefully take over direction of the patient's life. Neither is it helpful technique to hold oneself out as an example of how to live. If identifications do come about, they are chosen by the patient, and these are useful in ego and superego building. They are internalizations which lead toward independence and ultimately toward termination. But they can never be attained at the therapist's behest. When the patient has corrected his distortions and needs new identifications, he will find them. These will be characteristics of the therapist that the patient has experienced and admired. Never are they examples for emulation proposed from the therapist's own life experience. Mr. Baker feared for a long time that the therapist would dictate a way of life. This was consistent with the wish for perpetuation of the paternal domination. After two years of therapy, he became convinced that the therapist was more willing to provide the autonomy than he, the patient, wanted at that point. This helped him struggle with his own conflict over independence. Ultimately, he realized that the therapist would not direct his life. Only then could he venture the truth—that he was more intelligent than the therapist and could find his own ways. This statement employed neutralized aggression in the service of growth. It was not an offense to the therapist, but recognition of a fact. It came about because the therapist, unlike the father, maintained autonomy even

when the patient begged for repetition of the growth-thwarting paternal interference.

Guardianship of autonomy is not an active technique; it is rather an attitude. We have described how we do make decisions which are in the therapist's domain—about diagnosis and determination of the form and frequency of treatment. But this merely distinguishes overpermissiveness from autonomy. By guardianship we mean that, even at the point when the patient telephones for his first appointment, the therapist has in mind that this person is to be helped to leave in a state of independence some day. That he is not independent at the outset is one of the factors that brings him into therapy. That he becomes dependent upon the therapist need not be feared. That he grows increasingly independent as therapy proceeds is the result of the therapist's professional use of himself to promote growth. It is not as contradictory as it appears that, where necessary, the therapist permits himself to be used for "dependency"—that is, for transient symbiotic experiences and transmuting internalizations—if he is alert to the moment when the need for this is over and the patient, often with reluctance, is ready to be encouraged to take the next step. The ultimate developmental step is termination.

11. *Criteria for termination* of psychotherapy are different from those of psychoanalysis. In psychotherapy, we do not have the greater certainty of established psychoanalytic rules. We find guidelines in features other than resolution of the infantile conflicts (especially the oedipal one) and of the transference neurosis. A number of factors influencing termination are not even amenable to therapeutic alteration. Principal among these are reality factors, such as change in residence, marriage, motherhood, loss of income, or the more positive change of promotion on a job—all of which may remove the cathectic investment in treatment. Many of these may be resistances to be dealt with by interpretation. But there is no magical assurance that interpretation will motivate the patient to remain in treatment. The social isolate who had been fearful of heterosexual relationships and, after five years of therapy reaches a higher level of object relations leading to marriage, may have more therapeutic work left to do. But if he disregards the remaining problems in the excitement and

triumph of his dramatic improvement, his resistance can be difficult to work through. It is far better to terminate temporarily, on agreeable terms, thus leaving the door open for future resumption, than to reach an uncomfortable impasse which will feel quarrelsome to the patient.

Also, as Freud said in *Analysis Terminable and Interminable,* not all conflicts come to light in the course of treatment. They may remain unseen and unsuspected, or they may not be of sufficient interest to the patient to bring up. And we cannot continue to work on problems which seem more important to the therapist than to the patient. Here again, we recommend that the therapist not impose his values and ambitions.

We do not wish to leave the impression that, because psychoanalytic procedures are more clearly established, the psychotherapist is entirely at sea with regard to recognition of criteria for termination. We do have the following guidelines to offer.

Since autonomy has been safeguarded throughout treatment and since Mahler's concepts of separation-individuation and object constancy have been employed as criteria for establishment of identity, we await the patient's expressed wish to terminate. This is usually to be expected as he experiences identity. We then evaluate with him the extent of his readiness. Is this a reflection of the practicing subphase, in which instance rapprochement should be anticipated by the therapist before termination is encouraged too enthusiastically? Will separation anxiety be too severe if the therapist is too quick to end? There is a Scylla-Charybdis quality to the therapeutic responsibility. It is damaging to terminate too soon, but perhaps more damaging to cling to the patient too long. When the patient first announces a desire to terminate, the therapist can agree with this opinion and discuss arranging for a terminal phase during which the patient himself will get to know how ready he is and what it will feel like. The external arrangements are of little value. Attainment of identity is an internal process that has little or nothing to do, ultimately, with the physical presence of another person. It is best attained in the context of the dyadic transference where there is opportunity to use neutralized aggression in the service of that goal. We do not advocate tampering with the frequency of the sessions—a mechanical and ineffective device. When the patient is ready to terminate, he should do so and not prolong dependency by "tapering." As an art, psychotherapy will always be inexact. And so, despite the therapist's responsibility to protect the patient, some cases will be terminated prematurely. This, we think, is the lesser evil. The prematurely terminated patient can always return. For those borderline structures where identity is attained, it is even desirable for time to elapse during which the patient tries himself out in life, after which he might return.

Often, close to termination, the patient will express a desire to maintain friendship with the therapist. This is to be interpreted while the treatment is in progress, usually as some facet of separation anxiety. Even in psychoanalysis, but far more markedly in psychotherapy, separation anxiety is a predictable feature of the terminal phase. Whatever fantasies the patient has about "after treatment is over" are to be dealt with while treatment is still in progress. Attempts at social contact after treatment must always be regarded as countering separation anxiety. The patient is better left to work this through with the knowledge about it that he has attained during treatment. The door is kept open for him to return if he feels that termination was premature or that he needs the therapist to help a little more in the difficult process of working through the termination. We sometimes see terminated patients sporadically to give the process a boost.

The therapist should give careful thought to treating a spouse, sibling, or child of the patient even after termination, for if he does so, the door is closed to the patient. It is never desirable to accept, let us say a spouse, to fill the hours that the patient is vacating. A man may send his wife in his place as another form of attenuating his own separation anxiety. He may mention such a plan shortly before he gives up his hours. It is flattering to the therapist if the patient leaves on a wave of positive feelings. These may shift in a negative direction after he has left, or better still, they may reach a more realistic equilibrium. While the patient may believe, temporarily, that his therapist is the only one in the world to treat his wife, the therapist's narcissism must be held in check lest he agree. We systematize criteria for termination of psychotherapy as follows.

1. Attainment of identity.
2. Relief from the presenting problem. This goal is frequently de-

preciated as a symptom cure (without resolution of conflict), as a flight into health, or perhaps worse than those, as a transference cure. While such dangers do indeed obtain, there are many instances when the patient, relieved of the presenting problem, sees no further need for treatment. We cite two examples.

a. The marital couple who have used the marriage as the arena for projection of individual, internal conflict may, in psychotherapy, decide to terminate when they realize that fact and cease to use the marriage in that way. Alternately, one or both spouses may decide to go into individual treatment.

b. The individual who has had object relations unsatisfactory to him, such as social isolation, homosexual contacts, inability to marry, and the like, may feel satisfied (even if the therapist is not) that a suitable point of termination has been reached. In some such cases, the structural damage is so severe that ideal cure is not possible even if treatment were to be prolonged.

Mr. Cole had been a brilliant high school student and had had his pick of scholarships at leading universities. Separation anxiety became so severe in his first college semester that he had to return home. He began treatment concurrently with completing college in his home city. During treatment, he won a coveted graduate scholarship at a famous scientific institute, fortunately also in his home city. During his work on his doctorate, however, he abandoned his studies in favor of working out the compelling realities of effecting permanent separation from the parental home and becoming financially self-supporting.

Mr. Cole's severe separation anxiety was understood as resulting from the fact that, in early childhood as well as later in his life, his mother suffered from chronic, and at times acute, depression. He remembered his loneliness because of her libidinal unavailability. Nor had his father been able to provide adequate object cathexis. As a young adult, Mr. Cole was physically mature, but he was unable to make social contact with young men or social and sexual contact with young women. The therapeutic effort was directed largely to prevention of massive dedifferentiation. Concomitantly, the therapist constituted a stable, consistent, reliable object over many years. These measures saved this brilliant young man from lifelong psychosis.

Object-seeking outside of the therapeutic relationship was begun with trepidation. Where there had been no overt sexuality, not even autoerotic, sexual and social interests became important. Having found a modicum of object cathexis with the therapist, along with drive attenuation and some ego strengths which the therapist "excavated" from the good conflict-free sphere, Mr. Cole began to look for a life partner. He was not "cured" even to the extent of firm differentiation of self and object representations, although much progress had been made along this developmental line. He found a young woman he wished to marry and he decided to terminate treatment. While, in psychoanalysis, such a move might be regarded as resistance and as flight into heterosexuality, in psychotherapy the therapist must weigh the extent of therapeutic gain that might be anticipated if such a case were to continue in treatment against what may be lost in continuing interminably. The therapist was guided by lessened anxiety in heterosexual contact, diminished separation anxiety which dictated the wish to terminate, and decided to "go with" the patient's life plan. Problems will continue to abound in a person who has had a brush with psychosis, but he needs an opportunity to try to live with his problems if he so chooses.

3. Acquisition of a more competent defensive capacity. Traumatic anxiety diminishes in favor of signal anxiety. More effective defense mechanisms are employed. Denial and projection, for example, are abandoned in favor of reaction formation and the like. Even if this results in an obsessional defense, in some cases of impending psychosis this constitutes marked improvement. In more favorable cases, adaptation by means of change in function becomes operative; not only is secondary autonomy achieved, but ego functions derived from the conflict-free sphere are developed.

4. Object relations approach object constancy. In some instances true object constancy is attained. But, short of that, the level of object relations is raised. The objectless person, such as Mr. Cole, begins to need other persons. The individual on a need-gratifying level begins to value the object. The formerly aggressively cathected object can be "forgotten," as in the case of Mr. Forrester, without fear of object loss. The therapist is no longer needed to help the patient perform his own ego functions. Miss Epstein, for example, can begin to deal with the office manager without the therapist.

5. All the above are indications that structuralization, too, has proceeded and that higher levels of internalization have been reached.

6. The ego exercises more and more of its own functions, leaving the therapist behind because he is no longer needed to serve the auxiliary purpose of aiding a less competent ego.

The overall recommendation is that indications for termination present themselves when increments in structuralization impel the patient toward independence. Often this may resemble symptom cure, but that is only the external appearance. When structuralization has proceeded, symptoms such as overwhelming anxiety do indeed diminish. It is most important to consider that the patient who never had identity begins to think, as he approaches it, that its acquisition ends the relationship. This accounts for the excessive separation anxiety that many such patients suffer. It brings about a particularly "sticky" reluctance to use therapy toward progress. However, the therapist can relieve this fear by explaining that, when one possesses identity, relationships do not end—they change. Since the patient has not before experienced other than passive dependence upon the preoedipal object, he has no knowledge of object relations in the active mode. Not only is it necessary for him to be apprised that relationships change rather than end, but such information usually forestalls premature and ill-advised termination based on the misconception that, with acquisition of identity, the end must come. With this new knowledge, patients such as Miss Carroll decide to continue treatment.

Also forestalled by such explanation is the stalemate that comes about when the patient, fearful that the end will come before he can tolerate it, prefers to remain ill rather than work toward cure. Mr. Forrester's case illustrates this. The fear of the end of the relationship is to be interpreted not as the wish to remain ill, not as secondary gain, not as a negative therapeutic reaction, but as lack of experience with object constancy—that the self and object representations exist whether the real persons are physically separate or apart. With Mr. Forrester, this fear was a transitional phase in the acquisition of identity. Ultimately, new relationships replace the therapeutic one. It is important not to rush the patient toward termination at the beginning of this phase. He has to be permitted to linger until he is fully assured that the therapist and he will exist apart comfortably. Then, outside interests will absorb the libidinal energy. When such patients decide to terminate, it should be permitted even though problems remain unresolved. The goal of resolution of the oedipal conflict, as in psychoanalytic treatment, usually will not have been reached. But the goal of acquisition of identity, just as valid for the borderline structure as is resolution of the oedipal conflict for the neurotic, suffices if the patient feels comfortable with it. Some patients prefer to terminate at such a point; some return for psychoanalysis later; some choose to continue in psychoanalysis upon acquisition of an ego structure that can now tolerate that form of treatment.

Psychoanalytic developmental psychology describes the process of growth and the nutrients it requires. Out of this theory arise the specific techniques we have described and illustrated. Behind the specificity stands the philosophy of therapeutic growth promotion as the patient's road to identity and the freedom to approach the potential for which his apparatuses of primary autonomy have endowed him.

BIBLIOGRAPHY

Abraham, K. "Notes on the Psycho-Analytic Investigation and Treatment of Manic-Depressive Insanity and Allied Conditions," in *Selected Papers on Psycho-Analysis*, pp. 137–56. London: Hogarth Press, 1927.

Adler, M. H. (reporter), "Psychoanalysis and Psychotherapy," *International Journal of Psycho-Analysis*, 51 (1970), 219–31.

Alexander, F., and T. M. French, *Psychoanalytic Psychotherapy*. New York: Ronald Press, 1946.

Alexander, F., T. M. French, and G. H. Pollack. *Psychosomatic Specificity. Vol I., Experimental Study and Results*. Chicago: The University of Chicago Press, 1968.

Alexander, F., and H. Ross. *Dynamic Psychiatry*. Chicago: The University of Chicago Press, 1952.

Altman, L. L. *The Dream in Psychoanalysis*. New York: International Universities Press, 1969.

Apfelbaum, B. "Ego Psychology, Psychic Energy, and the Hazards of Quantitative Explanation in Psycho-Analytic Theory," *International Journal of Psycho-Analysis*, 46 (1965), 168–82.

————. "On Ego Psychology: A Critique of the Structural Approach to Psycho-Analytic Theory," *International Journal of Psycho-Analysis*, 47 (1966), 451–75.

Appelgarth, A. "Comments on Aspects of the Theory of Psychic Energy," *Journal of the American Psychoanalytic Association*, 19 (1971), 379–416.

Arlow, J. A. "Silence and the Theory of Technique," (*The Silent Patient*) *Journal of the American Psychoanalytic Association*, 9 (1961), 44–55.

———— (reporter). "Perversion: Theoretical and Therapeutic Aspects," Panel Discussion of the American Psychoanalytic Association, *Journal of the American Psychoanalytic Association*, 2 (1954), 336–45.

————, and C. Brenner. *Psychoanalytic Concepts and the Structural Theory.* New York: International Universities Press, 1964.

Bak, R. C. "Aggression and Perversion," in S. Lorand (ed.), *Perversions: Psychodynamics and Therapy,* pp. 231–40. New York: Random House, 1956.

————. "Comments on Object Relations in Schizophrenia and Perversions," reported by W. A. Stewart in *The Psychoanalytic Quarterly,* 34 (1965), 473–75.

————. "Fetishism," *Journal of the American Psychoanalytic Association,* 1 (1953), 285–98.

————. "The Phallic Woman and the Ubiquitous Fantasy in Perversions," *The Psychoanalytic Study of the Child* (New York: International Universities Press), 23 (1968), 15–36.

Bell, A. I. "Additional Aspects of Passivity and the Feminine Identification in the Male," *International Journal of Psycho-Analysis,* 49 (1968), 640–47.

Bellak, L., and L. Small. *Emergency Psychotherapy and Brief Psychotherapy.* New York: Grune and Stratton, 1965.

Benedek, T. "Parenthood as a Developmental Phase," *Journal of the American Psychoanalytic Association,* 7 (1959), 389–417.

Benjamin, J. "The Innate and the Experiential in Child Development," in H. Brosin (ed.), *Lectures on Experimental Psychiatry,* pp. 19–42. Pittsburgh: University of Pittsburgh Press, 1961.

Berezin, M. A. (reporter). "The Theory of Genital Primacy in the Light of Ego Psychology," *Journal of the American Psychoanalytic Association,* 17 (1969), 968–87.

Bergman, P., and S. K. Escalona. "Unusual Sensitivities in Young Children," *The Psychoanalytic Study of the Child* (New York: International Universities Press), 334 (1949), 333–52.

Bergmann, M. S. "The Intrapsychic and Communicative Aspects of the Dream," *International Journal of Psycho-Analysis,* 47 (1966), 356–63.

————. "The Place of Paul Federn's Ego Psychology in Psychoanalytic Metapsychology," *Journal of the American Psychoanalytic Association,* 11 (1963), 97–116.

Bibring, E. "The Mechanism of Depression," in P. Greenacre (ed.), *Affective Disorders,* pp. 13–48. New York: International Universities Press, 1953.

————. "The So-Called English School of Psychoanalysis," *The Psychoanalytic Quarterly,* 16 (1947), 69–93.

Blanck, G. "Crossroads in the Technique of Psychotherapy," *The Psychoanalytic Review,* 56 (1970), 498–510.

————. "Some Technical Implications of Ego Psychology," *International Journal of Psycho-Analysis,* 47 (1966), 6–13.

————, and R. Blanck. "Toward a Psychoanalytic Developmental Psychology," *Journal of the American Psychoanalytic Association,* 20 (1972), 668–710.

Blanck, R. "Factors in the Growth of a Professional Self," *Address to National Conference on Social Welfare,* May, 1964.

————, and G. Blanck. *Marriage and Personal Development.* New York: Columbia University Press, 1968.

Blos, P. *On Adolescence: A Psychoanalytic Interpretation.* New York: The Free Press, 1962.

Bonaparte, M. "Passivity, Masochism and Feminity," *International Journal of Psycho-Analysis,* 16 (1935), 325–33.

Brenner, C. "The Psycho-Analytic Concept of Aggression," *International Journal of Psycho-Analysis,* 52 (1971), 137–44.

————. "Some Comments on Technical Precepts in Psychoanalysis," *Journal of the American Psychoanalytic Association,* 17 (1969), 333–52.

Breuer, J., and S. Freud. *Studies on Hysteria,* Vol. II of James Strachey, *et al.* (eds.), *The Standard Edition of the Complete Psychological Works of Sigmund Freud.* London: The Hogarth Press, 1955.

Brierley, M. "Affects in Theory and Practice," *International Journal of Psycho-Analysis,* 18 (1937), 256–68.

Bromberg, W. *The Mind of Man.* New York: Harper & Brothers, 1959.

Buhler, C., and F. Massarik (eds.). *The Course of Human Life.* New York: Springer Publishing Company, 1968.

Clower, V. L. (reporter). "Panel on the Development of the Child's Sense of His Sexual Identity," *Journal of the American Psychoanalytic Association,* 18 (1970), 165–76.

Deutsch, F. (ed.). *On the Mysterious Leap, from the Mind to the Body: A Workshop Study on the Theory of Conversion.* New York: International Universities Press, 1959.

Deutsch, H. *The Psychology of Women.* New York: Grune and Stratton, 1944.

Edelheit, H. (reporter). "Panel on Language and Ego Development," *Journal of the American Psychoanalytic Association,* 16 (1968), 113–22.

Eissler, K. R. "The Effect of the Structure of the Ego on Psychoanalytic Technique," *Journal of the American Psychoanalytic Association,* 1 (1953), 104–43.

Eissler, R. S., and K. R. Eissler. "Heinz Hartmann: A Biographical Sketch," in R. M. Loewenstein, L. M. Newman, M. Schur, and A. J. Solnit (eds.), *Psychoanalysis—A General Psychology.* New York: International Universities Press, 1966.

Ekstein, R. "Historical Notes Concerning Psychoanalysis and Early Language Development," *Journal of the American Psychoanalytic Association,* 13 (1965), 707–31.

————, and E. Caruth. "Levels of Verbal Communication in the Schizophrenic Child's Struggle Against, For, and With the World of Objects," *The Psychoanalytic Study of the Child* (New York: International Universities Press), 24 (1969), 115–37.

————, and R. S. Wallerstein. *The Teaching and Learning of Psychotherapy.* New York: Basic Books, 1958.

Ellis, H. *Psychology of Sex: A Manual for Students.* London: Heinemann, 1933.

English, O. S. (reporter). "The Essentials of Psychotherapy as Viewed by the Psychoanalyst," Panel Discussion of the American Psychoanalytic Association, *Journal of the American Psychoanalytic Association,* 1 (1953), 550–61.

Erikson, E. H. *Childhood and Society.* New York: W. W. Norton, 1950.

————. "Identity and the Life Cycle," *Psychological Issues.* Monograph 1. New York: International Universities Press, 1959.

————. "On the Sense of Inner Identity," in R. P. Knight and C. R. Friedman (eds.), *Psychoanalytic Psychiatry and Psychology,* pp. 351–64. New York: International Universities Press, 1954.

Escalona, S. K. "Patterns of Infantile Experience and the Developmental Process," *The Psychoanalytic Study of the Child* (New York: International Universities Press), 18 (1963), 197–244.

Federn, P. *Ego Psychology and the Psychoses.* New York: Basic Books, 1952.

Fenichel, O. "The Ego and the Affects," in *The Collected Papers of Otto Fenichel,* Vol. 2, pp. 215–27. New York: W. W. Norton, 1954.

————. *Problems of Psychoanalytic Technique.* New York: Psychoanalytic Quarterly, Inc., 1941.

————. *The Psychoanalytic Theory of Neurosis.* New York: W. W. Norton, 1945.

Ferenczi, S. "The Nosology of Male Homosexuality (Homo-Erotism)," in *Sex in Psychoanalysis,* pp. 250–68. New York: Dover Publications, 1956.

————. "Thalassa: A Theory of Genitality," *The Psychoanalytic Quarterly,* 2 (1924), 361–403.

Ferreira, A. F. "Empathy and the Bridge Function of the Ego," (*The Silent Patient*) *Journal of the American Psychoanalytic Association,* 9 (1961), 91–105.

Fisher, C. "Psychoanalytic Implications of Recent Research on Sleep and Dreaming," *Journal of the American Psychoanalytic Association,* 13 (1965), 197–303.

————, and I. H. Paul. "The Effect of Subliminal Visual Stimulation on Images and Dreams: A Validation Study," *Journal of the American Psychoanalytic Association,* 7 (1959), 35–83.

Freud, A. "The Concept of Developmental Lines," *The Psychoanalytic Study of the Child* (New York: International Universities Press), 8 (1963), 245–65.

————. *Difficulties in the Path of Psychoanalysis: A Confrontation of Past with Present Viewpoints.* New York: International Universities Press, 1969.

————. *Normality and Pathology of Development in Childhood: Assessments of Development.* New York: International Universities Press, 1965.

————. "Obsessional Neurosis: A Summary of Psycho-Analytic Views as Presented at the Congress," *International Journal of Psycho-Analysis,* 47 (1966), 116–22.

————. *The Writings of Anna Freud, Vol. II, The Ego and the Mechanisms of Defence.* New York: International Universities Press, 1966.

————. *The Writings of Anna Freud, Vol. VIII, Problems of Psychoanalytic Training, Diagnosis and the Technique of Therapy.* New York: International Universities Press, 1971.

————, H. Nagera, and W. E. Freud. "Metapsychological Assessment of the Adult Personality: The Adult Profile," *The Psychoanalytic Study of the Child* (New York: International Universities Press), 20 (1965), 9–41.

Freud, S. *The Standard Edition of the Complete Psychological Works of Sigmund Freud.* Edited by James Strachey, *et al.* London: The Hogarth Press, 1953–64.

————. *Analysis of a Phobia in a Five-Year-Old Boy.* Vol. X of *The Standard Edition,* 1955.

————. *Analysis Terminable and Interminable.* Vol. XXIII of *The Standard Edition,* 1964.

————. *On Beginning Treatment.* Vol. XII of *The Standard Edition,* 1958.

————. *Beyond the Pleasure Principle.* Vol. XVIII of *The Standard Edition,* 1955.

————. *Character and Anal Erotism.* Vol. IX of *The Standard Edition,* 1959.

————. *A Child is Being Beaten: A Contribution to the Study of the Origin of Sexual Perversions.* Vol. XVII of *The Standard Edition*, 1955.

————. *The Dynamics of Transference.* Vol. XII of *The Standard Edition*, 1958.

————. *The Economic Problem of Masochism.* Vol. XIX of *The Standard Edition*, 1961.

————. *The Ego and the Id.* Vol. XIX of *The Standard Edition*, 1961.

————. *Female Sexuality.* Vol. XXI of *The Standard Edition*, 1961.

————. *Fetishism.* Vol. XXI of *The Standard Edition*, 1961.

————. *Formulations on the Two Principles of Mental Functioning.* Vol. XII of *The Standard Edition*, 1958.

————. *Fragment of an Analysis of a Case of Hysteria.* Vol. VII of *The Standard Edition*, 1953.

————. *From the History of an Infantile Neurosis.* Vol. XVII of *The Standard Edition*, 1955.

————. *Further Remarks on the Neuro-Psychoses of Defence.* Vol. III of *The Standard Edition*, 1962.

————. *Group Psychology and the Analysis of the Ego.* Vol. XVIII of *The Standard Edition*, 1955.

————. *The Infant Genital Organization: An Interpolation into the Theory of Sexuality.* Vol. XX of *The Standard Edition*, 1959.

————. *Inhibitions, Symptoms and Anxiety.* Vol. XX of *The Standard Edition*, 1959.

————. *The Interpretation of Dreams.* Vol. IV/V of *The Standard Edition*, 1953.

————. *Lines of Advance in Psycho-Analytic Therapy.* Vol. XVII of *The Standard Edition*, 1955.

————. *Mourning and Melancholia.* Vol. XIV of *The Standard Edition*, 1957.

————. *On Narcissism: An Introduction.* Vol. XIV of *The Standard Edition*, 1957.

————. *Negation.* Vol. XIX of *The Standard Edition*, 1961.

————. *Neurosis and Psychosis.* Vol. XIX of *The Standard Edition*, 1961.

————. *New Introductory Lectures in Psychoanalysis.* Lecture XXXIII, "Femininity." Vol. XXII of *The Standard Edition*, 1964.

————. *Notes upon a Case of Obsessional Neurosis.* Vol. X of *The Standard Edition*, 1955.

————. *Observations on Transference—Love*. Vol. XII of *The Standard Edition*, 1958.

————. *An Outline of Psycho-Analysis*. Vol. XXIII of *The Standard Edition*, 1964.

————. *Papers on Technique*. Vol. XII of *The Standard Edition*, 1958.

————. *Psychoanalytic Notes on an Autobiographical Account of a Case of Paranoia (Dementia Paranoides)*. Vol. XII of *The Standard Edition*, 1958.

————. *The Psychogenesis of a Case of Homosexuality in a Woman*. Vol. XVIII of *The Standard Edition*, 1955.

————. *The Question of Lay Analysis*. Vol. XX of *The Standard Edition*, 1959.

————. *Recommendations to Physicians Practicing Psycho-Analysis*. Vol. XII of *The Standard Edition*, 1958.

————. *Remembering, Repeating and Working-Through*. Vol. XII of *The Standard Edition*, 1958.

————. *Repression*. Vol. XIV of *The Standard Edition*, 1957.

————. *Resistance and Repression. Lecture XIX of Introductory Lectures on Psychoanalysis*. Vol. XV of *The Standard Edition*, 1963.

————. *Some Neurotic Mechanisms in Jealousy, Paranoia and Homosexuality*. Vol. XVIII of *The Standard Edition*, 1955.

————. *Some Psychical Consequences of the Anatomical Distinction Between the Sexes*. Vol. XIX of *The Standard Editon*, 1961.

————. *The Splitting of the Ego in the Process of Defence*. Vol. XXIII of *The Standard Edition*, 1964.

————. *Three Essays on the Theory of Sexuality*. Vol. VII of *The Standard Edition*, 1953.

————. *The Unconscious*. Vol. XIV of *The Standard Edition*, 1957.

————. *"Wild" Psycho-Analysis*. Vol. XI of *The Standard Edition*, 1957.

Friedman, L. "The Therapeutic Alliance," *International Journal of Psycho-Analysis*, 50 (1969), 139–53.

Fromm, E. *The Forgotten Language*. New York: The Grove Press, 1951.

Gill, M. M. (ed.). *The Collected Papers of David Rapaport*. New York: Basic Books, 1967.

————. "Psychoanalysis and Exploratory Psychotherapy," *Journal of the American Psychoanalytic Association*, 2 (1954), 771–97.

————. "Topography and Systems in Psychoanalytic Theory," *Psychological Issues*, Vol. 3, no. 2, Monograph 10. New York: International Universities Press, 1963.

Gillespie, W. H. "The General Theory of Sexual Perversion," Panel on Perversions, 19th International Congress on Psycho-Analysis, 1955, *International Journal of Psycho-Analysis,* 37 (1956), 396–403.

———. "Neurotic Ego Distortions," *International Journal of Psycho-
Analysis,* 39 (1958), 258–59.

———. "Symposium on Homosexuality," Panel Discussion, 23rd International
Congress of Psycho-Analysis, 1963, *International Journal of Psycho-
Analysis,* 45 (1964), 203–209.

Gitelson, M. "On Ego Distortion," *International Journal of Psycho-Analysis,*
39 (1958), 245–57.

Glover, E. "The Concept of Dissociation," in *On the Early Development of
the Mind,* pp. 307–23. New York: International Universities Press,
1956.

———. *On the Early Development of the Mind.* New York: International
Universities Press, 1956.

———. "Ego Distortions," *International Journal of Psycho-Analysis,* 39
(1958), 260–64.

———. "Examination of the Klein System of Child Psychology," *The Psychoanalytic Study of the Child* (New York: International Universities
Press), 1 (1945), 75–118.

———. "Grades of Ego-Differentiation," in *On the Early Development of
the Mind,* pp. 112–22. New York: International Universities Press,
1956.

———. "Metapsychology or Metaphysics. A Psychoanalytic Essay," *The Psychoanalytic Quarterly,* 35 (1966), 173–90.

———. "The Psycho-Analysis of Affects," *International Journal of Psycho-
Analysis,* 20 (1939), 299–307.

———. "The Relation of Perversion-Formation to the Development of
Reality-Sense," in *On the Early Development of the Mind.* New York: International Universities Press, 1956.

———. *The Technique of Psychoanalysis.* New York: International Universities Press, 1955.

Greenacre, P. "Certain Relationships Between Fetishism and Faulty Development of the Body Image," *The Psychoanalytic Study of the Child* (New
York: International Universities Press), 8 (1953), 65–78.

———. "Certain Technical Problems in the Transference Relationship,"
Journal of the American Psychoanalytic Association, 7 (1959), 484–502.

———. "The Childhood of the Artist," *The Psychoanalytic Study of the
Child* (New York: International Universities Press), 12 (1957), 47–72.

————. "Experiences of Awe in Childhood," *The Psychoanalytic Study of the Child* (New York: International Universities Press), 11 (1956), 9–30.

————. "The Fetish and the Transitional Object," *The Psychoanalytic Study of the Child* (New York: International Universities Press), 24 (1969), 144–64.

————. "Further Considerations Regarding Fetishism," *The Psychoanalytic Study of the Child* (New York: International Universities Press), 10 (1955), 187–94.

————. "Perversions: General Considerations Regarding their Genetic and Dynamic Background," *The Psychoanalytic Study of the Child* (New York: International Universities Press), 23 (1968), 47–62.

————. "The Predisposition to Anxiety," *The Psychoanalytic Quarterly,* 10 (1941), 66–94 and 610–38.

————. "Problems of Overidealization of the Analyst and of Analysis: Their manifestations in the Transference and Countertransference Relationship," *The Psychoanalytic Study of the Child* (New York: International Universities Press), 20 (1972), 209–19.

————. "The Role of Transference," *Journal of the American Psychoanalytic Association,* 2 (1954), 671–84.

————. "Special Problems of Early Female Sexual Development," *The Psychoanalytic Study of the Child* (New York: International Universities Press), 5 (1950), 122–38.

————. "The Transitional Object and the Fetish," *International Journal of Psycho-Analysis,* 51 (1971), 447–56.

————. *Trauma, Growth and Personality.* London: The Hogarth Press, 1953.

Greenson, R. R. "Comment on Dr. Limentani's Paper on Acting Out," 24th International Congress of Psycho-Analysis, 1965, *International Journal of Psycho-Analysis,* 47 (1966), 282–85.

————. "Empathy and its Vicissitudes," *International Journal of Psycho-Analysis,* 41 (1968), 418–24.

————. "The Exceptional Position of the Dream in Psychoanalytic Practice," *The Psychoanalytic Quarterly,* 29 (1970), 519–49.

————. "On Homosexuality and Gender Identity," Symposium on Homosexuality, 23rd International Congress of Psycho-Analysis, 1963, *International Journal of Psycho-Analysis,* 45 (1964), 217–19.

————. "On the Silence and Sounds of the Analytic Hour," (*The Silent Patient*) *Journal of the American Psychoanalytic Association,* 9 (1961), 79–84.

————. *The Technique and Practice of Psychoanalysis.* New York: Hallmark Press, 1967.

————. "That Impossible Profession," *Journal of the American Psychoanalytic Association,* 14 (1966), 9—27.

————. "The Working Alliance and the Transference Neurosis," *The Psychoanalytic Quarterly,* 34 (1965), 155—81.

————, and Wexler, M. "The Non-Transference Relationships in the Psychoanalytic Situation," *International Journal of Psycho-Analysis,* 50 (1969), 27—39.

Grinker, R. R., and J. P. Spiegel. *Men Under Stress.* Philadelphia: Blakiston Co., 1941.

Hartmann, H. *Ego Psychology and the Problem of Adaptation.* New York: International Universities Press, 1958.

————. *Essays in Ego Psychology.* New York: International Universities Press, 1964.

————. "The Mutual Influences in the Development of Ego and the Id," *The Psychoanalytic Study of the Child* (New York: International Universities Press), 7 (1952), 9—30.

————. "Notes on a Theory of Sublimation," *The Psychoanalytic Study of the Child* (New York: International Universities Press), 10 (1955), 9—29.

————. "Psychoanalysis and Developmental Psychology," *The Psychoanalytic Study of the Child* (New York: International Universities Press), 5 (1950), 7—17.

————. "Technical Implications of Ego Psychology," *The Psychoanalytic Quarterly,* 20 (1951), 31—43.

————, and E. Kris. "The Genetic Approach in Psychoanalysis," *The Psychoanalytic Study of the Child* (New York: International Universities Press), 1 (1945), 11—30.

————, E. Kris, and R. M. Loewenstein. "Comments on the Formation of Psychic Structure," *The Psychoanalytic Study of the Child* (New York: International Universities Press), 2 (1946), 11—38.

————, E. Kris, and R. M. Loewenstein. "Notes on the Theory of Aggression," *The Psychoanalytic Study of the Child* (New York: International Universities Press), 3/4 (1949), 9—36.

————, and R. M. Loewenstein. "Notes on the Superego," *The Psychoanalytic Study of the Child* (New York: International Universities Press), 17 (1962), 42—81.

Hatterer, L. J. *Changing Homosexuality in the Male.* New York: McGraw Hill, 1970.

Van der Heide, C. "Blank Silence and the Dream Screen," (*The Silent Patient*) *Journal of the American Psychoanalytic Association,* 9 (1961), 85–90.

Heiman, M. "Female Sexuality: Introduction," *Journal of the American Psychoanalytic Association,* 16 (1968), 565–68.

———, J. S. Kestenberg, T. Benedek, and S. Keiser. "Discussion of Mary Jane Sherfey: The Evolution and the Nature of Female Sexuality in Relation to Psychoanalytic Theory," *Journal of the American Psychoanalytic Association,* 16 (1968), 406–56.

Hoffer, W. "Mouth, Hand and Ego-Integration," *The Psychoanalytic Study of the Child* (New York: International Universities Press), 3/4 (1949), 49–56.

Holt, R. R. "Ego Autonomy Re-evaluated," *International Journal of Psycho-Analysis,* 46 (1965), 151–67.

——— (ed.). *New Horizons for Psychotherapy.* New York: International Universities Press, 1971.

Horney, K. *New Ways in Psychoanalysis.* New York: W. W. Norton, 1939.

Isakower, O. "A Contribution to the Pathopsychology of Phenomena Associated with Falling Asleep," *International Journal of Psycho-Analysis,* 29 (1938), 331–45.

Jacobson, E. "Depersonalization," *Journal of the American Psychoanalytic Association,* 7 (1959), 581–610.

———. *Depression.* New York: International Universities Press, 1971.

———. *The Self and the Object World.* New York: International Universities Press, 1964.

———. "Sullivan's Interpersonal Theory of Psychiatry," *Journal of the American Psychoanalytic Association,* 3 (1955), 149–56.

Joseph, E. D. (ed.). *The Place of the Dream in Clinical Psychoanalysis.* (H. F. Waldhorn, reporter; C. Brenner, chairman.) Monograph 2 of the Kris Study Group, pp. 52–106. New York: International Universities Press, 1967.

Kaplan, D. M. "Comments on the Screening Function of a 'Technical Affect,' with Reference to Depression and Jealousy," *International Journal of Psycho-Analysis,* 51 (1970), 489–502.

Katan, M. "Contributions to the Panel on Ego Distortions," *International Journal of Psycho-Analysis,* 39 (1958), 265–70.

Kernberg, O. F. "Borderline Personality Organization," *Journal of the American Psychoanalytic Association*, 15 (1967), 641–85.

──────. "A Contribution to the Ego-Psychological Critique of the Kleinian School," *International Journal of Psycho-Analysis*, 50 (1969), 317–33.

──────. "Early Ego Integration and Object Relations," *Annals of the New York Academy of Sciences*, 193 (1972), 233–47.

──────. "Factors in the Psychoanalytic Treatment of Narcissistic Personalities," *Journal of the American Psychoanalytic Association*, 18 (1970), 51–85.

──────. "Prognostic Considerations Regarding Borderline Personality Organization," *Journal of the American Psychoanalytic Association*, 19 (1971), 595–635.

──────. "A Psychoanalytic Classification of Character Pathology," *Journal of the American Psychoanalytic Association*, 18 (1970), 800–22.

──────. "The Treatment of Patients with Borderline Personality Organization," *International Journal of Psycho-Analysis*, 49 (1968), 600–19.

──────, et al. *Psychotherapy and Psychoanalysis*. Bulletin of the Menninger Clinic, Vol. 36, 1972.

Kestenberg, J. S. "Vicissitudes of Female Sexuality," *Journal of the American Psychoanalytic Association*, 4 (1956), 453–76.

Kinsey, A. C., W. B. Pomeroy, and C. E. Martin. *Sexual Behavior in the Human Male*. Philadelphia: W. B. Saunders, 1948.

──────. *Sexual Behavior in the Human Female*. Philadelphia: W. B. Saunders, 1953.

Klein, M. *Contribution to Psycho-Analysis*. London: The Hogarth Press, 1948.

──────. *Envy and Gratitude*. New York: Basic Books, 1957.

Knight, R. P. "Borderline States," in R. P. Knight and C. Friedman (eds.), *Psychoanalytic Psychiatry and Psychology*, pp. 97–109. New York: International Universities Press, 1954.

──────. "A Critique of the Present Status of the Psychotherapies," in R. P. Knight and C. Friedman (eds.), *Psychoanalytic Psychiatry and Psychology*, pp. 52–64. New York: International Universities Press, 1954.

──────. "Evaluation of Psychotherapeutic Techniques," in R. P. Knight and C. Friedman (eds.), *Psychoanalytic Psychiatry and Psychology*, pp. 65–76. New York: International Universities Press, 1954.

──────. "Psychiatric Issues in the Kinsey Report on Males," in R. P. Knight and C. Friedman (eds.), *Psychoanalytic Psychiatry and Psychology*, pp. 311–20. New York: International Universities Press, 1954.

Kohut, H. *The Analysis of the Self.* New York: International Universities Press, 1971.

Krafft-Ebing, R. *Psychopathia Sexualis.* Stuttgart: Ferdinand Enke, 1924.

Kramer, P. "On Discovering One's Identity: A Case Report," *The Psychoanalytic Study of the Child* (New York: International Universities Press), 10 (1955), 47–74.

Kris, E. "Ego Psychology and Interpretation in Psychoanalytic Therapy," *The Psychoanalytic Quarterly,* 20 (1951), 15–30.

———. "On Some Vicissitudes of Insight in Psychoanalysis," *International Journal of Psycho-Analysis,* 37 (1956), 445–55.

———. "The Personal Myth," *Journal of the American Psychoanalytic Association,* 4 (1956), 653–81.

———. *Psychoanalytic Explorations in Art.* New York: International Universities Press, 1952.

———. "The Recovery of Childhood Memories in Psychoanalysis," *The Psychoanalytic Study of the Child* (New York: International Universities Press), 11 (1956), 54–88.

Van der Leeuw, P. F. "Comment on Dr. Ritvo's Paper," *International Journal of Psycho-Analysis,* 47 (1966), 132–35.

Levin, S. "Some Suggestions for Treating the Depressed Patient," *The Psychoanalytic Quarterly,* 34 (1965), 37–65.

Levy, J. "Silence in the Analytic Session," *International Journal of Psycho-Analysis,* 39 (1958), 50–58.

Limentani, A. "A Reevaluation of Acting Out in Relation to Working Through," *International Journal of Psycho-Analysis,* 48 (1966), 274–82.

Loewald, H. W. "Internalization, Separation, Mourning and the Superego," *The Psychoanalytic Quarterly,* 31 (1962), 483–504.

Loomie, L. "Some Ego Considerations in the Silent Patient," *Journal of the American Psychoanalytic Association,* 9 (1961), 56–78.

Ludwig, A. D. (reporter). "Psychoanalysis and Psychotherapy: Dynamic Criteria for Treatment Choice," Panel Discussion of the American Psychoanalytic Association, *Journal of the American Psychoanalytic Association,* 2 (1954), 346–50.

McLaughlin, J. T. "The Analyst and the Hippocratic Oath," (*The Silent Patient*) *Journal of the American Psychoanalytic Association,* 9 (1961), 106–23.

Macurdy, J. T. *The Psychology of Emotion.* New York: Harcourt, Brace, 1925.

378 Bibliography

Mahler, M. S. "Autism and Symbiosis, Two Extreme Disturbances of Identity," *International Journal of Psycho-Analysis,* 39 (1958), 77–83.

———. "On Child Psychosis and Schizophrenia: Autistic and Symbiotic Infantile Psychosis," *The Psychoanalytic Study of the Child* (New York: International Universities Press), 7 (1951), 286–305.

———. "On the First Three Subphases of the Separation-Individuation Process," *International Journal of Psycho-Analysis,* 53 (1972), 333–38.

———. *On Human Symbiosis and the Vicissitudes of Individuation.* New York: International Universities Press, 1968.

———. "Notes on the Development of Basic Moods: The Depressive Affect in Psychoanalysis," in R. M. Loewenstein, L. M. Newman, M. Schur, and A. J. Solnit (eds.), *Psychoanalysis—A General Psychology,* pp. 152–68. New York: International Universities Press, 1966.

———. "On Sadness and Grief in Infancy and Childhood: Loss and Restoration of the Symbiotic Love Object," in *The Psychoanalytic Study of the Child.* New York: International Universities Press, 16 (1961), 332–51.

———. "On the Significance of the Normal Separation-Individuation Phase," in M. Schur (ed.), *Drives, Affects, and Behavior, Vol. II,* pp. 161–68. New York: International Universities Press, 1965.

———. "A Study of the Separation-Individuation Process: And its Possible Application to Borderline Phenomena in the Psychoanalytic Situation," *The Psychoanalytic Study of the Child* (New York: Quadrangle Books), 26 (1971), 403–24.

———. "Thoughts about Development and Individuation," *The Psychoanalytic Study of the Child* (New York: International Universities Press), 18 (1963), 307–24.

———, and P. Elkisch, "Some Observations on Disturbances of the Ego in a Case of Infantile Psychosis," *The Psychoanalytic Study of the Child* (New York: International Universities Press), 8 (1953), 252–61.

———, and M. Furer. "Certain Aspects of the Separation-Individuation Phase," *The Psychoanalytic Quarterly,* 32 (1963), 1–14.

———, and B. J. Gosliner. "On Symbiotic Child Psychosis: Genetic, Dynamic and Restitutive Aspects," *The Psychoanalytic Study of the Child* (New York: International Universities Press), 10 (1958), 195–212.

———, and K. LaPerriere. "Mother-Child Interaction During Separation-Individuation," *The Psychoanalytic Quarterly,* 34 (1965), 483–98.

Masters, W. H., and V. E. Johnson. *Human Sexual Response.* Boston: Little, Brown and Company, 1966.

————. *Human Sexual Inadequacy*. Boston: Little, Brown and Company, 1970.

Meissner, W. W. "Notes on Identification. II. Clarification of Related Concepts," *The Psychoanalytic Quarterly*, 40 (1971), 277–302.

Menninger, K. *Theory of Psychoanalytic Technique*. New York: Basic Books, 1958.

Moore, B. E. "Frigidity: A Review of Psychoanalytic Literature," *The Psychoanalytic Quarterly*, 33 (1964), 323–49.

————. "Panel Report: Frigidity in Women," *Journal of the American Psychoanalytic Association*, 9 (1961), 571–84.

————, and B. D. Fine. *A Glossary of Psycho-Analytic Terms and Concepts*. New York: The American Psychoanalytic Association, 1967.

Morgenthaler, F. "Disturbances of Male and Female Identity as Met with in Psychoanalytic Practice," Panel Introduction, 26th International Congress of Psycho-Analysis, 1967, *International Journal of Psycho-Analysis*, 50 (1969), 109–12.

Mullahy, P. *Psychoanalysis and Interpersonal Psychiatry*. New York: Science House, 1970.

Murphy, William F. *The Tactics of Psychotherapy*. New York: International Universities Press, 1965.

Nacht, S. "Causes and Mechanisms of Ego Distortion," *International Journal of Psycho-Analysis*, 39 (1958), 271–73.

Niederland, W. G. "The Role of the Ego in the Recovery of Early Memories," *The Psychoanalytic Quarterly*, 24 (1965), 564–71.

Nunberg, H. *Practice and Theory of Psychoanalysis*. New York: International Universities Press, Vol. 1, 1948; Vol. 2, 1965.

————. "The Synthetic Function of the Ego," *International Journal of Psycho-Analysis*, 12 (1931), 123–40.

Pasche, F. "Symposium on Homosexuality," *International Journal of Psycho-Analysis*, 45 (1964), 210–13.

Patterson, C. H. *Theories of Counseling and Psychotherapy*. New York: Harper and Row, 1966.

Pearce, J., and S. Newton. *The Conditions of Human Growth*. New York: Citadel Press, 1965.

Piaget, J. *The Language and Thought of the Child*. New York: Macmillan Books, 1955.

Pine, F., and M. Furer. "Studies of the Separation-Individuation Phase: A

Methodological Overview," *The Psychoanalytic Study of the Child* (New York: International Universities Press), 18 (1963), 325–42.

Pollack, G. H. "Mourning and Adaptation," *International Journal of Psychoanalysis,* 42 (1961), 341–61.

Rangell, L. "The Intrapsychic Process and its Analysis: A Recent Line of Thought and its Current Implications," *International Journal of Psycho-Analysis,* 51 (1970), 195–209.

———. "The Nature of Conversion," *Journal of the American Psychoanalytic Association,* 7 (1959), 632–62.

——— (reporter). "Psychoanalysis and Dynamic Psychotherapy— Similarities and Differences," Panel Discussion of the American Psychoanalytic Association, *Journal of the American Psychoanalytic Association,* 2 (1954), 152–66.

———. "Similarities and Differences between Psychoanalysis and Dynamic Psychotherapy," *Journal of the American Psychoanalytic Association,* 2 (1954), 734–44.

Rapaport, D. *Emotions and Memory.* New York: International Universities Press, 1942.

———. "An Historical Survey of Psychoanalytic Ego Psychology," Introduction to *Psychological Issues,* Vol. 1, no. 1 (1959), 5–17.

———. *The Organization and Pathology of Thought.* New York: Columbia University Press, 1951.

———. "On the Psycho-Analytic Theory of Affects," *International Journal of Psycho-Analysis,* 34 (1953), 177–98.

———. "Some Metapsychological Considerations Concerning Activity and Passivity," in M. M. Gill (ed.), *The Collected Papers of David Rapaport,* pp. 530–69. New York: Basic Books, 1967.

Ritvo, S. "Correlation of a Childhood and Adult Neurosis: Based on the Adult Neurosis of a Reported Childhood Case," *International Journal of Psycho-Analysis,* 47 (1966), 130–31.

Ross, N. "Affect as Cognition." Paper presented before the Topeka Psychoanalytic Society, February 22, 1973.

———. "An Examination of Nosology According to Psychoanalytic Concepts," *Journal of the American Psychoanalytic Association,* 8 (1960), 535–51.

———. "The 'As If' Concept," *Journal of the American Psychoanalytic Association,* 15 (1967), 59–82.

———. "The Primacy of Genitality in the Light of Ego Psychology: Introductory Remarks," *Journal of the American Psychoanalytic Association,* 17 (1970), 267–84.

Rubinfine, D. L. "Notes on a Theory of Depression," *The Psychoanalytic Quarterly,* 37 (1968), 400–17.

Sarlin, C. N. "Feminine Identity," *Journal of the American Psychoanalytic Association,* 11 (1963), 790–816.

Saul L., and A. Beck. "Psychodynamics of Male Homosexuality," *International Journal of Psycho-Analysis,* 42 (1961), 43–48.

————, and J. W. Lyons. "Acute Neurotic Reactions," in Alexander and Ross (eds.), *Dynamic Psychiatry.* Chicago: The University of Chicago Press, 1952.

Schafer, R. *Aspects of Internalization.* New York: International Universities Press, 1968.

————. "An Overview of Heinz Hartmann's Contributions to Psychoanalysis," *International Journal of Psycho-Analysis,* 51 (1970), 425–46.

————. "The Psychoanalytic Vision of Reality," *International Journal of Psycho-Analysis,* 51 (1970), 279–97.

Schur, M. "Comments on the Metapsychology of Somatization," *The Psychoanalytic Study of the Child* (New York: International Universities Press), 10 (1955), 119–64.

————. *The Id and the Regulatory Principles of Mental Functioning.* New York: International Universities Press, 1966.

Sharpe, E. F. *Collected Papers on Psycho-Analysis.* London: The Hogarth Press, 1950.

————. *Dream Analysis.* London: The Hogarth Press, 1937.

Sherfey, M. J. "The Evolution and the Nature of Female Sexuality in Relation to Psychoanalytic Theory," *Journal of the American Psychoanalytic Association,* 14 (1966), 28–128.

Silverman, M. A. "The Growth of Logical Thinking. Piaget's Contribution to Ego Psychology," *The Psychoanalytic Quarterly,* 40 (1971), 317–41.

Socarides, C. W. "Psychoanalytic Therapy of a Male Homosexual," *The Psychoanalytic Quarterly,* 38 (1969), 173–90.

———— (reporter). "Theoretical and Clinical Aspects of Overt Female Homosexuality," *Journal of the American Psychoanalytic Association,* 10 (1962), 579–92.

Spiegel, N. T. "An Infantile Fetish and its Persistence into Young Womanhood," *The Psychoanalytic Study of the Child* (New York: International Universities Press), 22 (1967), 401–25.

Spitz, R. A. "Aggression: Its Role in the Establishment of Object Relations," in R. M. Loewenstein (ed.), *Drives, Affects, Behavior,* New York: International Universities Press, 1953.

————. "Anaclitic Depression: An Inquiry into the Genesis of Psychiatric Conditions in Early Childhood," *The Psychoanalytic Study of the Child* (New York: International Universities Press), 2 (1946), 313–42.

————. "Anxiety in Infancy: A Study of its Manifestations in the First Year of Life," *International Journal of Psycho-Analysis,* 31 (1950), 138–43.

————. "Autoerotism Reexamined: The Role of Early Sexual Behavior Patterns in Personality Formation," *The Psychoanalytic Study of the Child* (New York: International Universities Press), 17 (1962), 283–315.

————. "Bridges: On Anticipation, Duration, and Meaning," *Journal of the American Psychoanalytic Association,* 20 (1972), 721–35.

————. "The Evolution of the Dialogue," in M. Schur (ed.), *Drives, Affects, Behavior, Vol. II.* New York: International Universities Press, 1963.

————. *The First Year of Life.* New York: International Universities Press, 1965.

————. "On the Genesis of Superego Components," *The Psychoanalytic Study of the Child* (New York: International Universities Press), 13 (1958), 375–404.

————. *A Genetic Field Theory of Ego Formation: Its Implications for Pathology.* New York: International Universities Press, 1959.

————. "Hospitalism: An Inquiry into the Genesis of Psychiatric Conditions in Early Childhood," *The Psychoanalytic Study of the Child* (New York: International Universities Press), 1 (1945), 53–74.

————. "Hospitalism: A Follow Up Report," *The Psychoanalytic Study of the Child* (New York: International Universities Press), 2 (1946), 113–17.

————. *No and Yes.* New York: International Universities Press, 1957.

————. "The Primal Cavity: A Contribution to the Genesis of Perception and its Role for Psychoanalytic Theory," *The Psychoanalytic Study of the Child* (New York: International Universities Press), 10 (1955), 215–40.

Sterba, R. "The Fate of the Ego in Analytic Therapy," *International Journal of Psycho-Analysis,* 15 (1934), 117–26.

Van der Sterren, A. A. "Life Decisions During Analysis," *International Journal of Psycho-Analysis,* 47 (1966), 295–98.

Stoller, R. J. "A Contribution to the Study of Gender Identity," *International Journal of Psycho-Analysis,* 45 (1964), 220–26.

———. *Sex and Gender.* New York: Science House, 1968.

Stone, L. "The Widening Scope of Indications for Psychoanalysis," *Journal of the American Psychoanalytic Association,* 2 (1954), 567–94.

Sullivan, H. S. *Conceptions of Modern Psychiatry.* New York: W. W. Norton, 1953.

Tarachow, S. "Interpretation and Reality in Psycho-Therapy," *International Journal of Psycho-Analysis,* 43 (1962), 377–87.

———. *An Introduction to Psychotherapy.* New York: International Universities Press, 1963.

Tolpin, M. "On the Beginnings of a Cohesive Self: An Application of the Concept of Transmuting Internalization to the Study of the Transitional Object and Signal Anxiety," *The Psychoanalytic Study of the Child* (New York: Quadrangle Books), 26 (1972), 316–52.

Waelder, R. *Basic Theory of Psychoanalysis.* New York: International Universities Press, 1960.

———. "Neurotic Ego Distortion: Opening Remarks to the Panel Discussion," *International Journal of Psycho-Analysis,* 39 (1958), 243–44.

———. "The Principle of Multiple Function," *The Psychoanalytic Quarterly,* 5 (1936), 45–62.

———. "The Structure of Paranoid Ideas," *International Journal of Psycho-Analysis,* 32 (1951), 167–77.

Waldhorn, H. F. "The Place of the Dream in Clinical Psychoanalysis," *Kris Study Group Monograph, II,* pp. 96–105. New York: International Universities Press, 1967.

Wallerstein, R. S. "Psychoanalysis and Psychotherapy. (The Relationship of Psychoanalysis to Psychotherapy: Current Issues)," *International Journal of Psycho-Analysis,* 50 (1969), 117–26.

Wangh, M. "Structural Determinants of Phobia: A Clinical Study," *Journal of the American Psychoanalytic Association,* 7 (1959), 675–95.

Webster's Third New International Dictionary. Springfield, Mass.: G. & C. Merriam Co., 1966.

Weinshel, E. M. "Some Psychoanalytic Considerations on Moods," *International Journal of Psycho-Analysis,* 51 (1970), 313–20.

Weisman, A. D. "Silence and Psychotherapy," *Psychiatry,* 18 (1955), 241–60.

Weissman, P. "Structural Considerations in Overt Male Homosexuality," *International Journal of Psycho-Analysis,* 43 (1962), 159–68.

Wexler, M. "Schizophrenia: Conflict and Deficiency," *The Psychoanalytic Quarterly,* 40 (1971), 83–99.

Wiedeman, G. H. "Survey of Psychoanalytic Literature on Overt Male Homosexuality," *Journal of the American Psychoanalytic Association,* 10 (1962), 386–409.

————. "Symposium on Homosexuality," Panel Discussion, 23rd International Congress of Psycho-Analysis, 1963, *International Journal of Psycho-Analysis,* 45 (1964), 214–16.

Winnicott, D. W. "Comment on Obsessional Neurosis and 'Frankie'," *International Journal of Psycho-Analysis,* 47 (1966), 143–44.

————. *The Maturational Processes and the Facilitating Environment.* New York: International Universities Press, 1965.

————. "Transitional Objects and Transitional Phenomena," *International Journal of Psycho-Analysis,* 34 (1953), 89–97.

Wolberg, L. *The Technique of Psychotherapy.* 2 vols. New York: Grune and Stratton, 1969.

Zeligs, M. A. "The Psychology of Silence: Its Role in Transference, Countertransference and the Psychoanalytic Process," (*The Silent Patient*) *Journal of the American Psychoanalytic Association,* 9 (1961), 7–43.

Zetzel, E. R. "Additional Notes Upon a Case of Obsessional Neurosis: Freud 1909," *International Journal of Psycho-Analysis,* 47 (1966), 123–29.

————. "Concept and Content in Psychoanalytic Theory," *The Psychoanalytic Study of the Child* (New York: International Universities Press), 11 (1956), 99–121.

———— (reporter). "Defense Mechanisms and Psychoanalytic Technique," Panel Discussion of the American Psychoanalytic Association, *Journal of the American Psychoanalytic Association,* 2 (1954), 318–26.

————. "The Depressive Position," in P. Greenacre (ed.), *Affective Disorders,* pp. 84–116. New York: International Universities Press, 1953.

INDEX OF NAMES

INDEX OF SUBJECTS

Undoing, *see* Ego, defensive function of

Vacation, 180-82
Ventilation, 147, 157, 161, 216, 261, 272, 316, 341, 351
Verbalization, 111, 162, 214, 219, 267, 348-49
Violence, 49, 148

Vocalization, *see* Communication, preverbal
Volition, *see* Ego, adaptive function of

Working alliance, 56, 98, 102, 125, 144, 149, 152, 153, 170, 171, 198, 199, 203, 222, 236, 296, 314, 322
Working through, 236

INDEX OF CASES